Aceh, Indonesia

THE ETHNOGRAPHY
OF POLITICAL VIOLENCE

Cynthia Keppley Mahmood, Series Editor

*A complete list of books in the series is available
from the publisher.*

Aceh, Indonesia

Securing the Insecure State

ELIZABETH F. DREXLER

PENN

University of Pennsylvania Press

Philadelphia

Published by
University of Pennsylvania Press
Philadelphia, Pennsylvania 19104-4112

Printed in the United States of America on acid-free paper
10 9 8 7 6 5 4 3 2 1

A cataloging-in-publication record is available from the Library of Congress
ISBN-13: 978-0-8122-4057-3
ISBN-10:0-8122-4057-X

Contents

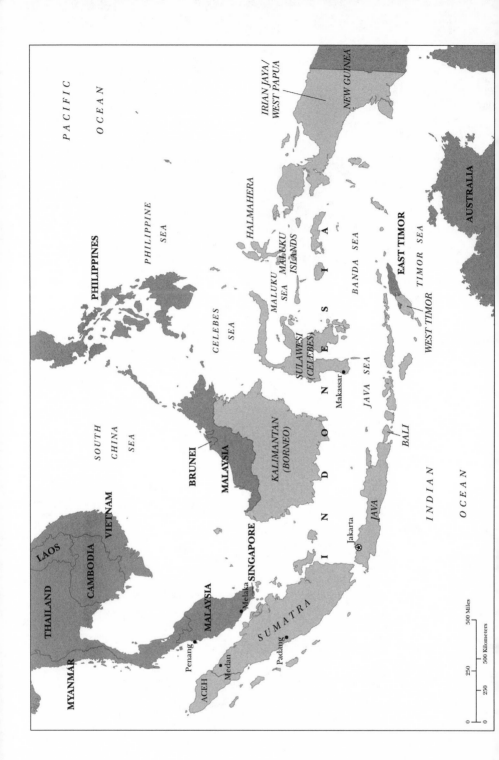

Map 2. Aceh. Kabupaten (regency) boundaries are approximate based on 2003 data, thus reflecting only some of the new kabupaten created after 1998 (e.g., Nagan Raya) and not others (e.g., Pidie Jaya).

Introduction

Indonesia under Soeharto was a fundamentally insecure state. Securing such an insecure state was impossible to accomplish, but was nevertheless continually attempted. Indeed, the strategies through which the state sought security actually generated and extended insecurity. The state was not held accountable for renewing insecurity, or even for failing to maintain a monopoly on force and to subordinate coercion to the rule of law. Rather, the state's chronic inability to create a stable political framework was treated, not as a reason to question the project, but as a justification for continuing it. Latent dangers, organizations without shapes, masterminds, provocateurs, puppet masters, and other mysterious figures recalled the regime's inaugural massive anticommunist violence in 1965–1966 and threatened to recreate those traumas in the present. Constant hypervigilance turned all dissenters into subversives and targeted them for state violence. Order and economic development miracles were secured by a powerful military with an institutionalized political and governance role. Ghosts of the past, imagined enemies, and indeterminate threats were constantly renewed to justify military repression. Spectral threats metamorphosed into deadly violence in a seemingly endless spiral. In Aceh, the cycle spun out of control and an imagined enemy came to life as actual armed separatist rebels.

While conducting field research between 1998 and 2000, the activists, journalists, intellectuals, and members of nongovernmental organizations with whom I spoke expressed wonder, as well as some pride, at how powerful soldiers with automatic rifles could be afraid of ordinary people, students, and other seemingly insignificant threats. Rereading latent dangers and arbitrary arrests as signs of military cowardice failed to quell the pervasive sense of anxiety of those who were intermittently targets of the regime.[1] An outpouring of testimonies and documentation of past violence followed the fall of Soeharto in 1998. Indonesian efforts to "straighten [out] history" initially focused on Soeharto's role in the supposed communist coup attempt.[2] Political and scholarly attention focused on the subsequent mass killings of suspected communist party members in 1965–1966[3] has diverted attention from the conditions of possibility for the killings and their more insidious legacies and logics that continue into the present, enabling other killings.[4] Most important, most public discussion of the killings failed to question the assumption that internal state enemies should be eradicated.[5] At the same time that public discourse scandalized the founding myth of the New Order (1966–1998)—that the army had saved the Republic from an attempted communist coup[6]—the logic of the insecure state continued to work, compounding its effects in the post-Soeharto period despite promises of greater transparency. The press documented both ongoing state violence and continued "engineering" or manipulation of conflicts between citizens by the military. As shocking as revelations of past state violence were, far greater consensus and popular protest were directed toward "trying" and "hanging" Soeharto for corruption, collusion, and nepotism (in Indonesian, signified by the acronym KKN). Outbreaks of violence between citizens, even if orchestrated by the military, were called "horizontal" violence, in contrast to "vertical" or state violence. Fears about the Balkanization of Indonesia in the face of separatist movements from Aceh to East Timor suggested to some anxious observers and members of the reform-minded elite that the Indonesian nation might have been held together only by a strong central state.

Even as the crimes committed by the military were publicly exposed after Soeharto's fall, corruption generated more sustained and widespread public outrage than the massive violence and systematic human rights violations that were committed in Aceh. Some human rights organizations, both locally and in Jakarta, agitated for justice and reform, but their demands were soon overwhelmed by more politicized campaigns and by the resurgence of violence of indeterminate origin. This book demonstrates the falsity of the reigning assumption of international human rights organizations: that the exposure of past violence promotes accountability and reconciliation rather than the repetition of abuses. The ample documentation of violence in Aceh did not lead to judicial proceedings that held the identified perpetrators responsible. Instead, responsibility was displaced onto a shadowy "third force" operating in the indeterminate space between the armed forces and their supposed antagonists, the separatist rebels.

Having heard and read many accounts of state violence in Aceh, I have deliberately refrained from trying to represent its graphic horror, but rather analyzed how it enters into political and discursive constructions. After the initial explosion of news following the end of the military operations zone that most people referred to as DOM (1989–1998), victims' voices were surprisingly absent from analyses of the conflict. What captures the problem of "DOM" for me is the silence that hovers around all of the narratives and media accounts of violence. The human rights violations of the state security operations have been documented, yet the alienation from neighbors, unspoken horrors, and survival by betrayal are less often iterated. This silence is not simply the mark left by trauma. Rather, I argue, it indicates the persistent doubts and suspicions about the loyalties of hearers, and the mistrust that divides speakers and listeners. The legacies of systematic betrayal and polarization are more damaging socially than individual trauma because they ramify through relationships in the present and extend patterns and logics of the past instead of merely creating an unspeakable gap between past and present.

Eventually, I came to understand that the dynamics of revelations and silences are related: what truth telling there has been in and about Aceh since the fall of Soeharto revealed the existence of probable conspiracies, collusion between the military and its supposed enemies, and complicity and betrayal at all levels of society. Mutual distrust has been exacerbated by these revelations, and the seemingly paranoid thinking that pervades some segments of Indonesian society appears rational. Impunity has compounded paranoia. The tribunal that was set up to hear one prominent case in Aceh and facilitate the transition from an arbitrary, authoritarian regime to a civil society under the rule of law let the acknowledged perpetrators and suspected masterminds escape indictment, while prosecuting only a few low-ranking members of the Indonesian military. The lack of justice confirms and compounds Aceh's historical grievances: promises from Jakarta are never to be trusted. Just as the Indonesian master narrative characterizes the Acehnese as by nature violent, vengeful, and subversive, so the Acehnese resistance narrative characterizes Jakarta and Javanese as by nature greedy, corrupt, and unjust.

In Aceh and Indonesia, I came to understand this preoccupation with corruption as arising from the pervasive and profound disjunction among words, actions, and consequences that renders institutions incapable of accomplishing their stated purposes but prone to being hijacked into the service of violent conflict. Such rampant corruption multiplies mistrust. Americans generally understand corruption as dishonest graft, as those in power profiting personally through the covert diversion of public resources. In Jakarta and Aceh, reformers were outraged over the extent to which public resources had been stolen by those in power. But discourses of corruption entailed much more than simple graft. In this book, I develop an analytic of corruption to guide my ethnography of an insecure state. What follows is not an account of how graft, bribery, and nepotism structure daily life for Indonesians,[7] but an ethnographic mapping of the state as refracted through indeterminacy and impunity. I use corruption in a double sense to indicate the erosion of memory and the lack of legitimacy of institutions of law and governance. Moreover, the logic of corruption echoes the proliferation of distortions that ramify through systems when one element is askew. In my examination of the dynamics of the Indonesian state's insecurity, I consider how historical narratives are technologies both of governance[8] and of violence.[9] I follow James Siegel's examination of an Indonesian state threatened by specters renewed in history, especially as he outlines the dynamic of vengeance: "Vengeance is not claimed by the murderers themselves; it is the one whom one kills, who, it is said, wants revenge" (1998, 5). He notes that fear of vengeance has focused on imaginary enemies and elaborates an analysis of the spectral fears that the state cannot name.[10] Ariel Heryanto (2006) examines the dynamic of how "victims" of arbitrary state arrest coauthor wider plots and conspiracies with their military torturers, providing a detailed analysis of state anxiety and excessive, arbitrary force related to the master narrative of the army saving the nation in 1965. The Aceh case is related to the dynamics that Heryanto and Siegel describe, but profoundly differs in the emergence of a visible force that steps up to claim the power of latent dangers imagined by the New Order. In Aceh, the imagined separatists became actual rebels, and they agreed with their military state antagonist on a retroactively constructed narrative of the conflict.

Specters of the past certainly play a role in violence in Aceh, but the "figures that reside both inside and outside the law" appear as "practices embedded in everyday life in the present" (Das and Poole 2004, 13). Productive indeterminacies in Aceh structure the conflict dynamics, and daily existence is refracted through uncertainty, suspicion, and paranoia.[11] Most Acehnese are well aware of the law's dependence on extralegal violence that Walter Benjamin described in his famous critique of violence (1986). Jacques Derrida's commentary on Benjamin examines the mystical force of law and impossibility of justice, using an analysis of the performative to highlight the law's lack of legitimation (1992). These insights have been extended by scholars considering everyday life in violent states. My analysis resonates with Veena Das's conceptualization of illegibility (2004). Observing "instability introduced by the possibilities of a gap between a rule and its performance," Das argues that the legibility and iterability of the state's signature introduce opportunities for forgery and other unauthorized performances of the state's power. Das looks to the margins where the state does not have enough authority to make a felicitous statement or a performative utterance that produces a social or political effect by virtue of its being stated by a specific speaker in a particular context (for example,

the judge's pronouncement of a marriage).[12] Das points to the significance of situations in which that state's saying so does not make it so,
and others might appropriate the state's power to say otherwise.[13]

In Eric Santner's analysis, the performative leads not to a problem of
forgery or imitation but rather to a problem of paranoia. In his argument, paranoia is the "bottoming out" of the chain of performatives
that exposes the arbitrary authority of institutions, especially the law
(1996, 11). Santner does not look at the state from the margin, but explores what happens when the judge realizes his or her authority is
based on an arbitrary chain of performatives. I am concerned here with
how institutions, especially law, narrate the past in order to produce effects of legitimacy, and I draw on the work of these scholars to develop
an analytic of corruption.

What I call corruption indicates a fundamental feature of social
relations; it distorts politics, inverting means and ends, causes and effects. Nothing is quite what it seems; no one is who they pretend to be.
Corruption creates constant epistemological conundrums, inhibits solidarity, and undermines the very foundations of social action. Just as
corruption pervades the present, the corruption of memories of the
past makes it impossible to obtain legal redress for human rights violations or to stop the replication of violence. An analytic of corruption
points to how the logics of the insecure state proliferate. When institutions of governance and social institutions are themselves corrupt, they
can no longer guarantee distinctions between truth and falsity, or validate certain actions and choices while invalidating others. Mistrust permeates everyday life and shapes institutional logics. In societies marked
by long periods of corrupt governance and massive violence, revelations are not therapeutic and societies are not self-healing.[14] Any testimony or evidence that circulates through these institutions becomes
corrupt because of the corrosive, destabilizing power of suspicion. Just
as truth cannot be proven, falsity cannot be demonstrated; by definition, conspiracies cannot be disproved.

It was during the euphoric period of "reform" that separatist rebels
in Aceh were transformed from an accusation used by the security
forces to justify repression and torture to a visible armed force challenging the centralized Indonesian state. During this period, many people
suggested that the rebels had been fabricated by the military to restore
their importance. People described the conflict in Aceh as directed by
"remote control," most often from Jakarta. In an interview with a retired general who had been responsible for intelligence in Aceh during
the 1980s, I broached the issue of the overlap between military forces
and rebels by asking where violence was being directed from. Almost
everyone I knew had referred to it in veiled terms, including this man.

In our previous conversations he had been surprisingly open. Now he responded with outrage. He admonished me that the military was losing men; how could I think they were directing anything? He said that the situation was out of control; no one, especially not the military, liked the situation now, but no one could control it. Then I mentioned a recent newspaper article indicating cooperation between the military and the separatist rebels in Aceh (GAM). He visibly relaxed and affirmed "that . . . yes, of course, in the beginning. . . ." His voice trailed off, and he threw his hands up in the air and reiterated that it is "out of control now." "During the New Order," he reminisced, "we cultivated the rebels, it was profitable." The volatile mixture of violence and profits and the corrupt combination of imagining and engineering threats that characterized the New Order has left complicated legacies. Knowing that enemies were manufactured and that innocents were wrongly killed as enemies has not undone patterns of insecurity. Incidents of widespread "horizontal" violence convinced many people that Indonesia was still endangered and the military was still necessary. Insecurity intensified and perpetuated political violence.

To explore the logic and legacies of cultivated threats in an insecure state, I examine corruption as a source of public outrage and as a metaphor for the logics of collusion and betrayal that laid the conditions for perpetual violence. Looking through the lens of corruption, it becomes easier to see why the strategies of exposure which underlie international human rights advocacy efforts did not end cycles of violence and injustice in Indonesia. Middle-class Indonesians who avoided politics in order to benefit from Soeharto's development regime saw their savings disappear during the 1997 economic crisis. Analysts often linked the foreign exchange value of the Rupiah to the level of popular protests, reminding elites that political expression was at odds with prosperity. Even long-standing NGO activists reiterated that when people are starving the economic crisis must be resolved before the crimes of the past can be addressed. Propagating the impression that political and economic issues can be disaggregated and pushing aside political issues in the name of economic development indicated that the logics of New Order governance persisted even after Soeharto's fall. A year after Soeharto fell, some elite Indonesians recalled the New Order nostalgically. Then, they said, there was order, life was better, we could afford things; then we knew who was friend and who was enemy. But returning to that order is impossible; everything is contaminated by corruption. The rhetoric of national development became untenable, while the rhetoric of latent dangers, international conspiracies, and pending national disintegration used to secure compliance became all the more real. These fears created a longing for a time when it was possible to establish order, even if it required violence. Seeing political violence as independent of the New Order system of development incorrectly implies that violence and corruption were aberrations rather than core features of the system.

Directly linking the issue of corruption and human rights violations, the attorney general of Indonesia asked: "How do we draw the line between amnesty and ending human rights violations and separate that from the issue of corruption?"[15] His position resonates with arguments regarding other crimes of the New Order: it would be impossible to bring to trial all those who have been involved in corruption. It would be difficult to find a civil servant who had not taken a bribe, or a citizen who had not bribed an official to facilitate the tasks of daily life, such as making an ID card. Establishing a functioning system of law is crucial, but it seems nearly impossible. In 2000, one member of the national human rights commission put it this way: In the New Order "the concentration of power was with the military, bureaucracy, conglomerates, and political parties. They all maintain that they were instruments when they were perpetrators and beneficiaries in a system made by injustice. That the criminal justice system is inadequate to deal with all the injustices of the past is not a coincidence: it had to be weak justice for effective corruption, collusion and nepotism."[16] This analysis points to the complications of efforts to "strengthen law" in a regime that is systemically complicit with corrupting the law.

Corruption discloses that language and referent have become severed and shows why the law is not working. One commentator noted, "We are already used to corruption without a corruptor, and therefore corruption without end" ("Korupsi Tanpa Koruptor," *Majalah Interview*, year 2, no. 18, 20 January 2001). This statement highlights the difficulty of assigning liability for corruption in a system in which corruption structured daily life for all citizens. Goenawan Mohamad, one of Indonesia's foremost essayists, extended the statement that in South Africa law and justice were distant cousins and commented, in Indonesia, "law and justice are not even on speaking terms."[17] This chasm is deeply problematic, vitiating arguments that presume a relationship between disclosure and justice as the basis for reestablishing law. In a system where institutions no longer function, the military is believed to disrupt order to preserve its own powerful role, and where corruption pervades society, it is almost impossible to imagine how justice could be pursued legally, not through mob violence or campaigns of revenge. Corruption pervades even attempts to eradicate it.

Violence, like corruption, spread uncontrollably after Soeharto's fall, and the law and its enforcers were unable or unwilling to control it, and they remain unable to hold anyone accountable for it. In the absence of functioning institutions of justice, the existence or nonexistence of spectral and actual enemies cannot be decided, endlessly reproducing the state's insecurity. Criminalizing political expression and believing that the state is endangered have destroyed the mechanisms that might be used to address the problem. In Aceh, indeterminate boundaries between state forces and their enemies corrupted the law and foreclosed possibilities for resolution until the devastating Indian Ocean tsunami in 2004.

This book analyzes political violence and, by extension, nationalisms as both discourse and materiality, tracing how each converts into the other in an escalating spiral of conflict. It maps how the Indonesian state has sustained itself through anxieties and insecurities activated and extended by historical and human rights narratives about previous violence. Exposure of state violence without a process of judicial accountability has perpetuated pervasive mistrust that undermines civil society.[18] Despite the repeated failures of the law, arbitrary excesses of power, and proliferating corruption of Soeharto's New Order, documentary evidence of injustice and efforts toward legal resolution remained powerful ideals for civil society groups. Aceh has been a limit case for human rights advocacy. Exposure without justice fails both to redress past grievances and to establish the trust necessary for social peace.

To consider the politics of neutrality and the circulation of expert knowledge about violence, I document how an international intervention failed to resolve conflict in Aceh because, in mistaking "public secrets" for truth (Taussig 1999), it unwittingly reinforced the polarization of groups into advocates of regional autonomy via independence versus the agents of the centralized state as embodiment of national integrity. This effectively abolished the possibility of neutral and nonviolent positions that alone could broker a settlement. Failed interventions are more dangerous than neglected conflicts, since the international stage amplifies grievances and provides access to resources from outside the region.

One critical lesson that the Aceh case provides is that ethnocultural nationalism is constructed retrospectively by political leaders who mobilize populations on the basis of new narratives of past grievances, rather than existing in prepolitical form as a primordial feature of divided societies. The centralized state, as well as advocates of regional autonomy, plays a crucial role in the construction of ethnocultural nationalism, since as an internal enemy it justifies repressive military rule. These conflicts are intractable not because of "undying hatreds" but because of the substantial economic resources and geopolitical interests at stake in these regions. Violent conflict itself becomes a crucial re-source, reinforcing the apparent intractability of the situation.

A second lesson is that in some postcolonial states, the central gov-ernment may actually create, arm, and exercise some control over key elements of the opposing guerilla forces, both to discredit the actual advocates of regional autonomy, who are often nonviolent in principle and practice, and to terrorize the civilian population in the region and provoke a "security" emergency. Shadowy forces, even if they begin as irregular soldiers and provocateurs, tend to escape central control and act as criminal gangs amid the resulting chaos, making political settle-ments difficult to negotiate and impossible to enforce.

Finally, this research challenges traditional understandings of narra-tion and trauma. I situate this work in the literature on transitions from authoritarian regimes, as well as the literature on trauma and history, by carefully documenting the relationship between acknowledgement and narration of past state violence and the social legitimacy of judicial institutions. The global rise in violence over the past two decades has been accompanied by a proliferation of transnational, post-conflict justice and reconciliation institutions. Guided by psychoanalytic theory and practice, in which individuals resolve traumas by narrating past ex-periences and integrating them into their present so they can move for-ward free from the fractures in memory, spoiled identities, and paralysis that trauma imposes, national and transnational institutions have been designed to facilitate a collective resolution of traumatic political vio-lence during transitional periods. Yet, some narrations of the past fail to resolve the legacies of massive state violence, but instead reinforce and perpetuate it.

A common assumption is that the opportunity to tell one's story and to have it heard promotes personal healing (Hayner 2001; Minow 1998; Brison 2001; Felman and Laub 1992; cf. Hamber and Wilson 2002; Ross 2001, 2003). Institutions of transitional justice—trials and tribunals no less than truth commissions—attempt to develop narratives about past violence intended to settle accounts and fill in missing pieces that cre-ate traumatic rents in the social fabric. It is often assumed that these narratives, and their ability to demonstrate the truth, play a powerful role in legitimating political institutions and mending social relations (Popkin and Roht-Arriaza 1995; Rotberg 2000; du Toit 2000; Kritz 1995). In contrast, the repeated narration, documentation, and expo-sure of past violence in Aceh have contributed to the extension of vio-lence rather than its resolution. In situations like Aceh where no formal institutional process attends to past violence, particular narratives are institutionalized through everyday practices in the present. This work maps the implication of testimony and representation of violence in the extension of violence.

Dominick LaCapra distinguishes working through trauma from acting out and the compulsion to repeat by the victims' ability to "gain critical distance . . . and to distinguish between past, present, and future" (2001, 143). According to LaCapra, by "working through" the past and distinguishing it from the present, a person who has been victimized and traumatized by violence "acquires the possibility of being an ethical and political agent" (144) recovering the ability to act in his or her own life with the expectation that justice and accountability, rather than terrifying randomness, cycles of vengeance, and naked force, prevail. Since one of the primary goals of transitional institutions is to establish the rule of law, it is important to consider how they facilitate working through the past, providing critical distance from its violations for both victims and perpetrators—and, indeed, for those who have occupied both positions—and enabling people to become ethical, political agents.

How do various transitional institutions—commissions of inquiry, fact-finding missions, truth commissions, criminal trials, and tribunals—create the conditions of possibility for knowing, narrating, and acknowledging the past such that it can be worked through rather than endlessly repeated or acted out? In Aceh, mediations and interventions have produced the conflict configuration they intended to resolve. Similarly, trials may reproduce the patterns of violence and social polarization that are judicially illegible (Felman 2002a) in the courtroom. Rather than seeking psychosocial or ethnocultural explanations for the repetition of trauma and extension of violence, I suggest considering how everyday practices, institutions, and politics shape memories and perpetuate conditions in which past patterns are replayed. Often, the indeterminacies and complexities that extend violence are public secrets, but even if officially acknowledged they remain beyond the grasp of the law.

My research in Aceh demonstrates that the overlap between state and separatist enemy not only extends violence but also corrupts the judiciary and makes law impossible. An analytic of corruption explains the failure of various transitional narrations to legitimate law and end cycles of violence. Legal institutions are corrupted when they fail to establish appropriate relationships between narrative meanings and social consequences. When legal processes grant immunity to identified perpetrators, fail to recognize known victims, and confuse these two categories of action, corruption becomes systemically contaminating. In social-historical contexts in which violence is widely presumed to have been carried out through conspiracies as well as conflicts between groups of suspicious loyalties and to have involved personal vengeance as well as political principles, corruption makes legal institutions a means of extending the problem instead of an alternative.

In contrast to analyses informed by theories of trauma, an analytic of corruption reveals how inadmissible truths return to unsettle institutions and societies. In a corrupt system, distortions in knowledge, narration, and action ramify through the system in what becomes an endless loop. Situating LaCapra's notion of individual working through trauma at the societal level demonstrates that it is impossible for a society to work through the legacies of mass violence through narration alone. A critical component of societal working-through depends on restoring accountability for individual actions at the same time that pervasive complicity is acknowledged. Inviting the indeterminacy and other unsettling truths into the courtroom is the only way to resolve systemic corruption. Inadmissible truths are far more threatening to postauthoritarian transitions than are traumatic repetitions. I outline the process through which the judiciary itself has been corrupted by narratives and judgments that fail to capture the indeterminacy of the conflict situation and demonstrate that law is implicated in reproducing the conflict it is called upon to resolve.

The situation in Aceh has taught me to be suspicious of histories about conflicts, wary of projects to expose pain and suffering, and sensitive to the circulation of testimony in international contexts.[19] It has vividly demonstrated the limitations and outright failures of the law as understood by international bodies and humanitarian agencies. Additional research on responses to similar violence perpetrated by the Indonesian military in East Timor has demonstrated to me that even well-funded, internationally supported transitional institutions, including both tribunals and a truth commission, failed to address the complicated legacies of conflicts in which violence is "horizontalized" and "engineered" (Drexler 2006c). Yet, without justice, past wrongs haunt the present, not only leading to private revenge in the guise of politics but also perpetuating the pervasive mistrust, or even paranoia, that undermines social relations, civil society, and law. While some Acehnese pragmatically argued that examining the past could undermine the current peace, I contend that each repetition of a politically expedient narrative that does not align with past experiences can diminish the social legitimacy of new institutions. The past haunts the present, and inadmissible memories corrupt the social, political, and judicial institutions that are necessary to end violence. Just as silence and silencing fail to ensure peace in the future, initiatives and institutions for reconciling memories of the past do not resolve its complex legacies.

Fieldwork and Archival Research

This book is deeply informed by fieldwork among well-educated, cosmopolitan, predominantly young Acehnese and Indonesian activists as they considered the possibilities of reform in Indonesia and/or what it meant to be Acehnese. I have known most of them for at least eight years. I first visited Aceh in 1996, during the infamous military operations period known as DOM. My time in Aceh was spent primarily with NGO activists. I was impressed with their strong solidarity and their innovative projects, which focused on the environment and women's empowerment, as well as legal aid. Many of them expressed shock when they discovered the extent of human rights violations that were occurring in Aceh. Although these activists addressed human rights issues only through their ongoing projects, they sought to attract attention to the situation in Aceh and talked freely with researchers like me. I decided to conduct my dissertation research in Aceh, planning to examine the development of civil society through environmental activism. After the fall of Soeharto in 1998, these NGOs' work became more explicitly political, and many other organizations and activists appeared to represent Aceh and protest the violence perpetrated there. The individuals whom I had met in 1996 introduced me to a very different context. The insights I gleaned and the understandings of the conflict articulated in this book were possible only because I was able to return to meet with these contacts and be trusted at a time when Aceh was flooded with outside attention.

The contrast between testimonies I heard in 1996 and in 1998 was striking. In 1996, I was taken to see several grassroots groups that NGOs had organized outside of Lhokseumawe to develop an awareness of human rights. One used a duck-raising project to document conditions in the community and to disseminate information about human rights. A group of widows recorded the daily events of their village life in traditional poem form. The majority related the difficulties of extortion and harassment by the military. Most of their husbands had been "disappeared." The widows did not know any members of the rebel forces, nor did they seem familiar with the movement's ideology. They noted that the military was violent without offering graphic personal narratives, and they discussed the problems of making a living without a husband and sending children to school so they would have a better future.

After Soeharto's fall, the NGOs I was studying expressed interests in human rights and justice more directly. This manuscript is based primarily on fieldwork and research I conducted from February 1998 to December 2000 in Jakarta and Aceh, as well as at national workshops of civil society organizations and discussions of human rights in other places. During thirty months of field research (in addition to eight months of predissertation research in 1994 and 1996), I conducted interviews in Indonesian with cabinet members, members of parliament, and regional government officials; high-ranking military and intelligence officials; leaders and supporters of the Free Aceh Movement, or GAM; and civil society activists, intellectuals, academics, nongovernmental groups, human rights investigators, journalists, witnesses, and bystanders. I interviewed victims of rape, torture, kidnapping, and imprisonment without trial; I met with surviving family members of victims of political violence; and I heard firsthand the defense of some accused perpetrators. Because most of my interviews took place with Acehnese elites and NGO activists as well as other leaders in Jakarta and Aceh, I conducted my research in the Indonesian language, the lingua franca of political activities that span Aceh and Jakarta. Most human rights workshops and advocacy events were conducted in Indonesian. In rare cases where individuals were unable or unwilling to speak in Indonesian (e.g., in some meetings with community groups or victims' support groups in rural areas), I was always with Acehnese activists who explained the process and translated accounts for me. We often discussed particular Acehnese expressions at great length after these meetings. These accounts serve as useful background and context but do not form a substantial part of my analysis, which is more concerned with the production of the "Aceh Problem" in an Indonesian context.

In collecting data through participant observation at NGO workshops and seminars, I devoted special attention to efforts to resolve past crimes, both in Aceh and more broadly. One initiative supported by the national human rights commission brought together community members across Indonesia to use scenario-building techniques to consider what kind of future Indonesia might choose. As a policy analyst in Jakarta (April–September 2000), I had frequent contact with international humanitarian aid organizations and the foreign diplomatic community. I participated in international discussions and forums regarding legislation, international models, funding, and possible outcomes for truth, justice, and reconciliation strategies. I attended parliamentary sessions and hearings held by national investigative teams related to the resolution of the conflict in Aceh.

My interview data and observations are supported by extensive textual documentation. I followed a range of Aceh-based and Indonesian print media, which represented a wide spectrum of interests and biases, including two military newspapers, throughout the transition period to compile a 70,000-page archive of reports related to incidents of violence, efforts toward resolution, rule of law, human rights, justice, reconciliation, and related issues. I researched collections of Acehnese media and military media through the entire New Order period. I collected a range of primary source materials, investigative reports, and relevant legislation and parliamentary transcripts. Copies of classified material were given to me by advocates who wanted to make sure that the truth was known, even if they could not proclaim it; they trusted that I would share this information widely. My selection of the particular documentary sources cited here is informed by my interactions with a range of individuals during fieldwork; some articles say publicly what particular individuals did not want attributed to them. Finally, I draw on short fiction, poetry, theater, and other creative means of addressing the trauma of unresolved injustice.

My desire to avoid negative repercussions to those who generously gave me their insights, without which this book would not have been possible, made it necessary to render individual comments and identities anonymous. In addition, I have refrained from presenting particular cases that encapsulate how military intelligence operations worked, describing their common patterns instead. The personal nature of the information required to trace cycles of betrayal over time renders it impossible to protect the identities of those involved. Not only was cross-checking such slippery sources difficult, but engaging in that endeavor would have amounted to engaging in the conflict itself. The mere reiteration of the betrayals visited upon families and individuals could provoke questions of honor and vengeance or complicity, potentially making the inquiry itself an extension of the military operations' social polarization. I have adhered to my aim to analyze rather than replicate conflict in the method, as well as substance, of this work. The disclosure of some sensitive information, which is known by a limited number of people, would betray its source. Rumors, information that cannot be substantiated, and dire predictions are always incomplete and often produce the feeling that something else is not yet revealed or known. Those with the power to produce information often deliberately generate the idea that something else lies "behind" what is visible and that conspiracies are on the verge of becoming known. Because Aceh is a conflict situation where for most people there is no space beyond politics and "neutral" or "nonpolitical" speech has sometimes been fatal, I have been very cautious in trying to prevent the circulation and documentation of what may later prove to have been dangerous statements.

One of the far-reaching and insidious microlegacies of New Order governance by terror has been the imbrication of the political and the personal in vengeance. The state could not have so successfully diminished the opposition of its critics without the assistance of members of the "depoliticized" floating masses who were willing to offer evidence of the misdeeds of others to spare themselves punishment or gain privileges. The "branch system," described in accounts of torture victims both from 1965 and in Aceh, worked by a series of substitutions and displacements. The person who can no longer stand the torture betrays another community member and, according to many accounts, remains in the protection of the security forces out of fear of vengeance by betrayed community members or their families. This chain of violence isolates victims and fragments society and, most importantly, deflects rage from the state and military apparatus to other civilians.[20] The pattern is then repeated without the direct involvement of the state. I have left out the details of how personal conflicts were politicized because I did not want this account to participate in the conflict or to be read as a collection of anecdotes that "horizontalizes" the violence and contributes to the perception of the Acehnese as irrationally violent and out for vengeance. Directing my attention to the ways in which state violence has been implemented, I do not want to make the state seem more competent than it is, or to give it an overwhelming presence that would diminish individual agency and reduce everything to a master conspiracy narrative.

Mapping Histories and Memories of Violence

Chapter 1, "Analyzing Conflict," centers on my meeting with Abdullah Syafi'ie, the putative commander in chief of the rebel forces, who appeared with an old AK-47, a black box containing ammunition, and a sheaf of photocopied historical documents in English. Substantial evidence suggests that the not-so-elusive Syafi'ie operated with the military's protection, although not entirely under its control. Syafi'ie represents the constructed rebel opponent par excellence. This chapter considers how the existence of the rebel force GAM (Gerakan Aceh Merdeka, Free Aceh Movement) is the ammunition that extends the conflict in Aceh. Syafi'ie's weapon and ammunition create the possibility of violence, while his preoccupation with historical narratives constitutes the grievance around which GAM is formed. Through this discussion of how GAM came into existence as a necessary protagonist of armed conflict, the chapter explicates principles for analyzing ethnopolitical conflict. I draw on my professional experience as a policy analyst in Jakarta in considering how knowledge about violence is produced and disciplined.

Chapter 2, "Struggling with History," takes off from and returns to the airplane that Aceh donated to the national multicultural theme park, "Beautiful Indonesia in Miniature." This nationalist project, designed to depoliticize regional conflicts by reducing them to culture and recasting them in a pluralist aesthetic, is disrupted by Aceh's donation, not of a distinctive house, shrine, and set of such artifacts as "native" costumes, but of an airplane Aceh initially donated to the nation in 1948. Reminding the center of Aceh's commitment to Indonesian self-determination from its protracted resistance to Dutch colonialism through its determined struggle for national independence in the aftermath of World War II, this airplane has, ironically, been reduced to a symbol of "bravery," a transhistorical quality of Acehnese culture that, at the end of the chapter, turns ominous when it is interpreted, not as a sign of Aceh's longstanding commitment to the Indonesian national project, but as a symbol of this people's intractable penchant for separatist violence in opposition to the inclusive predisposition of the nation. This reading symbolically casts Aceh out of Indonesia and constitutes it as the "other" within that disrupts national integrity and threatens state security.

Chapter 2 draws on a vast archive to document the discontinuous history of various groups opposed to Jakarta, from early Islamists concerned with spiritual and social purity to the secular socialist intellectuals concerned with inequitable development who issued the AM (Aceh Merdeka, Free Aceh) manifesto in 1976. None of these distinct political groups were large, and they were not aligned in terms of personnel or program, much less strategy or tactics. The analysis of exiled separatist leader Hasan Tiro's reinterpretation of treaties with the Dutch to provide a basis for the assertion of autonomy for Aceh from Indonesia exemplifies the ways in which historical narratives are constructed and deployed to constitute a political subject and assert its claims. Jakarta, too, propagates a historical narrative that sees Aceh as a serious threat to national unity and elides all local opponents into one vast, continuous state of rebellion. While everyone talks about the relatively remote past, everyone avoids confronting its more proximate ghosts: the human rights abuses and atrocities that took place from 1989 to 1998, during the period of special military operations generally known as DOM. The "official" history positing Aceh as a place of rebellion against the nation-state appears as the center's construction of an enemy in the present, which justifies its past and future military repression not only in this region but also throughout the country.

Chapter 3, "Threat and Violence," documents incidents of actual violence and analyzes shifts in the classification of violence that constitute Aceh as a threat to Indonesia. The original group, Aceh Merdeka (Free Aceh), was a small group of left-wing intellectuals primarily concerned with resource exploitation and revenue redistribution. The central government's policies and representations of the group exaggerated it as a widespread separatist threat. The dozen or so members of this movement were systematically assassinated by 1983. However, the military campaign was transformed into a program to militarize society to defend it against latent, shadowy subversives, variously identified as criminal gangs, security disruptors, and separatist rebels. The campaign involved thousands of human rights violations; many victims were targeted by informers for private reasons or denounced by their personal enemies under torture. This protracted period of state violence had serious, although mixed consequences: it laid the groundwork for conflicts between informers (*cu'ak*) and their victims' kin, or created conditions in which mysterious deaths and extrajudicial killings might be explained as vengeance, and it crushed the political opposition while constituting a guerilla threat that, pronounced to be an imminent danger, justified continued military repression. Key separatist figures were apprehended and cultivated by the military and sent out to infiltrate the shadowy criminal or subversive gangs in Aceh. In the midst of public exposure of the excesses committed by the military in the past, the level of violence actually increased after the state's withdrawal of troops.

Chapter 4, "Translating Violence into Politics," considers the problem of achieving justice in the absence of a judicial system, human rights protections, and a functioning state with a monopoly on lethal force. The conditions of violence that made legal accountability necessary also made it impossible. This chapter analyzes the one attempt at judicially accounting for state violence in Aceh, the Bantaqiah case. The trial demonstrated that the military was implicated not only in the massacre of more than thirty unarmed civilians, but investigations also revealed that there was a "dark pattern" in which various elements of the military contributed to the creation of a separatist enemy to cover up the fact that the military was the "single bad guys". The failure to hold perpetrators accountable compounded the pervasive sense of injustice articulated by many Acehnese. Furthermore, both advocates of justice and state apologists often translated demands for individual accountability into policies of compensation, according the region a greater share of the revenues produced from its resources. While glaring economic inequities certainly underlay discontent in Aceh and anxiety in Jakarta, the redistribution of wealth is not a solution to a legal problem. With equally fatal results, both parties also translated the demand for justice into the question of a referendum, which rapidly became a question not of democracy but of secession. Both responses failed to address the violence, although the second justified the international intervention critically analyzed in the next chapter.

Chapter 5, "Neutrality and Provocation," examines the first international intervention in Aceh, diagramming not only its failure but how it changed the conflict. The brief cease-fire, called the Humanitarian

Pause (2000–2001), did not offer a political solution to the conflict in Aceh, or even create conditions for a process of mediated negotiation. The agreement had only two parties, and in consolidating the "dark force" of *provokator* that it excluded from negotiations it legitimated a unitary command structure—GAM—to correspond with the state; thus contributing to the rebel group's actual consolidation under the leadership of armed forces, and abolishing the possibility of a neutral position in spite of the women's congress efforts not to take sides. While outside interventions attempt to appear neutral in order to obtain access to conflict regions, interventions are never neutral, and they often make it impossible for local agents to preserve their neutrality. In Aceh, NGOs that had advocated human rights were marginalized. The Humanitarian Pause intensified polarization and sowed the seeds for the resumption of armed conflict. Captive to narratives that proclaimed this conflict intractable, this international intervention contributed to making it irresolvable. After 2000, political violence in Aceh exceeded previous bounds and swept up all of civil society in its destructive wake until the December 2004 tsunami.

The sixth and final chapter, "The Tsunami and the Cease-fire," returns to the argument posed in the first chapter to consider whether and how the 2005 cease-fire agreement will disarm the ammunition of the rebels' existence. Considering the logic of agreement and subsequent policies, this chapter demonstrates that, once again, the existence of GAM has made pursuing justice for past violations through the law impossible. It is the condition of the cease-fire that past crimes will not be judicially processed. The convergent interests of GAM rebels and Indonesian Security Forces (TNI) foreclose investigation of human rights violations, especially during DOM. Without reviewing the past, the logic of an insecure state will persist. GAM will remain a threat—the M for Merdeka will always recall a separatist desire—and the TNI will remain necessary rather than a threat. The law will continue to be subordinated to the power of violence. I extend this analysis to consider the corrosive culture of paranoia in which the trust necessary for collective action is eroded and paralysis in the face of overwhelming, yet invisible, opponents prevents the formulation of political programs. If the state security forces constantly extend and reproduce insecurity in their efforts to combat it, what will finally produce a state of legitimacy?

Chapter 1

Analyzing Conflict

How can anthropologists contribute to the generation of knowledge about violent conflicts that uncovers rather than recapitulates the dynamics that perpetuate them? I am interested not in writing a truer history that implies a link "between past identities and the legitimacies of present political claims" (Scott 1999, 103), but in analyzing the work that historical narratives do in conflict dynamics. I am interested in how accounts shift over time and in the gaps, contradictions, and collusions among those narratives. An anthropological perspective on political violence offers the possibility of seeing the social and cultural grounds on which political narratives rest and making visible the dynamic interactions that shape them. Yet the task poses serious problems, from the dangers of undertaking an ethnography of continuing violence, especially for those who shared their thoughts at different moments in the conflict, through the conundrums involved in analyzing the suffering experienced. In addition to the practical difficulties of conducting "fieldwork under fire" (Nordstrom and Robben 1995; also Greenhouse, Mertz, and Warren 2002), the conditions, or even the impossibility, of representing violence have challenged analysts (Scarry 1985; Friedlander 1992; Kleinman, Das, and Lock 1997; cf. Jeganathan 2000). Anthropologists and other scholars have also debated appropriate ethical and political responses to violence encountered in the field and to the suffering of our subjects (Goodale 2006; Warren 2000).

In contrast to conceptualizing "violent events as breakdown, as the absence of sociality or the evacuation of meaning," Daniel Hoffman argues that "the constitution of violent moments, in fact their very demarcation as 'events,' are social processes." "Too often violence is rendered analytically meaningless because we fail to see in it the kinds of feedback loops of representation and imagination more easily discerned in other social dramas" (2002, 333). This chapter traces these feedback loops and explores the kinds of political work they do in conflict situations, what futures they foreclose, and what analytic devices might untangle them. It abstracts a series of principles to highlight the social life of representations and narratives about conflict produced by conflict protagonists, policymakers, and humanitarian workers. Based on my experience as a policy analyst as well as an ethnographer, these principles point to how we might discern and document the "looping effect" (Hacking 1995) while working in conflict situations. Heryanto quotes an intelligence agency director describing how they start to believe their own propaganda:

> The funny thing about the world of intelligence is the technique of psywar [psychological warfare]. As intelligence officers we make up issues, and we disseminate them in the press, radio or television. We treat them as if they are real. When they are already widespread, usually people will talk about them and they tend to add to and exaggerate the issues. Finally the issues will come back [to the intelligence bodies] in reports. What is so funny is that these reports incline us to believe that these issues are real, hahaha. In fact, we get terrified and begin to think, 'what if these issues are real?' Hahaha." (Heryanto, 140–41)

Although it is not as clearly acknowledged, a similar "looping effect" operates in the Aceh conflict.

I begin with a telling ethnographic moment, a meeting with a rebel commander in Aceh, Indonesia. Rather than read this as the performance of a powerful, charismatic individual, I explore the strange coauthorships that allow conflict protagonists to emerge. Writing a genealogical account (Foucault 1977) of conflict in Aceh involves tracing the twists and turns through which this protracted, but discontinuous, conflict between the military government and imagined separatist rebels developed and questioning the structure imposed on this complex conflict by an international humanitarian intervention. My experience as a policy analyst demonstrated the difficulties of moving from the messy accounts that anthropological fieldwork discloses to the executive summaries and recommendations that policymakers demand. Observations of the Aceh conflict over the last ten years show that oversimplified analyses of conflicts extend and even intensify violence.

Regimes of understanding that impose teleological narratives on violent conflicts not only reduce the possibility of understanding and addressing the causes and conditions of possibility for violence but may also perpetuate the conflict itself. Anthropologists have concentrated on exploring the context of state violence and human rights abuses and have pointed to the importance of factors that are often left out of human rights reporting (Wilson 1997). Like many anthropologists, I discovered that it was crucial to recognize the complex indeterminacy of conflicts rather than reducing them to two independent protagonists with clear identities. In this chapter, I have suggested analytic approaches that could be used by scholars and policymakers to explore conflict situations, narratives, and representations in places beyond Aceh and Indonesia. Precisely because it takes into account the messiness or "epistemic murkiness" (Taussig 1984) that attends violent conflicts, anthropological knowledge offers a valuable perspective for analyzing representations of conflict situations. In contrast to scholars who suggest that massive state violence defies representation and explanation (Scarry 1985) or seek to document how testimonies of some experiences of violence are marginalized or silenced (Ross 2001, 2003; Arextaga 1997) or how the experience of violence shapes social subjectivity (Kleinman, Das, and Lock 1997), I analyze how violent conflicts are represented and explained, both by those immediately involved and by interested outsiders. These narratives do particular kinds of work and produce effects that merit investigation. I am especially concerned with how conflict expertise is produced and circulates (Mitchell 2002).[1]

My interest in exploring how conflict protagonists come to exist and structure common understandings and human rights interventions developed during more than thirty months of fieldwork in Indonesia focused on the conflict in Aceh between 1996 and 2000 and subsequent visits in 2002, 2003, 2004, and 2006. In 1999, human rights defenders, whom I had initially met in Aceh during the military operations period three years earlier, told me that they were suspicious of the emergent rebel group. Our conversations rehearsed varying interpretations of well-known violent events and were punctuated by unanswerable questions regarding perpetrators, collaborators, victims, and witnesses whose identities were not clearly distinguishable. In 2000, I worked as a policy analyst for an international organization examining violent conflict and transitional justice issues in Indonesia, especially in the Aceh case. At that time, an international humanitarian intervention promoted a "humanitarian pause" cease-fire between the government and rebel forces. In the world of policy analysis, the interpretations and logics that supported policy recommendations required details of particular violence at the same time that they overwrote more nuanced analysis of the contradictory processes by which those situations developed.

Conversations with a range of individuals and observation of how conflict dynamics play out through locally, nationally, and internationally mediated contexts guide my attention to, and analysis of, the work that conflict narratives do. I have spent a significant amount of time discussing the Aceh conflict with human rights activists working locally and nationally. In developing these analytic principles, I am less interested in joining these actors' discourse about what should or should not be done than in considering the analyses and representations utilized by international humanitarian organizations that intervene in conflicts while claiming to be neutral. I argue that stable conflict protagonists are created and consolidated through discourses and narratives that elide the dynamics that underlie their existence. In Aceh, the binary opposition of conflict protagonists required for "peace" negotiations is actually the ammunition that perpetually renews and extends violence.

Meeting the "Commander"

In 1998, Indonesia was filled with euphoria and violence after the fall of its longtime authoritarian ruler, Soeharto, and his New Order regime. Hope centered on establishing the rule of law, securing civilian control over the military, and ending corruption. At the same time, the legacies of New Order violence threatened as regions demanded greater autonomy and a larger share of resource wealth from the central state. International observers and Jakarta-based elites were anxious about the possibility of Indonesia's disintegration as political grievances from East Timor, Irian Jaya, and Aceh were invoked to demand justice and resource-rich regions that had been relatively stable, such as Riau, began to press the center for greater revenues as well. "The Aceh problem" posed a particularly serious threat to the integrity and stability of the Indonesian state.

Definitions of "the Aceh problem" and the threat it posed varied for nationalists, political elites, military figures, nongovernmental activists, and reformers. The seriousness of the problem was not disputed. The commander in chief of the Indonesian military, Wiranto, apologized for thousands of "excesses" committed by soldiers in Aceh during a decade-long (1989–1998) operation to secure the region and its valuable natural resources, especially oil reserves and a productive natural gas field (see "Dicabut, Status 'DOM' Aceh*Panglima ABRI Jenderal Wiranto Mohon Maaf," *Kompas*, 8 August 1998). Soeharto's authoritarian New Order regime (1966–1998) perpetrated much violence by proxy to protect its own legality (Ryter 1998). The 1998 public apology marked a crucial shift from a government policy of denying any responsibility for violence in Aceh and refusing to deal with citizens' demands. For many elite Jakarta reformers as well as civil society activists, the Aceh problem seemed open to legal resolution. The acknowledgement of state violence seemed to promise that the military would be held judicially accountable. As he apologized, the commander in chief invited members of the Free Aceh Movement—Gerakan Aceh Merdeka, GAM—who had fled the military occupations to return from the neighboring countries where they had taken refuge. During 1999, the Aceh problem metamorphosed from the impossibility of providing political, legal, and economic justice for widely known crimes to the possibility of negotiating with armed separatists organized as GAM and addressing nonviolent popular demands for a referendum on secession from Indonesia.

For international donors and policymakers, the first post-Soeharto elections in June 1999 were an important test of democratization. Most international observers and analysts considered the elections a success. In June 1999, I monitored the Indonesian national elections in Aceh,[2] which were a site of struggle over the central state's legitimacy. Most people I interviewed spoke cautiously about threats made to deter them from participating in the election. When I asked about the source of these threats, most people said they came from people claiming to speak "in the name of GAM." The Indonesian government modified various national election procedures in response to these threats. For instance, throughout Indonesia voters' fingers were dipped in dye to prevent repeated voting. In Aceh, because of threats that forefingers with the dye would be cut off, no dye was used.[3]

I mentioned to a friend at the local election-monitoring group that I would be interested in speaking to a representative of GAM regarding their strategy of boycotting the election to demonstrate that "the will of the Acehnese people was not to legitimize the Indonesian state." Most taxi drivers were not willing to risk driving outside of the provincial capital, Banda Aceh. I found a willing driver and shared the taxi with two other international monitors and two Acehnese students. As we approached the city limits and the edge of cell phone coverage, I received a telephone call with directions for meeting the GAM. We stopped at the appointed gas pump and were taken into a small building, pieced together from sections of corrugated roofing with frayed fabric covering open sections serving as windows. I had not noticed many people along the road, but the building suddenly crowded with people. We were seated at a table, asked our names, where we were from, and if indeed we wanted to meet Abdullah Syafi'ie, the GAM commander. Finally a young man wearing a white crocheted cap stood up. According to the students, the cap, along with his language inflection, indicated that this man had recently returned from Malaysia. He would lead us. He sped off on his motorcycle trailing a cloud of brown dust, and our car rattled along behind, seemingly in circles, for half an hour.

We drove up to the edge of a camp of solidly built sky-blue wooden structures raised on stilts anchored in concrete foundations, close to the main road. The buildings circled a tall pole from which the GAM flag flew. As soon as the taxi stopped, several men in camouflage approached us. They held walkie-talkies, their mouths bent to the speakers and the antennae flying above their heads. Focused on their "handy-talkies," they said very little to us as they led us up the narrow stairs of the largest building to an open-air meeting room. We sat on bamboo mats covering the wooden floor. Men, women, and children in ordinary clothing watched us climb the stairs. We were seated near the front. An older man with graying hair leaned against the low wall at the edge of the platform; his eyes scanned the compound for anyone who might be approaching.

A large man wearing camouflage entered carrying an old AK-47, a small, black rectangular box, and a thick sheaf of photocopied newspapers stapled with a green cover curling on the right corner. He said, "My name is Abdullah Syafi'ie. I am forty-three years old. I am the commander in chief of Aceh Merdeka [Free Aceh]."[4] Syafi'ie explained that the goal of Aceh Merdeka is "none other than to restore the sovereignty of Aceh from the past era."[5] He claimed that the Dutch colonizers had "stolen Aceh's independence on March 26, 1873," when they declared war on Aceh to assert their claim over the entire island of Sumatra. He faulted the international community for allowing this denial of sovereignty to continue when Indonesia became independent: "The international world further erred in 1945 by recognizing the name of Indonesia, and as a result our nation[6] has been colonized until now. We request the attention of the international world's justice for our independence. We want our nation, Aceh, to return to its original sovereignty." He pointed to the photocopied English-language newspaper sources as evidence that Aceh had negotiated as a sovereign nation and was not part of the Netherlands Indies. Because the "international world failed to honor its laws," he continued, "Acehnese have been treated cruelly by the Dutch and then the Javanese." The "Javanese now bring rifles and threats to our people so that they will participate in their election." Reiterating that "these acts violate international law," he asked: "why is the international world still silent? . . . where is the justice of the UN?"[7] He stressed that the Acehnese people's desire for independence was not founded in "forming a new country, rather it was a continuation of the country of our ancestors." He implied that Aceh had always been a distinct country and that Indonesia current occupation was illegal.

Syafi'ie summoned the "worst cases" to testify to injustice and abuse. The people who had been waiting below swiftly and solemnly climbed the stairs and sat on the mats behind us. We turned to watch as these individuals delivered concise sound bites of horror about their victimization by the Indonesian military. They focused on the immediate acts of violence; they did not speculate on motives or causes. Their statements were delivered in rapid succession with no time for questions or interaction. The stories reminded me of the media accounts of similar violations. Most individuals bore physical scars that matched the stories they told. He encouraged us to photograph them. With the other female monitor, I was shown to a small, empty room that measured about four feet by six feet to hear two young women tell their stories of rape. The first woman exclaimed, "we are suffering" and recounted the events she had experienced, even reenacting certain moments in the attack. The other woman spoke with difficulty, voicing concern about her social status and marriage prospects as a known rape victim. We were then encouraged to photograph the victims. After these photographs, the commanders posed with the flag and the community of supporters behind them. The students were particularly eager to have copies of these photographs to document their meeting with rebels. Syafi'ie's performance relied on the photocopied histories, the black box, and the gun, along with the victims whom he called upon for testimony.

The black box contained ammunition, or so we were told. One of the Acehnese students explained to me that Syafi'ie carried the ammunition to counter rumors that GAM had only older weapons left from the 1950s and no ammunition. From 1948 to 1963, the Darul Islam/Tentara Islam Indonesia (DI/TII) movement, based in West Java but with significant support in South Sulawesi, South Kalimantan, and Aceh, rebelled against the central government. This armed movement sought to establish an Islamic state throughout Indonesia; it was not a separatist movement, and it was not limited to Aceh. Most chronologies of conflict in Aceh link the DI/TII rebellion to later radical and separatist movements. All these movements have distinct characteristics, but their conflation is itself significant, whether the linkage is made by the central government to rationalize its tight control of Aceh or by Free Aceh rebels such as Abdullah Syafi'ie to demonstrate the historical continuity of their struggle for sovereignty. To be credible threats in 1999, however, archaic guns needed live ammunition. Thus the black box, an inscrutable container whose contents were not open to inspection but whose existence attested to the contemporary power of GAM.

I suggest that the ammunition is in fact the existence of "GAM." Unpacking this description of the Aceh problem is like trying to look inside a black box that is impossible to open or, if pried open, reveals a mechanism whose workings are utterly incomprehensible. While Abdullah Syafi'ie points to the black box to attest to the power of Aceh Merdeka to challenge the Indonesian government, the violence that this ammunition signifies—even if the box turns out to be empty—simultaneously authorizes the forces of government repression. GAM exists because it commits acts of violence that are met with state violence, delivered both directly by the Indonesian military and indirectly through other armed forces. The violence of the state demonstrates the existence of GAM. Does GAM exist in order to justify state violence? The black box is inscrutable, but the conflict continues with live fire being exchanged from both sides. Perhaps the ammunition even changes hands in the shadows.

To explore how the existence of GAM is produced and maintained as a "black box" of ammunition, I extend Bruno Latour's notion of the black box drawn from cybernetics to indicate a social phenomenon whose inner workings are so complex that they are impossible to analyze.[8] The phenomena Latour characterizes as "black-boxing" fuse discursive and material resources into well-established facts and unproblematic objects that take on lives of their own. Seemingly immune to scrutiny, critique, and intervention, "black boxes" produce new results that extend discourses, replicate institutional practices, and produce material effects. I link the concept of the black box with ammunition to emphasize the importance of the existence of the conflict protagonist GAM for the extension of violence in Aceh and to underline the importance of an analytic approach that considers the social lives of conflict narratives and the work they do in extending conflict, foreclosing some futures and limiting liability for past violence. Developing this notion of the black box contributes to an analysis of the relationship between violence and history, which is critical in the Aceh case.

Syafi'ie claimed both Aceh's historic greatness and its prolonged suffering for his movement. He relied on two interlocked claims: one, that Aceh rightfully should be an independent, sovereign nation based on internationally recognized treaties; and two, that as the commander in chief he spoke for Free Aceh, a movement founded in 1976 by Hasan Tiro. He bypassed several other equally significant events between 1873 and 1976. Many Acehnese take pride in their people's prolonged resistance to Dutch colonization after 1873 and their active participation in the Indonesian movement for independence before and after 1945; indeed, these stories of anticolonial struggle are often told as a single narrative. Syafi'ie appropriated this tradition to buttress his claims for Aceh's independence. Second, he collapsed the complex history of Acehnese resistance to Indonesia by proclaiming the identity of GAM with the movement led by Hasan Tiro in the late 1970s, which was quickly crushed by the Indonesian armed forces (initially ABRI, later TNI). Conflict narratives created retrospectively, by international mediators as well as by Aceh Merdeka spokesmen, posit unbroken continuity between these two groups despite Hasan Tiro's flight to Sweden in 1979. Furthermore, by wielding the AK-47 to appropriate the mythic bravery and just struggle of DI/TII for GAM, Syafi'ie was engaged in the process of casting the current rebellion as an extension of DI/TII struggles (on DI/TII, see Sjamsuddin 1985 and on DI/TII leader Daud Beureueh, see Siegel 2000). In dominant conflict narratives, Acehnese participation in DI/TII during the 1950s plays an important role in enlivening Jakarta's anxieties about rebellion in Aceh,[9] but figures more as a provocation for repression than as a cause of the later uprising. The history Syafi'ie was constructing by splicing together different episodes of resistance and bravery posits an essentially continuous anti-colonial struggle from the advent of the Dutch until that moment, collapsing significant distinctions and contradictory meanings in its proclamation of Aceh's national sovereignty.

Syafi'ie's narrative of Aceh Merdeka consolidated the grievances of the recent past and the greatness of the distant past into an identifiable group as the representative around which a people's dissatisfaction could coalesce. This history both overwrites and is underwritten by the testimony of suffering victims. The existence of GAM requires the historical narrative performed by Syafi'ie, but this narrative of its continuous struggle also provides an unending supply of ammunition to animate and extend the conflict.

The Indissolubility of Conflict Discourses from Acts of Violence

The process by which GAM's existence became a black box of ammunition in an ongoing conflict demonstrates that representations and historical narratives are part of the conflicts they depict. The discursive dimension of conflict is not merely rhetoric that can be distinguished from urgent, on-the-ground events; these narratives are among the key conditions of possibility for conflict. I suggest a first principle: *It is impossible to separate the discourse from the materiality of the conflict.*[10] All conflicts have narratives that constitute protagonists, proclaim grievances, construct histories, and legitimate the conflict for actors on various sides.[11] The existence of identifiable conflict protagonists is critical for analysis, policymaking, negotiation, resolution, and international intervention. Grievances mobilize supporters and antagonists, and their interplay sets the agenda as negotiable—or not. Conflict situations are produced and perpetuated by various narrations of successive events that stand, not as object and description, but as spirals of interpretation and action. That some narratives come true is not evidence that those particular narratives are correct representations of the conflict, but rather signs of their discursive power to reproduce it. Historical events attain their importance through policies and successive acts that are shaped by discursive constructions of the conflict. In the case at hand, GAM exists, but like the black box, its inner workings and the processes that brought GAM into existence defy comprehension despite their having substantial consequences. Reversing the commonsensical notion that violence occurs because a group of rebels against a militarized state exists, I argue that GAM exists because violence is committed. That this violence is committed mostly against ordinary people, often in the name of defending Indonesia against GAM and the violence attributed to it by the security forces, is a central, rather than accidental, feature of the problem.

The Global Dimensions of Local Conflicts

The conflict in Aceh might be characterized as a sub-state conflict, since in 1959 Aceh was granted the status of "special territory" (*daerah istimewa*) within Indonesia and allowed a degree of autonomy in the conduct of local affairs. However, the conditions that have made it possible for an independence movement to exist in Aceh are global. Syafi'ie addressed his demands to "the international world" and demanded the "justice of the UN" to restore Aceh's rightful sovereignty. The movement rested its claims on international law and pursued a strategy of international recognition. Our visit was part of this effort, as were GAM's frequent contacts with the Indonesian and foreign media. Although Syafi'ie and GAM claim to represent the people of Aceh and set forth their demand for self-determination, the legitimation strategy of the movement has an international base. The knowledge and experience that Hasan Tiro acquired abroad as the exiled leader of Aceh Merdeka enabled GAM to obtain a hearing and assistance from foreign mediators. The validation of Acehnese aspirations by international institutions would, GAM hoped, bring justice to Aceh at last.

GAM quite literally cannot be recognized outside of an international context. Claiming to represent the people of Aceh in a popular liberation movement despite the prominent, nearly exclusive role of Hasan Tiro in prior actions, Syafi'ie points to the brutality of the occupying forces and calls on victims to support this claim. Syafi'ie elaborated on the group's local legitimacy when I asked him to comment on its membership: "Since the birth of Aceh Merdeka, everyone has been Aceh Merdeka. But before there was attention from the international community, like there is now, our people could not act because of the cruel abuse by Javanese colonialists. Truly, since the founding on 4 December 1976, everyone has become Aceh Merdeka."

When I asked Syafi'ie about the history of his organization, he emphasized the international component of the struggle as he located the origins of Aceh Merdeka in the Javanese extension of Dutch colonization and Hasan Tiro's education in international affairs:

Java continued the colonization of the Dutch and they did not have the right to our sovereignty. Out of that our struggle was born, by our leader, the venerable

Hasan di Tiro. That is our beloved leader whom we adore. Before he came home from the United States, where he went to school, our people did not know anything. Because we had been colonized and all of our leaders had been butchered by the Dutch, and then by the Javanese, we did not know how to establish a legitimate movement that was recognized by the international world to restore our history. Thus, with the homecoming of the venerable one, Aceh Merdeka was founded and has existed until now. We love and adore our leader.

Under the mantle of its eighty-year-old founder, Syafi'ie asserted the continuous existence of Aceh Merdeka from Hasan Tiro's tumultuous sojourn in Aceh in 1976–1979 until the recent emergence of Gerakan Aceh Merdeka.[12]

In this account, the movement seeks to restore sovereignty to the nation of Aceh which has been oppressed by Dutch and Javanese colonialism. Pursuant to international law, Syafi'ie emphasized that his group does not seek to form a new state, but rather to redress past injustices. In order to make internationally valid arguments, Syafi'ie's statements neglect the period of Indonesian anticolonial liberation struggles in which Acehnese played a prominent, even heroic role. Moving from Acehnese struggles against the Dutch in the name of Indonesia to Acehnese struggles against Java in the name of Acehnese sovereignty bypasses the complexities of Aceh's relationship to Indonesia from 1945 to 1976.

While Syafi'ie pointed to historically distant events, the resurgence and rhetoric of Free Aceh were inseparable from the situation in East Timor, in which international institutions played a decisive role. In 1999, East Timorese were granted a UN-supervised referendum to decide if they would accept special autonomy within Indonesia or choose independence. The distinguishing feature of East Timor for activists and policymakers in and outside of Indonesia was that the United Nations had never recognized Indonesia's occupation of the territory. Aceh had always been recognized as part of modern Indonesia. Thus, in pointing to historical treaties that distinguished Aceh from the rest of the Netherlands Indies, Syafi'ie attempted to cast his struggle in terms that followed international precedents. For policymakers in Jakarta, on the other hand, the East Timor case increased their anxieties about the sprawling island state's potential for disintegration and reinforced their tendency to understand the Aceh problem as a separatist threat and not as a case of extended human rights violations that needed legal resolution, especially with international involvement.

The second principle I suggest is: *Local conflicts are always linked to global geopolitical conditions and shaped by prevailing understandings of other conflicts.* Even contemporary conflicts that appear to be locally produced and reproduced take place in a global context that affects the mobilization, organization, duration, narration, and mediation of conflict. Appealing to international institutions requires opposition movements to make their case in terms of the prevailing paradigms of international law, national sovereignty, and human rights (Merry 2006). Arguably, conflict can become a resource for international as well as local and national political actors. A succession of powerful international discourses on the threats of "communism," "ethnocultural" conflict, "Islamist" movements, and "terrorism" have recast the legitimacy of particular conflicts, and in some cases strengthened states against a range of critics and challenges.

What Makes Conflict Protagonists Exist?

Enacting and articulating conflicts, developing policy directed toward intensifying, resolving, or managing them, and studying, analyzing, and intervening in conflicts all assume the existence of identifiable forces whose violent opposition defines the terrain and terms of conflict. To develop my argument that the existence of conflict protagonists serves as ammunition that extends conflicts under conditions like those prevailing in Aceh, we must ask how they achieve an existence in the first place. So I suggest a third principle: *Conflict protagonists exist because there is violence; violence does not occur because conflict protagonists exist.* A fourth principle follows: *The existence of a conflict protagonist obscures the process of distinguishing the group from others and consolidating various interests into a single force.*

While this phenomenon is most apparent in the coalescence of historically distinct moments and groups into the continuous narrative of Aceh Merdeka, the rule applies to the Indonesian government as well. Before 1999, Jakarta and the TNI denied the existence of a campaign of state violence directed against an independence movement in Aceh, even as they carried out systematic repression in order to stamp out "criminal" gangs there and periodically acknowledged appallingly violent actions carried out by gangs and other shady forces allegedly not under central control. Both state and opposition forces are subject to this rule; neither conflict protagonist forms a self-evident unity with well-defined limits in action or discourse. In some black-boxed situations, indeed, state and resistance forces may not necessarily be clearly distinguishable from one another on the ground.

Recognizable conflict protagonists are brought into being through naming, telling origin stories, and classifying groups; through mobilizing resources, spokespeople, and media; through witness testimony, official documents, and policy decisions; and, even in the case of opposition movements, through recognition by the state.[13] Defending the state against an opposition group requires repetition of its name and demands, even if these more powerful actors simultaneously deny its existence as well as its legitimacy and distort its message. Above all, conflict protagonists are brought into being through grievances to complain about and acts of violence to narrate, lament, and remember.

Naming is part of black-boxing; names consolidate a series of properties and collapse distinctions into a singular identifiable object. When I met Abdullah Syafi'ie in 1999, he spoke in the name of Aceh Merdeka (AM, Free Aceh), which declared independence in 1976, not Gerakan Aceh Merdeka (GAM, Free Aceh Movement), which emerged as the Indonesian state's shadowy antagonist during the late 1980s. Syafi'ie claimed all Acehnese as members of his movement, but suggested that they had been unable to express their true beliefs before international observation protected them from reprisals by state forces. The previous silence and inaction of most people in Aceh is interpreted and appropriated by Syafi'ie as an indication of repression by the state and international inattention. This claim echoes the logic of the security forces' threat perception system, which often justifies repression in the name of latent dangers.

Origin stories anchor names and retroject the existence of current political configurations. Since 1999, GAM leaders, international observers, and Indonesian military officers reiterate that GAM has been fighting for independence since 4 December 1976. Elaborate televised anniversary celebrations on 4 December 1999, demonstrated that this armed rebel organization had a twenty-three-year history. The anniversary celebration simultaneously underscored the longevity of the organization and elided the circuitous route by which the organization came to be. The precision of the date suggested a definitive event. According to official GAM documents, Hasan Tiro, as the head of the Aceh Sumatra National Liberation Front (ASNLF),[14] issued a proclamation declaring Aceh Merdeka, Free Aceh, on 4 December 1976. ASNLF included other regions of Sumatra and ethnic groups other than Acehnese. As the name National Liberation Front suggests, Hasan Tiro's declaration was situated in an international context of decolonization and the right to self-determination. He became familiar with international law while working at the UN as a representative for Indonesia in the 1950s. Tiro lost this position when his statements on behalf of the movement for an Islamic state became an embarrassment to Indonesia (see "H. Muhammad Tiro Rupanya Wakil D. I. di Amerika. Visa USA Baginya Tidak Berlaku Lagi," *Waspada*, 16 September 1954). Prior to declaring Aceh Merdeka, Tiro contributed to efforts to shape postcolonial Indonesia; he wrote extensively to advocate federalism and decentralization within the framework of the Indonesian state (Tiro 1948, 1958).

Despite its origin story, GAM was not founded in 1976 but developed from subsequent events in which the Indonesian state was intimately involved and through political transformations enabled by a historical narrative that invoked previous state violence and brave popular resistance. The black-boxing of GAM requires this origin tale. The original acts that constituted its formation, however, relied on histories of several distinct incidents of "rebellion" in Aceh, the Indonesian military's perception of threats to the state (see Honna 2003), a set of supplemental terms positing various incarnations of GAM as well as unidentified criminals, and a pattern of recurrent, but indeterminate violence.

In contrast to histories published in the Indonesian and international media after 1999 about the founding of GAM, Eric E. Morris, who conducted historical research in Aceh and interviewed political figures in Aceh and Indonesia from late 1974 through July 1977, described the group's origin in these terms:

> Immediately following the 1977 election, a separatist movement emerged in Aceh that claimed much attention but only a limited number of active participants. In May 1977 Hasan Muhammad di Tiro issued a declaration of independence of Negara Aceh Merdeka (Independent State of Aceh) and announced the establishment of the National Liberation Front of Aceh. Pamphlets issued by the Aceh Merdeka movement made a straightforward ethnic appeal to rise up against Javanese colonialism. Attention was focused on Aceh's natural wealth. Islamic appeals were noticeable by their absence. (1983, 300)

Newspaper accounts coincide with this chronology; no mention is made of AM, ASNLF, or Hasan Tiro in national media until mid-1977.

The black-boxing of GAM hides the series of events that transformed a political-economic critique launched by an exiled leader and a handful of intellectuals into the current separatist group. Official reports on the group, especially statements by military spokesmen about the threat it presented, contributed to the consolidation of GAM. The repetition of the names Aceh Merdeka and Hasan Tiro and stories that chronicled the success of the security forces in killing the ten individuals named as members of AM strengthened the idea that the state was under threat, even after the last person identified as belonging to AM was reported dead in 1983. Under the Indonesian military threat perception system, the G for Gerakan, movement, was added to Aceh Merdeka.

Despite the eradication of Aceh Merdeka's known local adherents, in 1990 military operations were initiated in Aceh to control what the state characterized as "criminality." At the time, official statements emphasized that the danger was only criminal. However, the security forces cast criminal dangers as a "Security Disruptors Gang" (GPK) and initiated systematic operations to militarize society against it. In 1992, GPK and GAM were linked through trials. Many civilians who were not involved in politics or criminal enterprises were accused of being GPK or GAM to justify their detention, torture, disappearance, and extrajudicial killing. The term GAM was extended well beyond the original members, and its organizational capacities were expanded in the minds of its state antagonists.

For many years, Hasan Tiro was the primary voice of Aceh Merdeka, issuing frequent letters to the UN from his exile in Sweden. During the period of intense state violence from 1989 to 1998, commonly called "DOM" for special military operations zone but defined more narrowly by Jakarta as "Operation Red Net," his connections with armed rebel forces in Aceh were unclear. But both sides of the conflict propagandized this tenuous linkage between AM in Sweden and rebellion in Aceh.[15] Hasan Tiro spoke on behalf of the imagined nation of Aceh in international forums, and the Indonesian state carried out violent acts in the name of combating a movement identified with his name in Aceh. The Indonesian military often accused groups it called GAM, GPK-Hasan Tiro, or GPK-Aceh of committing acts of violence that provoked its own violently repressive campaigns. This cycle of reprisals spiraled seemingly out of control until 1998. When Indonesia ended "Operation Red Net" and the TNI commander in chief invited exiled members of GAM to return to Aceh, the military commanders who emerged from this black-boxed conflict proclaimed themselves Hasan Tiro's followers, implicitly endorsing the security forces' definition of the situation. Abdullah Syafi'ie, GAM's commander in chief, claimed Hasan Tiro as his leader and spoke with the national and international media in the name of GAM.

In 1998 and 1999, I met and interviewed many of those originally accused of being members of Aceh Merdeka. None of them identified with the GAM that appeared after DOM. One person had heard of an armed group in the 1990s while in jail; the leader of the group he referred to was widely acknowledged to have links to the military. Other than this, he said, he did not know much about the armed wing of GAM. In 1999, I asked several of them if they knew Abdullah Syafi'ie, the commander of the armed wing of GAM, who became publicly visible that year; none of them did.

Moving from Conflict Narratives to Conflict Dynamics

Unraveling the shared narrative that has been assembled by the Indonesian state and the current Acehnese opposition from such disparate political currents and distinct instances of violence in Aceh's past demonstrates the four principles I have suggested so far about such conflicts: *that discourses and acts of violence are inextricably connected; that seemingly local conflicts have international dimensions; that conflict protagonists come into existence through acts of violence; and that conflict narratives repress differences among historical actors and paper over chronological and geographical gaps and chasms to construct stable protagonists, perennial grievances, and chronic antagonisms.* That they accomplish sweeping consolidations, elisions, and deceptions almost invisibly does not make them any less powerful. Concealing the tell-tale signs of their construction within black boxes enhances conflict narratives' self-evident "truth" value and enables them to serve as ammunition in conflicts that are perpetually renewed. Because conflict protagonists are a consequence, not a cause, of collective action, they are constituted in violent interactions with their enemies. The fifth principle I suggest is: *The struggle between conflict protagonists obscures narrative convergences that consolidate both state and enemy.*

Conflict chronologies, on which both antagonists and international observers may agree, reiterate a set of terms and apply it to changing conflict situations as if the groups involved and grievances at issue were stable over time. These chronologies appear not to have any narrative or point of view, but they transform a series of contingencies and choices into outcomes that appear inevitable. That this teleological perspective is a retrospective order imposed upon the past by interested contemporary actors is seldom acknowledged by those involved in the creation and propagation of conflict chronologies, whether they are national protagonists or international mediators. Yet this act of interpretation, too, wields enormous power, since it structures these conflicts as deeply rooted in the past, embedded in fundamental ethnocultural and national identities, and by definition impossible to resolve in the present. On the basis of such assumptions and through such constructions, the "undying hatreds" and "inevitable conflicts" issuing in (un)civil, even genocidal warfare are made. Alternative, more peaceful outcomes become literally unthinkable, and liability for actions cannot be assigned because all protagonists' choices are regarded as predetermined. If the state is perpetually insecure and justice becomes ensnared in vengeance, then conflict logics become embedded in negotiations intended to defuse them. This conundrum is familiar to scholars and practitioners of international human rights and conflict resolution and bedevils most efforts to control, let alone resolve, particular sorts of conflicts within states.

In order to construct accounts and conduct analyses of intractable conflicts that do not participate in the discourses that define those conflicts as inevitable and inadvertently support policies that perpetuate rather than end spirals of violence, critical approaches must move from the replication of conflict narratives to the analysis of conflict dynamics. Protracted, violent conflicts develop through specific dynamics whose "inputs and outputs" can be recorded and assessed, even if the system that transforms one into the other remains hidden in a black box. In Aceh, examining conflict dynamics during the period of most intense violence in the 1990s reveals a continuous process of interchange between the state and the "rebels." The security of the Indonesian state and the existence of Free Aceh were predicated on one another, as violent conflict was acted out between groups purported to be their armed forces. Close scrutiny of both the violence and victims' testimony suggests that, in many cases, the lines between these supposed antagonists were blurred. Shadowy forces maneuvered on uncertain, shifting ground, engaging in suspicious exchanges with the enemy under the cover of secrecy.

Victims' Testimony Obscures the Conditions That Produce Violence

Visual and empirical evidence of violence, such as photographs and eyewitness testimony, is composed, interpreted, and deployed as pointedly and strategically as the photocopied newspaper stories from the 1880s that Hasan Tiro probably assembled and Abdullah Syafi'ie carried with him alongside the gun and "ammunition" box. Producing testimony and circulating documentation is premised on the assumption that seeing and hearing about atrocities is so disturbing to observers that it arouses concerted action to end them; the acts of violence represented are such egregious violations of human rights that they must be halted in order to restore onlookers' sense of social order and human interconnection. But the linkage between images and words, on the one hand, and conflict narratives and dynamics, on the other, is multivalent and manipulable rather than fixed or given. I suggest a sixth principle: *Documentary evidence can mislead analysts by obscuring the conditions of possibility for violence and representation in the first place.*[16] Factual details and snapshots are mobilized to support various narratives at the same time that they distract our attention from the conflict logics themselves. Criminality appears as a set of events without apparent causes and lying outside of narratives, but the forensic residues of criminality can later be turned into evidence for different narratives.

Most of the GAM supporters whom Syafi'ie called up to testify the day I visited the camp were victims of an officially unacknowledged but widely recognized Indonesian policy of military repression commonly called DOM. DOM, the acronym for Military Operations Zone, signified the special status conferred by the central government upon the "troubled" regions of Indonesia during Soeharto's rule, including Aceh, East Timor, and Irian Jaya. Within those "unstable" zones, the military and its proxies conducted widespread, systematic campaigns of terror against civilians in the name of security.[17] Wiranto apologized on behalf of the individual members of the armed forces and the Indonesian military for "excesses" committed in Aceh by soldiers during the period between 1989 and 1998, while denying direct governmental responsibility for a policy of systematic human rights violations. In 1998–1999, DOM violence was widely known and reported in Indonesia: Acehnese victims of human rights abuses gave widely publicized testimonies to investigative teams, high-ranking state officials, and mass media.[18] Testimonies about sexual violence perpetrated by Indonesian soldiers in Aceh underlined the "sadism" and "arbitrariness" of the military.[19] The "hill of skulls" and "village of widows" provided vivid illustrative detail for reports that the excavation of mass graves indicated possible "massacres."[20] Testimonies also found their way into literature, drama, and nonfiction books that circulated widely during this period (Eda and Dharma 1999; Sukanta 1999b; Surampaet 2000). Media, politicians, and reformers all used the phrase "DOM victim" to emphasize the innocence of the victims and the systematic nature of the military operations in this zone.

No one expressed much doubt that the acts of violence recounted by victims had occurred. The national human rights commission documented 781 extrajudicial killings and 163 forced "disappearances" (Independent Commission 1999). Other governmental and nongovernmental teams documented serious abuses, including torture; estimated totals ranged between 5,000 and 7,000 victims. As "excesses" expanded into accounts of atrocities and evidence of systematic crimes piled up, high-ranking military officers denied the existence of the classification "DOM" without denying that individual members of the military had committed these acts ("Try: Tak Pernah Ada DOM di Aceh," *Republika*, 30 November 1999). Just before GAM's televised 1999 anniversary, military commanders addressing a special parliamentary session asserted that there was no policy called DOM, but that from 1989 to 1998 a strong military presence had been necessary to secure Aceh for development of its gas fields and to protect Indonesia from armed separatists who threatened national integrity. They again acknowledged that the implementation of these security operations had been marked by "problems" and "excesses," but defended them as a necessary response to the dangers in Aceh at that time (*Risalah Rapat* 1999). Ordinary Acehnese and archival sources tell a different story about threats and violence during the DOM period.

In 1990, most military spokesmen described the security problem in Aceh as apolitical and unrelated to previous opposition movements. Try Sutrisno, the same general who told the 1999 parliamentary session that DOM never existed, stated in 1990, as head of the Indonesian Armed Forces, that "the security disturbances in Aceh have no connection with politics; they are nothing other than acts of pure criminality" ("Pangab Try Sutrisno: Gangguan Keamanan di Aceh tidak ada Kaitan Politik," *Kompas*, 10 July 1990). Military spokesmen classified the security danger in Aceh as a criminal movement (Gerakan) and identified it by the acronym GPK or GPK-Aceh. In military statements about Aceh, GPK was commonly defined as a disorganized gang: "It is not clear who their leader is, and they are not tightly organized. . . . They are not all Acehnese, but are mixed with people from other areas" ("GPK Aceh: Kucing, Ganja dan Teror," *Majalah Tempo*, 30 June 1990, 23). Military sources explicitly distinguished GPK disturbances from the 1950s DI/TII movement to establish an Islamic state in Indonesia and the 1976 declaration of Free Aceh. Instead, they found a plausible explanation for criminality in conflicts over the valuable marijuana grown in Aceh: "Security disturbances in Aceh don't have any link with the problem of DI/TII or what has been called Free Aceh [Aceh Merdeka]. These security disturbances are not organized, but only 'revenge' between individuals because there was an operation to destroy marijuana fields" ("Pangab Try Sutrisno: Gangguan Keamanan di Aceh tidak ada Kaitan Politik," *Kompas*, 10 July 1990). Official statements about the composition of GPK specified the differences between dangers in 1990 and previous movements. One national media source explained that, according to the military, Hasan Tiro "used regional sentiment as a motivation"; "in contrast, the majority of this group [GPK] are not even people from this area," that is, Acehnese ("GPK Aceh: Kucing, Ganja dan Teror," *Majalah Tempo*, 30 June 1990, 25).

In 1990, an important Acehnese figure from DI/TII also surmised that GPK was not a political movement. He asked: "if this is a political movement, how come the victims killed are small children and low-ranking soldiers?" ("GPK Aceh: Kucing, Ganja dan Teror," *Majalah Tempo*, 30 June 1990, 26). The presence of non-Acehnese elements among the "security disruptors" and the discontinuity between this disturbance and previous political movements in Aceh were emphasized by both military and Acehnese community leaders. Most reports indicated that the GPK enjoyed neither social nor political legitimacy, and GPK-associated activity was not widespread.

At the same time, the GPK was a matter of serious concern to the Indonesian state, and its evident expertise in technologies of violence required explanation. Prior to the emergence of a visible GAM in 1999, the Indonesian military often accused GPK-Hasan Tiro or GPK-Aceh of authoring violence that only the military was capable of perpetrating. The same military official explained: "Because some of them [GPK] are ex-ABRI [former members of the Indonesian Armed Forces], it is not strange that this group is professional in their use of firearms" ("GPK Aceh: Kucing, Ganja dan Teror," *Majalah Tempo*, 30 June 1990, 23). A gang that made such effective use of violence had to be countered by a well-organized and powerful military force and by a concerted campaign to mobilize the populace to defend the state—or so the Indonesian armed forces contended.

In media accounts that reported military statements in 1990, the term GPK-Aceh refers to a disorganized gang comprised of military deserters, who possessed the means and techniques of violence that the Indonesian military should have monopolized, along with non-Acehnese, common criminals, and unidentified others. Even as GPK was the name used to designate an unorganized group, it gathered incidents of criminality into a threat that required a systematic response.

The military responded to the GPK problem in 1990 by training civilians to "defend" the nation and by "cultivating" GPK members to renounce the GPK and assist the military in its operations to eradicate the group. Geoffrey Robinson (1998) accurately described the military's exaggerated reaction to the GPK, outlining how civilians were militarized through paramilitary national defense groups (see also "Dilepas Dengan Surat Annisa," *Editor*, 6 October 1990).

In 1990, reports of corpses discovered in Aceh by foreign human rights monitors drew attention to the military's plans to eradicate GPK. Suggestions that the military had been summarily executing those it labeled as GPK were met with vehement denials and detailed explanations by regional and national military spokespeople. One published interview with a regional military commander included an explanation of the corpses that is worth detailed examination:

Tempo [Interviewer]: What about the corpses identified as members of GPK?
Pramono: Okay, I read that in *Tempo*. So, actually, they [the corpses] are in fact victims of the GPK itself. Sometimes, it's like this, the ones who surrender or the ones who help us are murdered by the GPK. That's true. I am not making this up. If you say that those corpses are tied like this (then Major General Pramono held up his two thumbs) what you would say is that can't be done by an ordinary person [*orang awam*, non-expert]. How would that kind of person know how to tie them up like that, the reason is there are deserters. [You might also ask,] don't a number of them wear camouflage, even though they are GPK. But camouflage fatigues are easy to get, for example in Bandung. Those deserters may be one or two people but they know the techniques, don't they, and they can teach them. So, they do it that way because it will look like we did it. So, they work hard to use our weaknesses and discredit us, so that the people

will hate the army. . . . So it happens that there is a member of GPK who surren-
ders, he is considered a traitor by the GPK. After we train him, we release him.
But in the middle of the road, he is killed by GPK. ("Rakyat Jangan Jadi Korban: Wawancara Tempo dengan Pangdam I/Bukit Barisan Mayjen Pramono,"
Majalah Tempo, 17 November 1990, 33)

This passage discloses the difficulty of knowing who was who in this conflict. There were overlaps between the military and its GPK enemy; the
signs that might normally confirm the identity of military members—
possession of a weapon, uniform, or expertise—could be used by either
side creating an atmosphere of extreme insecurity and distrust for most
people. State violence in Aceh during this period was extreme and arbitrary, but it was also perpetrated through more familiar informers,
collaborators, spies, and counterspies in a shadowy world of double
agents and doubled identities. Many individuals who experienced the
conflict first hand confirmed the apparent collusion between military
and its enemy. In addition to creating conditions of generalized fear
and suspicion, this practice made it extremely difficult to assign responsibility for violence and criminal acts to any individual or group.

In 1990, military sources narrated violence in Aceh as acts perpetrated by a criminal gang, not an ideological or separatist movement,
that possessed weapons and expertise transferred from the military
itself through deserters. The military had a program to eliminate this
threat by training members of society as paramilitaries and by cultivating members of GPK as military informants. Corpses were evidence of
GPK revenge upon traitors—not, or so they argued, evidence of the
military's own campaign of violent repression. GPK imitated the military in order to discredit and alienate it from the people it sought to
defend.

Archival sources disclose that these public distinctions strongly
drawn in 1989–1990 between the two threats, GPK and GAM, were contradicted after 1998 by policy reports, GAM leaders and spokespersons,
and military officials and analysts who stated that the two groups were
always the same. Consolidating acts of indeterminate violence and social critique as the same movement, GPK/GAM, justified past policies
and focused present anxieties. This construction emerged most visibly
after 1998 in official discourse, but was also echoed in GAM histories.

The victims' accounts that circulated in 1998–1999 testifying to arbitrary and sadistic violence committed by the Indonesian military provoked widespread outrage. An independent commission was appointed
by presidential decree issued by Habibie to investigate the abuses and
provide a foundation for a judicial process of accountability. The final
report, handed over to President Wahid in December 1999, explained

not only the thousands of victims who had receded from public view but also the armed fighters who were more often pictured. The commission report described the violence experienced by DOM victims, finding a pervasive pattern: victims were abducted and tortured based on accusations that they were assisting the GAM. After listing twenty-five types of violent acts done by the military at strategic posts in Aceh and devoting an equal amount of space to acts of sexual violence, the report concludes that "every type of violence which was done by the side of the [state security forces, military and police] points to a model of violence which was systematic and planned as an effort to intimidate the people for their attitude (or belief) and their choices in politics, in which [they] were always suspected as a member of GAM" (Independent Commission 1999, 21). The report explains the violent excesses of the early 1990s as part of a conflict in which citizens were arrested and persecuted for their political choices in the context of an already existing separatist movement. Stating that people were criminalized for their political "attitude" or "belief" implies a level of political resistance that was absent from previous narratives of criminality.

Although some individuals and groups may have organized politically in Aceh during the New Order, most individuals who were accused of being GAM did not choose to become politically active. Many described to me how they were implicated in politics through the accusation of a neighbor or business rival. According to the report, people accused their personal enemies of being associated with GAM in order to provoke the military to take action against them: "there was a pattern when there was a conflict between citizens, the rich citizen would use the military to torture the person who happened to be 'poor' with the excuse that he was involved with GPK/GAM" (Independent Commission 1999, 43). The state security forces collaborated with this misuse of their power for personal gain. The report concludes that, rather than stopping this pattern, the military cultivated and extended it.

Evidence that victims made political choices is largely absent from archival sources and initial discussions of DOM excesses. Indeed, most people I spoke with in 1999 expressed suspicions about what was then being called GAM. They often remarked that there were several varieties of GAM, imitation GAMs, and members of the military's Special Forces unit (Kopassus) who acted as GAM. They also noted that many GAM heroes appeared suddenly without a track record. Yet the conflict discourse, policy, and interventions rapidly became structured by understandings of the conflict as an armed separatist movement led by GAM, rather than unresolved state violence and regional economic inequalities (Drexler 2006b). I suggest a seventh principle here: *Narrative logics can corrupt forensic evidence and limit state liability for acts of violence its agents have acknowledged perpetrating.*

International Interventions and Alternative Analyses of Conflict Dynamics

On 12 May 2000, the government of Indonesia and representatives of GAM, meeting in Geneva, signed a "Joint Understanding on Humanitarian Pause for Aceh." This intervention, facilitated by the Henry Dunant Centre for Humanitarian Dialogue (HDC), an international NGO that mediates and promotes the resolution of armed conflicts, produced an agreement only six months after the presidential commission's report on human rights violations in Aceh. For the Humanitarian Pause, the HDC chose GAM as its negotiating partner, bypassing more complex coalitions of civil society groups and human rights advocates that had recently organized in Aceh. In the context of the "pause" agreement, citizens who wished to critique the state or military and participate in the mediations had to identify themselves as members of GAM, a stigmatized, illegal, and violent separatist group. Legalizing GAM as the only opposition group and consolidating political critique with violent struggle made GAM appear to be a solid movement with a continuous history and social legitimacy. The terms and consequences of the agreement obscured GAM's relationship to the military and popular suspicion of many Acehnese toward these reputed rebels (Drexler 2006a).

This intervention was followed by an HDC-brokered Cessation of Hostilities Agreement (COHA), but the military declared a state of emergency after it broke down. The most recent Memorandum of Understanding (MOU), signed in August 2005, validated and institutionalized the historical narrative on which the Indonesian state and GAM agreed, which constitutes them as the sole protagonists and legitimate representatives of the aspirations of the peoples of Aceh and Indonesia. Although the relative quiet temporarily brought about by the Humanitarian Pause and Cessation of Hostilities Agreement and recently established by the MOU has been a boon to the people of Aceh, especially after the devastating Indian Ocean tsunami, what this resolution has obscured and denied may still have the power to shape events. Most people I spoke with in early 2006 were wary of looking too closely at the past for fear of disturbing a fragile peace, yet what they knew about events on the ground made this narrative seem at best incomplete and at worst a continuation, rather than resolution, of the problem.

I conclude by suggesting an eighth principle: *Interventions are never neutral. How conflicts are understood shapes strategies for their resolution and may re-*

produce the very conflict formation that the intervention was designed to resolve.
The prevailing understanding of the conflict as violent separatism that
structured interventions and renewed military operations now structures
conflict resolution and reconstruction programs, which are aimed primarily at the reintegration of violent separatists and the transformation of
their armed struggle to a political struggle. A plethora of internationally
and nationally sponsored programs have been designed to reintegrate
ex-combatants into communities: amnesty has been granted, land has
been provided, and stipends have been promised. Yet conflict victims
have been marginalized from political and social initiatives.

In early 2006, I talked with many human rights defenders who had
been working in Aceh for a decade or more to ensure accountability for
acts of violence. Instead of reporting progress, many nongovernmental
organizations were unable to secure funding for their justice projects.
Some groups had to design psychosocial recovery programs to serve
tsunami victims and well as conflict victims, eliding human rights violations with a natural catastrophe. I was stunned to discover that individuals who had spent the last decade documenting the damages of the
conflict had now fallen silent about the past. In private conversations
they told me that now was not the time. They repeated dominant rationales that the people just want peace. Some told me that it was still too
dangerous. As activists became preoccupied with moving their struggle
for justice into democratization and policymaking, the old fears of violence underscored their reluctance to probe the disquieting legacy of
the past.

Decommissioning Weapons and Disarming Existence

Post-conflict reconstruction has its own regime of expertise and institutions. As a trained anthropologist who also served on occasion as an international observer and policy advisor, I am especially sensitive to the
assumptions imported by the nonviolent army of experts that arrives to
keep the peace in the aftermath of protracted state terror and armed
resistance. Mechanisms of transitional justice, international tribunals,
criminal trials, truth commissions, and commissions of inquiry have
gained increasing importance as tools of post-conflict rebuilding. In
recognition of the haunting presence of historical grievances, trials and
tribunals, no less than truth commissions, attempt to rewrite historical
narratives in order both to settle accounts and to fill in missing pieces
of the story. The expanding role of international institutions in pursuing justice after instances of mass atrocity has sparked public debate on
the function of trials for war crimes and crimes against humanity for
creating historical memory and public awareness of history (Osiel 1997;

Douglas 2001), as opposed to adhering strictly to the requirements of the judicial process for determining criminal accountability or reestablishing legitimate judicial institutions (Arendt 1964; Buruma 1994; Malamud-Goti 1996). Recent research examining international transitional justice mechanisms demonstrates that these processes often fail to achieve meaningful justice, accountability, or truth, and that these goals do not necessarily lead to reconciliation or the reconstitution of the social (Shaw 2007; Ferme 2006; Drexler 2006c; Ross 2003; Wilson 1997; Kelsall 2005; James and van de Vijver 2000). Demands for justice and institutions for achieving it are often based on global politics instead of local needs and practices; when states use these mechanisms to "attribute culpability to others, including their past selves, they often, paradoxically, legitimize ongoing injustices" (Sundar 2004, 145).

Historical and collective memory are often linked to the process of moving beyond trauma (Caruth 1995; LaCapra 2001). Memory is often positioned against forgetting in the struggle for justice. Jelin (2003) argues that rethinking the relationship between memory and politics or memory and national identity is an important component of working through trauma. Anthropologists have demonstrated that memory is shaped by complex social processes and everyday practices (see, for example, Steedly 1993, 2000; Stoler and Strassler 2000; Bal, Crewe, and Spitzer 1999; Mueggler 2001). Even if there are no official institutions for addressing violent pasts in Aceh, memories will be shaped by everyday practices that enforce certain narrations and recollections of the past while rendering others unthinkable or unsayable.

Disarming the existence of conflict protagonists that I have argued serves as the ammunition to extend the conflict entails more than the symbolic decommissioning of weapons; it requires a scrupulous review of the past. I have proposed in this chapter that the existence of GAM has been the ammunition for extending the conflict in Aceh. At the same time, the recognition of GAM's existence has made legal examination of the past impossible. The most recent peace agreement, the MOU, is predicated on the existence of GAM as a negotiating partner, though it simultaneously proposes to disarm it as a military force. Reconstruction processes are structured around GAM as the legitimate and sole representative of the Acehnese people. As a result of the December 2006 elections, "ex-GAM" will fill many positions in institutions of provincial governance.

Just before the elections, as the Aceh Monitoring Mission (AMM) wound down, heated debate emerged on the public display of GAM symbols. The head of the monitoring mission, Pieter Feith, called upon GAM to disband and said that the existence of GAM did not help the peace process (see "Kapan GAM Harus Bubar?" *Kontras* 343,

20–26 July 2006, 4). Nationalist lawmakers in Jakarta declared that GAM was no longer relevant once the conditions of the MOU had been fulfilled (see "Atasi Ganjalan RUU PA. Pertemukan GAM dengan Pemerintah. AMM dituntut segera ambil langkah penyelesaian," *Republika*, 13 July 2006). In his capacity as GAM representative to the AMM, Irwandi, who has since been elected as Aceh's governor, explained that there was nothing to worry about because GAM had already promised not to struggle for independence and that the weapons that GAM possessed, which had previously scared the Republic of Indonesia, had all been destroyed ("Irwandi Yusuf. Perwakilan GAM di AMM: GAM tak Relevan 2, 5 Tahun Lagi," *Kontras* 343, 20–26 July 2006, 6). He stated that GAM was not a problem for the Indonesian military ("Irwandi dan Feith Berbeda Pendapat Bendera GAM Bukan Simbol Militer," *Kompas*, 15 December 2006), a contention that the military later denied (see "Pangdam Bantah Pernyataan Irwandi," *Serambi Indonesia*, 16 December 2006, 1, 11). Finally, GAM representatives asserted that if GAM disappeared, so would the peace that had been signed between GAM and the Indonesian government. The military disagreed and hung banners in front of the barracks stating otherwise (Figure 1).

The inauguration of "ex-GAM" members to elected office ensures that GAM will persist under whatever name its party adopts. In addition to my reservations about the absence of institutions and processes for addressing the legacies of past violence, I remain concerned about what may happen politically if the past is not reviewed. Unless the corruptions of the past are examined, the logic of an insecure state will continue to replicate itself. Because the letter M in GAM stands for Merdeka, the organization's name will always recall the independence claimed by separatists from the Republic. Without considering the logics of the insecure state, even though all the existing GAM weapons may be decommissioned and their ammunition destroyed, the existence of GAM as a latent danger may never be fully disarmed. It may remain a threat that the state calls upon to name the insecurity it cannot quite locate but still feels compelled to combat (see Siegel 1998).

"Ghost Science"

The multiple deaths of named leaders demonstrate the difficulty of disarming the existence of conflict protagonists. The terms and logics that structure a particular conflict exceed the control of individuals, even those who appear to lead the movement. I met Abdullah Syafi'ie at the beginning of his public campaign as the leader of GAM's armed

Figure 1. "Since the MOU there is no longer the word Free Aceh, NKRI is non-negotiable." Banner in front of military complex, Banda Aceh, January 2006.

forces. Six months later, the televised December 1999 anniversary of GAM featured Syafi'ie reading a statement from Hasan Tiro, as well as delivering his own remarks. In January 2000, after President Wahid ordered the military to guarantee Syafi'ie's safety, a new military campaign was launched—an event that indicates the state's inability to control the military and enforce its policies. National military spokesmen reported that Syafi'ie had been shot by the military and was now "dying" (*sekarat*) ("Kapuspen TNI: Panglima AGAM Sekarat," *Kompas*, 22 February 2000, English in original). The news was publicized a month after the shooting incident upon confirmation from a captured member of the GBPK (Armed Movement to Disrupt Security) under torture. The TNI's evidence that Syafi'ie had been incapacitated was his disappearance from the public eye. Military spokesmen were quoted: "after that *Pak* Abdullah was not heard from anywhere. Usually, he receives SCTV, maybe NGOs."[21] The same day that these statements were published, Syafi'ie issued a counterstatement that on the day of the attack his group "had already received a leak from a friend in TNI so that his forces were ready and immediately ambushed them." He accused "the TNI [of] using cheap propaganda to distract the world's attention away from the human rights violations that the TNI had perpetrated on the people" ("Kapuspen TNI: Panglima AGAM Sekarat," *Kompas*, 22 February 2000).

Two days later, the TNI denied that the story "was engineered, as if it were a psychological war done by the TNI" ("Soal Tertembaknya Panglima AGAM, Bukan Untuk Perang Psikologis," *Kompas*, 24 February 2000). The local military even issued a sympathetic statement that they would provide health care to Abdullah Syafi'ie and promise not to arrest him. A week later in a televised interview, Syafi'ie opened his shirt to demonstrate that he had not been wounded. Casting doubt on his bodily authenticity, the report noted, "Abdullah Syafi'ie, who appeared older than he did in December of last year because his moustache is thicker, denied that his troops were trapped" ("Panglima Perang AGAM Segar Bugar," *Kompas*, 1 March 2000). The report doubled the doubt cast upon Syafi'ie by noting that he appeared infuriated when faced with the "rumor" that he was a "deserter (*desirtir*) of the RPKAD in 1976." Syafi'ie claimed that this rumor was "intentionally spread to divide the people of Aceh" because the RPKAD was the precursor to "Kopassus which was intensely despised by the people of Aceh because of all the human rights violations it perpetrated during the DOM." Around this time, I heard whispered stories that Abdullah Syafi'ie had been killed, and more cynically, that he had been replaced by the TNI and his name and role filled by a double. No evidence ever conclusively resolved this question, and it faded from public discourse.

Whoever embodied the leadership of the Armed Forces of GAM (AGAM) under the name of Abdullah Syafi'ie met with the Indonesian secretary of state two weeks later. Bondan Goenawan initiated communication to open the possibility of negotiations between Wahid and the rebels and conveyed two calves to Abdullah Syafi'ie on behalf of the president's family ("Panglima AGAM Bertemu Bondan Gunawan. Tonggak Sejarah Baru Dalam Konflik Aceh," *Kompas*, 17 March 2000). At that time Bondan, who appeared without military escort, asked the military to guarantee the rights of civilians, to be respectful of our "national relatives," and to appear in uniform.[21] The military said that there would be no sweeping, but twenty people were beaten early the next morning ("Aparat Obrak-abrik Empat Desa," *Kompas*, 18 March

2000). The police chief expressed skepticism that the person who met with Bondan was the real Abdullah Syafi'ie, based on his style of speech and appearance ("Kantor Kejari Bireun Dibakar," *Republika*, 20 March 2000). When I spoke with Bondan sometime later, he assured me that he had met the real Syafi'ie.

Rumors about Abdullah Syafi'ie were subsequently displaced by new scandals, other uncertainties, and more immediate violence. Disappeared but not resolved, the issue returned in June 2001. Following yet another "armed contact,"[23] a GAM regional commander was reported shot dead by the TNI ("Panglima Pase GAM Ditembak Mati Dikepung Saat di Rumah Istri Keempat," koridor.com, 5 June 2001). Despite denials, I heard reports that "TNI is more accurate to its target now, and the person they killed was someone who was intimidating and extorting the local people."[24] A week after the exchange of fire, the military reported that "acquaintances of GAM" had informed them that Abdullah Syafi'ie had once again escaped (Sad Harun, quoted in "Ratusan Anggota GAM Masuk DPO Gerakan Separatis Makin Terpojok," koridor.com, 12 June 2001). At the same time, an "influential figure" had been wounded and was likely already dead. The strategy of a group identified by yet another acronym, GSB or Movement of Armed Civilians,[25] was to "use a ghost science (*ilmu hantu*) to deceive the people of Aceh by bringing to life again figures who are already dead" ("Ratusan Anggota GAM Masuk DPO Gerakan Separatis Makin Terpojok," koridor.com, 12 June 2001). Military and police sources reported that Syafi'ie had fled to Malaysia. In the second cycle, the lack of appearances in the media fueled speculation. An Acehnese tabloid reported rumors that Syafi'ie "had been picked up by a helicopter and evacuated to Jakarta" or that he had suffered a coup ("Kontak Terkini Abdullah Syafi'ie," *Kontras*, 26 September 2001; "Mengendus Jejak Panglima AGAM," *Kontras*, 26 September 2001). Rumors of his evacuation implied his cooperation with the central military command.

In January 2002, there were reports of yet another armed contact that Syafi'ie had escaped. A few days later, there were reports that Syafi'ie had been killed and the body, in a regular button-down shirt rather than military clothing, had been evacuated to the hospital where hundreds of people crowded to view the corpse ("Panglima GAM Tewas Tertembak," *Kompas*, 24 January 2002). In reports following his death, Syafi'ie was said to be a moderate who favored negotiations and had forbidden his followers to commit violent acts in Jakarta. Indeed, some reports suggested that the security forces located the elusive Syafi'ie through a "microchip" embedded in a letter from the governor of Aceh inviting him to a dialogue to resolve the conflict ("Pemerintah Kurang Koordinasi.

Kasus Tewasnya Tengku Abdullah Syafei," *Media Indonesia,* 24 January 2002; "Bisa Melacak Posisi Sasaran Lewat Sinyal. *Chip* Untuk Syafi'ie Sebesar SIM *Card* HP," *Republika,* 25 January 2002). Analysts hypothesized that the death of Syafi'ie would lead to two possible outcomes: increased anger and a radicalization of the movement, or a weakening of GAM ("Kematian Syafi'ie Timbulkan Persoalan Baru," *Republika,* 25 January 2002). Most agreed that it would be significantly more difficult to negotiate without a "partner" for dialogue. In the chapters that follow, I consider the complexities of analyzing and resolving a conflict in which even proper names did not securely adhere to embodied singular referents.

Chapter 2
Struggling with History

As demonstrated by the collaborative construction of a dominant conflict narrative by the Indonesian state, its separatist opponent Gerakan Aceh Merdeka (GAM), and international mediators, historical narratives have contemporary consequences, validating a particular configuration of protagonists and defining a specific set of issues for consideration while ruling others out of order. Alternative conflict narratives, especially those stressing the discontinuity of parties and multiplicity of issues involved over time in Acehnese resistance to the Indonesian state, would authorize alternative approaches to conflict resolution, especially attention to the state's repeated violations of human rights and to consistent inequalities of resource distribution. Historical narratives are not only imposed retrospectively to secure stakes in the present and shape agendas for the future but also constructed, contested, and reconstructed. In this chapter, we turn from the conflict narrative currently shared by the Indonesian state and GAM to the opposing narratives of the relationship among Aceh, the rest of Indonesia, and European powers during the struggle against colonialism that were articulated and modified by Indonesian and Acehnese leaders from that time until the present.[1]

Soeharto and others in Jakarta understood the importance of historical narratives as did Abdullah Syafi'ie, who waved a sheaf of documents, perhaps compiled by Hasan Tiro, to legitimate the claim of Acehnese independence. Soeharto articulated a historical narrative to justify the permanent place of the military as defender and guarantor of the Indonesian state. The New Order origin story emphasized the heroic role of martyred generals defending the nation from the threats of disintegration and communist takeover. At the same time, it deemphasized the widespread mass killings of suspected communist party supporters that inaugurated the regime's rise to power. Most rural people throughout Indonesia, especially in Java, Bali, and Sumatra, were victims, perpetrators, and/or witnesses of this murderous repression. So the legitimation of the militarized state rested on two simultaneous moves: positioning "enemies within" as traitors to the nation, and constructing an ahistorical vision of Indonesia as united in cultural diversity.

In the mid-1970s, the president's wife, Mrs. Tien Soeharto, built a cultural theme park designed to complement economic development with "spiritual welfare" and serve as a "cultural inheritance" that denied the existence of historical conflict. John Pemberton's insightful analysis of the deployment of culture to enforce New Order stability discloses how the idiom of cultural diversity is used to obscure historical specificity and political difference (1994). I build on, and depart from, Pemberton's analysis in order to consider remnants of history and difference that lie outside the continuum of acceptable diversity prescribed by the theme park. In particular, I examine Acehnese efforts to attain historical recognition for their role in saving a threatened nation during the early independence period and for their prolonged refusal to bow to the yoke of Dutch colonialism. The central government has withheld the historical recognition that the Acehnese demand, attempting instead to appropriate their struggle to validate the Indonesian state. Equally important, Jakarta has been unwilling to hold anyone accountable for the crimes perpetrated since the imposition of the New Order. The national military concentrated on securing the state's access to resources throughout the archipelago in the name of a national unity that differs profoundly from the nation that the Acehnese struggled for in the anticolonial revolution. In response to the center's inability to provide justice and historical recognition, many Acehnese have sought independence via a referendum vote to secede from Indonesia, and some have supported armed separatism. New Order histories have transformed Acehnese bravery and contributions to the nation into an essentialized Acehnese character that can be invoked to justify military repression.

This chapter begins at the theme park, "Beautiful Indonesia in Miniature" (Taman Mini Indonesia Indah), with a review of Pemberton's and Siegel's analyses of New Order tactics of culturalizing the Indonesian nation in order to depoliticize differences (Pemberton 1994, 9; Siegel 1997). I focus in particular on the Acehnese contribution to this cultural project, an airplane that Aceh initially donated to the Republic in 1948 and gave to the new park in 1975, tracing the narratives evoked by this contribution in the context of seemingly intractable separatist violence since the end of the New Order in 1998. I was surprised by how many people pointed to the airplane in 1999 and 2000, when state violence and Acehnese resistance were prominent topics of discussion. In 2006, when discourses of separatism via armed struggle and referendum had replaced historical narratives of Aceh's contribution to Indonesian independence, the airplane itself remained, but was rarely mentioned. I explore the extent to which the cultural frame of the miniaturized nation has succeeded in translating the Acehnese history of struggle into a cultural attribute of bravery serving the Indonesian national project. Jakarta reinterpreted Acehnese resistance as a manifestation of culturally based intransigence and used it to justify forcible repression in the interests of preserving the unity of the nation. Acehnese leaders, on the contrary, shifted the terms of their historical narratives from a struggle for independence from the Dutch to a struggle for independence from the Javanese, creating an equally intractable narrative of separation. This chapter considers the legacies of deploying culture to contain historical difference and asks whether ahistorical narratives have taken its place in creating new forms of polarization and violence.

Modal Bangsa, Cultural Capital for the Nation

Among the authentic houses and crafts of Indonesia's various regions gathered in the Beautiful Indonesia in Miniature Park (Mini), a somewhat dilapidated bomber plane intrudes. President Soeharto's wife conceived of the park on a visit to Disneyland in 1971. Mini was not to be an imitation of Disneyland; rather, it was to be "complete spiritually" as well as "materially" and to embody Indonesian national culture (*Pendjelasan Tentang Projek Miniatur Indonesia "Indonesia Indah"* 1971 quoted in Pemberton 1994, 152). The plan met with objections both from the residents who were evicted from their land to provide the space for the park and by groups throughout Java who argued that it was an inappropriate use of the people's money ("TMII: Menggugat Monumen Dinasti Keropos," *Majalah Tempo,* 24 December 2000, 33; see also Pemberton 1994, 153). The Soehartos were adamant that they would bequeath this cultural inheritance to the future generations of Indonesians even if that required force. In dedicating the park, Soeharto argued that it represented an investment in the nation: "Economic development alone is not enough. . . . One's life . . . will be calm and complete only when it is accompanied by spiritual welfare. The direction and guidance toward that spiritual welfare is, in fact, already in our possession; it lies in our beautiful and noble national cultural inheritance" (*Kenang-kenangan Peresmian Pembukaan Taman Mini Indonesia Indah* 1975, 70, quoted in Pemberton 1994, 154).

Taman Mini constitutes the cultural legacy that Soeharto concluded "makes us proud to be Indonesians" (*Kenang-kenanangan Peresmian Pembukaan Taman Mini Indonesia Indah* 1975, 70, quoted in Pemberton 1994, 154). The park features a combination of full-sized traditional houses from all of the regions, models of ancient and modern monuments, and a range of halls, museums, and other facilities surrounding an 8.4 hectare pond filled with miniature versions of each island in the archipelago. As James Siegel notes, an overhead tram provides visitors with the vantage point to appreciate the mini archipelago in the pond and, to Mrs. Soeharto's chagrin, the dilapidated Dakota airplane (Siegel 1997, 3).

The plane was relegated to the periphery of the park and received very little comment in official histories. Both park and plane have featured prominently in anthropological analyses of New Order culture. John Pemberton argues that the park aimed to domesticate diversity and assert continuity between cultural pluralism and the Indonesian revolution. Pemberton argues that the "power of Mini-ization is . . . not simply a matter of force dressed in cultural guise and imposed from above, but an effect continuously constituted at the local . . . level" (1994, 12). He asserts that villagers themselves want to identify with the cultural imagery provided at Mini. Siegel suggests that because the plane is datable, it threatens the theme park's aim to create a timeless and distant past. Building upon these perceptive analyses, I return to the airplane itself to look at translations between culture and history as post-New Order Indonesia attempts to deal with the inheritance of both park and plane. Though the park attempts to turn history into a form of cultural diversity, this airplane demands historical rather than cultural recognition from the nation-state.

Originally, the plane was donated by the Aceh province, on the northern tip of Sumatra, to the Indonesian Republic during the struggle for independence. On 16 June 1948, President Soekarno visited Koetaradja, now called Banda Aceh, the capital of Aceh.[2] Merchants asked President Soekarno what they could donate to the new nation, which was fighting the Dutch army and seeking international recognition. President Soekarno responded:

Merchants are the economic pillars of our country; therefore help the efforts and plans of the central government to improve the national economy. The best step is for the merchants to create a link between one island and another, between one region and another. . . . I recommend before we strengthen and repair the roads for automobiles and trains or even ocean links, now we should strive to open connections through air traffic. Here I suggest that you merchants buy an airplane, best if it is a Dakota, and I will not mind if you gentlemen want to name it yourselves. The regions that I have visited are already capable of buying an airplane for their region. The plane can be used to serve your needs and purposes. For those merchants who can afford to give that money today will be granted permission to fly over Koetaradja with our airplane in Lhok Nga [the airfield outside the capital]. (*Perkundjungan Presiden Soekarno ke Atjeh*, 1948, 45)[3]

In a matter of days, enough money and gold were collected to purchase two planes. One was to be donated to the Republic in the name of the people of Aceh (*rakyat Aceh*), while the other was a donation from the merchants' association (GASIDA).[4]

When President Soekarno visited Aceh in 1948, the new republic faced many threats from within as well as without. Indonesians could not yet recognize themselves in their particular regional variations without threatening the unity of the nation. Soekarno sought to praise the distinctiveness of Aceh and its history at the same time that he subordinated it to Indonesia. Speaking to hundreds of thousands of people gathered in Koetaradja, Soekarno and his Interior Minister, Dr. Soekiman, praised the brave resistance of the Acehnese to Dutch colonial rule. Dr. Soekiman called this heroic resistance a "page that was beautiful and good in history." He told the crowd: "Brothers and sisters because of all this [anticolonial resistance] the leaders of the Indonesian movement . . . have the desire to meet face to face with all of you" (1948: 32). Echoing Soekiman, Soekarno said they "had come from thousands of kilometers away to this place specially to meet with the people of Atjeh who were famous as the one people who always struggled for independence, who always were the champions and vanguard of the struggle for independence of the people of Indonesia" (1948, 33).[5]

The independence and tenacity that Soekarno praised could swiftly become a liability rather than an asset if not harnessed to the national project. Dutch colonialists had hoped to turn the distinctness of Acehnese identity to their advantage in the 1930s. Governor Goedhart stated, "The exclusiveness of the Acehnese and his strongly developed sense of his own worth will, I predict, in the long run persuade him of the advantage of being bound to us rather than being absorbed into one Indonesian people" (quoted in Reid 1979, 26). Goedhart's erroneous prediction contained a grain of truth: an independent-minded people who so staunchly rejected "being bound" to a foreign power might also resist "being absorbed" by their neighbors. The relationship between Indonesian independence and Acehnese resistance could be conceived in more than one way. Many Acehnese said to me in 1999, "Without Aceh, Indonesia would not exist." While this might be true, Soekarno sought to reverse that dependence. In 1948, in the political course for leaders in Koetaradja, he said: "For more than twenty-five years I have always said to the people of Indonesia: Be one, be one, be one. The absolute requirement to win the National Revolution is national unity, the unity of all the revolutionary strengths" (1948, 26). Soekarno emphasized that lack of unity would endanger the Republic:

The people who are not united are the same as dry sand. I say to you, brothers and sisters, be united. Go to the beach, pick up sand that is dry, it numbers in the tens of thousands, brothers and sisters, but it is dry and there is no connection between one and the other. When there is a sudden storm or a cyclone, then that dry sand is sent flying to the left and the right. It is chaotic. But, whenever we fill this dry sand with the cement of unity and the iron of strong desire/will, this sand takes on the quality of concrete. Brothers and sisters, this concrete becomes a weapon; even if shelled by the enemy it is not going to be destroyed, brothers and sisters. That is the picture of a unified people. (1948, 35)

Soekarno implied that without unity there would be no independence; the Acehnese resistance must support the new Republic of Indonesia.

The Acehnese displayed none of the separatist tendencies that were prominent in other regions of the nation, but Soekarno warned political leaders in Koetaradja that the Dutch would exploit any divisions within the people. Noting that the Dutch occupied two-thirds of Java and one-fifth of Sumatra, he said: "I can tell all of you exactly where the Dutch in Java have broken through. Exactly where there are divisions between and among us, that is where the Dutch will enter" (1948, 23). He repeatedly urged the people to avoid "regional sentiments." He repeated that there was no nation (bangsa) other than the Indonesian nation. He made a special plea for unity to the Acehnese gathered to hear him speak: "I ask the entire people of Atjeh, be tightly unified with the other people of Indonesia, feel the brotherhood, think of them as your own brothers and sisters. Brothers and sisters from Tapanuli, from East Sumatera, from Minangkabau, from Lampung, from the entire island of Sumatera and from the entire islands of Java, and from Madura, and from Kalimantan, from Sulawesi, from the islands of Lesser Soeunda, all of them are your own brothers and sisters. Be one with them" (1948, 35).

The cries of "merdeka" that greeted Soekarno's speeches were for the whole of Indonesia. In the political courses, he reminded leaders of their national goals:

It is not that we aspire to Atjeh merdeka, Minangakabau merdeka, Djawa merdeka, or Greater Batak merdeka, or Soenda merdeka, or Kalimantan merdeka. No, not that. We have national aspirations [Nationaal] that is for all the entire nation [bangsa] of Indonesia to live throughout the thousands of islands of this Indonesia, to live independently as one nation (bangsa), in one state, under one government under the protection of one flag. (1948, 17)

Soekarno emphasized that Aceh should not stand alone, even if it could. If Aceh was all that remained of Indonesia, what remained was not Aceh, but Indonesia. The idea of Indonesia must be maintained at all costs.

Speaking to political leaders in Koetaradja, Soekarno asked the people of Aceh to continue to lead the struggle for Indonesian independence:

I know that the people of Atjeh are heroes. Atjeh has always been an example of the independence war, an example of the struggle for independence of all the people of Indonesia. Brothers and sisters, I know this, in fact, all of the people of Indonesia look to Atjeh, they seek to strengthen their inner spirits from Atjeh, and Atjeh continues to be the flame that guides [obor] the struggle of the people of Indonesia, in the same manner, I also hope that the people of the entire Republic will become examples, will become the vanguard of the struggle of the people of Indonesia. (1948, 26)

Soekarno called the Republic the vanguard and capital for the struggle, but when he spoke directly to the hundred thousand Acehnese people gathered to hear his speech in Koetaradja he exhorted them to rescue the Republic:

The main thing is, brothers and sisters, you must now struggle to save the Republic, the Republic that has now become quite small after there was a colonial war on 21 July last year. But this small Republic must, persistently, persistently, persistently, persistently, persistently become the vanguard, constantly be our capital [modal]. Even though the area has now become smaller than before, do not let your hearts, enthusiasm, inner spirit, resolve, mind and soul become small. This Republic must constantly stand; we must constantly defend it. In fact, even if it is no longer the size that it is now, if for instance it becomes smaller than this, if for instance, it becomes smaller than an umbrella, we must defend our state. Once independent, always independent. (1948, 34)

On the last day of his visit, Soekarno was presented with an Acehnese dagger (*rentjong*) "as a sign of their love for the Head of State . . . and as a symbol of the unity of the people of Atjeh who are going to preserve the independence of the Republic with this weapon" (1948, 75). Throughout his visit, Soekarno invoked the idea of capital (*modal*) for the struggle. Most often recalled is the idea that Aceh was the region of capital (*daerah modal*) for the struggle for independence.

Later sources quote from Soekarno's speech in Biruen (North Aceh), which extends and specifies his comments from the previous day's speech in Koetaradja:

My brothers and sisters, it is true that our area is small, but we will preserve the Republic. This republic will continue to be capital (*modal*) for the struggle of the Indonesian people. Even if the area of Indonesia remained only as wide as an umbrella, even if the Republic remained only Aceh, we will defend this Republic with Aceh as the capital (*modal*). Aceh is the region of *modal* for the Republic, *modal* for the struggle of the entire people of Indonesia. (quoted in Talsya 1990, 351)[6]

Through a set of elisions that obscured the substitutions and equivalences that were evident in his earlier speech, Aceh became an example of independence for all of Indonesia. The plane is tangible evidence of

the donation Aceh made, but Soekarno's declaration of Aceh as "capital for the nation" (*modal bangsa*) encompassed more than the wealth
Aceh had donated to Indonesia.[7]

Soekarno elaborated on the importance of this kind of *modal* in a
1959 speech in Meulaboh. After the crowd of people who had stood
waiting to hear him since morning greet his appearance with cries of
"merdeka," Soekarno asks rhetorically why they have given him such an
outstanding welcome. Attributing his own opinions to another speaker,
he answers his own question:

> The answer: Yes, it is true, what has been written there and pointed out by Mr.
> Chaerul Saleh: The region of Meulaboh, *daerah modal*, the region of Atjeh is the
> *daerah modal* and will always be the *daerah modal*. Not just *modal* like gold, not
> just *modal* in the form of money, but especially in the form of the soul that ex-
> cites the spirit. The people of Atjeh have a spirit that truly is a spirit that lights
> the fires, and that spiritual modal which lights the fires and enflames the spir-
> its, that is the modal which was most important to seize our independence, to
> uphold our independence, to protect our independence and to continue our
> independence until the end of time, in accordance with our oath: Once In-
> dependent, Always Independent! (Speech of President Soekarno, Meulaboh,
> Atjeh, 4 September 1959, 2)

Soekarno continued that without such a spirit, even thousands more
battleships and soldiers would be useless.[8] It is likely that in this speech
Soekarno sought to give the impression that the people maintained enthusiasm for the Republic at a time when the government was reporting that Aceh was secure and Daud Beureueh had only a few remaining
troops ("Tinggal Tiga Kompi Jang Masih Setia pada Daud Beureueh
menurut Overste Sjamaun Gaharu," *Warta* 7 August 1959).

Soekarno expanded the economic idea of capital investment to include
the symbolic importance of Acehnese bravery in the revolution and enthusiasm for the nation. The Republic is the capital (*modal*) for the people's
struggle for independence; Aceh and the Republic are interchangeable in
this equation. Aceh played an important role in governance of the new republic when the Dutch occupied other areas, although Soekarno had no
intention of shifting the center of governance to northern Sumatra. In
1999, many Acehnese proudly recalled their prominence during this
period, when they contributed money and gold and bought airplanes to
support the cause.

In the 1970s, when Mrs. Soeharto asked the regions to contribute artifacts representing their region to the Beautiful Indonesia in Miniature Park, the Acehnese again donated the airplane to the nationalist
project. The gift could not be refused, but it was hardly what the First
Lady had in mind. The specificity interjected by the plane and the history it carried was "dangerous" precisely because it threatened to dis-

rupt the carefully crafted timeless past of the nation.[9] At the same time, the plane's celebration of Indonesian patriotism offered an opportunity to subsume the brave resistance for which the Acehnese were known to the Indonesian nation-building project.

From a History of Struggle to a Culture of Bravery

Aceh has lent much symbolic capital to the Indonesian nation. Central Jakarta is filled with streets named after Acehnese heroes: Tengku Cik Di Tiro, Teuku Umar, and the extraordinary female fighter, Tjoet Nyah Dhien. Aceh's mythic resistance to the Dutch is recalled as an Indonesian victory.

Acehnese bravery and rebelliousness are inscribed in stories of the Aceh War (1873–1912), which is also known as a "Holy War" (Perang Sabil) (Reid 1979, 7–37; Siegel 2000, 75–77). A large-format commemorative volume titled *The Dutch Colonial War in Acheh* (*DCWA*) appeared shortly after the plane landed at Mini (Alfian et al. 1997). Complete with a foreword by President Soeharto dated 10 November 1977, this book chronicles the protracted conflict and features photographic reproductions of maps, telegrams, drawings of battleships and equipment, information about troop deployments, and portraits of both Dutch and Acehnese fighters. President Soeharto claimed the Acehnese struggle as "our own" and linked it to national development.[10] Soeharto explained that an awareness of history promoted a sense of national dignity, not unlike the artifacts at Taman Mini:

> We need a more intimate knowledge of our own history because it contains all of our aspirations with regard to a future which we are developing at this time. It also reflects all of our sufferings in the past, which have led to our present state of being an independent nation. Our people have struggled for independence so that with the independence the Indonesian Nation can enjoy a dignified life, progress, prosperity and justice. Therefore the most important call of history for us who live at the present time and for the coming generations is to enrich the independence that we have today with national development. (11)

The rhetoric is similar to that of the opening of Mini: the past has become timeless and national; the Acehnese struggle for independence should be directed toward and expressed through national development.[11] History itself is vacated except as it validates the present and endorses the dominant vision of the future. This history no longer belongs to Aceh; it has become Indonesia's. Is this the historical recognition that the Acehnese seek and the Dakota demands, or have the Soehartos flattened the distinction between culture and history, denying the Acehnese desire for historical recognition? What role will these histories have as they are handed down to future generations?

The text of *DCWA* provides a seemingly straightforward chronology of events. The first step toward the Dutch declaration of war was the Sumatra Treaty of 1871, in which "the Dutch were 'given the freedom to expand their authority'" on the island by the British. This treaty ended any obligation of the Dutch to respect "the rights and sovereignty of Acheh," which had been recognized by the Netherlands and Great Britain in the London Treaty of 1824 (Alfian et al. 1997, 57). *DCWA* recognizes the London Treaty's historic significance as the first, and only, treaty signed by the Netherlands and an independent sultanate in the archipelago; however, the authors declare it "nothing more than a broken promise" after the Sumatra Treaty (58).[12] That the Dutch followed with a declaration of war against the sultanate in 1873 confirms the view that European recognition of Aceh's autonomy had been withdrawn. To many Acehnese, on the contrary, the treaty remains more than a broken promise; it confirms Aceh's historical sovereignty, and even obligates the international community to support Aceh's struggle for independence.

Contemporary historians of colonialism explain these events not as evidence of Aceh's political importance and military prowess but in relation to Aceh's pivotal role in international trade. Not only was valuable pepper grown there, but the Malaka Straits were of strategic importance to European trade with China. Constellations of European economic, colonial, and political power had important repercussions in Southeast Asia. Anthony Reid's *The Contest for North Sumatra* (1969) provides a useful analysis of context for the London and Sumatra treaties. In the early nineteenth century, British colonial officers, including Governor Raffles, favored unified local powers under their empire. In 1819, the British entered into a treaty with the Acehnese sultanate Jauhur stipulating that Aceh would make no treaties with foreign powers without British consent; that the British were allowed to trade in all ports; and that Aceh and Britain were entering into a defensive alliance. At the same time, the Dutch sought to extend their dominance throughout Sumatra, including Aceh. The British were concerned with protecting both their trade in Southeast Asia that fell outside the areas occupied by the Dutch (Java and Maluku) and their access to the straits route to China. After several years of negotiations, the Dutch and British signed the 1824 London Treaty transferring British settlements in Sumatra to the Dutch and Dutch possessions on the Indian subcontinent and the Malay Peninsula to the British. The British were bound to make no treaties with Sumatra, which obviously contradicted their 1819 treaty with Aceh. In a series of notes, the British agreed to modify the treaty to "a simple Arrangement for the hospitable reception of British vessels and subjects in the Port of Acheen. But as some of the provisions of that Treaty [1819] will be conducive to the general interests of Europeans established in the Eastern seas, they trust that the Netherland Government will take measures for securing the benefit of those provisions. And they express their confidence that no measures hostile to the King of Acheen will be adopted." The Dutch accepted and replied: "That their Government will apply itself without delay to regulate its relations with Acheen in such a manner that that State, without losing anything of its independence, may offer both to the sailor and the merchant that constant security which can only be established by the moderate exercise of European influence" (quoted in Reid 1969, 12). While the British were adamant about guarding Aceh's independence, these notes had little effect. Reid shows that British authorities never followed through on their promise to modify their agreement with Acheen, fearing that recognition of the sultanate could be dangerous. The subsequent rulers in Aceh were never informed that Raffles's treaty was no longer valid. In 1857, Sultan Ibrahim signed a treaty with Holland that declared friendship and guaranteed commerce but did nothing to end their mutual distrust (Reid 1969, 22). The expansion of the Netherlands into areas formerly independent and protected by treaties with the British created tensions during the 1860s, as the 1824 guarantee of Aceh's independence, long forgotten in Europe, was invoked in Southeast Asia. Holland's desire to expand unencumbered by these earlier treaties ultimately led to the Sumatra Treaty of 1871 in which the British received commercial concessions in exchange for accepting Dutch territorial claims.

Reid argues that during the negotiations the British drew attention to the Aceh issue, not to fulfill their obligations, but rather to increase their bargaining power with the Dutch (1969, 63). In notes that were kept secret to avoid alarming the Sultan of Atjeh, the Dutch asked the British to annul the 1824 treaty. Language that the British suggested to ensure a peaceful transition for Aceh was deleted without British protest (67–68). In Holland, this treaty, called the Siak Convention, was sharply criticized because the notes regarding Aceh were not included and it appeared to grant too many commercial concessions to the British. A revised treaty, which "annulled British objections to Dutch expansion anywhere in Sumatra, and referred specially to the Atjeh reserve of 1824," was then drafted. Sumatra was seen as compensation for possessions on the Gold Coast of Africa that the Dutch ceded to the British (72–73). Making the Dutch intention to colonize Aceh obvious accelerated the battles between the Acehnese and the Dutch. In 1873, a Dutch force attacked Aceh and was forced to retreat in a matter of weeks; another colonial war began on the Gold Coast, setting off strong criticism in Britain. The linkage of these two cases provoked outrage in Britain, generating the London *Times* editorial criticizing the exchange that was among the articles in Syafi'ie's packet (quoted in Reid 1969, 76).[13]

In describing the efforts of religious leaders to inspire a holy war to repel the Dutch invasion, *DCWA* notes that young people had been "indoctrinated" by their religious teachers "to sacrifice their lives for the sake of Islam" (Alfian et al. 1997, 64). *DCWA* reports the findings of Dr. C. Snouck Hurgronje, the Dutch expert on Islam commissioned to study the Acehnese problem: "the Dutch were facing a people's movement which was fanatic by nature, led by religious leaders, and which could only be overcome by the force of weapons" (68). Interpretations of the conflict as "fanatic" obscure the sense of justice that animates many Acehnese narratives of their culture, identity, and history. They emphasize that Aceh was the only part of the archipelago that never submitted to colonial conquest.

Accounts of the long war between Dutch and Acehnese forces differ with regard to when and how it was concluded. Some sources contend that the war officially ended with the surrender of the Sultan Muhamad Daud Syah in 1903 (Alfian et al. 1997, 72). Others note that isolated attacks and guerilla resistance continued, extending the war to 1912 and beyond. Still others argue that the Dutch misunderstood the statement of surrender because of their ignorance regarding Islam.[14] *DCWA* poses the question of when the war ended as a controversy over the meaning of the Sultan's surrender and leaves it unresolved, while citing several sources that suggest it never ended. Anthony Reid argues that the Dutch had effectively conquered Aceh by 1913 (1979; see also Morris 1983).[15]

DCWA details violent resistance in Aceh that continued into the 1910s, and abruptly moves to link this armed struggle with civil efforts in Java:

The war against Dutch colonialism was not only fought with military forces, as related on earlier pages, but Acehnese also took part in actions of non-violence by participating in national movements and forums. The effects of political movements in Java had made themselves felt in the Western part of the archipelago. (Alfian et al. 1997, 74)

This passage echoes Soekarno's comments in Biruen many years before, but with an important difference. The authors of *DCWA* assert that "national unity was a vital prerequisite for the country's independence," in contrast to Soekarno's plea for national unity during the struggle for independence. In the New Order version, the project of national unity is seen to predate independence. This account nationalizes Aceh's past struggles.

After transforming Acehnese history into an Indonesian asset, *DCWA* concludes that Acehnese bravery is universally admired. The words of the Dutch soldier who killed Teungku di Barat, one of the last Acehnese warriors to die in 1912, are invoked: "is there any nation on the face of this earth that would not write about the death of these heroic figures with a deep feeling of respect in their history books?" (quoted in Alfian et al. 1997, 294). Most books written under the New Order, especially about Aceh, do not express respect. The sense of justice that is prominent in Acehnese accounts of their history does not come through in this chronicle of battles. Those who die become national heroes by name and fanatics by group, but never attain the venerated status of the religious martyrs revered by the majority Muslim population in Indonesia.

Acehnese heroism threatened official histories, which concentrated on the bravery of Soeharto and his associates in saving the nation from the 1965 coup attempt. Yet, the history of Acehnese resistance to the Dutch was essential to national identity and narratives of liberation from the colonizer.[16] In his introductory comments to *DCWA*, the Minister of Culture and Education articulated the lesson to be learned from this history: "The series of pictures and words in this book *The Dutch Colonial War in Acheh* are the facts of history, studying them intensely one will obtain an understanding from experience that independence is a human right." After describing the evils of colonialism and imperialism, he concluded:

The history of the Indonesian people's struggle against colonialism or imperialism is an important experience where one can learn the unconquered spirit of the firm unity and solidarity, which could be an example and principal capital (*modal*) to accomplish our planned and continuous development according to the Five Principles (*Pancasila*) and the 1945 Constitution. (Alfian et al. 1997, 19)

In this passage, the exemplary Acehnese spirit of resistance is transformed from rebellion to solidarity in the name of national development. Soekarno's mention of the puppet states has disappeared along with the task of establishing national identity, and the assumption is made that without national unity, there would not have been independence. This version of history solidifies Indonesia as more than a colonial construct.

The 1990 foreword to *DCWA* by Ibrahim Hasan, then governor of Aceh,[17] reflects a shift in the demands made of history to do national work. Hasan defined history not as a determinate sequence of significant events in the past but as a repository of cultural values that can be applied in an indeterminate present:

> History is a series of notes, a mirror where we see human life either in the past and in the present day, it is a lighthouse which guides our course of life for the future. Hence history is not only notes of important events, it is a process which narrates our life and the role of each of us, or in a group as a nation in a certain time and in a certain place. It is history that has led us to the present conditions. (Alfian et al. 1997, 23)

The verbal slippage between individual, group, and nation is telling. The phrases are not simply parallel ("in a group as in a nation"), but constitute the group as nation or even subsume the group within the nation. Hasan continues:

> This book is not only a commemoration of those heroes and martyrs, it is also one of our endless efforts to maintain their values and their spirit of fighting, and to inspire the coming generations with it. They did what they could do but they left the work unfinished, before it could give significance and meaning. It is up to us to give meaning to what they have already done. (23)

It is not the national revolution that is unfinished; rather, past struggles can be used to create new meanings. In the context of increasing violence in Aceh at the end of the 1980s, the emphasis on fighting spirit and completing the task of previous generations of martyrs can be interpreted in ominous terms. It may be a deliberate effort to increase the perception of Aceh as a dangerous place requiring military attention; or, it may be linked to the military's efforts to teach the "Acehnese to defend the nation" by arming them to combat other Acehnese.[18] The tone of this passage marks the completion of a shift in the discourse about the Acehnese past: the conversion of the history of Aceh from anticolonial resistance to bravery as a cultural attribute of the Acehnese people.

The redeployment of Acehnese anticolonial resistance in the service of Indonesian nationalism evident in *The Dutch Colonial War in Acheh* appears in the mass media as well. An epic made-for-TV movie, *Tjoet Nya' Dhien*, filmed in the mid-1980s, was extremely popular.[19] The film chronicles a woman's effort to continue her husband's struggle against the Dutch after he was killed.[20] Long battle scenes are punctuated by intrigues and betrayals, as some members of the group become spies for the Dutch and others traitorously reveal plans; the climax is a scene of cooptation and compromise when Dhien is surrendered to the Dutch. The brave Acehnese speak in Malay rather than Acehnese for the convenience of the actors and the national audience. Most of the costumes and props are appropriate to the period, but in the battle scenes the

Acehnese carry an Indonesian national flag rather than a traditional banner, though this was used in other scenes.[21]

This classic film, like *The Dutch Colonial War in Acheh,* places Acehnese anticolonialism in the service of Indonesian nationalism. As the symbolic capital of struggle was appropriated by the nation, the histories of specific struggles were transformed from instances in a holy war against the "Dutch infidels" into a generalizable cultural attribute of brave resistance. In a particularly significant example, an elementary school history book described the determination of the legendary leader Cik Di Tiro by declaring that "for him peace meant failure" (Hasan and Imran 1997, 121). Taken out of the historical context of the Acehnese struggle for independence, Tiro's resistance was reduced to an emotional commitment.

This version of the past does not represent a hijacking of history. The airplane enshrined at Mini cannot be hijacked; it stubbornly insists on the distinct Acehnese contribution to the struggle for independence. Many Acehnese I spoke with did not distinguish their struggle from Indonesia's, despite the fact that their struggle long predates the existence of the nation.[22] Some Acehnese claim "bravery" as their cultural attribute. Otto Syamsuddin Ishak, an Acehnese intellectual and activist, posed a challenge to his people: "Culturally, Acehnese are indeed truly brave. If people want to see a value become a reality, then like it or not, they must do something with that value" (1999, 258). Bravery is not a timeless cultural attribute; it must be renewed in action. Perhaps it must always be generated in history.

The pride, bravery, and rebelliousness of the Acehnese are now both cultural attribute and historical fact. The specificity of the airplane, which cannot quite be converted to a cultural artifact, retains the power of history and indexes the revolution (see Siegel 1997). In 1975, the historical referents that the plane triggered disrupted the aim of Mini to create a timeless, "authentic," and peaceful portrait of cultural diversity within a unified Indonesian state. In 1999, many years after the Dakota's donation to Mini, the historical referents again became dangerous, not because they inspired memories that confronted the institutionalized version of the past but precisely because they recalled that "truth" in juxtaposition to current events. Many Acehnese felt that their contribution to the struggle for Indonesia's independence had been disregarded. Immediately after the fall of Soeharto and before the conflict between Aceh and Jakarta had been constructed in polarized terms of armed separatists versus the center, these historical referents were dangerous because the miniaturized culture of bravery was read back through history to prove that Acehnese are violent by nature and must be treated with violence. The notion that Acehnese people fanatically pursue revenge, which justified and pervaded military repression during DOM, continued after the TNI's public apology for its "excesses," constituting a continuing threat to the unity of the nation.

Campaigns to suppress the perceived dangers to the state posed by Acehnese history have produced historical grievances that compounded the initial threats to the unity of Indonesia. Geoffrey Robinson has astutely argued that the intractability of the conflict in Aceh has been the result of state policies rather than Acehnese culture.

The violent conflict in Aceh after 1989 was not the inevitable consequence of primordial Acehnese sentiments, nor a manifestation of a venerable Acehnese tradition of resistance to outside authority or Islamic rectitude. Instead . . . it was the unintended, but largely inevitable, consequence of certain characteristic policies and practices of the New Order state itself. The argument is not that the culture and traditions of the people of Aceh were of no importance in stimulating demands for independence there, or in generating the conflict that followed. Rather, . . . the policies and practices of the New Order regime, and the unique historical circumstances which shaped them, gave these incipient demands a much wider credibility than they might otherwise have had, and also ensured a rapid escalation from resolvable political disagreement to widespread violence and political conflict. (1998, 153)

The past slides between history and culture as differently positioned actors mobilize the past for a variety of interests and ends.

Capital Flight to Banda Aceh

While the original Dakota airplane remains at Mini, a replica of it proudly rests in the provincial capital of Banda Aceh. In 1948, money was raised for the donation of two planes. The plane that was to be from the people of Aceh never materialized because the money disappeared through corruption (Polim 1996, 68). Along with the Great Mosque built by the Dutch to win the hearts of the Acehnese, the replica plane is a monument to Aceh's brave and glorious history. These objects enliven stories of successful struggles. Many Acehnese people I met in 1999–2000 repeated such stories: "Unlike the rest of the archipelago, Aceh was never conquered by the Dutch"; or, "Without the contributions of Aceh, Indonesia might not exist today"; and especially, "Acehnese collected enough gold to buy the planes in a matter of hours, for the struggling nationalist effort." This plane evokes stories of past greatness, both from the very young and from those old enough to remember the events. In Aceh, most airplane stories I heard ended with the phrase, "we gave milk and Indonesia reciprocated with poison." The plane, which fifty years before had symbolized Aceh's commitment to the nation, in 1999 became to many people in Aceh the symbol of why Aceh must have a referendum with the option of independence. Even those who remained committed to Indonesia and said they would not vote for secession sought a referendum so that the choice would be theirs, rather than having their national fate imposed upon them. The Acehnese people found themselves in a complicated dilemma, especially when they struggled with histories that could not easily be forgotten.

On 8 November 1999, as many as one million people marched peacefully in Aceh to demand a referendum on their future. During the year after the fall of Soeharto, violence in Aceh had not only increased but had became more indeterminate, difficult to narrate, and impossible to account for. At that point, polarized conflict protagonists had yet to emerge. Many journalists, policy makers, and combatants described this violence as part of a long, continuous conflict that had varied in intensity since 1976 or even earlier. Memories and chronologies of violence are critical in understanding this conflict, but the struggles over history are shaped at least as much by conflicting contemporary interests as by historical events. These historical narratives join together discontinuous struggles to prove retroactively that latent dangers existed even when conflict was not overt. These latent dangers were created by anxieties about controlling historical difference. Perhaps the architects of the New Order, who understood the profound importance of historical narratives, recognized that Aceh's claims to revolutionary nationalist struggle exceeded their own. The grievances in Aceh are many and specific, but the most enduring may be that they have not been acknowledged for their founding role in the Indonesian nation. Campaigns to repress these phantom dangers have created unresolved historical grievances that have become a source of actual dangers to national unity in the present.

Prior to the fall of Soeharto, Aceh's fidelity to Indonesia was not in question. In the national media, stories of a separatist movement requiring military attention appeared only sporadically, as isolated incidents. National military discourse on violence in Aceh was slippery, defining the continuing threat as a matter of criminality but occasionally raising the specter of separatism. New Order rule by fear of latent dangers and threats of national disintegration mandating military interventions did not emphasize Free Aceh Movement (GAM) separatists. Throughout the late New Order period, most Indonesians would not have considered the possibility of Aceh separating; nor would most Acehnese have done so. As late as 1997, during the economic crisis, when citizens were asked to donate gold to the nation, Aceh gathered the largest donations ("Siapa Bertangung Jawab," *Panji Masyarakat* 34, 8 December 1999). Initially, after the fall of Soeharto, people I spoke with both in Jakarta and in Aceh did not describe the problem between Jakarta and Aceh as separatism. Typically, it was cast in terms of economic injustice and military-state violence. Natural resources from Aceh fueled Indonesia's economic development, but most Indonesians were unaware of Aceh's large contribution. Most Indonesians were also unaware of the scale of military operations in Aceh that safeguarded natural gas fields. The historical image of Acehnese rebellion enabled the military to suggest the danger of separatism in order to justify a very lucrative campaign, as the army profited by protecting industrial complexes. Public discourse in Aceh demanded an end to state-sponsored violence and a more equitable distribution of natural resource wealth between Jakarta and Aceh. After Soeharto's fall in 1998, Aceh became increasingly visible in national political discourse focused on trying to come to terms with the legacies of New Order violence. At the time when many Acehnese mobilized for a referendum, many in the Jakarta elite pointed to the airplane and other anecdotes from the revolution to prove that, unlike recently independent East Timor, Aceh belonged both to and with Jakarta.

Many Acehnese pointed to the plane as a symbol of the long train of deceptions they have suffered: first, Soekarno's violation of his promises to make Aceh a province and allow it autonomy in education and religious affairs;[23] the marginalization of Islam as a political force in Indonesia; the massive human rights abuses which occurred from 1989 to 1998 while Aceh was a "military operations zone" (DOM); and finally the abuses that continued after the commander in chief of the armed forces, General Wiranto, and Indonesian President Habibie apologized for military excesses in 1998. Habibie commissioned reports, made promises, and implemented a few substantive changes. For example, DOM victims had a special opportunity to become civil servants. On the other hand, people I spoke with were outraged that students had been beaten by mobile police brigades when they protested Habibie's visit to Aceh. His ineffectual gestures added to long-standing disappointment in Aceh; despite the passing of the New Order, justice seemed impossible to attain.

In 1999–2000, Acehnese chronicles of disappointment with the central government typically began in 1950. Aceh's status as a province, granted in 1949 in recognition of Aceh's valiant efforts in the revolution, was withdrawn less than a year later.[24] In 1950, Aceh was joined to other residencies in Sumatra to form the province of North Sumatra. In addition to loss of administrative, economic, and security privileges, Aceh lost its distinction as a Muslim area. Soekarno developed the national ideology of *pancasila*—which mandated that all citizens profess faith to one of the five major religions—to replace the Jakarta Charter in the Constitution, which would have stipulated that all Muslims were subject to Islamic law.

When the Acehnese donated the plane to Soekarno in 1948, Acehnese leader Daud Beureueh extracted a promise that if the Acehnese joined Soekarno's efforts to maintain the Republic, Aceh would be allowed to practice Islamic law. The dialogue is cited in Sofyan Tiba's book on the legal aspects of the referendum issue and in a parliamentary discussion on the implementation of the regulations on Aceh's status as a special region. In recruiting Beureueh's support, Soekarno appealed to Acehnese history and Islamic identity: "I mean a war such as those fought by the famous Acehnese heroes such as Tgk Cik Di Tiro and others, a war in which there is no retreat, a war with the slogan 'independence or martyrdom'."[25] In these recollections, Beureueh's support is conditional on Soekarno's written promise that Aceh will have Islamic law. Soekarno guaranteed his promise with tears, crying "until his shirt is wet" because he was not trusted by his people.

In the wake of Soekarno's broken promises, Daud Beureueh withdrew his allegiance from Soekarno's government and in 1953 declared Aceh part of the Islamic State of Indonesia (DI/TII).[26] Many Acehnese explain the origins of the DI/TII armed and guerilla resistance as a reaction to the insult of losing their status as a province and with it the possibility of instituting Islamic law.[27] After almost five years of violence, the DI/TII conflict was resolved by negotiations. In 1959, the central government proposed granting Aceh special status and autonomy in religion, civil law, and education. Initially Beureueh refused, but a compromise was finally achieved in 1962 (Syah and Hakiem 2000; see also *Panji Masyarakat*, 8 December 1999).

The DI/TII uprising has taken on various interpretations in current discourse (Siegel 2000, Sjamsuddin 1985). Many Acehnese in Jakarta argue that this was an extension of Acehnese battles for justice that occurred within the framework of Indonesia ("Aceh Yang tak Kunjung Padam," *Panji Masyarakat*, 8 December 1999, 30–31). At other times, this incident is called upon to demonstrate the longevity and fanaticism of Acehnese desire to separate from Indonesia. Those involved in current violent struggles seek to attach themselves to the moral legitimacy of Beureueh's martyrdom.

Alternative Histories of Acehnese Resistance

Just a year after Beautiful Indonesia in Miniature Park was inaugurated in 1975 with the First Lady's exclamation "Freedom" (*merdeka*), Hasan Tiro reportedly returned to his home in Pidie, Aceh, proclaiming

"Merdeka" and the independence of Aceh from the "colonialist-Java-Indonesians" on 4 December 1976. GAM, which engaged in an armed struggle to separate from Indonesia until the August 2005 peace agreement, recognizes Hasan Tiro as its leader and as the *wali Negara*, head of state, of the kingdom of Aceh that he seeks to restore.

The emergence of Aceh Merdeka (AM)—and its putative offspring, Gerakan Aceh Merdeka (GAM)—is often linked with the earlier DI/TII. Hasan Tiro was involved in the broader movement to make Indonesia an Islamic state, but important discontinuities between these revolts are often overlooked in current discussions. The post-Soeharto GAM rhetoric based its separatist demands in historical assertions that Indonesia has no legal right to claim Aceh as part of the nation. GAM, following Hasan Tiro's claims, argues that the Dutch should have restored sovereignty to the independent sultanate of Aceh, rather than granting authority over Aceh to Indonesia.

Hasan Tiro's political career before the proclamation of Aceh Merdeka included activity in both the Indonesian revolution and DI/TII (Sulaiman 2000, 11–14). Tiro's earlier political writings all considered Aceh in an Indonesian frame. In 1958, in *Democracy for Indonesia*, Tiro advocated a federal system with Islam as a basis for national identity. In 1965, in *The Political Future of the Malay Archipelago*, Tiro criticized Soekarno's handling of separatist movements and the concentration of economic development in Java. He called for people in "Aceh, Sumatra, Kalimantan, Sulawesi and Maluku to come together to retake their power and respect which had been taken by the colonialist Javanese over the last 20 years" (quoted in Sulaiman 2000, 15). These are differences within Indonesia, not from Indonesia. The movement that claims Tiro as its leader seeks to root itself in earlier Acehnese resistance, but stumbles where the glory of that past is joined to Indonesia.

The relationship between Acehnese independence and the establishment of Islamic law was never clearly articulated in political terms. The issue of Islam is reiterated in Tiro's writings. For example, he took issue with Soekarno's proclamation of the principle of religious unity amid diversity: "*Pancasila* is not a philosophy, or an ideology, which is alive and deeply rooted in Indonesian society. Acknowledgment of Islam as the basis for the unity of Indonesia does not mean we will separate out the Indonesians who are Christian, Hindu etc from the Indonesia we are dreaming of" (quoted in Sulaiman 2000, 14). Yet the movement for Acehnese independence from Indonesia never acquired religious legitimacy. Eric Morris, who interviewed AM participants and sympathizers in 1977, observed "an inherent instability in the ethnic separatist position. When asked if they were given a choice between an independent

Aceh and an Indonesia which was truly based on the dictates of Islam, most replied that what they really wanted was an Islamic Indonesia. Others, after holding forth on the inevitability of Acehnese independence, would add that the real purpose of the Aceh Merdeka movement was to achieve some sort of 'federalist' solution" (1983, 301).[28] Morris concluded that the military repression of Aceh Merdeka may have been "used as a pretext to move against Islamic activists not connected to the movement." In his view, "the meaningful ideal which had mobilized the Acehnese into political action was the hope of realizing Islamic goals in this life. This ideal has been the defining characteristic of Aceh within the Indonesian nation-state, to which Acehnese have maintained a commitment and by which they are yet disappointed" (301–2). Tiro may have been correct in positing continuity between DI/TII and AM, but the appeal to Islamic law did not necessarily lend support to demands for separation from Indonesia. The depth of Acehnese disappointment with the Indonesian state is also a measure of their seeing themselves as Indonesian—indeed, as the embodiment of the spirit of national independence.

Tim Kell's analysis of Acehnese rebellion points to economic inequality as the core issue under the New Order (1995). While economic issues may have been his main motivation, Hasan Tiro legitimated Aceh Merdeka in history and international law. He argued that the "Republic of Indonesia-Java is nothing but a continuation and extension of the Dutch colonization, and the legacy of the illegitimate surrender of the colonial war" (quoted in Sulaiman 2000, 15). In 1964, fifteen years after the fact, Tiro contended that in 1949 the Dutch should have returned sovereignty to the individual nations that originally were sovereign, such as the Acehnese and the Sundanese,[29] rather than turning it over to the new Republic of Indonesia. Ordinary Acehnese and those who identify as GAM often repeat such claims. When I asked how such histories circulated, people told me they were repeated primarily by word of mouth, but Hasan Tiro's writings are also available on the Internet. Publications issued by Aceh Merdeka (those I saw were dated 1995 and 1996) circulated much more widely after DOM, and most people said that they did not have or see documents supporting separation during DOM.

Tiro's platform requires historical dexterity. Tiro cannot abandon the capital of previous historical struggle; his movement is dedicated to recuperating the glory of Aceh's past. At the same time, Tiro's demand for independence is founded on his interpretations of norms and precedents of international law that would require denying the legal validity of Indonesia's claim to Aceh. Among other logical difficulties, Tiro must account for how the heroes of the past relinquished

Aceh's sovereignty. He attacks the earlier leaders of rebellion for what he calls a half-hearted struggle carried out within the frame of Indonesia, which can be considered "separatist" but not revolutionary (Sulaiman 2000, 17).

Capitalizing on a lineage of rebellion from the Aceh War through the DI/TII uprising, Tiro traces his own ancestry to Teungku Cik Di Tiro M. Saman, an Acehnese hero whose authority was slighted by those who surrendered to the Dutch.[30] In his 1948 history, Hasan Tiro dates the Aceh War from 1873 to 1937. He denies the authority of Sultan Muhammad Daud Syah to surrender and make peace with Dutch military governor Van Heuzt in 1903, because his own ancestor, Saman, had received the title of king when he took over the resistance movement in 1885–1891. National authority follows to his descendants, culminating in Hasan Tiro himself. The treaty the sultan signed is not valid according to international law, because the hereditary chiefs (*uleebalang*) who were coopted by the Dutch were not the legitimate heirs to the kingdom. But the claim Hasan Tiro asserted in 1948 is subject to the critique he offered in 1968, since he himself held positions in the Indonesian government and participated in pan-Indonesian Islamic rebellions. If Hasan Tiro were the rightful king, then his own career would void the historical-legal basis on which he claims the right to independence. So would the history that he wrote in 1948 declaring Aceh indivisibly linked to the Republic of Indonesia.

In April 1948, Hasan Muhammad Tiro wrote a fifty-page pamphlet, *Perang Atjeh 1873M.–1927M.* (*The Atjeh War 1873–1927*), in which he explained the importance of Aceh's history to the Indonesian nation:

Just as the region of Atjeh is one part which is not separate from the State of the Indonesian Republic, also its history even is an inseparable part of Indonesian history, for a motto (*semboyan*) we are one nation (*bangsa*), one language (*bahasa*) and one fatherland (*tanah air*). To guarantee the continuation of this strong resolve (*tekad*) as best as possible, we not only have to struggle in the field of political understanding but also in the field of national (*bangsa*) culture. (1948, 3)[31]

Recognizing the vulnerability of the nation, Tiro seeks to bring the strengths of Acehnese history into Indonesian national culture in much the same way Soekarno did when soliciting the donation of the Dakota, but Tiro envisions a more central role for himself and his people in the Indonesian state than Aceh was allowed to play.

Tiro elaborates the importance of understanding history as he embarks on writing the history of the Aceh war:

This is where great responsibility sits on the shoulders of all our leaders, education and especially the writers of our history. The responsibility of the historian is to create the spirit of "unity" (*kesatuan*) from all areas in understanding politics as well as understanding culture and history. Harmonious unification of all elements of the body, which constitutes our unity is our source of strength especially in facing the future. In this relationship the writers of our history will play the most important role. They have an obligation and responsibility that is heavy, to create o n e history for o n e Indonesian nation (*bangsa Indonesia*)! (1948, 3)[32]

National unification is understood as involving politics as well as culture and as a task that has not yet been accomplished. Rewriting the history of Acehnese resistance to the Dutch is essential, Tiro explains, because Dutch historians had created a "false picture" of Aceh and its inhabitants "with the intention of playing us against each other and to justify the acts of raping the independence of Atjeh, the final bastion from the fortress of independence of the Indonesian nation (*bangsa Indonesia*)" (4). In this work, Aceh stands as an example of and to the Republic of Indonesia.

Tiro's history of Acehnese resistance to Dutch colonialism begins in the mid-nineteenth century, with international treaties recognizing the independence of Aceh and the Acehnese vigorously defending their sovereignty. Tiro had apparently not yet found the 1824 Treaty. After stating that Dutch efforts to divide the kingdoms of Aceh in East and West Sumatra without a doubt violated the Treaty of Friendship, Tiro explains that the "Kingdom (*keradjaan*) of Atjeh still demonstrated goodwill and was prepared to negotiate with the Dutch to repair relations if the Dutch would truly fulfill their promises . . . thus, in the year 1857, the peace agreement was signed between the Dutch and Aceh which also included trade agreements as well" (1948, 13). This treaty was violated by the Dutch declaration of war on Aceh in 1873.

Hasan Tiro contends that the war against the Dutch ended no earlier than 1937. The sultan's surrender does not matter because the religious leaders of Tiro were still fighting: "In 1903 M. Sultan Alauddin Muhammad Dawod Sjah, Teuku Panglima Polem, Tuanku Radja Keumala, Tuanku Mahmud, etc, and the Sultan's family were forced to surrender. But this issue does not have any consequence for the path of the war because the Teungkus of Tiro had already taken responsibility to lead the war continuously no matter how many lives must be sacrificed" (1948, 29). Battles continued after 1908, and even after Cik Di Tiro's death in 1911: "The leaders of Atjeh remained determined . . . to struggle until the last drop of their blood was gone. One by one they martyred themselves as heroes who supported and followed by their friends from the struggle until 1927M. after Teuku Tjut Ali the last commander in chief died, and the big battles ended, at that time, Atjeh could be occupied, but Atjeh was already deserted because the beloved leaders had gone, they all chose to die as heroes instead of live under colonialism" (31).

Tiro maintains that, although the Dutch occupied Aceh, the Acehnese never surrendered: "Even though the war had ended but the dignity and spirit (*hakekatnya djiwa*) of Atjeh never submitted to the Dutch. This fact is not hidden for those who know the actual conditions in Atjeh, even the Dutch themselves know and acknowledge it. Zentgraff states in his book 'that the people of Atjeh never will submit wholly to our government'" (1948, 32).[33] In this account, the people of Aceh exemplify continued resistance to Dutch colonialism. Tiro's history of the Aceh war seeks to demonstrate that the Acehnese are not fanatics but rather committed nationalists defending Indonesia from aggressive colonizers. He contends that the Dutch misrepresented the Acehnese struggle, but he extracts enough lines and points from Dutch texts to make his own case. Using Dutch words, he shows that this dignified struggle was similar to other defenses of the nation Europeans have valorized and that the Dutch, not the Acehnese, were the aggressors. This aspect of his 1948 work demonstrates his intention to appeal to the international community.

At the same time, Hasan Tiro asserted a claim relative to the emergent Indonesian state. The Acehnese exemplified the struggle for independence, but with a significant difference from the rest of Indonesia. Tiro insists that Aceh was not colonized for as long as other places, and that this distinction must be acknowledged:

It is a fact that at the start of the twentieth century there was still a part of the Indonesian fatherland which still maintained independence. Because of this it is not true, not just, and rapes their history at the same time that it is an insult to themselves if our nation says absolutely that Indonesia has been colonized for three hundred fifty years by the Dutch. We recognize that indeed there were parts of our fatherland that had to experience such a fate, however, this was a local phenomenon and if we do not want to deny the history that has been written by our heroes with blood and lives then we must make it absolute. (1948, 48)

Aceh's distinction was Indonesia's glory, but only as long as this history "written . . . with blood and lives" was acknowledged by the nation-state as the universal truth, while capitulation to colonial rule was treated as a merely local phenomenon. In 1948, Tiro's writing might have been a call to arms against the remaining Dutch. However, the history can as easily be mobilized as a call to shed blood to defend the achievements of the ancestral martyrs against those who deny them.

How did Indonesia recompense this debt to Aceh? In 1965 Hasan Tiro criticized the state's first twenty years, labeling the regime Javanese rather than Indonesian and colonialist rather than nationalist. He lamented that the people are starving and that there is no freedom of religion, speaking, or writing. Tiro encouraged the people of Aceh, Sumatra, Kalimantan, Sulawesi, Maluku, and other regions to reclaim their dignity, which has been stolen by the Javanese colonialists. If they do not, Tiro warns: "In the present and in the future, we and our descendents will vanish without a trace" (quoted in Sulaiman 2000, 15). Although Tiro was increasingly critical of the shortcomings of earlier generations, he did not relinquish their history. Rather, that historical uniqueness is the basis on which he exhorts other *bangsa* to exercise their right to self-determination.

We Acehnese are one nation in the world like other nations . . . we have a country of our own, that is Aceh. We have a language of our own, that is Acehnese . . . and we have our own biography (*riwayat*), the history of Aceh which was made by our ancestors . . . is an heirloom (*pustaka*) that cannot be forgotten night and day, evening and morning wherever we Acehnese are, if we are in Aceh itself or out of the country. (quoted in Sulaiman 2000, 15–16)

This equation of nation and language with Aceh rather than Indonesia directly contradicts the statements he made in 1948.

In 1968, Tiro argued that Aceh had been colonized for fifty-seven years, from the death of the last king in 1911. The latest colonization, by the Javanese, was accomplished without a single battle, because of the "stupidity" of Acehnese leaders who in 1945 "no longer understood Aceh's history as a nation" (quoted in Sulaiman 2000, 17). According to Tiro, there was a political conspiracy between the Dutch and the Javanese in 1949. The Dutch should have surrendered power to each nation (*bangsa*) that was originally sovereign, including Aceh and Sunda. Tiro fails to recall the version of history that he wrote in 1948, or the role he himself played in the roundtable negotiations that resulted in this transfer of sovereignty to the Republic of Indonesia. Contemporary Acehnese historian Isa Sulaiman found no evidence to suggest Acehnese dissatisfaction with the negotiations at that time. In retrospect, Hasan Tiro's evaluation of the relationship between Indonesian nationalism and Acehnese independence had changed.

Tiro sought to attract support for his idea by calling for a return to Aceh's historic greatness, as well as an end to economic disparities. His call to remember history continues today. A cartoon from an Acehnese newspaper on the anniversary of Tiro's proclamation of independence, 4 December 2000, features Tiro saying: "Remember always the greatness of your history, our ancestors were brave and strong." The referendum is, in this sense, a vote on the past.

AMANAH WALI PADA MILAD ACHEH MERDEKA
(Minggu 3 Desember 2000):

Figure 2. "Remember always the greatness of your history, our ancestors were brave and strong." *Kontras*, 4 December 2000.

In recuperating this long-ago past, Tiro attempts to submerge the disappointment, deception, and destruction that occurred while Aceh was part of Indonesia. However, it is precisely this disappointment and disillusionment, along with the more recent history of DOM abuses, that the current incarnation of GAM uses to recruit people to its cause. Tiro cannot point to the plane, or to living memories of specific historical events; he must call upon an imagined history through distant ancestors and vanished kingdoms. Many other Acehnese would like to forget the period of Indonesian humiliation as well, but they draw their legitimacy and moral claims from their status as victims of human rights abuses and Indonesia's disregard for the capital Aceh once invested in the nation. While the details of what happened in the past are not disputed, these historical narratives differ markedly in interpretation and trajectory, especially in the futures that are projected as their inevitable or logical outcomes. This struggle over the meaning of the past, para-doxically, reinforces the power of history to legitimate the nation—whether Indonesian or Acehnese.[34]

Culture as Justification for Military Action, History as Ground for Resistance

When the governor of Aceh was writing in the foreword of *The Dutch Colonial War in Acheh* that the task of the past heroes must be finished, he was requesting additional military troops to "secure" Aceh. So successful was the New Order culturalization of Acehnese history, so legendary was their bravery, so ferocious was their rebelliousness, that in 1990 the Indonesian Army launched a campaign to deal with "Security Disruptors Gangs" (GPK).

Media reports that accompanied the military operations relied on historical imagery to explain the scale of violence. One report began with a recitation of Dutch colonial expert Snouck Hurgronje's caricature of the Acehnese as "fanatic Muslims, full of deceptive tricks, [who] hate non Muslims, delight in war, and since long ago devote more attention to war than other ethnic groups in the archipelago" ("Mengamankan Aceh: Wawancara dengan Pangdam I Bukit Barisan," *Majalah Tempo*, 17 November 1990). In answering the question why "Aceh is always restless," the report says that the explanation lies in "the violent character of the Acehnese, their pride in their past, and the role of culture and religion." It concludes that the development of Aceh from an isolated area with unskilled labor to an industrial zone with skilled laborers from outside the region inevitably generated social inequality, which made it "very easy to fan the flames of sentiment, especially if it is decorated with the flowers of pride in the past." Yet military spokesmen noted at the time that the criminal gangs were often not all Acehnese.

The ostensible mission of the military operations (*Operasi Jaring Merah* 1) retrospectively labeled DOM was to secure public safety for ordinary people. The military relied on the participation of the ordinary people it sought to protect in killing anyone suspected of being a security disruptor. Countless people became victims of misrecognition. Malign indeterminacies developed as a result of this strategy. General Zacky Anwar Makarim, a prominent Army intelligence officer involved in the design and implementation of the operations in Aceh, explained the problem of distinguishing ordinary Acehnese people from GPK-GAM, conflating "security disruptors" with separatists: When Free Aceh guerillas chased by the army run into the crowd, "they turn into women holding babies to protect themselves" (*Panji Masyarakat*, 8 December 1999, 3).

Victims of DOM tell a different story of the difficulty of separating ordinary people from separatists. In a striking first-person narrative collected, fictionalized, and published by an NGO after the end of the violence, a woman whose husband was killed in 1991 recalls the arrival of strange outsiders, military personnel from Java and elsewhere:

> From one of my younger brothers, I knew that they [the strangers] came here to look for and arrest Acehnese who had become a member of the Free Aceh Movement. I did not know what that meant. Wasn't Aceh already free (*merdeka*)? Hadn't Teuku Umar, Cut Nyak Dhien, Teungku Chik Di Tiro and the other Acehnese warriors (*pejuang*) already battled until Indonesia was free (*merdeka*) in the year 1945? From elementary school even I knew that. There were no more *kafir* (non-Muslim) colonialists here. (Mariati 1999, 125)

Some Acehnese treated as separatists understood their historical struggle to be joined to Indonesia's struggle for independence from colonial domination. The same historical myth of bravery was used by the military to justify its repression of "dangerous separatists."

The arbitrary and excessive state violence and human rights abuses that occurred during this period created deep frustration, dissatisfaction, and even hatred toward the central government. Coupled with what Geoffrey Robinson has termed the "shared memory of struggle" (1998, 132), the legacy of DOM accelerated the drive for referendum and independence in Aceh. Military officials invoke the popular expression of desires for the referendum in the less repressive post-Soeharto period to prove retroactively that there has always been a separatist urge in Aceh. Although the military acknowledges its own excess, it maintains that it was justified in saving the nation from dangerous separatists.

Immediately following General Wiranto's public apology to the Acehnese, many discussions among Banda Aceh intellectuals, activists, and NGO members focused on the Acehnese "culture" of revenge, which some accounts linked to Islamic religious teachings that demand punishment equal to the crime. However, the consensus of these discussions was that the Acehnese people supported justice and a peaceful resolution of conflict instead of vengeance ("Dendam Bukan Sifat Masyarakat Aceh," *Media Indonesia*, 5 January 1999). At this point, it seemed that the specificity of abuses might not be forgotten, but skulls from the mass graves would not be contributed to future theme parks. The Acehnese self-image of bravery would be rearticulated not as failing to avenge wrongs but as following religious wisdom and forgiving enemies. Stories of the struggle for independence were told to demonstrate Aceh's fidelity and commitment to Indonesia, and perhaps to remind those who might favor more radical action what they would be giving up should they not make their own peace with more recent histories. These narratives emphasized that Acehnese could not simply leave the nation they had helped to create.

In the euphoria that followed the ending of the military operations zone (Daerah Operasi Militer, DOM) in 1998, stories of Acehnese bravery circulated to remind people of a past they could be proud of. Images of the more distant past were invoked to transcend the indignities suffered at the hands of an Indonesian army undeterred by Acehnese bravery. I asked many people in Aceh why the mythic Acehnese did not defeat the Indonesian soldiers as they had the Dutch. I was told that the Indonesians were also Muslims, so there was not the inspiration of a holy war. Perhaps there was also an unspoken shame that some Acehnese had informed upon and committed acts of violence against other Acehnese. Memories of defeats during DOM do threaten a sense of Acehnese dignity. For some, it may be easier to forget this period than to acknowledge that they failed to demonstrate the courage their ancestors exemplified.

Widespread support for a referendum in 1999 does not indicate that there was a real threat of secession that necessitated the brutal military campaigns. Many Acehnese told me in November 1999, privately and off the record, that they remained committed to struggling for justice within Indonesia. One older man who fought against the Dutch and was involved in human rights investigations told me, "We have invested too much in the nation. But, I am old, it is the younger generation's turn now, I can only pray they will not vote to leave Indonesia." Many Acehnese struggle with the history of their joined struggle with Indonesia, but few can forget their struggle against Indonesian forces both for justice and for a return to normal life, before there was a DOM, before there was a GAM.

By 2000, it was clear to most Acehnese that they would not be granted a referendum, and violence continued unabated. Many Acehnese regarded giving up what even they recognized was a hopeless cause as a betrayal of a long history of fighting for moral right against any odds. Without their fierce determination and will to struggle, they ask, how can Aceh get historical recognition for its contribution to the nation? Yet precisely that determination makes it impossible for them to attain historical justice. Many older Acehnese, holding fast to the historical myths of their people, struggled with the impossibility of leaving the nation they fought to liberate. Which histories can be remembered in the future and which ones will have to be forgotten, both in Jakarta and in Banda Aceh?

It is difficult to know what would fulfill the Acehnese demand for historical recognition. Many Acehnese say "justice," which Jakarta has been incapable of providing. As the 4 December 2000 anniversary of GAM's declaration approached, national media featured special articles and sections on Acehnese history ("Memandang Aceh Dengan Mata Baru," *Majalah Tempo*, 4 December 2000; "History," *Kompas*, 4 December 2000). These articles did not provide recognition of the nation's debt to Aceh. Instead of addressing injustices, they sought historical justification for character traits that would make the ongoing violence inevitable.

Nono Anwar Makarim, who has written on issues of truth and reconciliation, compiled a series of articles with the theme "Viewing Aceh with New Eyes" ("Memandang Aceh Dengan Mata Baru," *Majalah Tempo*, 4 December 2000, 68). He suggests "collective metamorphoses" so that the "history of Aceh can be written with ink instead of tears." He looks back to the Dutch government's use of Snouck Hurgronje to explain the culture and customs of the Acehnese as founded on fanaticism and committed to violence. It is precisely this understanding of Acehnese that Hasan Tiro sought to correct in his treatise so the Acehnese struggle against the Dutch could serve as an example for Indonesia.

According to Tiro's 1948 history, the Dutch baselessly accused the Acehnese of being pirates and thieves in order to justify their colonial war (4). When the Dutch encountered strong popular opposition and were unable to occupy Aceh as easily as they hoped, they accused the Acehnese of being bloodthirsty fanatics. Tiro suggests that the Dutch characterized the Acehnese as fanatics because "they love independence and they do not acquiesce to colonization." Tiro sees this condemnation as paradoxical, because "if 'love of the nation's independence and fatherland together with giving up one's life to preserve it' is called fanatic then truly every respectful nation is 'fanatic' and must be 'fanatic'" (5). The reason for the Dutch slander is clear:

it was Atjeh that was the last fortress of independence . . . of the *bangsa* Indonesia because the region of Atjeh was the one and only region of ours that was strong enough to persevere and hold on to independence to the final moment, long after all of Indonesia was colonized by the Dutch. Likewise, the war [in] Atjeh was a war that was forced by the Dutch upon the State of Indonesia which was independent and sovereign, and not just a rebellion. (5)

When Acehnese strength and independence is no longer the embodiment of Indonesian independence, it is again rewritten as fanatical, even drawing on colonial sources.

In the early twentieth century, the Dutch colonial expert Hurgronje declared violence the only way to resolve the Aceh problem. Makarim's article, titled "Orders to Governor Van Heutz," reads like a set of rules for the Indonesian military, even using contemporary terminology: "More than a hundred years ago, the Dutch Indies government gave instructions to the Governor of Aceh that that area should be treated as a military operations zone (Daerah Operasi Militer). The instructions were comprehensive, not just the order to annihilate the GPK (Gerakan Pengacau Keamanan)" ("Perintah kepada Gubernur Van Heutz," *Majalah Tempo*, 4 December 2000, 91).[35] Reading between the lines, a list of the excesses committed by the Indonesian armed forces in Aceh emerges from the Dutch prohibitions that Makarim cites: do not burn houses, do not treat people harshly, do not allow low-ranking soldiers to search houses or to steal things while searching, do not take food from local people, do not force people to labor, do not involve local Acehnese in military operations, do not allow firearms to be carried without a specific permission from the governor, do not impose heavy punishments on crimes with political motivations, and repeatedly, do not create hatred among the people. When Makarim wrote the article in 2000, news in Aceh featured frequent occurrences of these crimes by security forces. Historical evidence suggests that the Dutch soldiers were guilty of such excesses as well.

In a formulation popular in Indonesian media, Makarim asks: who are the masterminds or "intellectual actors behind" the political violence in Aceh? ("Mau Berunding Dengan Siapa di Aceh?" *Majalah Tempo*, 4 December 2000, 97). The two usual suspects, GAM's titular head, Hasan Tiro, and Mohamad Nazar, leader of the civilian movement for the referendum, are not considered on a par with the heroic martyrs before them. In Makarim's analysis, they mobilize the deep inner hatred of the Acehnese. In a logical maneuver that echoes the fourth-grade textbook, a struggle for justice has been transformed into pure emotion. If hatred represents the people of Aceh, then negotiation must be done with hatred, as it was a hundred years ago.

Makarim recognizes that Aceh is a nation of heroes. "Strange and miraculous," he writes, "the most respected of all the Dutch was the most harsh. Harsh, but just." He concludes: "Acehnese people understand the language of violence. In fact, it is respected as an aspect of masculinity" ("Mau Berunding Dengan Siapa di Aceh?" *Majalah Tempo*, 4 December 2000, 97). By making violence into a cultural attribute, Makarim misses the point of his own historical research. He does not factor into the equation the injustice of the recent past.

Figure 3. "Who is responsible, THE PAST." *Kompas*, 27 November 1999.

Holding the Past Responsible

A cartoon appeared in a national newspaper in November 1999. A large military jacket heavy with ranks and medals dominates the frame. The right breast of the jacket is adorned with two skulls hanging as medals: one reads DOM (Daerah Operasi Militer, Military Operations Zone), the other reads HAM (Hak Asasi Manusia, Human Rights). A man standing erect without a shirt, presumably the jacket's owner, says "Who is responsible? THE PAST."

This cartoon appeared while military officers were rebutting the charges brought against them for human rights violations during DOM. The image points to the lack of accountability and justice for past crimes, despite the official military apology to the Acehnese. Following Robinson (1998), I argue that certain articulations of the past have created the conditions of possibility for violence, but I extend his argument by suggesting that the reliance on the past for justification and grounding has a complicated legacy. If the "past" were indeed responsible for all the crimes committed in name of the nation, then a referendum would be its trial.

What kinds of histories hold the past responsible for recent violations? To date, efforts to address history have not decreased violence. Histories that compete to serve as a ground for the future have not quieted the ghosts of historical grievances (see Scott 1999). Aceh hovered on the edge of a state of emergency after the military operations zone status was lifted at the end of the New Order. Violence grew increasingly widespread and difficult to analyze, continuing throughout a series of international interventions and a formally declared state of emergency until a peace agreement was reached in 2005. The historical narratives that enabled the 2005 Memorandum of Understanding may also unravel this agreement. How can history be written that cannot be turned into renewable ammunition in a perpetual self-renewing conflict? How can anyone write histories as states of siege in perpetually pending states of emergency?

Michael Taussig remarks that to achieve Benjamin's command to see the "constancy of the state of emergency" requires "knowing how to stand in an atmosphere whipping back and forth between clarity and opacity, seeing both ways at once" (1992, 17–18). Such a vantage point may provide one way of writing histories that intervene in seemingly inevitable cycles of violence and repression. The optics of Taussig's "Nervous System" highlight the moments in which the normality of the abnormality of the everydayness of violence is disrupted suddenly by "something that even while it requires the normal in order to make its impact, destroys it." Turning the optics of the nervous system on the history of rebellion in Aceh discloses a logic by which the normalness of justification through reference to the past is ruptured by statements like this one, which was made to me in confidence by an Acehnese who lived through these events:

Then I would have been willing (*rela dan ikhlas*) to die. I had told everyone what happened . . . . If I disappeared, it would have been clear, there would have been others who would have sprung up and continued [the fight for justice], they would have known what happened. Now, now it is a different story. Now, I am not willing. It is not a good time to die. Now, it is an empty death. Community leaders die all the time now, and no one knows . . . it is not clear. There are suspicions that they might have been working for both sides, it is just not clear. Now people do not become martyrs. There are a lot of "heroes" and "martyrs" springing up now. They all say they are ready for death, they think it will really do something. They don't realize what this is about. They don't realize that they are trapped. . . . No, now I would not be willing.[36]

This explanation of why dying would no longer be a heroic act registers the senselessness and arbitrariness of violence, the hallmarks of New Order brutality.

Romantic identification with the bravery of the past produces, not martyrs and heroes, but "curious ghosts." A few months later the same person commented: "Aceh is full of curious ghosts (*hantu penasaran*). They don't know why they had to die so they return to the world to ask why they had to die." These curious ghosts and the mass graves of DOM persist in troubling the division between history and culture. They refuse the conversions of historical detail into cultural type. The confidence that bravery offers seems useful in an uncontrollable and uncertain present. Yet heroism and honor are impossible to attain, and continuing to choose bravery proves fatal by retroactively demonstrating the validity of the threat that justifies repression. Refusing the logic of history or identity has equally fatal consequences, branding a person as a traitor in a polarized conflict. These mass graves and continuously appearing corpses haunt the present. The remnants of DOM cannot be buried again, and it is hard to know quite where to put them. Evidence of violence compounds daily, like interest on the debt to history that is unpaid, or the future that history promised but has never come. As the Acehnese put it, "a promise is a debt which must be paid."

The New Order regime relied on history to justify the military's role in national politics. For at least a generation, Indonesians have been indoctrinated by a fabricated story of struggling against imagined enemies threatening to destroy their unity. The enemies have always been latent, invisible, and remembered. It is hard to imagine how Indonesia as a whole will come to terms with a threat that is real, or with a historical referent like mass graves. Though historical disclosures that have resulted from the freer press following Soeharto's fall have provided new information, they have not rewritten the cultural effects of this propagandized version of history.

Chapter 3

Threat and Violence

Tensions between Aceh and Jakarta are articulated historically and include significant historical grievances, although neither analysts nor participants have considered the histories and terms of violence in Aceh from a genealogical perspective (Foucault 1977). The narratives of Aceh's differences with the central government, ahistorically recast as timeless, produced violence as a cultural attribute. Suspicions of Aceh's disloyalty to the Indonesian Republic created the conditions in which criminal violence could be considered politically motivated and, subsequently, political violence could extend the conditions for criminal activity and extortion. Ultimately, a violent separatist movement emerged. This chapter documents the incidents of violence and the shifts in classification of violence that structure the discourse of Aceh and the threat it poses to Indonesia.

Violence Before GAM

Versions of history that emphasize DI/TII as a fanatic Islamist movement, an incarnation of the attributes of irrational resistance diagnosed by colonial ethnographer Snouck Hurgronje, obscure the constancy of Aceh's desire to have a greater say in the shape of the Indonesian nation. State nationalism, consolidated through constant fear of difference and disintegration, relied on the ghosts of DI/TII violence to mark Aceh with chronic suspicion. The violent means used by DI/TII are emphasized, while Daud Beureueh's compromise with the central government and the peaceful resolution of the DI/TII conflict are forgotten. Other regional identities articulated through armed struggle during the 1950s have been overwritten by narratives of cultural diversity, yet the possibility that the regions might be disloyal to the center remained fundamental to the military architects of New Order security.[1] DI/TII rebellion is frequently recalled to create suspicion that Aceh is violent and disloyal to the center ("Aceh Sudah Bosan Berperang," *Kompas*, 6 September 1990).

The anti-communist violence that accompanied the rise of the New

Order in 1965–1966 extended to Aceh,[2] but in these versions of history Acehnese violence that supported the regime is forgotten. In 1999, a national newspaper noted the common disregard of Aceh's loyalty to the center, emphasizing that when the communist party "created chaos with the 30th September Movement. . . . Aceh did not give a place to a movement like that" ("Memahami Aceh," *Media Indonesia*, 5 May 1999). Typically, all threats to the state, whether from communism or separatism, are conflated by a rhetoric of an imperiled national unity that must constantly be defended from internal enemies. To add the mass killings of suspected communist party members that inaugurated the New Order to a chronology of violence in Aceh would interrupt narratives of Aceh's dissatisfaction with the center. Yet it could also evoke them, since one of the fundamental problems between the center and Aceh was the broken promise to allow Islamic law in Aceh. Initially, violence was a way Aceh articulated its support for Indonesian-ness: against the Dutch, against a communist takeover, for an Islamic state in Indonesia. Violence in support of Indonesia was recast as a potential threat to Indonesia.

In 1968, after Acehnese Muslims had joined in the New Order's program to eradicate the communist party, President Soeharto went to Aceh to promote religious tolerance, warning that splits among groups were the entry point for the atheist Indonesian Communist Party (PKI) to divide the nation ("Presiden Soeharto di Atjeh: Djaga Toleransi Agama," *Kompas*, 2 September 1968). Strikingly, the religious "fanaticism" that was used to eradicate the PKI in Aceh was imagined as a source of danger. One man I spoke with in Banda Aceh recalled that in the early 1970s, military intelligence conducted operations in search of "Jihad Commandos," likely the same groups that had eliminated the PKI.[3] In the early New Order period, the threat of past violence used to secure the nation was projected into a future threat, and the power of violence itself was unsettling. From the start of the New Order, anxiety about the nation "splitting" echoed Soekarno's earlier anxieties, but with the difference that the sources of division were between ideological groups, not just between different islands. Miniaturized culture might eventually domesticate regional identities that potentially threatened Indonesia. But the problem of ideological difference created a flexible threat that could be mobilized to fragment and stigmatize, reducing the possibility that solidarity might form across and especially along the lines of group identities.

Repeated emphasis on the military's role in "saving the nation" obscured the fact that initially the military itself was suspected as an agent of division. Official ceremonies reminded soldiers that "excesses" might divide the people from the military. In 1970, military leaders warned their troops to "be aware and careful of instigations and agitations which might push members of ABRI [the armed forces] to take negative actions which could be the source of excesses (*ekses-ekses*) in ABRI's mission to be devoted to the people" ("Sasaran Memetjahbelah Kini Dipusatkan Kepada ABRI," *Kompas*, 20 March 1970). This statement located responsibility with ABRI members to avoid "provocations" at the same time that it introduced the idea that some elements might provoke ABRI. Anxiety about the armed forces' relationship to the people was underlined by warnings from Soemitro, a high-ranking military leader, that members of ABRI "must not misuse their uniforms for excess, or the excess that comes from special rights and privileges, as it [would] divide ABRI from the people." (The theme of misused uniforms returned later: as stolen uniforms and as the power of the uniform out of control.) The armed forces themselves were not exempt from splitting: "Each member of ABRI must be aware that targets to split [the nation] are centered on ABRI now, by creating division amongst the ranks and spreading a feeling of mutual suspicion amongst ABRI's battle array" ("Sasaran Memetjahbelah Kini Dipusatkan Kepada ABRI," *Kompas*, 20 March 1970). The anxiety that the armed forces were not "one" with the people persisted in narrations of the separatist conflict. However, warnings from high-ranking military officials to others in the military were replaced by suspicions that outside forces strove to alienate ABRI from the people, a possibility foreshadowed by the mention of potential "instigations."

Uneven economic development has often been invoked as an explanation for the tensions between Aceh and Jakarta.[4] In the mid-1970s, the discovery of liquid natural gas in the region and its exploitation by the state created new "social jealousies." The Acehnese clearly understood that the central state appropriated the lion's share of the wealth its rich fields produced. The issue of economic injustice is certainly a deeply sedimented foundation of the conflict between Aceh and Jakarta. The conflict was exacerbated by cultural differences, as the outside experts who flooded the area to develop this natural resource disrupted the strong Islamic values that predominated in Aceh (Kell 1995). The possibility that chronic instability and periodic uprising in Aceh would jeopardize its economic development returned in the early 1990s in a much stronger and more direct form. Military campaigns of vigilance focused on this "social gap" as a threat at the same time that they criminalized social critics who tried to address the issue.[5] Unequal development was regarded as a potential cause of resentment, violence, and disintegration, rather than a problem that should be attended to substantively.

Creating a Continuous Violent Separatism

Analyses of the relationship between the DI/TII movement and GAM link the two as indicative of Acehnese character. Daud Beureueh, an important religious leader prominent in the DI/TII struggle for an Islamic state, possessed the moral legitimacy that Hasan Tiro sought as the leader of the Free Aceh movement and future independent state of Aceh. Tiro criticized Beureueh for compromising with the Indonesian authorities and for conducting his struggle within the framework of Indonesia. He did not, however, criticize the use of violence against the central government; indeed, he sought to position his own movement as an extension of that morally sanctioned violent force. The aims of GAM and the state apparatus coincided in the erasure of the peaceful conclusion and negotiated compromise of DI/TII. Both Tiro and military sources linked disturbances during the New Order with Beureueh, activating a chain of violence to erase political differences between Jakarta and Aceh and to obscure the series of promises Jakarta had reneged on. Many accused members of the movement noted that Beureueh never supported it and that there were rumors that Tiro had betrayed Beureueh in an arms deal, which both distinguished their politics and linked their violent means.[6] Less often recalled is the absence of violence in the founding declaration of Aceh Merdeka.

Most national and international media reports on the conflict in Aceh feature a standard statement: "Separatist rebels have been fighting for independence since 1976." On this point, the security forces' version of history concurs with GAM's own.[7] The declaration of Aceh Merdeka on 4 December 1976 became much more significant in 1999 and 2000 than it was at the time. The process by which Aceh Merdeka was transformed into Gerakan Aceh Merdeka was obscured by the popular and official histories that emerged and were consolidated in the post-DOM period.

The first official mention of the formal declaration of Aceh Merdeka on 4 December 1976 appeared in June 1977—significantly, in an announcement by the security forces, not by the movement. Laksmana Sudomo, head of the national military Operational Command for the Restoration of Security and Order (Kopkamtib), noted that a document declaring Aceh Merdeka on 4 December 1976 had been found in May 1977 by the commander in chief of the Military Area Command Iskandar Muda, Brigadier General Rivai Harahap ("Terlalu Pagi Menilai 'Deklarasi Aceh Merdeka'," *Kompas*, 7 June 1977). Sudomo stated that it was not yet possible to ascertain whether there was any connection with DI/TII figures. In the same article, foreign minister Adam

Malik dismissed the threat with the comment, "A movement like Aceh Merdeka is a person dreaming."[8]

Two days later, Sudomo reported not a delusion, but a threat. He called Aceh Merdeka a "separatist and subversive movement" that possessed not only pamphlets but also weapons. Yet, he was still not able to give the details of exactly what kind of a movement it was ("'Deklarasi Aceh Merdeka'," *Kompas*, 9 June 1977). The newspaper noted that the government usually revealed findings in cases like this and emphasized that, in addition to legal investigations political observations were also needed, "so that rumors did not increase, and it did not create provocations," because if "that happened it would succeed in becoming subversive" ("'Deklarasi Aceh Medeka'," *Kompas*, 9 June 1977). Not only did the movement appear capable of creating a provocation, but the failure to treat the case transparently could also create a provocation. The editorial called the movement an anachronism in a nation that had moved into the unity and growth phase of its history. It posed two possibilities for the movement's existence: the development process in the region or "consistent ideological struggle." Such ideological struggle had to be separated from religion, noting that it was only the efforts of a small group of people.

In two more days, Sudomo invoked Aceh Merdeka as "a warning to the nation" that "the ideology of *Pancasila*"[9] was "still not understood and studied by all the layers of the Indonesian nation in the farthest corners of the archipelago" ("Kas Kopkamtib: Munculnya 'Aceh Merdeka' Peringatan Bagi Bangsa Indonesia," *Kompas*, 11 June 1977). National military rhetoric inserted AM into a sequence of threats to the nation that included DI/TII. As Sudomo put it, the "separatist movement is only one instance of ideological conflict . . . which tried to replace *Pancasila* as the ideology and philosophy of the nation."[10] This conflation of AM with DI/TII was erroneous: unlike DI/TII, Aceh Merdeka was not explicitly Islamic, and in the early years it was unable to attract the support of religious leaders.[11]

Only two days later, Sudomo did an about-face and echoed the foreign minister's dismissal of Aceh Merdeka: "Hasan Tiro's efforts [are] only the efforts of a person dreaming" ("Kesimpulan Kas Kopkamtib: Gerakan 'Aceh Merdeka' Hanya Petualangan," *Kompas*, 13 June 1977). Sudomo reduced Aceh Merdeka to mere "opportunist subversive separatists who are not supported by a powerful force." This article is the first instance in which official sources added the word "Gerakan" (movement) to the group's title, extending the threat at the very moment that officials were downplaying its significance. Asserting that those who had been captured for possession of flags and declarations of independence were "only influenced by Hasan Tiro," Sudomo declared that "whatever is done by Hasan Tiro and his movement does not have an influence on the Acehnese people, and the conditions in the region are peaceful."[12] Sudomo supported his assessment with characteristic New Order logic, arguing that "it is not possible that a separatist movement could work without the support of powerful force."[13] He denied earlier reports that the movement possessed weapons. In terms of New Order rhetoric on dangers and subversions, this shift was striking. The movement, even though it had a named leader who later would be called an "intellectual" or a "mastermind," did not have powerful external backing or arms.

Less often noted was Aceh Merdeka's newness. From late 1998 to early 2000, I interviewed most of the people arrested and detained in the first wave of GAM arrests.[14] One said he himself did not know much about the origins of the group, but had been arrested several times because the security forces suspected him on account of family connections. "At first, in Aceh, the Free Aceh Movement was proclaimed on December 4, 1976, and according to my observation, it did not get much of a response from people. The people were afraid of something that new, especially the ordinary people." The ideas espoused by Aceh Merdeka represented a rupture with the past, rather than a continuation of DI/TII. AM had drawn on the support of family and local (sub-district) loyalties. The "cabinet" of AM "did not have power; they just struggled through diplomacy." At this point, Aceh Merdeka was clearly not a mass-based "movement"; rather, it was a small group whose leadership was composed mostly of exiles. Hasan Tiro made a brief visit to Aceh at this point, but was in exile before and after the declaration.

I interviewed people who were apprehended in the first round of GAM arrests; all were detained without trial for more than a year. Army intelligence officers processed the detentions. Treatment was much more "humane" than it was later, under DOM. One person reiterated, "A lot of people were arrested then, but the conditions were not like in 1990." Those arrested were not "finished off" or "executed." Another person had a sense that the soldiers used excessive force out of insecurity: "There was the impression that they (*laksus*, interrogators) were afraid; the impression came from the fact that they were too repressive. They did not want to think how they could resolve this problem with wisdom; instead they used violence, though it was not as bad as it is now." When I asked whether GAM had weapons that the security forces were afraid of, he said "only very old ones."[15] I asked him why, then, the security forces feared GAM. He explained: "They feared, like this, if I use the example of an embryo, they were afraid that the embryo would get bigger, so they worked so that it could get bigger."[16] His comment is intriguing: the security forces are afraid of the movement, yet work so that it can become bigger. Aceh Merdeka itself may have been eradicated, but it was reincarnated as GAM, which became much bigger. Analysis suggests that the security forces wanted to preserve the movement as an embryo, neither completely eradicating it nor allowing it to escape their control. In this way, it remained a threat that justified their continued role as protectors of the state without endangering them. Developing Islam as a threat was considerably more dangerous, as it could provoke reactions from across the archipelago. A separatist threat by definition was limited to one region in opposition to the nation.

In 1998 and 1999, I met and interviewed many of those originally accused of being members of Aceh Merdeka. None of them identified with the resurgence of post-DOM GAM. One person said there was another group that worked "directly," implying the use of arms, which he referred to as "Arjuna's group."[17] He had learned of Arjuna in the 1990s when he was jailed with a person who had been arrested for sheltering Arjuna, who had himself escaped. Other than this, he said, he did not know much about the armed wing of GAM. (Many other people I spoke with suggested that Arjuna had strong connections with the military; they suspected he was a double agent planted in GAM by the TNI.) In 1999, I asked several people if they knew Abdullah Syafi'ie, the commander of the armed wing of GAM, who became publicly visible that year; none of them did. Of those I met from this early group, only one said he had flown the flag of AM in 1976.

The others were forced to acknowledge that they were GAM members after brutal interrogations. One person suggested that a business competitor had accused him of being a GAM member in order to destroy his business. None of them had been involved in violent acts. The violence of the interrogations quite literally made them GAM members as they were forced to confess. In their later recollections, the injustice of the state apparatus became a reason to embrace Aceh Merdeka, whose rhetoric, as they recalled it, focused primarily on economic injustice. The ideas and words of Aceh Merdeka became more powerful when they were attached to violence—that committed by the security forces in these interrogations above and that later committed in the name of the separatists.

Military Threat Perception and Dangerous Categorizations

New Order discourse of threats and subversion required some mastermind or powerful force behind them to become a real danger. Latent dangers had to be guarded against as well, but the discourse of latent danger, which had been used to recreate the threat of the PKI and the trauma of the 1965 killings, was not applied to Aceh. Aceh Merdeka was a real and visible danger, and "Wanted" posters named figures associated with it. The military may have feared that the danger of latent communism would galvanize a reaction from Aceh's strong Muslim community. Despite the difference in rhetoric, separatism was inserted into an array of dangers collectively referred to as "New Style Communism" (*Komunisme Gaya Baru*, KGB).

It is important to read the national military's shifting categorizations of the danger in Aceh in the context of the development and consolidation of its vigilance (*kewaspadaan*) campaign. Jun Honna notes that in the early New Order period, "continuous efforts were made to construct an image of instability" (1999, 143). In 1978, the National Vigilance Refresher Course was institutionalized within the armed forces. Formal indoctrination began in June 1978, following crackdowns on the student movement (144). This campaign marked a significant increase in the importance of military intelligence and a close relationship between President Soeharto and intelligence officers. By 1985, "the kewaspadaan [vigilance] project, which was first intended to standardize the military's (and the government's) threat perception regarding national stability, was . . . transformed into ABRI's security-intelligence project aiming to control political ideas in society" (145). In tracing the application of vigilance rhetoric to various threats, Honna shows that all forms of opposition to the government were construed as renewing the latent danger of communism. In 1988, military officials declared that the *kewaspadaan* campaign was almost complete, at which time the institutional apparatus (*Kopkamtib*) designed for implementing the campaign was abolished in order to reduce the influence and power of the campaign's architect, L. B. Moerdani (147). According to Honna, ABRI produced a strategic position paper that defined a new "internal security threat" it called New Style Communism. Four different kinds of threats were monitored under this new category: social organizations; fourth-generation communist groups that used "intellectual activities" and other means to "depoliticise ABRI"; "extreme groups which would try to use extra-constitutional ways—such as instigating mass riots—to further their political interests based on racial and separatist motivations"; and, finally, a "certain group of people who wanted liberal democracy with unlimited freedom" (150). Separatism—whether real or imagined—became the target of a military campaign.

The threat perception system was based on the idea that the military was capable of securing stability but stability was constantly threatened, paving the way for a constant state of vigilance. Despite differences of ideology between GAM and other threats classified as New Style Communism, they were joined in official threat perceptions by their use of methods that were disruptive of national unity. These imagined threats were met by real violence and danger in Aceh.

Honna demonstrates that globalization replaced the threat of communism, and factions in the military with opposing agendas used the vigilance campaign against threats of different natures. A military document of the campaign against the latent communist danger argued that, despite the collapse of the Soviet Union in 1991, the communist threat was still relevant (1999, 147–50). According to Honna, the document's argument is based on a logic whereby the values of globalism, especially human rights, pose threats to Indonesia's national resilience. As Honna points out, in 1993 Soeharto used the National Human Rights Commission (Komnas HAM) to remove certain officers in East Timor who had fallen out of his favor, or slipped out of his control. The discourse of human rights has, like the discourse of vigilance, been used by opposing parties to rein in the military. Freed from its substance, the logic itself becomes difficult to control.

One of the pivotal events in shifting GAM from a rhetorical threat to an actual problem was the killing of an American worker at the Arun gas field in North Aceh in 1977. At this point, vigilance training had not yet consolidated and standardized official threat perception. Distinguishing this murder from the ideological threat of Aceh Merdeka, Minister of Defense and Security Panggabean attributed it to a *gerombolan*, or "gang" of "disruptors" ("Menhankam: Peristiwa Aceh Dilakukan Gerombolan Pengacau," *Kompas*, 13 December 1977).[18] A few weeks later, military sources reported that forty-one members of an "Illegal Movement," who had declared themselves as part of DI/TII in Pidie and North Aceh, had been arrested and accused of murder, arson, and "terrorizing foreign workers" ("41 Pelaku Gerakan Ilegal Ditangkap," *Kompas*, 6 January 1978).[19] At this point, AM was not associated with violence, so a linkage with DI/TII would have been a more credible threat to the nation and the crime would have been viewed as more political. In response, the military initiated a strategy of patrols, intelligence-gathering, and interrogation to eradicate the movement. Although later the military cultivated a violent GAM, at this point a variety of other terms were used to describe the violence. AM was still viewed in exclusively ideological terms, and the attack on foreign gas company workers was marked as criminal, not ideological. Yet Aceh Merdeka became a target of the ensuing repression.

Eradicating Aceh Merdeka

By 1978, conditions in Aceh were officially reported as under control ("Keamanan di Aceh Masih Terkendalikan," *Kompas*, 12 May 1978). Criminal violence disappeared briefly from reports, and AM was characterized as neither the irrational dream of one individual nor a massive threat to the nation, but rather as a limited movement. In 1979, national news proclaimed that "what is called Aceh Merdeka, now has only six people remaining" ("Apa Yang Disebut 'Aceh Merdeka' Mereka Kini Tinggal Enam Orang," *Kompas*, 28 March 1979). An in-depth story about suspected AM member Ilyas focused on Hasan Tiro's familial connections to explain his recruitment strategy; it was based, a *Kompas* article argued, on his relationships with the parents of prospective members, cultivated while he was a commercial supplier during the DI/TII period. Though placing AM in a lineage with DI/TII, the article concluded that there was not sufficient ideological motivation for Tiro's followers to persevere in difficult conditions of isolation in the jungle. Hasan Tiro himself fled to Tiro "because it was the place where Cik Di Tiro fought the Dutch" and he hoped to "rekindle the sentiment of that struggle" ("Apa Yang Disebut 'Aceh Merdeka' Mereka Kini Tinggal Enam Orang," *Kompas*, 28 March 1979).

Despite reports of dwindling membership in AM, in March 1979 members of Parliament advocated a three-pronged solution in which the government would take a social and political approach, while ABRI would handle security problems in Aceh caused by the leftovers of the "Hasan Tiro's wild disruptors (*pengacau liar Hasan Tiro*)" ("Tiga Jalur Penyelesaian Keamanan di Aceh," *Kompas*, 27 March 1979). It is startling that such a large-scale campaign was thought necessary to eliminate the threat posed by six people in the forests who, according to the official story, lacked even a strong ideological commitment to sustain them.

A year later, the three-pronged strategy had resulted in the elimination of several AM figures. In May 1980, the minister of health of Aceh Merdeka, Dr. Zubair, was shot and killed by members of ABRI, who were informed by local people that he was in the area. Zubair refused to surrender, and in his attempt to escape, according to a report in *Kompas* newspaper, there was an exchange of fire in which Zubair's rifle failed to work. This explanation foreshadowed a style of reporting on the conflict in the post-DOM period in which most deaths were said to result from exchanges of fire that exceeded the ammunition and weapons capacity that the military acknowledged the enemy to possess.[20] Zubair's death, according to the article, reduced the total number of GAM members in the forest to six, who were requested to surrender.[21]

In August 1980, Dr. Muchtar, interior minister of Aceh Merdeka, was killed while he and his bodyguard rested in the middle of the night, unarmed and without incriminating articles on their persons ("Tertembak, Dokter Muchtar, 'Mendagri' Gerakan Aceh Merdeka," *Kompas*, 15

August 1980). A week before, Muchtar had escaped a gunfight, but not without ABRI finding an LE rifle and two hand grenades. Dr. Muchtar was reportedly the most influential figure in the movement after Hasan Tiro. The countdown continued slowly. In December 1982, one more "*tokoh* GHT" (leader of the Hasan Tiro Movement) was killed ("Seorang Lagi Tokoh GHT Ditangkap," *Kompas*, 12 June 1982). A *Kompas* article noted that Rachman Batee Puteh had joined Hasan Tiro "in forming a 'Free' Country," but did not refer to AM by name. The four remaining leaders and their positions were listed.[22]

According to the security forces, the final four were under great pressure because the "people (*rakyat*) have joined the effort to annihilate this Hasan Tiro Movement." As a result of "Operation Smile," in December 1982 the regional commander of what official military sources labeled the Hasan Tiro Movement (GHT) was caught, effectively finishing off the group ("'Panglima Wilayah' GHT Tertangkap," *Kompas*, 16 December 1982). The military proclaimed that the security operation was successful because the people exposed the hiding places of Hasan Tiro's followers. During the period of the military operations zone in Aceh, one of the most frequent reasons given for military violence was to force villagers to disclose rebels' hiding places.

Despite the eradication of the important figures of AM, the movement itself, the idea of it, and even its name did not disappear. Like the continually renewed communist threat, the movement was repeatedly "eradicated" and "reenlivened." New Order logic sought the masterminds, puppeteers, and brains who must be behind these constantly renewed threats. Their search created charismatic discourses that posed greater threats than the leaders whom they sought. These discourses had the power to renew conflict and threat even without identifiable leaders.

Between AM and DOM

Between AM's 1976 declaration and the period of the military operations zone (DOM) from 1989 to 1998, there was a critical disjuncture. After the majority of the named figures of the founding AM were arrested, security forces attributed the sporadic violence to gangs or groups associated with DI/TII or Hasan Tiro; for the most part, the terms "Aceh Merdeka" and "Gerakan Aceh Merdeka" were not used. Indeed, it appeared that there was a conscious effort to get rid of the idea of Aceh Merdeka and make the movement into an irrational, subversive dream of a solitary figure. Contemporaneous accounts by media and security forces, and even some retrospective accounts by security forces, emphasize that the problem had been resolved by the mid-1980s

(Tippe 2000). Yet, one GAM fighter I interviewed in 2000 told me it all started in 1985. The seeds of future violence were guns, money, and "cultivation" (*dibina*).

Many reports on the conflict in Aceh linked the security problems there with the cultivation of marijuana.[23] "Cultivation" also refers to the process by which criminals were arrested and released on the condition that they collaborate with the military by providing intelligence and serving as a constantly renewable threat. Both of these cultivations are widely acknowledged, but their exact details and scale are difficult to ascertain. No one I spoke with was able to estimate the value of marijuana to the conflict, but an illicit economy in marijuana enabled the rebels to mobilize substantial resources.[24] As the last rebel leaders were destroyed one by one, the national media reported on problems of marijuana smuggling. In 1981, the military launched Operation Authority to prevent the traffic.[25] In 1982, six members of ABRI were tried in a military court and jailed for buying and selling marijuana, evidenced by possession of 260.5 kilograms ("Kasus Ganja di Mahmil Aceh. Enam Oknum ABRI Dijatuhi Hukuman Penjara," *Kompas*, 23 March 1982). Six months later, five hectares of marijuana fields were burned under U.S. Drug Enforcement Agency supervision. Eight police officers and one civil bureaucrat received life sentences in 1985 for possession of 59 kilograms of dry leaf marijuana ("8 Anggota Polri Aceh Dituntut Maksimal Hukuman Seumur Hidup," *Kompas*, 3 April 1985). Despite stories that the rebels were financing their movement from an illicit trade in marijuana, arrests during the 1980s indicate state actors' exploitation of this resource.

Weapons linked different phases of the conflict in Aceh. Leftover guns seem to have been passed, literally as well as figuratively, from one cause or threat to another, as well as between the military and the supposed criminals, whom it identified by a dizzying variety of names and acronyms. In June 1980, weapons were stolen from a police post in Aceh. The police chief there reported positive signs that the thief was from Gerakan Pengacau Liar Hasan Tiro (Hasan Tiro's Wild Disruptors Movement, or GPLHT) ("Diringkus, Perampas Senjata Api di Pos Polisi Sabang," *Kompas*, 4 June 1980). The thief arrived in the middle of the night and was permitted to sleep in a room that had unlocked weapons with ammunition, which he tried to steal. The thief had been associated with GPLHT, but had been released upon signing a statement that he would not help GPLHT anymore. In such a high state of alert, it is striking that the military would have released someone they had caught stealing weapons and ammunition merely because he signed a pledge not to do so again!

Out-of-control weapons were one way to substantiate the threat to national security in Aceh. This gun theft was part of a resurgence of arrests of the GPLHT in the mid-1980s. Those arrested were *dibina*, cultivated.[26] There was no sense that they had been corrected or punished for their criminal or subversive ways (and it was not clear if the danger was subversive or criminal at this point); rather, the sense was that they had been captured, trained, and sent out. For example, in December 1986, thirteen GPLHT were arrested. All were released after they were "cultivated" because it was judged "that they still could live and return in a good environment" ("13 Anggota Gerombolan Hasan Tiro Ditangkap," *Kompas*, 11 December 1986). This pattern of arresting, cultivating, and releasing continued into the early DOM period.[27]

In 2000, I met a man who identified himself as a fighter who had been part of GAM "since the beginning." He looked barely thirty, so I asked how long he had been involved. He said, "For about fifteen years, since 1986." I asked him how he learned about GAM and why he joined at that time. I expected a story about Hasan Tiro and history, which I frequently heard from those who declared themselves GAM members or were prominent representatives of the movement. To my surprise, he said that in the mid- to late 1980s "outsiders" delivered "provocative (*hasut*) speeches at mosques in Acehnese." I asked who the outsiders were and how they learned to speak Acehnese. He said they were trained at Cilangkap (Special Forces Headquarters in Java). He hesitated slightly when I asked if they were Acehnese; some were, he said, but not all. He cut off my other questions about that period by saying, "We don't like to recall that now."

DOM and Operation Red Net

DOM, the special military operations zone officially carried out under the code name "Operation Red Net," refers to the period of intense human rights violations in Aceh that began in 1989 or 1990. The precise beginning of DOM cannot be ascertained because, despite Commander in Chief Wiranto's public apology for military excesses during DOM, the Indonesian officers in charge of security operations in Aceh refused to admit that the campaign even existed. When the generals thought to be the masterminds behind DOM were called to a parliamentary inquiry in November 1999, General Try Sutrisno asserted that "The government never declared Aceh as a DOM" (*Risalah Rapat Dengar Pendapat Umum Pansus Tentang Permasalahan di Daerah Istimewa Aceh* 1999). This denial was repeated throughout the news media. Numerous criticisms of the atrocities committed during the DOM period met with similar responses from other military leaders ("Korban Jaring Merah di Bukit Tengkorak," *Majalah Gatra*, 8 August 1998). Denying the existence of DOM left the violence unaccounted for and, when acknowledged, characterized it as "excesses" committed by individual agents (*oknum*), not by the military apparatus. At the parliamentary inquiry, I heard Sutrisno explain: "what there was, was ABRI doing its duty to maintain security according to the constitution and the parliamentary decree and other legal parameters" (*Risalah Rapat* 1999; see also "DPR tak Mampu Korek Para Jendral," *Kompas*, 30 November 1999). He contended that security had been threatened by Hasan Tiro's declaration of Aceh Merdeka on 4 December 1976, and underscored his belief that ABRI's "actions were in the frame of providing protection and security to all the people." In the 1999 investigation, Ibrahim Hasan, the civilian governor of Aceh, reiterated the position that in 1990 military action had been needed to defend the country from armed separatists.[28] The massive state violence popularly known as DOM was narrated by Indonesian military sources and political figures in strikingly similar terms, but only in retrospect was it constructed as a justifiable response to armed separatist rebels.

Media accounts at the beginning of the period, which quoted official spokesmen of the security forces and bureaucratic apparatus, document that Jakarta initially classified the violence as purely criminal. Contemporary descriptions parallel the military's threat categorization system and the strategies at the center, particularly through the discourse of the shifting relationship between the people and the armed forces. The obvious professionalism of these criminal acts meant that they had to be classified and given a plausible explanation. Criminality was consolidated into subversion under the new term, GPK, Gang or Movement of Security Disruptors, and specified as GPK-Aceh. This distinctly New Order term was widely used in 1989 to give regional problems a subversive and nationwide cast.[29] Subsequently, the "purely criminal" category disappeared from government discourse on violence in Aceh.

At the outset of what became DOM, national reports on a series of criminal incidents in North Aceh, the center of LNG development and exploitation, created a sense of danger and inserted these incidents into a discursive frame of "pure crime" ("GPK di Aceh Kriminal Murni," *Angkatan Bersenjata* 26 June 1990). In June 1990, the situation was reported to have "returned to normal" in Aceh ("Pangab: Keamanan Di Aceh Mantap dan Makin Terkendali," *Suara Pembaruan*, 7 December 1991). The security forces blamed GPK (Gerakan Pengacau Keamanan), which had been "claiming victims both civil and security apparatus since last May" ("GPK Aceh: Kucing, Ganja dan Teror," *Majalah Tempo*, 30 June 1990, 22). The establishment of checkpoints and other security measures implied a certain kind of instability and threat at the same time that it was rhetorically countered. Inserting the possibility of political danger through its denial,[30] *Majalah Tempo*, relying on information from military sources, wrote that the "terror, intimidation, and disruption which [had] been done by GPK since last May [turned] out not to be a political movement like many people guessed." General Try Sutrisno, who in 1999 stated that the 1990 operations were aimed at securing national integrity, denied at the time that the threat was political. In the military's own newspaper, he stated:

Destructive actions, which have been done by the GPK in Aceh, seem to be very low level, and there is very little disturbance to development security. Also, they do not have any background of social or political nature whatsoever; they are nothing but the evil of a gang of Security Disruptors (GPK). They are not this or that. Purely criminal. ("GPK di Aceh Kriminal Murni," *Angkatan Bersenjata*, 26 June 1990)

The suspicion that this was indeed a political movement was not easily documented, except for military denials (see also "Pangab Try Sutrisno: ABRI akan Tuntaskan GPK Aceh Secepatnya," *Kompas*, 5 July 1990).

The types of crimes committed during this period included drive-by shootings at local police offices, threats to Javanese transmigrants, attacks on military posts, and random attacks on civilians. National media compiled long lists of incidents. In one published account, a surviving civilian recounted that unidentified visitors arrived and identified themselves as members of the regional military command (*kodim*). When the resident asked for identification, one reportedly drew a Colt pistol and said, "If you don't believe, look at this" ("GPK Aceh: Kucing, Ganja dan Teror," *Majalah Tempo*, 30 June 1990, 25). Then he fired, injuring his questioner.

The New Order state sought to maintain a monopoly on the means of violence. A weapon should have been proof of the legitimate authority of the possessor. Through the expertise with which these crimes were committed, violence took on an imagined and actual power that did not always adhere to the state, but was not divorced from it either. A former DI/TII figure, Haji Hasan Aly, doubted GPK's political agenda: "If they are a political movement, why do they kill low-level soldiers and children?" (quoted in "GPK Aceh: Kucing, Ganja dan Teror," *Majalah Tempo*, 30 June 1990, 26). The national military emphasized the incidents of violence toward its members and, at the same time, deflected suspicions that violence in Aceh was political. Official ABRI spokesman, Brigadier General Nurhadi, stated: "In Jakarta there are police or other members of ABRI who are killed by criminals. . . . whoever gets in the way of what they are doing using unsavory means to get what they want, they finish off" (quoted in "GPK Aceh: Kucing, Ganja dan

Teror," *Majalah Tempo*, 30 June 1990, 23). Local commanders, however, regarded the violence as intended to discredit the military by showing its vulnerability to attack.

Initial reports described instances of violence serious enough to be threatening, but not so overwhelming as to cast doubt on the military's ability to guard the nation. In June 1990, official sources amplified the threat the group posed, but suggested that it aimed mostly to frighten people. According to official sources, the indication that GPK sought to spread terror was that most of its victims did not understand why they had been targeted ("GPK Aceh: Kucing, Ganja dan Teror," *Majalah Tempo*, 30 June 1990). Nurhadi stressed that GPK intimidated ordinary people so that they would not give the security forces information regarding GPK's whereabouts. According to national media reports based on military sources, in Lhokseumawe the campaign of terror included spreading rumors of killings, which, upon investigation, were found not to have happened. The military's statements that the killings had not occurred did not eliminate anxieties. Deaths could be left unaccounted for and attributed to terror and rumor; in addition, such statements might discourage the reporting of deaths to authorities.

According to *Majalah Tempo*, interviews with residents in Banda Aceh suggested that "most people in the city believed that GPK was indeed not a political movement, and was nothing more than a criminal group" ("GPK Aceh: Kucing, Ganja dan Teror," *Majalah Tempo*, 30 June 1990, 23). Local government officials, such as Bupati Ramli Ridwan, stated that the government and economy were functioning fine, but people were afraid to go out at night. A. Hasjmy, head of the Majelis Ulama Indonesia (MUI), the Indonesian Council of Ulamas, linked the issue with AM explicitly, but, like Nurhadi, he did so to deny its significance. After touring several villages in troubled spots, he emphasized, "All the people of Aceh want to live peacefully. They are already bored and don't want to have problems anymore." The GPK are "people who are resentful. There are also robbers in Jakarta and Medan, who hitchhike on the name of Aceh Merdeka" (quoted in *Kompas*, 6 September 1990).

The identity of the perpetrators was as indeterminate as the type of violence, political or criminal, they committed. GPK appeared to be capable of obtaining and utilizing weapons. The violence that seemed to be out of the military's control, but relied on the means it monopolized, was explained by the figure of the deserter who transferred both knowledge and equipment to produce violence, which in turn created narratives that obscured this transfer of violence from legitimate to separatist. The denial of rumors that GPK had trained in Libya introduced further confusion. In June 1990, Nurhadi accused GPK of spreading these rumors like "cats trying to use the mask of a tiger to enlarge themselves" ("GPK Aceh: Kucing, Ganja dan Teror," *Majalah Tempo*, 30 June 1990, 25). Rumors are empowered through reiteration and denial. Post-DOM statements by the military also enlarged the enemy, emphasizing that warriors were trained in Libya.[31]

Despite repeated references to these crimes as the work of a group or a movement, Nurhadi suggested that it was not clear who their leader was, and they were not tightly organized. He concluded: "These actions of terror do not have any political background and one of their perpetrators is named Robert" ("Kerusuhan di Aceh Kriminal Murni," *Angkatan Bersenjata*, 23 June 1990). "Robert" had been thrown out of the military a few years before because he had "deserted." He was stationed in a unit in Lhokseumawe, where he was infamous as a "drunkard, fighter and womanizer" ("GPK Aceh: Kucing, Ganja dan Teror," *Majalah Tempo*, 30 June 1990, 23). Nurhadi emphasized the GPK's pure criminality by underscoring that many of its members, like "Robert," were not Acehnese.[32] Their proficient use of firearms was not "strange . . . because among them there were ex-ABRI" ("GPK Aceh: Kucing, Ganja dan Teror," *Majalah Tempo*, 30 June 1990, 23). In 1990, General Try Sutrisno suspected that there were two groups who were directing the terror and killings. Despite the unified signifier that consolidates apparently nonsensical, inexplicable criminality into threat, the GPK were multiple movements united by one term.

A 1990 Asia Watch/Human Rights Watch report linked "Robert" to the marijuana syndicate. Since his discharge from the military in 1982,

Robert had attracted around him a group of about 120 people, according to the army, most of them deserters from the army and police who provided weapons for the group and formed part of the *ganja* (marijuana) syndicate. Acehnese interviewed by Asia Watch in November were divided as to whether "Robert" was a fiction of the security forces, a "new cadre" of Aceh Merdeka, or a disreputable element planted by military intelligence to discredit the genuine movement, but at least one source reported that Robert had been present at a meeting at a religious school in Peureulak, East Aceh, in September 1990, and narrowly escaped arrest. (HRW/AW 1990, 2)

Robert's presence at the meeting suggests that he may have been planted by the military to set up the meeting at which others would be arrested for identifying themselves as part of the "new cadre" of AM. The report notes in a footnote that Acehnese sympathetic to independence were concerned that the Indonesian government had created a "false" Aceh Merdeka to discredit the group that included criminal elements (HRW/AW 1990, 2).

A 1998 retrospective account elevated "Robert" to corporal and GAM's "Five Star War Commander." His relationship to violence, separatism, and criminality was recounted:

As the 1987 elections approached, the activities of GAM (the Free Aceh Movement) were absent from the map of security in this nation. Just two years later, or exactly 1989, a deserter ranking Corporal, suddenly appeared, who knows from what world. Using the non-Muslim code name, Robert, he stole weapons of unfortunate ABRI members. He shot people here and there, but on a small scale. But the conditions in Aceh at that time were likened to volcanic lava, which wants to explode, or in the military's terminology at a danger stage of a great war. Robert, who had called himself the Five Star War Commander of GAM . . . for the next two years went to Malaysia and became a street vendor in Kuala Lumpur. But Aceh as he left it had already become a DOM Red Thread [sic]. ("Laporan dari Aceh (1) Dari Belanda Hingga Mr. Robert," *Kompas*, 6 October 2000)[33]

This retrospective account notes that Robert's appearance is sudden, but it foreshadows or provokes Operation Red Net, which explodes and causes great destruction that Robert himself escaped.

Inspection of materials and public statements from that time disclosed "pure criminality" under the control of the military. Casting aspersions on both men identified as GAM leaders in the early DOM period, the retrospective account echoed the doubts that many Acehnese conveyed to me privately: "regarding the matter of Hasan Tiro and Mr. Robert himself, now it is not all that clear what color they are. There are those who speculate that they truly want independence for Aceh. But those who doubt their integrity are also not few" ("Laporan dari Aceh (1) Dari Belanda Hingga Mr. Robert," *Kompas*, 6 October 2000). The implication that these figures are unknowable, or unclassifiable, suggest concerns about their collusion with the Indonesian military. At present "Robert," a liminal figure between the military and GAM and an instigator of the violence that initiated DOM, has disappeared from public discourse in and on Aceh. A few people told me that Robert was still in Jakarta and had links to many groups in Aceh. I was never able to meet him.

The explosion of criminality that preceded and, indeed, laid the conditions of possibility for DOM functioned as an intermediary phase in accounts of violence. The violence did not immediately become attached to narratives of separatism; rather, through criminality and desertion, the power of violence was transferred from the military to the enemy. Subsequently, this nonpolitical violence could be resignified and inserted into military schemes of threat perception, consolidating an enemy force significant enough to blame for random violence and to further chronologies of Acehnese resistance.

Ordinary Acehnese people's deep suspicions about the security forces' role in the production of GAM were expressed in a simple story. I asked a child orphaned by DOM how it started. He said first there were traditional medicine sellers (*tukang jamu*) from Java who would ride through all the neighborhoods on bicycles. Some brought other goods from outside to sell. These people paid attention to everything and "put many people in their debt." He reasoned that they wanted to understand the grudges, tensions, and rivalries in each community so they could be exploited when the army opened its posts in each village. Those initially regarded as *tukang jamu* later were unmasked as ABRI.[34] This incident, which foreshadowed the implementation of a military operations zone in Aceh, demonstrates that DOM was not created in response to a sudden increase in perceived danger. The military, according to the stories of many DOM victims, understood and played upon existing conflicts. At the time, ABRI's own ideological platform viewed all citizens as informers.

Acehnese suspicions about the Indonesian military's responsibility for the violence it attributed to criminal elements, political forces, and "horizontal" conflicts among the people found grim confirmation after the end of DOM. In December 1990, the appearance of unidentified corpses in public areas and reports of international human rights advocates that 200 corpses had been found buried in one place drew attention to Aceh.[35] Regional military officials were no longer able to characterize the danger as separatist or criminal (Pramono, quoted in "Rakyat Jangan Jadi Korban: Wawancara dengan Pangdam I/Bukit Barisan Mayjen Pramono 'Sekarang GPK Sudah Terjepit'," *Majalah Tempo*, 17 November 1990). Popular suspicions abounded that this was another instance of "mysterious killings" (*petrus*) practiced in Java as a form of what Soeharto described as "shock therapy."[36] Military officials denied both the existence of mass graves and explanations holding the military responsible. They acknowledged that as many as twenty bodies had been found and suggested that these corpses were victims of GPK. Typically, the military would capture GPK members, "cultivate" or train them to assist the military, and release them; they could then be killed by GPK as traitors ("Dilepas Dengan Surat Annisa," *Editor*, 6 October 1990). In 1990, when the military estimated GPK's strength at 200, they recruited and trained as many as 1,500 local men as People's Forces and 300 more as Defenders of the Nation. Because of the difficulty of distinguishing "security disruptors" (GPK) from local people who might be sheltering them, Regional Military Commander Pramono commanded "people" to shoot on sight anyone suspected of being GPK. Given the difficulty of distinguishing GPK from the local population, it is possible the military was arming the GPK it sought to eradicate (see Robinson 1998).

Typically, rapid economic development was used to explain tensions in Aceh during this time. In a 1990 report, Pranomo commented on the disparity between local residents and the skilled workers who arrived with the development of the gas fields in North Aceh (the Lhokseumawe Industrial Zone development, or ZILS).[37] He denied that this was a valid reason for social conflict, stating that the Acehnese must not be dependent upon the government for everything and must see that they were not qualified for these jobs. Pramono pointed to other areas such as Irian Jaya and Kalimantan where conditions were more difficult, noting that there were no disturbances there.[38] In a surprising turn of rhetoric, he concluded with this statement: "The political awareness of Acehnese has to be increased. Especially their consciousness to defend the country and nation" ("Rakyat Jangan Jadi Korban: Wawancara dengan Pangdam I/Bukit Barisan Mayjen Pramono 'Sekarang GPK Sudah Terjepit'," *Majalah Tempo*, 17 November 1990).

The conversion of pure criminality to subversion was completed by trials in 1992 that coincided with the height of DOM's brutality. The relationship between GAM and GPK was clearly slippery. The media and security forces created a criminal, non-ideological problem that was distinct from the "people" (*rakyat*) and enrolled them in fighting the problem. Violence was understood as a problem of criminality and deserters striving to ruin ABRI's reputation and rapport with the people. If it were merely a problem of deserters, however, it would be more logical for ABRI to resolve the matter on its own rather than train and militarize five times as many villagers to eradicate a leaderless, nonpolitical threat. That the armed forces were served by the existence of an amorphous threat is a more likely explanation for its efforts to mobilize the people.

The 1992 trials of the initial members of Aceh Merdeka effectively made GAM and GPK synonymous. Indonesian NGOs and international human rights organizations linked GAM and GPK as well. An Acehnese daily newspaper headline read: "Trial of GPK Aceh: Has joined GPK because of a personal connection." The account indicated that the offense for which a member named Has was being tried did not correspond to the definitions of pure crime developed in 1990 for the term "GPK-Aceh." Has's crime was to shelter his brother and two other GAM members and escort them to exile in Malaysia ("Sidang GPK Aceh: Has Menampung Anggota GPK Karena Hubungan Pribadi," *Serambi Indonesia*, 15 January 1992). The article emphasized that the goal of GAM was to separate from Indonesia and replace the *Pancasila* ideology. My interviews with Has in 1999 and 2000 demonstrated that he was not a militant separatist.

The trials continued throughout 1992–1993, all following the same pattern of accusing the individual of being GPK, which had been created as a term of criminality, and then pointing to his involvement with GAM. An Indonesian Legal Aid Foundation report on these trials noted that according to the public prosecutor's indictment (*Dakwaan Jaksa Penuntut Umum*) the cases against GAM were divided into three categories: "the intellectual group, the operational group, and the sympathizers, which also included those who contributed money. In the intellectual and sympathizer groups most people had a high level of education, generally university. In the operational group, on average the education level was low (elementary school)" (1991, 1). The report proves that most alleged members of the "intellectual group" tried in Banda Aceh were forced to sign false testimony under the threat of indefinite detention by the Special Forces. A journalist explained to the judges that he had "confessed" to being a member of AM after torture; he denied that he ever joined AM, or accepted the task of collecting information for them. He did not even recognize the flag and symbols of AM (6). Another defendant was arrested based on the confession of another individual that they had attended an AM meeting at a coffee shop together. He denied that he had donated money or had been asked to support AM's struggle.[39] Of the nine Banda Aceh cases described in the report, all the witnesses had testified that five of the defendants were not involved in AM. Two other defendants who were lawyers stated that the trials had violated the presumption of innocence. Two others were unaware of the movement until their arrest and interrogation. All nine were highly educated.

In contrast, the eleven cases heard in Lhokseumawe and Langsa described in the report involved gun theft. The accused typically had only an elementary education and their occupation or employment was "unclear." Three denied any relationship to GAM; others regretted being involved. One retired police officer turned himself in for giving weapons to GAM. One man who sold rice in Medan said he had heard people discuss GAM, but he had never attended a meeting. The 40-page indictment accused him of being a primary actor for GAM. He was alleged to have three guns and 2,000 bullets for an M-16, but he said it was left behind by a GAM member from Libya. One individual was a well-educated former member of the regional parliament for the Islamic Party (PPP) who was recalled when he was accused of conducting GAM business while traveling overseas. He denied the charge, stating that he had traveled on business and met an Acehnese youth, but did not know that the youth was a GAM activist. Robert was never caught, so he was tried in absentia in 1992. He was declared to be involved in subversive activities and terminated from the military on 30 April 1990 at a low rank ("Robert, Gembong GPK Aceh, Dituntut Hukuman Mati," *Kompas*, 17 March 1993).

The declaration of GAM in 1976 did not produce a separatist threat. The incidents of violence in 1989, which may have been criminal acts of military deserters, were joined to the separatist ideology of Aceh Merdeka symbolized by Hasan Tiro. Only in retrospect has GAM been consolidated and projected continuously back to its 1976 origins and stretched further back to the DI/TII uprising.

Cultivating Informers

The relationship between GAM and ABRI during DOM was mediated by *cu'ak*, local operations support (TPO) informers. At the start of DOM, according to Tim Kell's account, some villagers felt that it would be better to sacrifice a few fellow villagers in the hopes that conditions would return to normal. Ironically, conditions of violence and betrayal became normal instead (Kell 1995). The *cu'ak* stories I heard followed two patterns: those who betrayed or informed on another person because they could not endure torture or to settle personal grudges; and those who became full-time *cu'ak* and lived with the military so they would be protected from the wrath of those they had betrayed. The second type was "cultivated" (*dibina*). Both patterns could be exploited for financial gain. Although this type of intelligence operation causes widespread polarization in society, it is extremely difficult to generalize relationships between *cu'ak* and those betrayed after the end of DOM. While there were frequent reports of *cu'ak* killings by mysterious figures immediately following Wiranto's apology, many people I spoke to suggested that the military had killed these individuals to prevent them from testifying about the intelligence operations. On the other hand, some of the most infamous *cu'ak* were not harmed and continued to perpetrate violence.

Although I read and heard detailed accounts of how the intelligence operations worked during DOM, I do not present specific cases here. The personal nature of the information required to trace cycles of betrayal over time renders it impossible to protect the identities of those involved. Not only was cross-checking such slippery sources difficult, but engaging in that endeavor would have amounted to engaging in the conflict myself. Local knowledge of betrayals saturated families and villages and was sometime shared with me, but airing it publicly, when questions of collusion and complicity still rend kin-groups and communities, would be destructive and irresponsible, potentially making the inquiry itself an extension of the military operations' social polarization. Nevertheless, the specifics of how the security forces implemented their operations are critical to understanding how the conflict dynamic worked and how its legacies challenge the fragile peace reached after the tsunami. My analysis draws, not on unspoken common knowledge, but on official military documents that were originally secret.

The Red Net Operations were composed of multiple units dedicated to intelligence, combat, and strategy. In 2006, an NGO passed on to me a bundle of photocopies of the special reports on the operations conducted by one of the Special Forces Intelligence teams that operated from November 1994 to November 1995, which it had obtained in conjunction with an official investigation. I was particularly interested in analyzing how *cu'ak* were used and how these polarizing tactics were conceived, implemented, and reported by the intelligence units. The nearly 500 pages of reports demonstrated that, although many of the decisions made and implemented were based on insufficient evidence, imagined enemies, and perceived threats, they ultimately reproduced the enemy that had been eradicated and yet continued to be imagined as a threat to the state. The discourse of "horizontal" violence used in the post-New Order period by a range of actors to characterize violence between individuals and communities appeared at that time to be a sudden threat of disintegration in the wake of strong state control. Close examination of operations in Aceh discloses how violence was "horizontalized" and how the ground was laid for conflicts between individuals, families, or others who occupied different positions in relation to the security operations. In other cases, the appearance of horizontal violence was a guise for continuing patterns of state-sponsored violence.

The letter of assignment for the team provided background and described the tasks and strategies for the operation. The definition of the enemy sets the stage for a particular kind of operation. The enemy is weak, but might potentially be a threat: "GPK-AM (Gerakan Pengacau Kemanan Aceh Merdeka) is a separatist movement that wants to separate itself from the unitary state of Indonesia [NKRI] . . . At the outset this movement was annihilated, and a few leaders fled overseas." However, with their "underground movement, they were able to recruit a few sons of the area [i.e., Acehnese] who were influenced by their ideas and went to train in a foreign country. At this point their strength is very limited, nevertheless, they still have the potential to become a threat to the union and unity (*persatuan dan kesatuan*) of the State, especially in the region of Aceh" (*Laporan Penugasan Pase 4 di Daerah Operasi Aceh Periode Nov. 1994 s/d Nov. 1995*, 2). The threat extends beyond Aceh, as statements about fighters coming in and out of the province suggest. The threat of the movement is more potential than actual, but the movement had reappeared after its annihilation in the past.

In describing the social and cultural conditions in the region, the report notes that the Acehnese are fanatic about Islam and their ethnic group (*suku*), but remarks that "the charisma of the religious leaders is decreasing because there is competition from the formal leaders and the results of development are beginning to be felt by the society" (*Laporan Penugasan*, 4). The lack of attention to the actual economic disparities experienced by most people implies that it is only of importance to attach the "formal leaders" or technocrats to Indonesia.

The shifting categorization of the security forces' characterization of their enemy is indicative of the process of splicing violence and ideology of the past into flexible current threats or potential threats. The report describes three types of GPK: "armed guerillas in the jungle; clandestine popular (*rakyat*) supporters, sympathizers"; and ideological leaders. The first group, "the outside/foreign branch . . . has received military training in Libya. This is the group with potential in military technologies, but they are not militant and not experienced." The domestic or inside branch includes "members of society who are provoked, resentful and have social jealousies, etc." In a move that makes dissatisfaction equivalent to sympathizing with GPK and furnishing logistical support the equivalent of taking up arms, the report continues: "This group will join the movement in the jungle and villages as clandestine or become a sympathizer." The third group comprises the "ideology leaders who play a role as motivator in general, they are former DI/TII and Aceh Merdeka who are still active" (*Laporan Penugasan*, 5). The military finds historical reasons to treat Aceh with suspicion; through links to past Islamic and separatist violence, the threat is more easily generalized to any or all Acehnese. Distinguishing the members of AM who are still active suggests that in 1995 military strategies made a distinction between GPK and AM. There was no inevitable progression from AM to the current GAM; GPK and GAM were not simply two names for the same group, and the GPK was a distinct element that was later fused with the AM to become the current GAM. One way this occurred was through the collaboration of ideological figures and the linkage of particular grievance narratives or ideological differences. The inclusion of DI/TII as a threat some thirty years after the movement had reconciled with the government is an important element of how the potential of violent threat to the state is spread throughout society, which the military operations themselves concretize.

After general statements of the problem, the report moves to specifics. The GPK AM has only four primary personnel "who lead different groups of GPK in the jungle. The supporters who have joined them in the jungle are estimated as 31 people" with approximately 27 weapons (*Laporan Penugasan*, 5). The report acknowledges the difficulty of collecting data on the "clandestine" group, but suggests that they connect with the movement overseas. While this formation might accurately describe the threats faced by the military in East Timor, there is very little evidence to suggest that there was an active clandestine movement in Aceh or that there was an overseas presence other than Hasan Tiro and a few deputies. As described by this report, however, the GPK-AM's abilities include high mobility between villages, rapid movement in the jungle, blending in with the people, and an ability to escape to the regions outside of the operation. Their weaknesses were limited weapons and ammunition, decreasing support from the people, dependency on the people for logistics, and the declining popularity of their ideology (*Laporan Penugasan*, 6). It is unclear what ideology is not popular; it seems in this analysis that Islam and DI/TII ideology have declined in popularity. In the face of widespread social jealousies and the evidence of uneven development, however, the economic justice approach expounded by AM should have been very popular. The fundamental contradiction of viewing all the people as potential threats at the same time that they are all potential allies or informants of the military permeates the reports and marks the implementation and expansion of the operations.[40]

Given the that the "main task of the operation is to find and destroy the leaders and members of GPK, demolish the clandestine GPK network in the city and villages, and to demolish the marijuana syndicate as a source of wealth for GPK," it seems peculiar that the first stage of operations "targets the clandestine supporters in the villages with the following activities" (*Laporan Penugasan*, 7):

1. Intelligence operations with continual investigation, infiltration of agents into the body of the enemy and cultivation of the people to create conditions
2. Battle operation attack and ransacking of houses
3. Collection of data on the clandestine
4. Forming and cultivating Agent[s]/Panah

In facing an enemy with fewer than thirty active fighters in the jungle, this team focused its immediate efforts on the "clandestine" or hidden supporters in society. As is only too obvious in retrospect, this repression produced a widespread and compelling grievance narrative that these reports disclose was missing before their campaign began. Only in the second stage will the actual enemy, the GPK groups in the forest, be targeted with the following activities:

(1) Intelligence operations continue the activities of stage one continuously
(2) Battle operations, conducted by working on targets in the form of attacks, reconnaissance patrols and ambush
(3) Gathering data on the clandestine, to develop larger operations, even though by the end of the assignment not all of the primary tasks can be accomplished.

Collecting data on the clandestine was carried out through a process of informing and betraying, often by means of torture. In light of later events, this passage suggests that the military was aware that the expansion of its enemy was a critical prerequisite for the expansion of its operations.

A primary figure of the operations is the "agent/*panah*." The Acehnese I interviewed use the term *cu'ak* more frequently than *panah* to describe informers. *Panah* literally means the arrow of an archer; the agent (*agen*) is the "child of the bow," also the arrow. One person explained that the *panah* is the agent of someone, whereas the cu'ak is more general. Most media reports use the term *cu'ak*. The military report notes that the use of agents was becoming less effective: "many of the agents very often have been used openly so that it is difficult for them to obtain information in a covert manner. In addition, many agents are now not paying close enough attention to the development because of economic needs. The GPK has also threatened the people and families of the agent" (*Laporan Penugasan*, 16). Four steps are outlined to overcome this problem:

1. New Agent[s]/*Panah* have to be shaped even though that will require a significant amount of time to achieve the maximal results.
2. Agent[s]/*Panah* must be continuously cultivated, both new and old to give them motivation and attention and especially economic support.
3. An intensive technique of support [literally, framework or girding] to the society so that they are bold enough to forward necessary information.
4. The conclusion of every battle must be absolute so that there are not any GPK who escape (who will later become a threat for the *panah*/people).

The slash marking the thin line between the people and informers indicates how the threat was generalized throughout society. The military suggested that corpses were the result of GPK's revenge on informants (16). The fourth point suggests that this problem will be corrected by more killings, and those dead will by definition be GPK. The pattern of recruiting agents to infiltrate the GPK enlarges the enemy. In conclusion, the report reiterates the importance of informers: "success of the operation in Aceh, especially the operation to oppose the guerilla is very much determined by the handle on the agent[s]/*Panah*, both the overt and the covert ones" (20).

The subsequent reports on specific operations are permeated by the paradoxical logic of military successes that produce greater threats that in turn justify the need for further operations. A special report on 22 April 1995, describing the team's success in obtaining one long-barrel weapon demonstrates how the logic of endless threat, the links to the DI/TII movement, and use of agents intersected in particular cases. The report begins by noting that "the conflict in Aceh has developed such that GPK is inclined to cover their tracks, often leaving their weapons in storage with others for later use, or burying them for later retrieval" (Laporan Khusus, No. R/08/LAPSUS/IV/1995, 1). In this instance, the team received information that there were modified weapons in a particular housing complex. The information came after an ambush of farmers in February; the captives stated during interrogation that people were coming from outside of Aceh (Medan) to join the conflict. Two months later, an agent was released to the area where the weapons were said to be. The report does not specify whether the information came from another agent, or the farmers who were victims of the original ambush were "shaped" as agents. Even though they had been modified for use in hunting, the weapons provide a potential threat and a link to a real threat in the past:

The modified weapons like the ones we got were often used by DI/TII in that era. With the eradication of the DI/TII movement, remaining weapons were [modified] in a condition that could be used for hunting, nevertheless, this does not foreclose the possibility that the aforementioned weapons could be misused for another kind of criminal activity. Since the explosion of GPK AM in the 1990s modified weapons of any form and collector's weapons (*parbakin*) must be collected at the Operations Implementation Command (Kolakapos), and with such an order, people who do not think to the direction of GPK can consciously collect all of the aforementioned guns, nevertheless people who are still on the side of the GPK will continue to make efforts to store their weapons and indeed are assigned to help the GPK at the time that they can be used. (Laporan Khusus, No. R/08/LAPSUS/IV/1995, 2)

Two months later, another report repeated that the weapons had to be collected, noting: "It is the fact that there are still rogue elements who do not want to turn over for collection such weapons and there is a great possibility that they are supporters of the GPK AM" (Laporan Khusus, No. R/12/LAPSUS/VI/1995, 3). The introduction of rogue elements introduced the possibility that these could be elements of the military itself. Every success increased rather than decreased the potential threat: "The discovery of these modified weapons does not close off the possibility that there are others which are stored by the families of the GPK, sympathizers or GPK AM who went overseas" (Laporan Khusus, No. R/08/LAPSUS/ IV/1995, 3).[41] This pattern of indeterminacy and collaboration with the security forces was likely the source of these weapons.

In 1992, the military held a series of courts martial to discipline soldiers accused of providing weapons to the GPK. Human Rights Watch described one case:

The prosecutor said that Private Samidon, born in Kutacane on July 5, 1952, was assigned in February 1990 to PT Gruti Krueng Tuan (a private company) to help eliminate the remnants of the GPK. He went on rounds with four colleagues, each equipped with a rifle and ammunition. On or about February 27, the accused, who had previously been sentenced to four months in 1988 for theft, was approached by another soldier, a member of the GPK whom he had known from their time together in prison. The soldier told him if he could get two rifles, he would become head of Aceh Merdeka operations with a salary five times larger than his present one. He persuaded his colleague, Private Danau Bangun, to go with him to get a payoff (*uang rokok*) from an illegal logger. Without permission from their squad leader, the two left their post in camouflage gear, carrying their guns. They went into the forest where Samidon had allegedly arranged a meeting with the GPK, unbeknownst to Private Danau. The soldier with whom Samidon had been in contact was waiting for them and faked an ambush; Samidon, according to press accounts, gave up his gun without protest, but Danau, not knowing the plan, resisted until he was knocked unconscious. The accused left him there and ran back to his post to report to his commander about the "ambush." Danau later died. (HRW 1992, 7)[42]

Similar scenarios are likely for many exchanges of weapons.

The possibility that weapons left over from DI/TII could be hidden and used for criminal purposes vastly expanded the threat faced by the military from a few dozen armed men with very little logistical support and in constant flight to a formidable force, and the supposition of such a threat justified the military's pursuit of weapons whose possession would identify a person as GPK. The military campaign looked for shadowy enemies who had changed their names and locations—anyone anywhere could be GPK.

According to the perverse logic of these documents, the military's success in enrolling "society" in its campaign to find and eradicate its shadowy enemies meant that the rebels were cornered and unable to obtain necessary logistical support from local people, so they were acquiring new identity cards with new names and places of origin, moving to more isolated areas, and blending in with the people. The report notes that members of the task force and two other soldiers had identified one ex-GPK AM and one ex-Libya (Laporan Khusus, No. R/10/LAPSUS/V/1995, 2). The label "GPK AM" was applied to a twenty-six-year-old farmer, who would have been only seven at the time of the AM declaration and about twelve when the last named AM leader in the country was assassinated. What the "ex" meant in this context is not clear. Was he a former GPK turned agent? This analysis would justify the arrest of anyone on suspicion of GPK affiliation.

At the moment that GPK was almost eliminated, military analysis and government policy reactivated and extended the scope of the threat and authorized an invasive mission to find unseen threats in areas previously not part of the conflict zone. The report completes this generalization of the threat throughout society by not only militarizing citizens through civil defense patrols but also conducting more intensive surveillance. The report concludes: "With the number of Ex GPK AM who escape out of the region of operations or indeed out of the country (to Malaysia) it is necessary to collect data that is much more detailed for each citizen (*warga*) in each territorial apparatus and to reactivate the local government for each district to collect data on their citizens to prevent the entry of Ex GPK AM to join with society" (Laporan Khusus, No. R/10/LAPSUS/V/1995, 3). As with the capture of weapons, the arrest of participants increases the threat rather than moving toward resolution of the problem.

In the span of a year covered by the documents, only two incidents concerned named ideological leaders. One report about the ambush of the Pawang Rasyid Group in Pidie observed that Pidie had the most militant and strongest GPK because the supreme leader of GPK AM, Hasan Tiro, is from there. Moreover, the district commander is deeply respected by the people. Pawang Rasyid had been affiliated with "GPK-AM since the first time there is rebellion in Aceh under the banner (*kobar*) of DI/TII in 1952, AM 1976 and AM 1990 and he appears to be a charismatic figure who is held in awe and respected by the society of Pidie so that the situation and conditions of Pidie are such that the people are very closed about giving information or any other kinds of explanations about the whereabouts of Pawang Rasyid." The report recommends that "tactics and techniques be implemented that would furnish the framework" for people to inform on this group (Laporan Khusus, No. R/13/LAPSUS/VI/1995, 1). The ambiguity regarding the situation of the region is striking. A later report on Pidie observed that "for this period there has not been any kind of rebellion that has been raised by the GPK AM, such conditions have two possibilities, this region is truly clean of GPK AM or in fact they are very strong and implementing closed mouth actions" (Laporan Khusus, No. R/18/LAPSUS/X/1995, 1). The absence of overt activity could be interpreted as a sign of the strength of resistance.

A report from September (Laporan Khusus, No. R/17/LAPSUS/IX/1995, 2) demonstrates the standards of evidence for determining who is who:

The report from the society that there were three unknown people with two guns who went by the edge of their village has a significant possibility that the people are GPK, because if the three people are not GPK there is a very small possibility that they would pass the edge of the village; in addition, if ABRI was doing a movement, usually they wear camouflage clothing and the people recognize them.

Based on the time of day they walked past, the report postulates that they were probably GPK members returning to their family's homes to pick up logistical support.

A year later, despite continuing lack of GPK actions, a report states that the GPK AM "still exists" because documents were discovered with the clandestine group demonstrating that they are members of GPK AM and remain committed to the movement: "Because the people in possession of the documents did not destroy them it indicates that they still hope to use the documents when the situation permits." The posts are continuing to do well in "cultivating" agents, including an "Ex GPK AM" who is loyal and willing to help (Laporan Khusus, No. R/ /LAP-SUS X/1996, Tertangkapnya Pendukung GPK-AM di Wilayah Sattis-B/Biruen pada bulan Agustus s/d Oktober 1996, 1–2). The existence of GPK documents is consistently invoked as evidence of ideological action.

I first met a *cu'ak* carrying a letter identifying him as a TPO (operations assistant for the special forces) in 1998 when I was trying to find GAM members to talk to. I was in Lhokseumawe in 1998, immediately following Wiranto's apology and the end of DOM. I asked friends at an NGO if it would be possible to talk to some GAM members. The person who accompanied me knew of only one village where some GAM members might be. We spoke to people there about their experiences during DOM; the village had lost many residents. One man identified himself as a GAM member and stated that he had come "from the mountains." He slowly removed a discolored letter that appeared to have been in his wallet for quite some time. The tattered official letter of explanation stated that he was helping the Special Forces (Kopassus) operations. He swore to me and all the other villagers, over and over, that he had done this so he could provide the rebels in the mountains with information on what the military was doing. He said no one ever suffered because of him. Curiously, he said that initially he had been arbitrarily arrested; only after that was he inspired to join the rebels. He was very anxious while talking. I sensed he wanted to say more, but he did not show up at the "four eyes" meeting—with only the two of us present—we had scheduled for the next day.

At that time, the *cu'ak* killings had just started. Placed in relation to published military interpretations and secret intelligence reports, this story very closely echoed the pattern of cultivation (*dibina*). It is likely that he was trained to eradicate GPK, perhaps even initially to "infiltrate," but in the end, he expressed sympathy toward "our brothers in the mountains." I heard scattered stories of other acquaintances who had cards or letters from the Special Forces through various connections; it is hard to know with any degree of certainty who had done what to obtain these letters.

Descriptions of violence were circulated by GAM. *Voice of Free Aceh*, published in 1995 (given to me in 1999), features a long description of torture inflicted upon one of its members. "I was treated like a domesticated calf which is stamped on the back with a number as an identity," recounted Djafaruddin, who was arrested by two Kopassus (Special Forces) members ("Tahanan: Terelak dari Bala," *Suara Acheh Merdeka*, 6 December 1995). A friend who was arrested could "no longer stand the torture" and betrayed him, and then was released "as bait." When Djafaruddin was with him, their vehicle was stopped; accused of driving a stolen car, they were brought to a guard post. Djafaruddin was beaten but refused to admit any knowledge of the troops' positions. The Kopassus members then stripped him naked and used hot iron stamps to brand him with their unit numbers: 9, 10, and 11. He lost consciousness several times and was finally taken to the military command (*Kodim*) in Lhokseumawe.

Djafaruddin informed readers that "they (Kopassus) thought that I would cooperate with them" and offered him "a million Rupiah, motorcycle, schooling in Jakarta, and a beautiful woman." Feigning willingness, Djafaruddin agreed to guide the Special Forces members to the Islamic boarding school of Teungku Bantaqiah. He told the Kopassus officer to wait while he scouted ahead. Djafaruddin gloated, "The stupid Kopassus officer believed my words." Not only was he allowed to leave alone, but the Kopassus also gave him a bulletproof vest. Identifying Bantaqiah's group with GAM,[43] Djafaruddin warned the people at the school that seventy-five Kopassus surrounded them, enabling them to escape. The article concluded, "Because they did not succeed in their task, Kopassus arrested my parents and held them ransom so that I would not take vengeance." A photo of Djafaruddin's chest with black marker circles highlighting his scars was captioned: "Torture still scars the body of Djafaruddin. Java may think that torturing the nation of Acheh can paralyze the strength of GAM." The GAM narrative of DOM torture transforms victimization into heroic outsmarting of the Special Forces.

This account portrays the typical features of military action. Betrayal through the branch system introduced Djafaruddin to Kopassus. He received equipment and knowledge—a bulletproof vest and information about the Kopassus plans. He passed the information to others considered GAM by both military and GAM accounts. His family suffered. The transfer of resources and the cooperative associations between victims and torturers were too widespread to ignore. GAM had to appropriate these events in the narrative of its ongoing struggle. In 1999, I asked Abdullah Syafi'ie, leader of the armed wing of GAM (AGAM), what would happen to the *cu'ak* if Aceh were to become independent. There would be no problem, he argued: the "TNI was worse." There has been very little public discussion about the role of *cu'ak* and other liminal figures in the conflict. Many of these figures were killed in the initial post-DOM period, with widely varying explanations given for their deaths. In the multiplicity of implausible reasons given for their murders, they do not differ much from DOM victims.

Post-DOM Violence and Second-Generation GAM

In the aftermath of DOM, the Acehnese were portrayed as victims of state violence, but soon their entire society (*masyarakat*) was represented as merged with GAM. Initially AM was described as an intellectual critique of the government and its economic policies that did not take violent actions and did not enjoy much popular support. Its supposed successor, GAM, was more indeterminate. Subsequently, through the consolidation of the criminal GPK and GAM, state violence perpetrated by the military, its agents, or deserters was resignified as separatist, ideologically motivated violence against the state. Rebel violence justified acts of violence toward anyone on the grounds that they were Acehnese. Through the exposure of state violence against innocent victims, the special military operations were ended. But, through the figure of the *provokator*, violence was decentralized and made an autonomous force, neither wholly state nor entirely society. Finally, the label "GAM/Society" (GAM/*Masyarakat*) produced the intellectual construct of a widespread, unified, violent rebellion against the state and conditions of rampant criminality. The application of this label justified more indiscriminate repression of the Acehnese, extending the reach of violence once more.

In response to the political pressures aroused by victims' testimony in Jakarta, on 7 August 1998 General Wiranto apologized to the people of Aceh for the "excessive" treatment they had received from ABRI while Aceh was treated as a military operations zone (DOM). Wiranto promised that the extra troops from outside of Aceh (known as non-organic troops) would be removed within one month; *oknum*, individuals from ABRI who were guilty of criminal acts, would be tried according to existing civilian law; GAM prisoners would be released on Indonesian independence day, 17 August 1998; and GAM members who had fled to Malaysia could return to Aceh. Wiranto suggested that the term GPL (Gang of Wild Disruptors) replace GPK, removing the term "security" to neutralize or deny the threat they posed to the state ("Dicabut, Status 'DOM' Aceh*Panglima ABRI Jendral Wiranto Mohon Maaf," *Kompas*, 8 August 1998). The term GPK persisted in military comments. Strikingly, at the same time that Wiranto welcomed the enemy back home, he proposed a new term to stigmatize them. The National Human Rights Commission's recommendations that reconciliation programs be undertaken to increase people's sense of security were not implemented ("Pernyataan Komnas HAM: Penanggung Jawab Kebijakan DOM Harus Diadili," *Kompas*, 3 September 1998). In the absence of justice, the resumption of violence recreated widespread separatist sentiment.

The explosion of violence after Wiranto ended the military operations zone and withdrew Indonesian troops from Aceh inaugurated a new phase of the conflict. Many Acehnese thought the violence was engineered by the military; they spoke of *provokator*, unidentified parties, or the "force that does not want Aceh to be safe." They argued that the military needed to create instability to recapture its former prominence. Many suspected that the security forces were trying to distract attention from the massive human rights violations that they had committed under DOM, since at the time it seemed as if perpetrators might be tried. In military discussions, the new violence was described as a resurgence of the rebel forces, or an indication that the people were no longer rational.

Initially, the violence that dominated post-DOM discussions was the "excesses" of the military during DOM. But when violence actually increased a short time after troops were withdrawn, it was interpreted as evidence for the military's claims that the ongoing violence was the work of irrational, resentful, vengeful, spiteful Acehnese. Indeterminate violence was used to demonstrate that separatist rebels would flourish in the absence of military repression and to prove retroactively that military action during DOM had been a justifiable response to a strong rebel threat. What had been acknowledged as "excess" was rapidly redefined as "proportionality." Indeed, in this period rebels seemed to emerge suddenly and become visible, identifiable figures. Patterns of state insecurity linked to the threat of communist vengeance relied on latent threats. What distinguishes the threats in Aceh is that separatists did step up to claim the state's projected threat. Although reports of violence became exceedingly indeterminate, recent incidents dominated public discussions. Consideration of who was responsible for DOM violence and how justice would be served was pushed aside. Past violence figured mostly to support the notion that the Acehnese people were irrationally seeking revenge, which served as a rationale for continuing state violence.

In order to analyze the conflict that ensured the repetition of patterns of violence after DOM, I have compiled a comprehensive chronology of violence during the period from August 1998 to January 2001. Here I focus on a few major incidents that drew the most outrage and public discussion. I am particularly concerned with the idea that the violence was "engineered" and with the various parties who were said to have engineered it. Criminal violence became provocation, and widespread evidence that the military was provoking violence produced no resolution of the cases. GAM reemerged, but many Acehnese during this period were careful to distinguish a GAM that had the interests of the people in mind from the many strains of imitation GAM, or GAM imposters.

The burning of Rumoh Gedong, a "strategic post" known as a "torture camp" during DOM, was the first major incident of violence following Wiranto's formal apology. Many of the thousands of Acehnese who were "missing" as a result of DOM were abducted and taken to Rumoh Gedong, where they were tortured and executed. The building was burned half an hour after a visit by a team from the National Human Rights Commission to conduct forensic investigations. The preliminary investigation revealed no complete skeletons, but many human bones and hair. Rumors circulated that the remaining detainees had been forced to unearth all of the remains prior to the end of DOM (Rahmany 2001). No investigation or legal process resolved who had burned the building. Most people were convinced that the military had burned the building to destroy evidence; military spokespeople suggested that the Acehnese had burned it.

The withdrawal of troops from Lhokseumawe occurred in two stages. The first occurred without incident, but the official ceremony on 31 August 1998 ended in rioting.[44] One account described the presence of a military-looking man who began yelling curses at ABRI and shouting "Long live Aceh Merdeka!" ("Aksi Perusakan Terjadi Lagi di Lhokseumawe," *Kompas*, 2 September 1998). The official speakers emphasized that the people of Aceh must take responsibility for Aceh's safety and resist being incited by irresponsible parties ("Ditangguhkan, Penarikan Pasukan dari Aceh," *Kompas*, 3 September 1998). Following the ceremony, people attacked various places in Lhokseumawe. The prison was set on fire, and there was a rumor that an Aceh Merdeka flag was found inside ("Aksi Perusakan Terjadi Lagi di Lhokseumawe," *Kompas*, 2 September 1998; "Ditangguhkan, Penarikan Pasukan dari Aceh," *Kompas*, 3 September 1998). One confidential report noted that a truck moved rioters from place to place and that, despite the presence of more than 1,000 soldiers, very little effort was made to prevent or control the riots.

In commentaries regarding the riots, two explanations were predominant. First was the idea that outsiders were involved; the riots were not the spontaneous actions of people who were "not yet recovered from the trauma of DOM." This theme emphasized the possibility that *provokator* or instigators engineered the riots. Second, the security forces did not take responsibility for preventing, controlling, investigating, or processing the incident. Eight high school (SMU) students stood trial in two cases related to these riots. The proceedings demonstrated that Sergeant Second Class Rizali of Military Sub-district Command (*Koramil*) Syamtalira Bayu had coordinated their actions; however, only the students were tried and sentenced to 37 and 45 days in jail.

The formal withdrawal of outside (non-organic) troops was followed by the return of GAM from Malaysia.[45] Many Acehnese I spoke with noted the sudden appearance of people who identified themselves publicly as GAM members and spoke about separating from Indonesia in various mosques, particularly in resource-rich North Aceh. Very few were convinced that these people had been in Malaysia throughout DOM.

No action was taken to prosecute those who had committed "excesses" under military rule. Despite continued demands by Acehnese citizens and public figures both in Aceh and in Jakarta, Wiranto proposed—instead of investigating crimes committed during DOM—to investigate only those crimes that had happened afterward. The police who were responsible for security during this period were opposed to the investigation of post-DOM crimes, however. Teams continued to collect testimonies and evidence regarding what had happened during DOM. During the exposure and circulation of testimonies, killings by "unknown forces" and "unrecognized persons" increased.

In the first phase of post-DOM violence, the victims were primarily *cu'ak*, local people who had assisted the military during DOM. While the media and official sources attributed these killings to vengeance for crimes committed during DOM (Tippe 2000, LIPI Research Team 2001), testimony of *cu'ak* and of family members of victims of violence during DOM suggested otherwise. One DOM orphan told me that he knew the *cu'ak* who had taken his father, but he did not have any desire to kill him. Instead, he said: "This *cu'ak*, the ones who kill the *cu'ak* are also ABRI, why, to me, because he [ABRI] wants to erase the evidence, his witness, because this *cu'ak* is a witness to the procedure, he is the witness as a spy."[46]

Evidence implicates the security forces in numerous killings of *cu'ak*. Some *cu'ak* or civilian military assistants (TPO) who wished to testify about their treatment by the military were killed by unidentified people in the immediate aftermath of DOM. One incident that occurred on 28 December 1998 was described in a confidential human rights report. Azhar bin Abdullah, twenty-nine years old, was waiting for a public van on the side of the road when four unidentified men on two motorcycles shot him as they rode by. The report notes the complexity of the victim's loyalties. Known during DOM as a TPO, he had testified about the human rights abuses that had led him to collaborate with the military before the national parliamentary fact-finding team at the regional parliamentary building. After being detained three times for reasons he could not understand, he became a TPO to guarantee his survival and because he could not stand the pressure. While serving as a TPO, he was arrested and tortured at the Special Forces post at Rancung because the military felt that one of his reports was not true (*Notes and Events of 1998*, 34). The police never resolved any of these cases. The *cu'ak* most likely to inspire the wrath of local people were the more "cruel" and professional ones, but they survived and continued to play a role in post-DOM violence. An infamous *cu'ak*, Thalib, was implicated in the December 2000 killings of humanitarian volunteers.[47]

The next phase featured random killings of active and pensioned military and Acehnese civilians. In February 1999, Daud Abubakar, a prison escapee who had been jailed on charges of gun smuggling for GAM, was killed by a mob of local people after a firearm went off accidentally during an argument he had with the village head.[48] In such conditions, people felt great uncertainty and lacked faith in the ability of the institutions of justice to resolve cases or offer due process of law. Instead, mass killings and unidentified armed persons enforced conditions of anxiety, terror, and frustration.

The figure of Ahmad Kandang, who was featured as a representative of GAM, personified the violence attributed to separatist rebels. Many Acehnese said that Kandang appeared from nowhere and remarked with suspicion upon his rapid ascent to fame and his adroitness in evading arrest and disappearing into the crowds he convened. Archival investigation revealed that Kandang's name first appeared in conjunction with an armed robbery of a Bank Central Asia (BCA) vehicle in February 1997.[49] A few days after the robbery, military sources stated that the robbers could be "ABRI agents (*oknum*), GPK or ordinary people with weapons (*rakyat bersenjata*)." In September 1997, Ismail Syahputra was charged for his role in the BCA robbery. He too became a prominent spokesperson for GAM in the post-DOM era and then suddenly disappeared without a trace, provoking much and often contradictory speculation as to his true identity. Both men appeared to be agents of the security forces as well as putative spokesmen for the rebels ("Soal Perampokan Bersenjata di Aceh: Ada Kelemahan Sistem Keamanan," *Kompas*, 8 February 1997; "Perampok BCA Dihukum 16 Tahun," *Kompas*, 18 December 1997).

In November 1998, Ahmad Kandang's name reappeared in reports of an armed conflict with security forces ("Dan, Kandang Pun Tak Bisa

Pulang Kandang," *Majalah Tajuk*, 26 November 1998). A detailed description of the event stated that what was advertised as a ceremony to pray together at the gravesite of a famous Acehnese hero, and which drew a large crowd, turned into a ceremony to bless (*pesijuk*) GAM weapons. Kandang introduced himself and three others as GAM leaders who had recently returned from Malaysia. The military arrived several hours later, after Kandang and others with guns had disappeared into the crowd. An ABRI member was reportedly being held hostage, but he later returned. Nevertheless, the incident resulted in orders to shoot on sight anyone who took down an Indonesian flag or performed any other subversive act. A regional military commander stated that the ABRI hostage had been released through "inside efforts," which were not elaborated upon ("Kantor Polsek Ditembaki," *Kompas*, 3 November 1998).[50]

Many prominent civilian figures in Aceh emphasized that this action did not represent the aspirations or attitudes of the Acehnese people. When security forces came to arrest Kandang at his home, he escaped, but 43 of his "followers" were arrested. The security forces alleged that captured documents confirmed his identity as a GPL member. Mimicking the rhetoric used during DOM to justify violence toward ordinary people, official reports emphasized that locals had protected him ("Dan, Kandang Pun Tak Bisa Pulang Kandang," *Majalah Tajuk*, 26 November 1998).

An incident interpreted as a violent reprisal against the security forces occurred in Lhok Nibong on 29 December 1998. A "mass," including a few people with rifles, stopped a public bus to inspect identity cards in a tactic known as "sweeping." This group was said to be led by a few men who declared themselves to be members of GAM ("Tujuh Anggota ABRI Dibunuh di Aceh," *Media Indonesia*, 30 December 1998). Seven ABRI members who were forced to get off the bus were tortured and beaten to death by the crowd. One body was hung on a roadside tree, while the others were dumped in the Arakundo River. Fourteen inhabitants of Lhok Nibong were detained for questioning, and thirteen were released; no further information appeared on the processing of the last suspect. The ABRI information center's press release declared that there were indications that the action was "motored" by a group of GPK ("Tujuh Anggota ABRI Dibunuh di Aceh," *Media Indonesia*, 30 December 1998). Wiranto asked that the National Human Rights Commission investigate and prosecute the perpetrators ("Wiranto Minta Komnas HAM Usut Pembunuhan Anggota ABRI di Aceh," *Kompas*, 31 December 1998).

Wiranto announced through the press that the murders had been committed by an "old group that wants Aceh to be independent." The next day the regional military commander in Medan stated: "ABRI is now chasing Ahmad Kandang who is the figure who provoked the masses and did many evil things in Aceh" ("Buntut Pembunuhan Anggota ABRI di Aceh: Diburu, Ahmad Kandang Dalang Penggerak Massa," *Sinar Pagi*, 2 January 1999). This article described Kandang as a member of Hasan Tiro's Gang of Wild Disruptors (GPL Hasan Tiro) and said that extra troops had been dispatched in search of him (see also "Pencarian Korban ke Sungai. ABRI Terus Buru Penculik," *Sinar Pagi*, 3 January 1999). In response to accusations that ABRI wanted to extend DOM in Aceh, Wiranto announced: "This is not engineered. Who would want to lose soldiers only to engineer something. ABRI also does not want DOM in Aceh" ("Buntut Pembunuhan Anggota ABRI di Aceh: Diburu, Ahmad Kandang Dalang Penggerak Massa," *Sinar Pagi*, 2 January 1999). Kandang was also said to be directing GPK Aceh's kidnapping of suspected military "ninja" ("Aparat keamanan berusaha negosiasi: 2 Sandera GPK Masih Hidup," *Poskota*, 4 January 1999).[51]

Another fatal exchange of fire reportedly occurred between the military and Kandang's group, which the military contended had forced women and children to the front to protect its fighters (Wahab, quoted in "Baku Tembak di Lhokseumawe, 5 Orang Tewas," *Republika*, 5 January 1999). This explanation for civilian casualties reproduced justifications the military used during DOM and in response to investigations afterward. The local military commander, Danrem Johny Wahab, stated that it was very difficult to search for the "opportunist GPL led by Ahmad Kandang" because local people who had been "provoked" were hiding them ("Kapuspen ABRI: Situasi di Aceh Dapat Dikuasai," *Republika*, 5 January 1999). According to Wahab, Kandang's group combined violence and ideology in military statements: its members were "willing to kill anyone" they thought of as an enemy, and they had "already stated their desire to form an independent country." Wahab underlined that "their acts are already sadistic and beyond the limits of humanity" thus, the military had to respond with violence ("Kapuspen ABRI: Situasi di Aceh Dapat Dikuasai," *Republika*, 5 January 1999).

Following heightened efforts to find Ahmad Kandang, a team from the National Commission for Human Rights (Komnas HAM) was asked to facilitate a resolution of the conflict.[52] Upon the team's arrival in Lhokseumawe, ABRI said they would not be able to guarantee the team's safety if they traveled to Kandang village. According to one report, security forces blocked people from attempting to reach Lhokseumawe from Kandang. Others who tried to travel by boat were prevented from landing. Security forces fired shots to disperse the mass at the blockade points. One hundred forty-five people were arrested and brought to the KNPI building; all but seven were released. National media estimated that "GPL Hasan Tiro, led by Ahmad Kandang" comprised only twenty to thirty people, but said it was difficult to capture Kandang because he hid behind women and children ("Warga Kandang Masih Lakukan *'Sweeping'*," *Media Indonesia*, 8 January 1999). Lhokseumawe military commander Johny Wahab said Kandang was "only a small rat, but the difficulty is that the small rat is already inside the house." At this point, Wahab noted that this group was not GAM but rather remaining GPL from Hasan Tiro's group.

Kandang escaped yet another raid on his house in which thirty-eight of his followers were arrested and the house was burned down ("Lhokseumawe Aceh kembali bergejolak: ABRI Serbu Rumah Ahmad Kandang," *Poskota*, 9 January 1999; "Aksi Pengosongan Desa Mencekam Penduduk," *Kompas*, 10 January 1999). Of the detainees held in the KNPI building, four died after being tortured by ABRI members ("Puluhan Anggota ABRI Menganiaya Tahanan," *Kompas*, 11 January 1999). The media counted tens of torturers, but the national research institute cited as many as a hundred (LIPI 2001). One human rights investigator noted that ten detainees were taken for questioning, reducing the original thirty-eight to twenty-eight. However, later reports put the number of wounded detainees at forty, indicating that the KNPI building had been used to hold other captives. Wiranto expressed regret over this incident and hoped that those responsible would be prosecuted ("Disesalkan, Penyerbuan Tahanan di Aceh," *Kompas*, 12 January 1999). A major was discharged for failing to prevent the incident ("Jeritan hati warga Aceh kepada ABRI: Jangan Lagi Lakukan Kekerasan," *Poskota*, 16 January 1999).

Following this series of events, Kandang became the subject of rampant media speculation. Some reports painted him as a hero, protector, and moral force who convinced villagers not to gamble and follow Islamic teachings after he returned from Malaysia. Kandang was also reputed to have magical powers that enabled him to disappear, as well as immunity from weapons (*kebal*) developed through his training in Libya with Hasan Tiro's group ("Kandang Diburu Kandang Menghilang," *Majalah Gatra*, 16 January 1999, 70). Another report linked Kandang to DI/TII hero Hasan Saleh, but stated that he had not been considered very important until his house and a mobile police brigade member were attacked ("Si Misterius Ahmad Kandang," *Majalah D&R*, 11–16 January 1999, 19). A local NGO member said that "we didn't know Ahmad Kandang's name, then suddenly it appeared"—creating suspicions, repeated in other interviews, that the ABRI inflated Kandang's importance to create a reason for their return. The military cited contradictory physical descriptions of Kandang as a difficulty in the search and as an indication of local support for him.[53]

The details of what came to be called the Idi Cut Tragedy, which took place on 3 February 1999, have led some analysts to consider it as retribution for the deaths of armed forces members killed at Lhok Nibong. Approximately 10,000 people were gathered at a mosque in Idi Cut, a community in East Aceh, for a *Dakwah Aceh Merdeka* (Aceh Merdeka religious event). One Acehnese youth I interviewed who attended the event recalled the speeches as "heating up the crowd" by calling the Javanese "immoral" and "Jews who had killed Islamic people." Three orators introduced themselves as local GAM members. Before the speeches were concluded, as people began trying to leave, the sound of a shot rang out. According to one report, a group of youths began to throw rocks toward the crowd and the nearby military command post, which was darkened, at which point the military started shooting ("Belasan Mayat Berserak di Idi Cut," *Majalah Forum Keadilan*, 8 March 1999, 75). Roads in all directions were blocked by the military, and the crowd was unable to disperse safely ("Rekaan 50 Jam Yang Mengerikan," *Serambi Indonesia*, 5 February 1999). Several hours later, according to eyewitnesses, military trucks dumped the bodies of seven civilians into the Arakundo River, in which the corpses of the six soldiers killed at Lhok Nibong had been discovered ("Diduga, Kasus Idi Cut Terencana," *Serambi Indonesia*, 7 February 1999). Military officials denied the widespread suspicion that the murders were retribution for the Lhok Nibong killings and stated that it was "unclear if the bodies that were found in the Arakundo River were victims of ABRI or the GAM/GPHLT." Later, the Independent Commission established by the presidential decree to investigate acts of violence in Aceh noted that most "guessed" the killings were motivated by revenge (1999, 282). The following day, people attempted to find the corpses in the river, many of which were in gunnysacks or barrels weighted with rocks, and all of which had bullet wounds. Also found at the edge of the bridge were bullets and projectiles bearing the imprint of Pindad, the Bandung arms manufacturer that supplied the Indonesian military (see "Peluru Pindad Berserak di Idi Cut," *Serambi Indonesia*, 9 February 1999). Fifty-eight individuals were arrested in conjunction with this event, and three accused as orators and members of Aceh Merdeka were detained for trial ("Tersangka Penceramah Kasus Idi Cut Diciduk," *Serambi Indonesia*, 14 February 1999).

In discussing his experience at the event, one youth told me that the GAM members he knew and recognized had disappeared when the violence started, despite the fact that one had bragged that night that GAM had killed many soldiers. He was convinced that the army was manipulating GAM. He explained:

I think, first, that this GAM is a manipulation of the army, because I asked GAM—the next day I asked the one that I mentioned that I knew before, I said, "Brother, where were you last night?" . . . He said, "Defending people who were shot there, running to there." For me that doesn't make sense, because there were so many people. . . . I say that GAM in Aceh now is not the same as DI/TII before; GAM now is mostly a plaything of ABRI. The military are manipulating it. The example is Idi Cut; it was proven to me when I was there. It is impossible that there is a victim who has been shot by the security forces and he [GAM member] doesn't defend that person, but instead he disappears. . . .[54]

This youth was not alone in his assessment that the activities of the new GAM evidenced unclear loyalties. This incident made it increasingly clear to many people I spoke with that the end of DOM "did not mean anything."

Thirty-nine civilians were fatally shot and 125 others were wounded at the intersection near the Kraft Paper Aceh factory (Simpang KKA), approximately 20 kilometers west of Lhokseumawe, on 30 April 1999, when a ceremony for an Islamic holiday (1 Muharram) turned into a *Dakwah Aceh Merdeka*, an AM religious event.[55] One of the speakers was Ismail Syahputra, who became known as a GAM member after he was arrested in the 1997 BCA robbery with Kandang.[56] According to one account, two TNI members arrived and identified themselves as GAM activists. They were equipped with two handguns and a "handy-talkie."[57] According to eyewitness accounts, these two were asked to leave by organizers; according to the security forces, the two had not returned since that night (Independent Commission 1999). The next day, 1 May, four trucks of military personnel searched for the two soldiers. In the process, residents were badly beaten ("Tentara dan Warga Bentrok di Aceh," *Kompas*, 4 May 1999). The regional military (Koramil) and the Red Cross (ICRC) negotiated a settlement of 8 million *Rupiah* to compensate the eight people injured in the military searches and interrogation, but the agreement was broken the same day with the arrival of more military looking for their lost members. On 2 May, according to one source, local people gathered in the intersection with whatever sharp items they had, aiming to approach the military and ask them to honor their agreement to conduct no further searches in the area. Thousands of people gathered at the intersection and nearby locations. Two motorcycles were burned in front of Koramil, and the office was destroyed. Six trucks arrived with a mass of people who joined the others. The unit that had lost members began to fire at the crowd of people, who had been forced by the military to lie on the ground for an hour; when they began to rise to run, they were shot again. On 11 May, five bombs exploded in the detachment area, in an incident that was said to be the work of an armed group that called itself GAM. Many people I spoke with in private, as well as media sources, were doubtful about this attribution.[58] Since the bombs did not do any damage, they reasoned, it was more likely that they were thrown by the military themselves.

In sum, violence that may well have been perpetrated by the military itself created the impression that there might be a GAM. Throughout this period, crimes were frequently attributed to "unidentified people," "*provokator,*" and other mysterious forces. The separatist movement has not been a continuous unitary force fighting a consistent battle for independence in Aceh. Anxious concerns about separatisms have been taken up by opposing groups and enlivened by incidents of violence that demanded narratives.

Chapter 4

Translating Violence into Politics

In the period of reform that followed the end of Soeharto's rule in 1998, widely publicized state violence and demands for justice made legal accountability in Aceh an urgent necessity, but the absence of a functioning court system, human rights protections, and a state with an effective monopoly on lethal force made justice impossible. As *Kompas* put it, "Law is camouflage clothing and guns" (*Laporan Dari Aceh (2-Habis): Bermula Dari Operasi Intelijen*, 4 August 1999). Every failed attempt to hold perpetrators accountable was followed by renewed instability, underlining the state's inability to subordinate violence to the law.

This chapter analyzes the one and only attempt at judicially accounting for state violence in Aceh, the Bantaqiah case.[1] In Jakarta as well as Aceh, demands for justice accompanied the exposure of DOM violence. The state-sponsored investigations that followed demonstrated not only that the military was implicated in the massacre of more than thirty unarmed civilians but also that, in what the report called a "dark pattern," the military conspired to create a separatist enemy to cover up its own involvement in violence. The joint civilian-military (*connexitas*) trial found low-ranking members of the military guilty of murder, but the main perpetrators evaded the tribunal.

Military and state apologists moved from demands for legal accountability to possible compensation, considering a policy to accord the region a greater share of the revenues its resources yielded. The security forces used the discourse of economic redistribution to focus responsibility for injustice on the government, aiming to obscure their own violence by pointing to popular grievances against Jakarta policymakers. Ironically, the state and military sought to address the economic issues originally raised by Aceh Merdeka after constituting GAM as a separatist threat. While glaring economic inequities certainly underlay discontent in Aceh and anxiety in Jakarta, the proposed redistribution of wealth did not, and could not, address the injustices of the past or free the legal system from corruption. The realization that no redress was available through the justice system prompted some Acehnese to take up the issue of economic redistribution. This move failed to address the conflict dynamic that allowed the military to continue to perpetrate human rights abuses in the name of phantom separatists. Indeed, military discourse converted their own "excesses" into a threat of retribution because of the "irrationality" of Acehnese ideas of justice. For the Acehnese, the calculations of economic redistribution only added to the list of unfulfilled promises.

Simultaneously, and with equally fatal results, all parties—the military and state in Jakarta, and prominent advocates of justice and NGOs in Aceh—translated the demand for justice into the question of a referendum on independence, which rapidly became a question not of democracy but of secession. The discourse of Referendum responded to and perpetuated the impossibility of legal redress and the incalculability of justice. The international intervention that resulted from the Referendum movement is analyzed in the next chapter, since it was not a popular demand and was not intended to offer a political solution to the conflict. Both economic redistribution and the Referendum represent political translations of grievances and do not address the questions of violence and law. Finally, returning to the problematic issues and themes of historical grievance raised in Chapter 2, I consider the implementation of Islamic law in Aceh.

Exposing Injustice

The "Aceh problem" was constituted by discussions both in the region and in Jakarta. Violent "excesses," inequitable economic arrangements, failed promises, and political constraints were highlighted in these discussions. Yet, despite shifts in rhetoric, new plans, and better promises, violence persisted. Violence meant dramatically different things at different times and was used by different groups to mobilize opposing interests. In Aceh, the recollection of violence most often demonstrated that the center (Jakarta) lacked credibility, control over the military, and the desire to hold anyone accountable for historical grievances and continuing atrocities. Some Acehnese emotionally asked: "Why are we hated [by the center]?" Although physical violence seemed to be the ultimate referent grounding these discussions, a closer examination revealed the violence done to Acehnese dignity by a long train of broken promises. The sense of persecution was linked directly to the problem of injustice by one banner that proclaimed, "Hatred is not a reason for injustice." The violence was troubling, but so too was the injustice of it. When repeated exposures of military-state violence against innocent Acehnese failed to yield justice, the sense of grievance compounded exponentially, and the possible avenues of resolution decreased precipitously. The images of violence that had not been brought to justice became another crime, symbolizing the government's lack of credibility. Exposure without justice exacerbated the problem.

In 1998, prior to the end of DOM, Acehnese NGOs organized groups of female DOM victims to raise awareness in Jakarta of what had happened in Aceh ("Forum LSM Minta Operasi Militer di Aceh Dihentikan,"*Kompas*, 5 June 1998). In addition to campaigning at the Indonesian Legislative Assembly (DPR), the victims presented their stories to the National Commission on Human Rights, Komnas HAM, which sent an investigative team to Aceh shortly thereafter ("Irian Jaya Subur Pelanggaran HAM,"*Kompas*, 13 June 1998). Simultaneously, students in Banda Aceh undertook a hunger strike to emphasize the seriousness of the ongoing violence. Following visits by Komnas HAM investigators and the publication of statistics and reports generated by Acehnese NGOs indicating the extent of abuses during DOM, the DPR dispatched several investigative teams to Aceh.[2] Despite intimidation and fears of repercussions from the security forces, dozens of victims described their experiences. After giving their testimonies, many asked for a security guarantee ("TPF Temukan Kondisi Memprihatinkan di Aceh,"*Kompas*, 28 July 1998). The head of the DPR fact-finding team, Lieutenant General Hari Sabarno, expressed his concern to the hundreds of DOM widows who had gathered to give their testimony "over the violence and cruelty done by rogue elements (oknum) of the security forces toward the people, including toward women" ("TPF DPR Prihatinkan Tindak Kekerasan di Aceh,"*Kompas*, 29 July 1998).

The role of female victims was critical in ending DOM. Rape victims disrupted the New Order pattern of casting victims as enemies of the state and isolating them as political contaminants. Coincident with attention to the rape of Chinese women in the May 1998 riots in Jakarta, significant international attention was directed toward the sexualized violence committed by the Indonesian military ("Pejabat PBB Benarkan Laporan Perkosaan Massal di Indonesia," *Suara Pembaruan*, 19 December 1998). Initially, much of the outrage in Jakarta centered on the plight of women who had been raped in conjunction with accusations that their husbands were sheltering or were themselves GAM rebels. These women symbolized the pure excess of military abuse of power and the profound injustice of violence in Aceh.[3] The security forces often accused GAM rebels of hiding behind or turning into women (as if they had shape-changing abilities), justifying the shooting of unarmed women.[4] The narratives of violence against women shifted following the Humanitarian Pause as women were increasingly photographed with guns as vengeful warriors for GAM.[5] After the tsunami, women disappeared from the ranks of combatants when re-integration programs were designed to provide compensation for ex-fighters.

In July 1998, Komnas HAM said that it would investigate the Aceh case, but noted that "if the DPR was already capable of opening up the case it would be better" ("Marzuki Darusman: Saya Yakin TGPF Mandiri,"*Kompas*, 29 July 1998).[6] Students demonstrated in front of the UN headquarters in Jakarta to draw international attention to the human rights violations that occurred during DOM. ("Solidaritas Mahasiswa Untuk Kasus Aceh Datangi Kantor PBB," *Suara Pembaruan*, 30 July 1998). As a result of this pressure, General Wiranto promised that the military involved in "excesses" would be tried according to existing civil law.[7] Immediately following his apology, national media focused on the military's role in killings. One magazine cover story was titled: "Killing Fields in Aceh: ABRI accused" (*Majalah Gatra*, 8 August 1998). The military ignored the visceral descriptions of the excesses it was accused of having perpetrated.[8] Despite military denials that Aceh had ever been a special operations zone, the term DOM gained popularity as a signifier for the systematic violence committed by the state against Acehnese. Many Acehnese I spoke with at that time pointed out that General Wiranto had apologized for DOM and asked if there had never been a DOM, then why did he use the term?

At the same time that the media focused on the brutality of the military, it reiterated the violence of GAM/GPK, particularly in 1990 when troops were killed ("Mereka tak Bisa Tersenyum," *Majalah Gatra*, 8 August 1998). Members of Parliament in 1998 said that it was not enough for the troops to be removed, but the "actors, and intellectual actors of the slaughter for eight years of the people, who in fact were not members of the GPK must be investigated and brought to the military court" ("Soal DOM Aceh, Pemerintah Harus Minta Maaf," *Suara Pembaruan*, 12 August 1998). In this first phase of demanding justice, certain victims were labeled as "not GAM/GPK," which distinguished victims who were not guilty from real separatists, at the same time implying that the separatist threat was not as grave as military imagined. At this point most people adamantly denied their alleged participation in GAM and even its existence. The arbitrary accusation that a person was GAM seemed more a justification for the exercise of power than an accurate political assessment. Not until the Humanitarian Pause were there widespread affirmations of affiliation with GAM. These belated and situational conversions indicate a discontinuity in the history of the movement, not false denials by accused GAM members.

After Wiranto's apology a broad spectrum of Acehnese people, from students to local politicians and elite in Jakarta, demanded justice

("Soal DOM Aceh, Pemerintah Harus Minta Maaf," *Suara Pembaruan*, 12 August 1998). Ultimately, the failure to fulfill the promise that the perpetrators would stand trial according to civilian laws compounded the sense of grievance and lack of faith in the central state. The military resisted being held accountable for specific crimes. By explicitly declaring the "evidence" of mass graves unearthed by Komnas HAM to be the remains of the 1965 mass killings of suspected communist party members, the military endeavored to return to its narrative of saving the threatened nation from imminent disaster through publicly sanctioned violence in which most survivors were to some degree complicit.[9] The Aceh case differed from the anti-communist campaign in the degree to which past violence was discussed and accountability demanded.

In Aceh, the status of the victim changed from contaminant to a kind of capital in the international circulation of humanitarian aid and human rights discourse. While the stories of violence inflicted on specific victims provoked anger, Wiranto's reneging on his promise to bring perpetrators to trial intensified and extended the betrayal, insult, and injustice to Aceh itself, consolidating and politicizing most Acehnese. The series of broken promises demonstrated the government's powerlessness over the military and convinced many people that "it was all engineered" and nothing was said in good faith. Ultimately, the string of broken promises and the violence for which no one was held accountable created conditions of corruption.

At the center, some politicians recognized that the civilian government's credibility was endangered unless justice was pursued "hierarchically" to reach higher up the chain of command ("Tim Depag Bergabung Cari Masukan Dari DI Aceh,"*Kompas*, 13 November 1999). Early recommendations by the National Human Rights Commission included accountability and trials for both policymakers and direct perpetrators, compensation and rehabilitation for victims' families, and a police enforcement of the law to restore feelings of safety and mutual trust among civilians. Finally, Komnas HAM noted there must be a redistribution of wealth between the center and periphery ("Pernyataan Komnas HAM: Penanggungjawab Kebijakan DOM Harus Diadili,"*Kompas*, 3 September 1998). The end of DOM created the opportunity for discussions of justice, but did not fulfill the demands for justice. Military statements alternately suggested that the apology of the commander in chief was sufficient to serve justice and emphasized a new narrative in which the injustices catalyzed the reappearing danger of separatists (Tippe 2000).

In Jakarta, elite reformers and NGOs invoked the case of Aceh as a reason to rein in the military.[10] Referendum had been introduced into debates, but initially the threat of referendum did not imply separatism and in public discourse seemed limited to angry youth. The idea that the nation might be in peril inspired some in Jakarta to express humility and sympathy. Ali Sadikin said that as a member of the 1945 founding generation he was "ashamed if it comes to the point that Aceh lets go of the [nation], because of our own actions" ("Ali Sadikin: ABRI Dendam," *Sinar Pagi*, 15 January 1999). As the violence continued and justice remained elusive, demands for a referendum on the question of secession increased.

At the point that demands for Referendum became more adamant, acts of violence made GAM increasingly visible; as several Acehnese told me, GAM "increasingly had an existence." NGOs in Jakarta were split on how to handle the "Aceh question." One vocal critic of the military distinguished the emergent force of GAM from the previous GAM that was stigmatized. He suggested that GAM had a right to political expression, but violent acts must be subject to law. He emphasized that the use of violence was limited to GAM and that other Acehnese should not be criminalized for it.[11] Most other NGO representatives were solidly opposed to the use of violent resistance. Once a violent GAM occupied a prominent role, some critics of the New Order were inclined to conflate all Acehnese criticism of the center under the rubric of separatism. It was difficult for nationalist reformers to accept that the Acehnese might secede. In very emotional conversations they would say that Aceh could not leave because they had helped found the country. After GAM became increasingly prominent, one Jakarta-based NGO leader abandoned her rhetorical efforts to play a role in Aceh, declaring that "if the GAM wants to violently separate, I can no longer support Aceh."[12] Others distinguished GAM from the Referendum drive, reiterating the importance of justice and noting that secession was forbidden by the constitution. It was difficult for Jakarta NGOs and elite reformers to come to terms with Acehnese as both victims of horrific violence and agents of armed struggle. In their comments, the violence that was most irreconcilable was not the violence of the security forces but the violent acts by supposed separatist rebels. For many Jakarta reformers, even the threat of separatist violence seemed to annul any moral right that Aceh had to make claims for justice. As long as there was a pretense of law enforcement, the separatist threat seemed to justify the military's authorized violence in the name of national unity. By April 2001, some reformers articulated a different way that violence absolved the nation from accountability for the past: "We have to fight to have the nation back, and if the Acehnese do not want to be a part of the nation any more they should go."[13]

Investigations

One year after the official apology, President Habibie commissioned a team to find the "facts, perpetrators and background to the acts of violence in Aceh" (Presidential Decree No. 88, 1999). The commission was charged with developing legal evidence to account for and resolve the "excess." In the year between the end of DOM and the commissioning of the report there were several incidents of large-scale violence. The report investigated five priority cases, two incidents that occurred during DOM and three post-DOM incidents.[14] The report, which was completed in December 1999, analyzed DOM cases to support understandings of the post-DOM violence regarded as more urgent by the government. A close reading of the Independent Commission's *Report on Acts of Violence in Aceh* discloses how knowledge and representation of conflicts produce the social realities that they predict or describe, and how certain logics interrupt the law and undermine seemingly factual evidence.[15]

The commission's report, though eagerly anticipated, was not circulated widely. Perpetrators were named and facts reported under a frame of confidentiality designed to protect the status of the contents as evidence admissible in future trials. Despite the secrecy surrounding this report, most of its contents were widely known; the reorganization of these facts was the report's critical intervention. Building on Ann Stoler's important insight that colonial commissions "organised knowledge, rearranged its categories, and prescribed what state officials were charged to know" (2002a, 95), I contend that this report narrates and limits the state's liability not only for past violence but also for present and future violence as it classifies and organizes the evidence that it documents and rewrites.

I carefully consider the logics and classifications developed by this report in its executive summary before diagramming how the evidence and analysis developed by this team not only failed to produce justice in the courtroom but also led to policies and decisions that produced a particular conflict formation that was not inevitable.[16] My analysis of this crucial report examines four main issues. First, I briefly note how the previous dangers in Aceh were consolidated by the team as a second-generation movement. I then consider how past actions were reclassified and future actions predicted, highlighting the logics of misidentification and regret. Next, I map how indeterminate violence became productive. Finally, I consider the dilemma the report names for itself, the problem of "single bad guys," the report's rhetorical "excess" that unsettles its carefully crafted analytic logic. The "truth" of the "single bad guys" was not judicially examined, paving the way to compounded injustice and corruption of state institutions. Existing separatist rebels, mysterious forces, and narrative logics linking discontinuous resistance all contribute to distorting evidence about the conditions that enabled this massacre of Bantaqiah and his followers to take place. The focus on individual actors who could be held accountable in trials was a legal necessity, but at the same time it constituted such a distortion of the situation that justice could not be done. The trial not only failed to examine the systematic nature of the dark pattern, reducing it to isolated criminal incidents perpetrated by individual agents, but it also did not challenge the rhetoric of an existing movement that threatened the state; rather, it depended on the logic of an existing GPK enemy figure.

Defining the Problem

The key to limiting state liability for previously acknowledged violence was not the contestation of facts but the way the report defined the problem in Aceh. The report's executive summary begins:

The Independent Commission observes that the acts of violence in Aceh cannot be separated (*dilepaskan*) from two root causes. First, the existence of a procedural error and political policies of the government, and second the appearance of a movement that the government calls the second-generation Security Disruptor's Movement (*Gerakan Pengacau Keamanan*) (GPK) and which several sides, and some literature, call the Free Aceh Movement (*Gerakan Aceh Merdeka*). The political policy error was to implement a security approach which was very repressive, even though, the military side "did not understand it as a state of military emergency," but almost all layers [of society] understood Aceh to be a Military Operations Zone (DOM). This understanding was based on the existence of operation Red Net 1, which was implemented by the Chief of the Armed Forces at that time in response to a request of the governor of Aceh who reported there was a Security Disruptor's Movement in 1989. (2)

The assertion of the second problem, the appearance of a second-generation movement that consolidated the previously distinguished political (GAM) and criminal (GPK) dangers in Aceh, was the condition for analyzing the military operations and their "excesses." After asserting the existence of a movement that joined all the previous dangers in Aceh, the report notes that Operation Red Net was initiated at the request of Aceh's civilian governor who reported criminality that threatened "development security." The problem highlighted in this definition is no longer the acts of violence or the appropriateness of a "security approach" to the situation in Aceh in 1989; rather, it is a procedural error and a misunderstanding. In an effort to address outrage over the military claim that DOM never existed, the report notes that the military did not consider Aceh a state of emergency, but everyone living in Aceh understood it to be a DOM. Debates on the status of DOM obscured other important shifts in the conflict discourse. Far less public attention was focused on the report's assertion of a second-generation movement. Making GAM and GPK two different terms for the same movement had far-reaching effects in terms of military responsibility for its past policies and acts.

The report's definition of the problem produces a historical narrative that posits essential continuity between first- and second-generation rebels. Archival sources draw clear distinctions between GPK and GAM, but the report joins them in a single movement. Consolidating acts of indeterminate violence and social critique justified past policies and focused present anxieties. The report's narrative of a second-generation movement became much more powerful when representatives of both GAM and the military converged in claiming this story as the truth as a result of international mediation.

After joining GAM and GPK in the past to establish a unified movement in the present, the report documents the extent of resource exploitation and economic injustice under the centralized New Order regime. The commission concludes its brief abstract and definition of the problem with what appears to be its central concern—the incidents of post-DOM violence and the political demands for a referendum: "After DOM was withdrawn, the escalation of the situation was increasingly reversed, when the points of dissatisfaction mixed with the 'ideology' of a wider movement, the society is divided into two groups (*kutub*) that are centered on a desire that is inclined toward separatism, through independence or referendum" (3). Although the report distinguished two groups here, it subsequently conflates all critique with separatism.

The Referendum movement had organized a peaceful mass rally attended by over a million people several months before the completion of the report ("Sejuta orang turun ke Banda Aceh," *Suara Pembaruan*, 8 November 1999). A number of prominent Acehnese had lent their support to the movement, and a range of diverse interests operated under the Referendum banner. These groups were aware that the strength of their position depended upon an appearance of unity. The banner hid many conflicting interests and imposed silence rather than dialogue. The report links this nonviolent coalition with the second-generation movement as an inevitable result of past state violence:

The opening of the desire to be separate from Indonesia, via these two options [referendum or independence], has to be understood as a process that is natural from the social structure in Aceh, which has already experienced oppression for too long. . . . What is happening now, this moment, appears to be the fruit of the past. (3)

In subsequent chapters, the report lamented the excesses of the past: if there had not been a DOM, the second-generation movement for independence would not have formed and post-DOM violence would not have occurred (40–41). A series of rhetorical questions develop the analysis:

Suppose there had not been a DOM, is it possible that those demands [for justice and for Referendum] would have been made? This logic is very important to begin to see in a comprehensive, integrated way that the violence which appears now is a consequence of the implementation of DOM in Aceh. (40)

In the report's logic, the fact that there was no legal resolution for widely publicized atrocities during DOM created conditions in which the second-generation movement was the only option for Acehnese. Reiterating and regretting the impossibility of changing the past substituted for considering how to account for the events of the past. What I call the logic of regret provided the independent team a way of acknowledging the magnitude of past violence and violations without acknowledging or addressing the conditions that made such violence possible and made justice impossible. Lamenting the errors and excesses of the past, the authors blame the past for causing the present instability. In this logic, every statement and exposure of the excess of DOM became a threat of what would return as justice or, in the event of its failure, as vengeance.

Based on the past violations, the report predicts states of insecurity that would not be resolved by the end of military operations:

The ending of DOM is not a guarantee that the problem in Aceh will resolve itself. Because of that, concrete steps need to be taken to try the perpetrators of violent acts, both horizontal violence done by the members of GAM and vertical violence done by the military, not only the members of the troops in the field, but also the policymaker. (3)

The report sees justice as the solution to the contemporary problem in Aceh: a separatist movement that is both violent and widespread and has a compelling grievance narrative that incorporates past abuses perpetrated by the state and a history of economic injustice. Justice, however, has proven unattainable because the problem of "single bad guys" was obscured by the convergent narratives shared by rebels and the state.

Single Bad Guys

Although the report's definition of the problem depends on two distinct sides in the conflict, as it analyzes the period after DOM the report emphasizes the difficulty of identifying the true perpetrator because of the "dark pattern":

Other perpetrators also exist: the third force which very often wears "Indonesian Armed Forces [TNI] uniforms" to conduct its operations in the *dark pattern*. In this case, it is extremely difficult for the commission to "show their faces" because the commission was not given the authority to arrest people. But it is a dilemma, because it can crush the morale of the TNI foot soldiers if TNI seems to be the *single bad guys* in Aceh. (25, italicized words in English in original)

The dark pattern encompassed not simply unauthorized individuals wearing military uniforms but also the legacies of the GPK: deserters and former, disavowed, or active military members. Archival materials demonstrate that the "dark pattern" operated during the early years of the military operations as well as during the violent period following the official end of DOM. The report endeavored to overwrite the history of the 1990s' "dark pattern" with the historical narrative of a unified, representative, second-generation movement that consolidated the earlier political-economic critique of GAM with the violence, military manipulations, and criminality of GPK. The historical narrative of the report added violence to political critique by fusing GAM and GPK in a similar way to the report's contemporary efforts to link the nonviolent coalition for Referendum with an independence movement that might be responsible for acts of inexplicable violence. The dark pattern introduced a powerful indeterminacy that corrupted the identities of and boundaries between the two acknowledged sides. The various elements of the military that comprised the "dark pattern forces" compromised but also supported the logic of the political causes and historical grievances that distinguished the two forces in the conflict.

The analytic frame of the report relied on a conflict between two sides. The dark pattern supports this bifurcation by distancing ongoing military misconduct from the legitimate forces as a distinct "dark force." In contrast to previous "rogue elements" (*oknum*) discourses that indicated that individual members of the military might have committed violations, the dark pattern introduces the possibility that perpetrators might be agents of either side. Likewise, GAM might be "pure" and engaged in a just struggle for the dignity of many Acehnese, a hope that was often expressed during this period. There might be other GAMs manipulated by the military. The dark force enabled each of the two forces to be conceived as "pure," but also corrupted their boundaries and indicated their ambiguous and indeterminate relationship.

Resolution, according to the report, was only possible through the exposure of truth in the context of the judicial apparatus through a special tribunal (26). In the report's logic, removing ambiguity and unmasking the "dark force" would end it. In a conflict of two sides, the dark force figures would be returned to their proper identity and the two-sided frame could be employed to resolve the conflict. A professional, disciplined, accountable military could easily "crush" the minor armed elements of the separatist forces, and political grievances could be addressed through special autonomy legislation that would return resource wealth to the region and allow for greater local control in cultural and political domains. Even as the importance of legal resolution was reiterated, its impossibility was acknowledged in the report: the true identities of the perpetrators could not be discovered without powers of arrest. The independent commission lacked the authority to make arrests, and the police lacked the willingness or ability to arrest powerful military perpetrators. The report suggested that arrest would fix the identity of the individual caught and presumably end the possible permutations and doubling of categorizations and identities. Therein lies the report's dilemma: "it can crush the morale of the TNI foot soldiers if TNI seems to be the *single bad guys* in Aceh," as well as corrupting the report's carefully crafted narrative logic of a violent second-generation movement opposing the state and national unity. This conundrum underlines the salient facts that the police do not control the military and the state does not have a monopoly on violence.

Mass media reported the capture of various *provokator* and unidentified figures during this period, but the identification and arrest of individuals did not stop the pattern. As individual perpetrators were disavowed by the military as deserters or double agents, the pattern reproduced with greater virulence (Drexler 2001; Sulistyo 2000). Once caught, these individuals became particular members of the military who had gotten out of line, not elements of systematic plan that could be addressed, legally or politically.

The dark pattern accurately described a social reality. The report pointed to a significant aspect of the perpetuation of violence in the ambiguity and overlap between the military and its enemy. But the law failed to provide resolution in the one case heard (Zamzami 2001; Rahmany 2001). In the Bantaqiah tribunal, the military was not held liable for this pattern, and the star witness who might have unraveled it disappeared. The dark pattern replicated and continued through the very suggestion of its existence, which called into question other seeming facts: Was it one renegade soldier committing a crime? Was it a turf war between the police and military? was it a separatist in a stolen uniform? Was it a disavowed military member posing as a separatist? Was it a military deserter now committed to the separatist side? Or was it a "pure" GAM member working to restore Acehnese dignity? The dark pattern enabled a relativist analysis of violence committed by the two sides at the same time that it obscured the inability of the transitional regime to control the powerful military.

The Bantaqiah Trial

The report emphasized the importance of trials to address the past violence. Of the five cases investigated by the independent commission, only one case was heard in a joint civilian-military tribunal. The incident occurred nearly one year after Wiranto ended DOM and declared the people of Aceh responsible for security in Aceh. The executive summary of the Independent Commission to Investigate Violence in Aceh summarized the incident as follows:

> This case of shootings occurred 23 July 1999 at the Islamic boarding school of Teungku Bantaqiah in the village of Blang Meurandeh Beutong, West Aceh and was done by the military from Regional Military Command (*Korem*) 011/Lilawangsa causing the death of 65 civilians who were studying the Koran (*pegajian*).
> Some surviving eyewitnesses said that in this incident there was no armed contact or resistance. The men who were studying the Koran descended from the second floor of the school and were ordered to hand over knives even though according to the version of Korem 011/Lilawangsa there was an attack on the military. (17)

The death of sixty-five civilians in an incident without armed contact challenged the emerging discourse of armed resistance in Aceh at the same time that it renewed outrage over military misconduct.

The killings were not reported in the national media until a week after the event. Initially, 31 fatalities were reported.[17] Military spokesmen defended the action of their troops[18] on the grounds that there was an exchange of fire as they attempted to confiscate weapons said to be in the possession of Bantaqiah and his followers. In the trial, the group was described by military informants as comprised of GAM members who controlled an extremely large marijuana operation in the area.

Who Was Bantaqiah?

Bantaqiah was accused of separatism, but his biography shows that his primary concern was Islamic piety. Through his Islamic boarding school in a remote part of West Aceh, Teungku (the title for a religious leader) Bantaqiah had developed a reputation for radicalism and piety through the anti-sin (*maksiat*) campaigns of the Jubah Putih movement. In 1984, the Jubah Putih movement was outlawed by Aceh's highest court ("Protes di Balik Jubah Putih," *Majalah Tempo*, 30 May 1987). In May 1987, Bantaqiah and approximately thirty followers descended from their residence in a more remote hill area[19] into the cities of Sigli and Meulaboh to campaign against drinking alcohol and engaging in other practices that were at odds with the teaching of Islam, such as gambling and selling food during fasting hours ("Protes di Balik Jubah Putih," *Majalah Tempo*, 30 May 1987). In some accounts, they argued that the "specialness of Aceh"—presumably, its status as a province that should be ruled by Islamic law—had been disregarded (Zamzami 2001). The protesters wore white and were armed with sharp knives. They carried a green and red flag that was different from both the Indonesian and the Free Aceh Movement flags ("Protes di Balik Jubah Putih," *Majalah Tempo*, 30 May 1987). The governor of Aceh, Ibrahim Hasan, denied that Bantaqiah and his followers were a political movement; he suggested that their style of Islam regarded anyone outside of their group as a non-Muslim (*kafir*) and that men had to kill a *kafir* to join (Zamzami 2001, 20–30; "Protes di Balik Jubah Putih," *Majalah Tempo*, 30 May 1987). Bantaqiah's interpretation and teaching of Islam were at odds with the institutionalized version of Islam disseminated and tolerated by the New Order and bureaucratically regulated through the Indonesian Council of Ulamas (MUI) (Zamzami 2001, 22, n. 16). New Order religious officials called the campaign a "show of force" without religious basis. Bantaqiah was not given a chance to defend himself against this ruling because "they are recalcitrant. It is difficult to dialogue argumentatively with them." Many of his followers considered Bantaqiah to have divine powers (*sakti*). Followers and detractors said he possessed special powers of invulnerability (*ilmu kebal*) (Zamzami 2001, 13; Independent Commission 1999).

At approximately this same time that the center was increasingly concerned with radical Islam, the chief of the armed forces, Pangab L. B. Moerdani, cynically said that this was a group of people with "not enough work to do," meaning, according to *Tempo* magazine, that it was "not a large, planned movement" ("Protes di Balik Jubah Putih," *Majalah Tempo*, 30 May 1987). Other Acehnese civil servants commented that it was a social protest of people who were "not happy with Aceh's progress."[20]

The central government's efforts to outlaw and discredit Bantaqiah's religious teachings failed, so there was an effort to co-opt him through the promise of development funds. This effort failed as well, when Bantaqiah refused to move to the more easily controlled lowland community that had been built in his name with money from the central government.[21] Often overlooked in characterizations of Bantaqiah as a separatist is his service to President Soeharto's Golkar party. Bantaqiah surrendered to the security forces in December 1989 and promised to be faithful to the 1945 Constitution and the *Pancasila* national ideology ("Tokoh Kelompok Jubah Putih Menyerahkan Diri," *Kompas*, 13 December 1989). The security forces said no punishment was necessary (see also Zamzami 2001). In 1990, Bantaqiah met with the governor to thank him for the promised development funds and to pledge his support for the government in security and order, and at the same time to deny that he was involved in the GPK ("Tokoh 'Jubah Putih' Akan bantu Pemerintah Jaga Keamanan di Aceh," *Angkatan Bersenjata*, 30 November 1990). Bantaqiah's relationship with the government was complex, though he was consistent in his principles and teachings of Islam. More recent analyses have linked Bantaqiah's religious struggles to Acehnese political resistance in an effort to attach current political movements to Islamic movements (Ishak 2003).

In 1993, marijuana cultivation in Aceh had become prominent nationally, and Bantaqiah was accused of being part of a large-scale syndicate.[22] He fled the authorities, but was arrested and tried for subversion (Zamzami 2001, 37). How an accusation of participating in the marijuana business was transformed into a charge of subversion for which a life sentence was demanded can only be explained by the power of the military and police during the New Order and the use of the courts to legitimize their arbitrary use of force. Bantaqiah was convicted after a trial marked by numerous procedural irregularities. Evidence included two GPK flags, forty-nine marijuana leaves, and two Toyota vehicles with police license plates for which no explanation was given. It was alleged that Bantaqiah assisted GPK's logistics and that he had sold 530 kilograms of marijuana to an unnamed source. Zamzami suggests that individuals in such an isolated location might not have known that marijuana cultivation was illegal and that they were growing it as a flavor enhancer, its traditional Acehnese use. Ishak suggests that the marijuana syndicate was not linked to GAM, but rather to the military and police (2003, 77–81). According to Zamzami's account, the trial was deliberately moved to the North Aceh court to coincide with that of known GAM figure Nyak Mariani; the local military command at the time linked the two cases (2001, 38–39). An article written after Bantaqiah's conviction in 1995 notes that he used his followers to tend the marijuana and used the proceeds to support his activities coordinating the logistics of GPK AM ("Gembong GPK-AM Divonis 20 Tahun," *Suara Karya*, 25 January 1995). Zamzami notes that the trial served the purpose of creating a history for the previous five years. He emphasized that the details of Bantaqiah's support for Indonesia, such as his public pledges witnessed by prominent civil and military representatives and reported in the local media, were disregarded, as was his role as a

Golkar functionary. In contrast, Ishak suggests that the marijuana syndicate operated in collusion with the military and police, who attempted to discredit GAM by associating it with this criminal activity. Bantaqiah served his prison sentence until Habibie released him in March 1999, along with other political prisoners as specified by Wiranto's apology at the end of DOM ("Napol Gerakan Aceh Merdeka Dilepas dari LP Tanjung Gusta Medan," *Republika*, 27 March 1999).

The Trial

Legal experts justified the use of a *connexitas*, joint military-civilian trial, because one of the accused perpetrators was a civilian informer, a TPO or *cu'ak*. Amran Zamzami, chairman of the Independent Commission, commented that this case was recommended to President Wahid for trial in the hope that it would be considered under the classification of crimes against humanity, which would have enabled the use of stronger laws, such as the pending legislation on a human rights court, or temporary legislation that was being used to investigate the East Timor case. The human rights court legislation had not yet passed, and an ad hoc tribunal was not convened. The military agreed to the joint hearing based on the civilian informer's involvement. Zamzami commented retrospectively that it was unfortunate that the case was rushed through under the *connexitas* formation. However, he noted that many complications had resulted from the government's delay in processing the case; the team's report was submitted to the president in December 1999, but the trial did not begin until April 2000. In the end, twenty-four members of various units and one *cu'ak* were indicted and tried under the criminal code. The primary charge was for individually and collectively following or acting with Lieutenant Colonel Sujono in the premeditated murder of Teungku Bantaqiah and as many as 57 of his followers on Friday, 23 July 1999, at his religious boarding school and on the road seven and eight kilometers from it. Sujono, who oversaw the operation, had disappeared, so he was not included in the indictment.

The indictment outlines the incident as follows: The military resort commander in North Aceh[23] obtained information that Teungku Bantaqiah and his followers possessed 100 guns, which were buried around his complex, and he had a force of approximately 300 men equipped with weapons. The single civilian indicted had reported along with one other informer that Bantaqiah and his followers often threatened to kill citizens who did not want to follow their group, which the indictment referred to as an armed movement to disrupt security (GBPK) as well as GAM. Based on this information, the Danrem, Colonel Syafnil

Armen, sent a telegram with these instructions: "Find, Meet, Approach and arrest/capture the GPK figure and his sympathizers alive or dead." According to the telegram, joint forces composed of as many as 215 men were formed under the leadership of Infantry Lieutenant Colonel Heronimus Guru as the field commander and Infantry Lieutenant Colonel Sujono, who served as the head of the intelligence section for Korem, as the overseer of operations. The field group was divided into the "arrest/attack" group (with three teams from various units, indicted numbers 1–10) and the "closing" group (indicted numbers 11–25). Sujono participated in both groups, as did the one civilian informer (indicted number 11). The first group had the duty to attack and arrest Bantaqiah, while the second group had the duty of securing the first group, locating the weapons that were supposedly hidden in Bantaqiah's complex, and guarding the road and bridge leading to the complex.

The complex is in a remote location. The troops departed Lhokseumawe on Wednesday, and the attack took place on Friday. In addition to students residing at the school, men from the surrounding area were present for Friday prayers. During one of the rest breaks, the indictment notes, the indicted civilian was instructed in the use of firearms; he was wearing a TNI uniform that he had previously been issued.

According to the indictment, one of the units from the attack group entered Bantaqiah's complex and asked someone if he was Bantaqiah; since he was not, he called Bantaqiah. The soldiers and Bantaqiah reportedly shook hands and chatted for five minutes. Sujono arrived and asked which man was Bantaqiah. The indictment states that indicted number 1 said, "This is the man." The indictment next states that Sujono said, "OO, so this is Bantaqiah," and then, "Let's kill them all." In the indictment it appears that Sujono said these things in the presence of Bantaqiah. Sujono communicated by radio to Heronimus Guru, who led the attack group, saying, "How about it, little brother, let's kill them all." Heronimus Guru did not reply. In his testimony, he stated that the connection was not clear and he heard only the word "kill." Sujono left the complex. Another soldier ordered subordinates to ransack the living quarters, while other soldiers herded the men into the courtyard where they were ordered to remove their clothes, ID cards, and weapons, and assume a squatting position. Sujono and the civilian informer approached the complex. Another team sealed off the road to prevent escape. Bantaqiah's son went to fetch a walkie-talkie that the military was looking for; when he returned with it, one of the soldiers struck him with a weapon. The indictment states that Bantaqiah then shouted, "God is great," and at the same time one of the soldiers shouted "attack." Testimony from the indicted soldiers accepted by the court and included in its deliberations suggested that Bantaqiah shouted "Attack *Pai*," using an extremely derogatory ethnic term for the non-Acehnese soldiers. The indictment describes the weapons and positions used by the indicted to kill Bantaqiah and thirty-four of his followers. Sujono shot a pistol from a squatting position in the direction of Bantaqiah's followers. The civilian informer used an M-16 to shoot three times in the direction of Bantaqiah and his followers.

Subsequently, Heronimus Guru commanded soldiers to dig up the ground behind the school and in a small prayer room in search of the hundred hidden weapons. No weapons were found. This team cleaned up the area and buried the dead. Sujono commanded another group of soldiers to load the twenty-three injured individuals onto two yellow and red civilian trucks. The indictment states that the wounded were told they would receive medical treatment in Takengon. According to the indictment, however, Sujono had already told indicted number 12 that they were to be taken onto the road and "schooled," that is, killed or disappeared. After thirty minutes on the road, six injured men were ordered to get off the truck; on the orders of indicted number 12, six soldiers shot them with M-16s. The corpses were thrown by the second group into the gully. After ten more minutes, the process was repeated. The indictment states that when the remaining injured men began to struggle, they were shot without orders by indicted numbers 12–25. Forensic examination of three unidentified corpses revealed extensive damage to their faces and skulls caused by violent force or gunshot with a high-speed weapon.

A thousand soldiers secured the trial. It was "public"; twenty-five special passes were available for the press, and the remaining fifteen seats were available on a first-come, first-served basis to anyone with a proper ID card. The trial failed to satisfy popular demands for justice, and most Acehnese I spoke with at the time told me they were not interested enough to listen to the radio broadcasts. NGOs and students protested the decision to conduct the trial as a *connexitas*, rather than a human rights, trial. The Minister of Human Rights stated that he was very disappointed that people were not participating in this legal transparency and that there were protests outside the courthouse ("Soal Pelanggaran HAM: Masyarakat Aceh Merasa Dibedakan,"*Kompas*, 15 February 1999). The victims' families did not attend because of insufficient witness protection. They said they had no hopes for justice through the state system at that point and preferred to think of Bantaqiah as a religious martyr (Zamzami 2001; "Bantaqiah Sengaja Dihabisi? Tragedi Beutong *Target* Siapa?," *Kontras*, 4 August 1999).

The details that emerged during the investigation and trial, especially in the military's objections, indicated a deliberate attempt to obscure all traces of the killings. Defense objections began with an effort to delegitimize the trial based on the absence of victims' identity documents and autopsy evidence. The defense objected that the police did not have the authority to investigate the military; documentation for the hearing was incomplete; and the trial should have been held in the location where the incident occurred. Crucially, the defense argued that Sujono, who had disappeared, should be the only person accused, since the others were following his command. The judge responded that the documentation was legitimate and followed procedure and that the criminal code permitted the trial to be held elsewhere given the instability of the area where the crime occurred.

The main problem of the trial was the disappearance of the key witness, Lieutenant Colonel Sujono. Sujono had controlled intelligence around the sensitive Lhokseumawe region since 1978. He told the Independent Commission that he had "done what Jakarta ordered" in the Bantaqiah case. He was present at the shooting of Bantaqiah and commanded the lower-ranking men charged with executing the wounded and disposing of them in a gully. Mysteriously, he disappeared while the trial's venue and procedure were being negotiated. The chronology of his absence betrayed several inconsistencies[24] and contradicted the military's stated efforts to find him as a gesture of their support for law enforcement. Before the trial, several people told me that they believed he was being protected and would be brought out for the trial. When, after the trial, I asked where Sujono had gone, many well-informed people put forward one or all of three scenarios. The first was that Sujono was a bad soldier; he was afraid to face the punishment and had run away. The second was that he had been reassigned and relocated for his own protection by the military. The third was that the military had "disappeared" him; they had killed him to destroy possible incriminating evidence. Sujono's documents went missing from Jakarta headquarters when properly authorized investigators requested them (Zamzami 2001, 138; "Insiden Bataqiah: Gelar Peradilan Krocositas," *Adil Tabloid*, 28 April 2000). The investigative team had recommended putting witnesses and suspects under "protection," which was not done.

At the trial, most witnesses were from the military, except for Bantaqiah's widow and a survivor from the complex. Surya, from the local intelligence unit, testified that the civilian informer (indicted number 11) had escaped a murder attempt by Bantaqiah and his group and had subsequently been protected and housed at the military intelligence unit. Surya also talked about the observations conducted on 12 July 1999 by his intelligence unit based on "information that there was a member of GPK Bantaqiah conducting a *jilbab* operation [checkpoint to make sure all women were wearing headscarves] and continuing with a GAM meeting at Mr. Aman Santi's house" (*Putusan, Pengadilan Negeri Banda Aceh, Nomor 11/PID/Koneks/2000/PN-BNA*, 17 May 2000; *Perkara Pidana, Terdakwa "Anton Yuliantoro dkk"*, 2000, 87). They found and arrested Kamaruddin for leading a GAM meeting with five people. Surya testified that a list of the persons supposed to be killed by Bantaqiah's group and a knife were obtained at the arrest. Kamaruddin was taken to the post where he acknowledged that he was a member of Bantaqiah's group in the capacity of "intelligence" and admitted to participating in an incident of arson. Surya testified that Kamaruddin was not detained but was cultivated by the intelligence unit. Indicted number 11 (the *cu'ak*) was on the list to be killed, as Bantaqiah's group had accused him of being a spy for the TNI/Polri units. According to Surya, Kamaruddin also stated that he was a member of Bantaqiah's group who had "taken an oath to become a member of GAM" (88). Kamaruddin had reported that Bantaqiah's group had approximately 100 weapons and 300 men. He alleged that Bantaqiah's force was financed through marijuana cultivation, claiming Bantaqiah had approximately ten hectares of marijuana; that Bantaqiah's group had committed murder and burned a school; and that they had threatened the local people that if they did not fly the GAM flag on the coming Indonesian Independence Day, their houses would be burned. The intelligence witness denied participating in the operation, but noted that conditions in the area had been safer since Bantaqiah was shot.

Colonel Armen testified that on 15 July 1999 he sent a telegram ordering the arrest of Bantaqiah, but neither stated nor denied that he had included "dead or alive" (*Putusan* 2000, 116–17).[25] He testified to receiving reports that there had been fatalities in the operation to arrest GBPK Bantaqiah because "the situation was extremely critical for the survival of the soldiers and there was no other alternative except to paralyze the enemy to the point that there were fatalities." He noted that women and children were part of Bantaqiah's forces and that Bantaqiah was hysterical and commanded "Attack *Pai*, kill" while attacking the military with a knife. He stated that Bantaqiah's followers were brutal and the arrest team was nearly killed, so there was no alternative (118). Armen confirmed the reports of Bantaqiah's weapons and forces from Kamaruddin, and cited another report suggesting that weapons entering central Aceh would supply Bantaqiah. His comments introduce the note that all security operations in Aceh at that point were under the coordination of the police (120).

As an expert witness, M. Yunus clarified that the operation was done under the umbrella of the national police. He reminded the court that in Aceh "the enemy faced is an armed group (GBPK) who utilize guerilla tactics and the police have not yet mastered the tactics to face the guerillas," so the operations were implemented by the military. He emphasized that the military always sought its own tactical superiority and conducted operations when it was sure to achieve maximum results; the dynamics of the field made it unavoidable that victims would fall. He confirmed that policies were followed in initiating the attack. He argued that the closing group members (indicted numbers 12–25) acted wrongfully in shooting enemies who were not resisting and were restrained, so they must face the applicable laws. His expert opinion was that the telegram[26] from the Danrem Armen ordering the soldiers to arrest Bantaqiah alive or dead did not constitute a justification for killing Bantaqiah and his followers; rather, it anticipated what could happen if there were a struggle that endangered the troops themselves. He noted that the arrest operations had been well prepared and followed normal procedure; however, dynamics in the field resulted in a deviation (*Putusan* 2000, 124).

From the testimony of the many military witnesses, especially the indicted men, several assertions stand out: that Bantaqiah was armed; that he shouted "attack"; and that there was a conversation between Sujono and Bantaqiah, but at such a distance that no witness could hear. The military reported that thirty knives were found along with a camera, passages written from the Koran, a telephone card, and radio antennae, as well as a modified pistol and a Colt pistol with no ammunition. One indicted platoon commander explained that he had not ordered the grenade to be fired, but that it was a "reflex/spontaneous reaction from the one who held the grenade launcher." The soldier who fired the grenade launcher agreed that he did so on his own initiative because he felt threatened.

Bantaqiah's widow did not include the story of the son fetching the walkie-talkie and did not state that Bantaqiah yelled anything. She noted that the men were gathered in the courtyard to surrender their IDs and sharp objects when a TNI yelled "attack" and grenades were launched into the living quarters, followed by shooting. She noted that the survivors were stripped to their underwear, ID cards were burned, and the military ordered them to bury the dead. She said that the injured were loaded on trucks and that they found the corpses seven and eight kilometers from the complex; people from the area brought the corpses back to the complex for burial. She stated that the only evidence taken from the complex was the cable for the walkie-talkie, excluding the notebook, photos, and gun that TNI claimed to have seized. The indicted contended that most of her testimony was not true.

Both of the civilian informers who attended to "show the way" testified. Only one was indicted; the other did not shoot. Number 11, Taleb, explained how he came to take part in the operations: he was introduced

to Sujono by the local intelligence officer Surya, to whom he was introduced by the commander of a lower-level military unit whom he met because he was pursued by Bantaqiah's followers. He said mysteriously
that "there was a meaning that he did not know" (*Putusan* 2000, 153).
Because he was afraid, he was taken to another town to meet with Surya.
He noted that Sujono was picked up by a civilian vehicle on the road
after the remaining wounded were killed.

The Verdict

Based on the evidence, including weapons as well as the statements in
court and during questioning prior to the case, the judges concluded
that the following facts had been established:

1. That it is true that Danrem 011/LW Colonel Syafnil Armen S. Ip. SH. MSC
   on 18 July 1999 has issued spoken orders to Heronimus Guru as DanYon
   328/DGH to attack the GBPK Bantaqiah group and followers in Meurandeh Beutong Ateuk, West Aceh. These orders were issued at the official
   residence of the Danrem 011/LW at night to guard against any leaks;
2. On 19 July 1999 a briefing was done for unit leaders who were involved in
   the planned operation to arrest Tgk. Bantaqiah and his followers in meeting room of Korem 011/LW with the following [names are listed].
3. That it is true that the operations were conducted on July 23, 1999 according to each unit's task that had been arranged in advance;
4. It is true that on 23 July 1999 at approximately 11:30 AM in the household
   complex of Tgk. Bantaqiah in Meurandeh, Beutong Atuek, West Aceh, the
   indicted 1–10 together and individually fired on Bantaqiah and his followers resulting in the death of thirty-one civilians and injuring others because Bantaqiah's followers had already attacked the indicted with knives
   (*rencong, parang*) suddenly and at close proximity, thus, the indicted shot
   them because there was no other way;
5. That it is true that on the orders of Lieutenant Colonel Sujono [Kasie Intel
   Rem 011/LW] indicted 12 through 25 shot wounded victims between
   seven and eight kilometers on the road to Takengon from the school with
   the result that 23 followers of Tgk. Bantaqiah were killed;
6. That Lieutenant Colonel Heronimus Guru then reported to the Danrem
   011/LW that the operation had been done, and that Danrem 011/LW gave
   Heronimus Guru telegram STR No. Str 232A/VII/1999 dated 15 July 1999;
7. That since August 7, 1998 DOM has ended and been replaced by operation *Sadar Rencong II* [Be Aware of the Acehnese knife] under the umbrella
   of the police.
8. That the area of the operations is not the jurisdiction of Korem 011/LW,
   but the area of Korem 012/TU.
9. And, that victims died as listed in the forensic reports attached [Lists numbers of the reports and who performed them]. (*Putusan*, 188–89)

The judges ruled that in order for the indicted to be found guilty of
the primary charge, four requirements had to be met: the act resulting

in the death of another person must be committed by a legal subject, intentionally, and planned in advance. For a case to be heard in a *connexitas* proceeding, it must be demonstrated that the crime was committed by military and civilians acting together.

Regarding the first requirement, the judges found that indicted numbers 1–10 individually and together committed the crime they were accused of. Number 11, the *cu'ak*, was a civilian perpetrator of the crime. Numbers 12–25 perpetrated the crime of killing the wounded on the bridge. So, the *connexitas* requirements were fulfilled. The judges ruled that intentionality was demonstrated for the first group who fired on Bantaqiah and his followers in the complex and for the second group who shot the injured on the road. With regard to advance planning, the second group was following orders issued at the time, not committing a crime planned in advance. The court cited the expert opinion that the telegram ordering the capture of Bantaqiah dead or alive was an appropriate anticipation of conditions that might develop in the field. The attack group explained that they shot because they were threatened and in a critical position. The *cu'ak* also fired because he felt his life was threatened. The judges concluded that the requirement that the killings were planned in advance had not been met. Thus, the judges were unable to convict the defendants on the primary charges. Next they considered the subsidiary charges of the "layered" indictment.

A section of the criminal code stipulates that if a legal subject commits an intentional act resulting in loss of life, both the person who does it and the one who orders him to do it are liable. Having already demonstrated the first two requirements, the court pointed to the ample evidence that lives were lost. The decision then turns to the principle that anyone who committed or ordered the crime is liable. The two groups are again considered separately. The attack group testified that they acted without orders because they felt threatened (1–11, 25); thus, they directly perpetrated the crimes. The judges considered whether they acted in self-defense, invoking a different section of the code (Pasal 49) stating that someone who is attacked cannot be punished. The decision then evaluated whether the indicted had to kill in order to defend themselves from attack. They observed that members of the military were trained in the use of weapons, were armed with automatic weapons (SS-I) when they were attacked, and were already in a formation designed to anticipate the worst conditions, while the attackers were armed only with knives and sharp objects. The judges also noted that the indicted did not fire warning shots or fire to disable rather than kill. Thus, they failed to fulfill the requirements for self-defense. Another section of the code was invoked (Pasal 51) regarding following orders, which stipulates that orders must be issued by rightful power. The decision concluded that Sujono was the overseer of the operation and that he ordered number 12 to have the injured victims killed. Formally, it was legitimate for Sujono to command number 12, who in turn commanded the others. Substantively, however, the decision notes that shooting those who are powerless violates the constitution and therefore no such order can be legitimate. Thus, the indicted do not meet these requirements. The decision states that number 12 had already questioned Sujono about the order.[27] The judges observed that the deeds of the indicted cannot be separated from the commander's telegram, the briefing meetings, and the division of tasks, which indicates that this operation was arranged systematically. The judges remarked that they considered these deeds a crime against humanity, but since they have fulfilled the charges that the prosecutor suggested, nothing else can be considered. Thus, the judges concluded that the lack of regret demonstrated by the accused as well as the fact that they fired on the victims with un-equal weapons worked against them; on the other hand, the fact that this was the first time that they had been sentenced and their youth was in their favor. The court ruled that all of the indicted were not guilty of the primary charge of individually and collectively following or acting with Lieutenant Colonel Sujono in the premeditated murder of Teungku Bantaqiah. They were all convicted of the secondary charge of individually and collectively committing murder. Indicted numbers 1 through 11 were sentenced to eight and a half years, num-bers 12 through 24 were sentenced to nine years and number 25 was sentenced to ten years. They were transported to Jakarta to serve their sentences. In a final irony, a large amount of dried marijuana was dis-covered with them, reportedly to be sold in Jakarta.

The testimony to the Independent Commission from Major Asro articulated the military's deep anxiety and inflated estimate of their perceived enemies' power. Media reports, international conspiracies, and the inability to control information created these anxieties. Major Asro accused the investigative team of looking only at a small slice of what had happened in the region and making things difficult by spread-ing rumors and misinformation to the press.[28] In response to a question regarding written orders and accountability for the detailed planning of the Bantaqiah operation, Asro explained what conditions in Aceh were like:

At this time we are facing many problems in eradicating GAM. Of the sixty-nine operations that have been undertaken, almost all of them were leaked. It is as if we are now facing a technology war. They already have a filter that is more so-phisticated [than ours] and imported. Second, if we change frequencies, we can communicate with them. So, here it has already occurred as an electronic war. They use code names [that change] from one second to another. Third from the arrests which we have made, we always get more than 500,000 Rupiah in cash, from people who don't have shoes. (Independent Commission, 1999)[29]

He described GAM's control of resources in the area. GAM acknowledged the overlap in communications technology and reported that they frequently escaped operations because information had been leaked, or they had overheard plans on the radio. Although no one offered this observation, perhaps the military was as likely to learn GAM's strategic secrets. Acehnese print media noted that the killings took place at the time when there was an effort to conduct a dialogue in Bangkok with Acehnese representatives and exiled leader Hasan Tiro ("Bantaqiah Sengaja Dihabisi? Tragedi Beutong *Target* Siapa?" *Kontras*, 4 August 1999). The prospect of international negotiations with separatist rebels made the military and some nationalist politicians anxious.

In conclusion, the investigative team advocated eradicating what it termed the "dark pattern"; accusations that the military was behind the violence left it unclear whether "ex-military," "deserters," or active military were involved.[30] The Independent Commission recommended that a trial bring those involved to justice so that the state apparatus would gain credibility among the people.

The failure of this case demonstrated the profound lack of political will among military and civilian elites to establish legal supremacy and accountability for past state violence. None of the other five cases investigated by the Presidential Commission has been brought to court. Human rights defenders have struggled to enact legislation that would authorize them to create ad hoc tribunals for investigating gross violations of human rights. The constitutional amendment on human rights, passed in September 1999, prohibited any retroactive legal action as a standard universal human right, but not without provoking suspicions from some Indonesians that the military had engineered this point to avoid being held accountable for past human rights violations. Legally, the only law not retroactively applied was the criminal code, which does not specify crimes of commission or omission. Following the Bantaqiah trial, no one I spoke with expressed any hope that the Indonesian legal system could provide justice. There were various expectations of what an international tribunal, inquiry, or other intervention might provide. A session of the national Parliament (Pansus Aceh) in which prominent generals were called to account for the abuses during DOM indicated to many Acehnese that national political institutions also lacked the desire or capacity to provide justice.

Referendum

How was the campaign for Referendum connected with the issue of justice? Repeated injustice and Jakarta's disregard for Aceh as an important part of the nation was demonstrated by the center's violent excess, economic exploitation, and failed promises to the province. When Indonesian judicial institutions failed, advocates searched for other means of redress. Efforts at economic compensation did not suffice. In November 1998, victims and NGOs demanded that the rule of law be upheld and justice be served: "the suffering experienced by the people of Aceh must be immediately and exhaustively treated" ("Dialog Mensos dengan Korban DOM: Perhatikan Kami, Tegakkan Hukum," *Kompas*, 7 November 1998). The proposed autonomy and revenue sharing programs were not enough.

As Referendum converted violence and suffering into the right of self-determination, the campaign refigured Acehnese identity, both consolidating and dividing the people in whose name it was demanded. The next chapter extends the discussion of how the Referendum movement as an explicitly and adamantly nonviolent movement based in civil society may, ironically, have reduced the political role of Acehnese civil society in negotiating a resolution to the crisis and, in the eyes of some, increased violence and made justice impossible. Here I examine how the failure of justice institutions fueled the demand for Referendum without effectively addressing the matter of violence.

Most chronologies of Referendum begin with the Congress of Acehnese Students and Youth from All Over held in February 1999. A month earlier, students from Aceh declared at a press conference in Jakarta that "the cases of violations during DOM must immediately be resolved by the central government. If these cases cannot be resolved before the election, then students, youth and the people of Aceh are going to boycott the national elections and demand a referendum" ("'Operasi Wibawa 99' Tangkap 38 Pengikut Ahmad Kandang," *Suara Pembaruan*, 10 January 1999). The congress was held just a week after President Habibie had announced that there would be a referendum with the options of autonomy and separation to resolve the East Timor problem.[31] This conference established SIRA, the Central Information Committee for Referendum Aceh, the organization that coordinated the campaign. Participants expressed the desire to "free themselves (*melepaskan diri*) from the Unitary Republic of Indonesia in a peaceful way through a Referendum" ("Relakan Aceh Merdeka," *Serambi Indonesia*, 3 February 1999). At this point, the word merdeka, independence, used by the armed separatist movement was first joined to the civil society coalition. Because Referendum was initially designed as a threat, it is likely that the word *merdeka* was chosen both to attach this campaign to the legacy of Aceh Merdeka and to appropriate the terms, language, and symbolism of the Indonesian Revolution, which would express the feeling of grievance that everything Aceh had done for the nation had been disregarded.

The statement issued by the congress began: "The government in Jakarta for this long has never wanted to hear the genuine voice and screams of the oppressed Acehnese people, despite the extremely great contributions which have been given by Aceh to the country since the time of colonialism in resisting the Dutch until the present." Cases of human rights violations during DOM had never been thoroughly investigated by the government. "Thousands of lives . . . have already flown without accountability" because powerful elites, both in Jakarta and in Aceh, "did not want to know about these events" ("Relakan Aceh Merdeka," *Serambi Indonesia*, 3 February 1999).

Some commentators in Jakarta acknowledged the role of the center in Acehnese dissatisfaction. One national newspaper posed the question: "Acehnese people were an integral part of the struggle to found the united Republic of Indonesia. But, after the country has been redeemed with the blood of founding heroes, why does a group of young Acehnese struggle to separate themselves?" The newspaper's answer pointed to the New Order predilection for violence: "The New Order never responded thoroughly and honestly to the desire of the Acehnese people. What the people of Aceh desired was justice. But we answered them with rifles" ("Aceh Butuh Keadilan," *Media Indonesia*, 5 January 1999).

In early 1999, justice seemed impossible to attain. Initial demands for justice might have been fulfilled by something less than Referendum or independence, but the failure of the center to hold high-ranking military accountable made Referendum the only possible route toward justice. It is not often recalled that amid the calls for Referendum in January 1999, a smaller demonstration met with President Habibie to express the continuing loyalty of the Acehnese people to the Republic, provided that there was an immediate investigation of human rights violations; a grant of broad autonomy, including an 80 percent share of Aceh's resource wealth to be controlled by Aceh; and consideration of the problem of Islamic law ("Pemerintah Didesak Usut Pelanggar HAM di Aceh," *Kompas*, 9 January 1999). While the meeting was going on, several students demonstrating outside were severely beaten by the security forces ("Habibie Datang, Aceh Bergolak," *Rakyat Merdeka*, 27 March 1999). The precedent of East Timor and the international support it received made a referendum seem a viable option. Referendum became an idea around which much frustration and many interests coalesced.

The presence of international observers in Aceh and Indonesia to monitor Indonesia's first post-authoritarian elections in June 1999 raised anxieties in Jakarta and hopes in Aceh. Students threatened to boycott Indonesian elections in favor of a referendum if there were no justice ("Rakyat Aceh Minta Secepatnya Ekses DOM Diselesaikan," *Suara Pembaruan*, 23 February 1999).

Elections had been a site of political contest in Aceh throughout the New Order. Abuses inflicted by the central government peaked around the elections, which occurred every five years. In contrast to the rest of Indonesia, where most protest was registered by voting "white group," not simply boycotting the election but also turning in blank or damaged ballots, in Aceh dissatisfaction was not always articulated through the boycott. Voters in Aceh supported PPP, the officially sanctioned Islamic party, and suffered serious reprisals. The partial boycott in 1999 was enforced more through intimidation and violence than through civil disobedience. One person I interviewed told me that the violence in Aceh during DOM could be correlated with the "election season" and "around the time of elections GAM is always a problem." In a deliberately ambiguous construction, he implied that GAM existed, but only sporadically, and that its appearance coincided with state violence. Aguswandi, a student leader, stated in a national daily that morally the elections were already handicapped, especially because of the *provokator* ("Pemilu di Aceh Harus Diboikot," *Media Indonesia*, 16 March 1999). National elections were heavily burdened by their historical legacies and the violence that continued to surround them (Aspinal, Drexler, and Johanson 1999).

By April 1999 the Referendum campaign had taken full force, and election preparations had been disrupted by mysterious killings, intimidation, destruction of polling places, and threats intended to prevent people from voting. Mysterious forces perpetrated the violence. In the midst of what was described as "referendum fever," one person observed: "Aceh is now more and more difficult. How will referendum be achieved if the election is rejected? The problem is who will advocate/struggle for the request of referendum later in the People's Consultative Assembly?" (Indonesia's supreme legislative institution, the MPR) ("Aceh Tambah Runyam," *Sinar Pagi*, 26 April 1999). Conditions in Aceh resulted in an unrepresentative ballot. Most Acehnese did not vote. The uncompromising stance required by Referendum as a threat and ultimately nonnegotiable demand foreclosed many options of participation in discussions and processes that subsequently had consequences for Aceh, especially the implementation of Islamic Law and Special Regional Legislation. Referendum had a specificity that other election boycotting strategies did not. Based on the precedent set by

Habibie's granting of a referendum to East Timor, the campaign assumed that the central government would agree to a peaceful and democratic resolution to the violence for which it had long been responsible.[32]

On 8 November 1999, an estimated one million people gathered in Banda Aceh to show their support for a referendum ("Sejuta Orang Turun ke Banda Aceh," *Suara Pembaruan*, 8 November 1999, 1). This massive demonstration was not attended by any violent incidents; it was simply an assembly of "the people" in whose name Referendum was demanded. Previously unknown figures emerged as orators demanding justice in the form of Referendum. Leaders issued rhetorical denials that this demand posed any threat to the nation. The head of SIRA, Muhammad Nazar, affirmed: "I challenge any theory or any opinion which says that this referendum is separatist" ("Presiden KH Abdurrahman Wahid: Aceh Takkan Lepas Dari RI,"*Kompas*, 9 November 1999). Other regional government figures expressed their support for Aceh to "determine its own fate."[33] Cut Nur Asikin spoke about the injustices of Indonesia toward Aceh.[34] The logistics of managing food, shelter, and facilities for so many people were coordinated efficiently; people brought with them stoves, pans, blankets, mats, food, and whatever else they might need.

Following this massive expression of popular support, everyone, including the Acehnese governor who had repeatedly refused to support the demand, endorsed Referendum. Many of the people I spoke with indicated that there must be a referendum now. They acknowledged that the demand had a logic and momentum of its own; it became a *harga mati*, literally a fixed price beyond which there could be no further bargaining, an unconditional and nonnegotiable matter. Many people admitted to me that they would not vote for independence and hoped that others would not either. At this stage, it seemed that Referendum would be an opportunity to decide, not a foregone conclusion.

After Referendum became a force to be reckoned with, the rhetoric of SIRA, GAM, and the TNI shifted. Reflecting on the 8 November "march," the regional military commander suggested that the peaceful character of the event was evidence of the ability of the TNI and SIRA to work together: "Even though there were so many people who attended, because we have built a good cooperation between the security apparatus and SIRA, who reported the event to the TNI in advance to coordinate security, it went safely and orderly" (Syarifudin Tippe, quoted in "Tiga Menteri Didaulat Serukan Referendum," *Suara Pembaruan*, 15 November 1999). Other military officials suggested that if there were to be a referendum, it would have to be conducted throughout Indonesia.[35] Some people I talked with in Jakarta at this time, while angry about East Timor's departure, were sympathetic to Aceh and suggested that if there had been that much injustice maybe they should leave the nation.

Following President Wahid's efforts to offer a referendum without the option of independence, for instance on the issue of implementing Islamic law, SIRA's rhetoric shifted and, as many people noted, the drive became "Independence via Referendum." Simultaneously, many reported feeling pressured to advocate *merdeka*, independence, instead of Referendum. SIRA president Nazar, responding to a reporter's question regarding the resolution of human rights violations, which was now the priority of Wahid's government, said: "Now the trials of human rights violations can no longer resolve the Aceh problem. Because of that the most important is a political resolution, which will be communicated through a referendum" ("Tanpa Opsi Merdeka. Tawaran Gus Dur Ditolak," *Serambi Indonesia*, 11 October 1999). Since Wahid reneged on his widely publicized statement that if Timor could have a referendum, so could Aceh, which most people interpreted as implying independence, the president's promises to pursue justice were regarded as empty and certainly not giving up the powerful bargaining position the Referendum movement had gained by its massive show of force in the march. The rapid shift in rhetoric of spokespeople does not indicate that popular support for Referendum was always veiled support for independence or that anything short of independence could not have resolved the problem. Nonetheless, the conviction that only a referendum could address Aceh's relationship with Indonesia became a self-fulfilling prophecy. The special regional legislation for Aceh was passed in 2001, but Acehnese civil society was not involved in designing the legislation.[36] For the most part, civil society organizations abstained from the Indonesian political process and devoted their energies to the Referendum campaigning.

While Referendum initially promised an alternative to the "hard attitudes" of GAM and Jakarta, it became a synonym for GAM's demand and Jakarta's rejection of independence, and justice was lost from the equation. Early in the campaign, some reformers in Jakarta were careful to distinguish Referendum from separatism in Aceh. Following the 1999 elections, several Jakarta NGOs came together to advocate that the Aceh problem be redefined not as a problem of separatism or fundamentalism but as a problem of justice: "Aceh is a symbol of strong resistance of the people against injustice which has been done by the nation and violent acts which have been done by the military to the people" ("Kasus Aceh, Simbol Resistensi Atas Kekerasan," *Kompas*, 17 June 1999). Echoes of separatist ghosts and suspicions of the legendary bravery of the Acehnese rendered it impossible for statements such as this to be heard. While the exposure of once-unspeakable violence and victimization may initially have provided evidence of the need for justice, the lack of justice, the constant reiteration of stories of human rights violations, and the frequent repetition of acts of violence transformed this into a matter of honor and dignity. The New Order logic of imagined enemies relied on threats of vengeance to justify repression. Long-cultivated anxieties about vengeance and latent dangers within the nation were triggered by Acehnese demands for justice. Justice itself became ensnared in the logic of vengeance. The denial of justice in the face of overwhelming evidence of wrongdoing convinced most Acehnese that dignity and honor were at stake. Their demand that wrongs be avenged only confirmed the center's anxiety.

Calculating Compensation

Discussions of justice initially focused primarily on the need for economic redistribution and on trials in which high-ranking military would be held accountable for DOM violence. During the first month after the end of DOM, demands from Aceh toward the center were often cast in terms of a more equitable distribution of the profits from the exploitation of the province's natural resources ("Aceh Bisa Peroleh Dana Rp. 22 Trilyun,"*Kompas*, 18 September 1998). Minister of Law and Legal Institutions Yusril Mahendra[37] equated the demands for justice with demands for an equal economic share. In opposing demands for federalism and human rights trials, he stated: "I see that what is desired by the people of Aceh is justice between the division of money for the center and regions" ("Aceh Butuh Keadilan Bukan Negara Federal," *Republika*, 8 February 1999). The Minister for Woman's Empowerment took the opposite view after a visit to Aceh: "Maybe if I had experienced the oppression that the Acehnese people have, I would do the same thing [advocate for a Referendum]. Even worms writhe if they are stepped on. I am certain that if the people of Aceh are offered money or dignity, they certainly will choose dignity" (Khofifah Indar Parawansa, quoted in "Gus Dur Akan Diterima di Aceh,"*Kompas*, 14 November 1999). Despite her unflattering metaphor, she correctly judged that the Acehnese people would choose dignity.

The governor of Aceh, Syamsuddin Mahmud, located injustice in the inequitable distribution of natural resource wealth between the center and the region, which had "wounded the hearts of the Acehnese people." In discussing Aceh's special status, he said: "The specialness which has been granted did not give the region the space to handle its own affairs. In fact, just the opposite, it gave freedom to the central government during the New Order to use the natural wealth of Aceh in a one-sided and unfair manner" ("Gubernur di Depan Mahasiswa dan Pemuda Aceh: Ketidakadilan Pusat Melukai Rakyat Aceh," *Serambi Indonesia*, 1 February 1999). In these discussions, the governor always stressed that Aceh should remain a part of Indonesia with wider autonomy, or in a federal state.

Older members of the political elite, who spoke forcefully in the name of an "Acehnese people" that had been degraded and humiliated by DOM, focused on justice as well as the demand for an equitable division of natural resource profits. Most agreed that there had been financial injustice, but many regarded financial compensation as insufficient in principle. In my interviews with members of the Acehnese political elite, both in Aceh and Jakarta, the injustice of Aceh's lack of economic development was always emphasized. The rhetoric they invoked to describe their indignation at the economic disparity (which they themselves had not often suffered), such as not having electricity in an area that was producing a majority of the nation's natural gas, was reminiscent of the security forces' description of the "social gap" that had occurred in the early 1980s as the Lhokseumawe Industrial Zone was being developed.[38] A cynical analysis is that the political elite preferred to discuss economic injustice because they would benefit directly as bureaucrats in a more autonomous system if they could establish their credibility by demanding justice for Aceh. However, as all forms of justice remained unattained, their positions shifted as well. An alternative analysis underlines their politically savvy understanding of the importance of the immediate, concrete, and symbolic concession from the center that economic compensation could provide while more abstract kinds of justice were sought. They advised the state to buy time and credibility until the military could be held accountable.

The problem of resource exploitation enabled by stability, secured through violence, and producing underdevelopment was the foundation of many analyses of the situation in Aceh. In his pioneering study of Acehnese rebellion against Soeharto's New Order, Tim Kell emphasized the prominence of economic grievances in local discourses of dissatisfaction (1995). Some Acehnese I spoke with pointed out that Hasan Tiro's initial grievances were economic. University professors arrested and ultimately tried as GAM recalled early discussions highlighting the problems of New Order development.[39] Promises of wealth gained from local control of natural resources were part of GAM's platform for recruiting support in the post-DOM period.[40]

In the lives of the ordinary Acehnese who had been disproportionately victimized by DOM violence, economic parity paled in comparison to other, more basic issues. The DOM victims with whom I spoke in Lhokseumawe and surrounding villages were euphoric that DOM had ended. Their demands were simple: they wanted to return to a normal life, health care, and education for their children. The fairness they sought could be found in the rehabilitation of their names and an end to their social isolation, a matter as much of national policy as of local reconciliation. At the disco that was burned in the riots that followed the end of DOM, most of the people I spoke with proudly told me they were "DOM victims" (*korban DOM*). They were no longer running from the label of GPK/GAM; they had been victimized, but they were no longer stigmatized.

In a long conversation in a remote village, a woman whose brother had been accused as GAM, abducted, and disappeared explained in a matter-of-fact tone the various maladies she suffered as a result of this trauma. Her sleep was often disturbed by visions of the abduction; she suffered a deep chest cough that often produced blood; her son had been forced to stop attending school because he was stigmatized by alleged association with GPK and had trouble socializing with other children. The woman seemed most emotionally committed to convincing me that neither she nor any member of her family had any tie to the rebels. When I asked her what she wanted now, her answer was simple: she needed medicine and a doctor to resolve her cough. She wanted to be free of the fear that every knock on the door meant someone was coming to turn everything upside down and threaten her. Her child would like to return to school and not be ostracized.

Analyses of the Aceh conflict that focus entirely on the economic aspects of the inequity, or that emphasize economic opportunism to the exclusion of genuine grievance, fail to address the complex conjunction of economic and political issues in New Order legacies. Economic inequity fueled demands for justice and constituted another form of injustice alongside the state violence documented, exposed, and circulated by NGOs and the media. It is impossible to ascertain whether the swift implementation of economic redistribution and compensation would have altered the development of this conflict. At the ending of DOM, the victims I spoke with wanted not independence, but justice and compensation. Jakarta's promises of economic redistribution and political-legal accountability for the violence proved empty. When injustice is cast as incalculable human suffering, justice figured in terms of economic wealth is not commensurate with the moral outrage of those who felt victimized as Acehnese. The central government can recognize gross economic exploitation more easily than the human rights violations that were deemed necessary to secure stability for resource extraction.

Security Forces Discourse on Excess and Justice

Military spokesmen commented on the issue of excess and injustice by pointing to the central government's mismanagement of economic development. The demand for justice figured in the security forces' discourse only as a force for independence that recreated the threat which originally produced the excesses of which the Acehnese complained. The military pointed to the civilian government's responsibility to divide natural resource wealth more equitably. On the eve of the national election, after Referendum had become a visible demand and violence and instability had increased through the figures of the *provokator* and "unknown persons," national media interviewed one regional military commander, Johny Wahab.[41]

Interviewer: "Which is greater, the desire for *merdeka* (independence) or the demand for the feeling of justice"?
Wahab replies: "Actually the people of Aceh are now already independent (*merdeka*). But they see much that is not just. Then they want to be *merdeka* again. They see the situation now as not yet *merdeka*."

The interviewer asks: what is the best solution to "fulfill the feeling of justice for people there?" Wahab responds: "I feel that the government has already made great efforts on this issue by drafting laws for economic balance between the center and the regions. So there is a distribution of profits between the center and region that is just" ("Rakyat Aceh Diajak ke Jalan yang Salah Oleh kelompok GAM," *Media Indonesia*, 7 June 1999). In Wahab's analysis, economic redistribution would suffice. National military spokesmen, in contrast, resisted any formulation in which the situation would be resolved by the economic legislation under consideration. They expressed anxiety that "the problem is no longer a demand for economic equality between the center and the region" ("TNI Kirim Pasukan Antirusuh ke Aceh," *Republika*, 7 May 1999). This formulation renewed the threat and danger for the future and obscured the initial injustice of military violence.

Unlike many other articles in which the military analysis of economic injustice remained unquestioned, the interviewer reminded Wahab of another kind of injustice: "what about the demands for justice from the victims of DOM which have not yet been fulfilled?" Wahab defended the government: "The efforts of the government, I see, are continuously done, but that still has not satisfied the Acehnese people. I think that if we demand justice continually, it will never be resolved" ("Rakyat Aceh Diajak ke Jalan yang Salah Oleh kelompok GAM," *Media Indonesia*, 7 June 1999). In the security forces' discourse, justice was often seen as a kind of vengeance.

At this point, the central government efforts had been limited to discussions of economic policy and "cultural" issues such as Islamic law. Komnas HAM had made investigative trips and NGOs had made statements, but there had been no concrete demonstration of a commitment to justice or to addressing human rights violations. Amid the intensification of indeterminate violence, Wahab challenged those who sought justice:

> if there truly is strong evidence/proof please go ahead. For example there is someone who has been raped, who is the rapist? I think that now the government is open, so if there really is proof, please report to the military police (POM ABRI, now TNI) about the deeds of the TNI members who were naughty so that they can be processed through the courts and punished. ("Rakyat Aceh Diajak ke Jalan yang Salah Oleh kelompok GAM," *Media Indonesia*, 7 June 1999)

Of the cases investigated by the presidential decree team, even a rape with DNA evidence has not resulted in legal action. Rape victims often reported that they had been harassed by the authorities to whom they sought to give evidence. Selecting the example of rape, Wahab dismissed all the crimes as the work of individual naughty boys, not a systematic plan. What constituted proof varied, depending on the person's proximity to power. In the Bantaqiah case, the security forces justified acting on rumors and misinformation from informers and reports extracted under torture, while the testimonies of victims only authorized further intimidation in a context where there was no witness protection. In such conditions, Wahab can be certain that the "evidence" will seldom be strong enough for legal action.

Colonel Syarafuddin Tippe, called the TNI's modern-day Snouck Hurgronje by many Acehnese, provided the most sustained analysis of the conflict in Aceh from an active military position. In his book *Aceh di Persimpangan Jalan (Aceh at the Crossroads),* Tippe refuted theories that popular support for Aceh's independence was based on history, distinguishing it from the Timor case, and suggested a different narrative for the excess and injustice that was damaging the military's image. In discussing the problem of injustice as the root of the movement to separate via referendum, Tippe emphasized intellectuals' criticism, not popular anger. For him the problem began with a meeting of Acehnese leaders, intellectuals, and other important political figures at the regional parliament (DPRD):

> Since that meeting the analysis of whether or not Aceh still needed to be in the frame of the republic became very critical. . . . The form of the Republic of Indonesia's betrayal that started with this sort of analysis included almost every issue, in the fields of economy, politics, government, as well as the treatment of Aceh as a DOM. . . . [In terms of economics] Aceh is likened to a candle. Itself

burned and finished off for the light of another. . . . [In terms of government]
the attitude of the government that is repressive and does not try to understand
the will of the people created DOM to end the reactions of dissatisfaction which
began to arise formally when Teungku Muhammad Hasan Tiro proclaimed
Aceh Merdeka. Thousands of lives have already been lost and this group sees
that there has not yet been a good faith/ethical effort from the government to
resolve these cases which have created a very deep wound. (2000, 35)

Locating the demand for injustice with intellectuals and not the people
repeats a New Order pattern of looking for the "mastermind" behind
popular actions. The demands of a small group of intellectuals were the
basis for Hasan Tiro's original 1976 declaration of Aceh Merdeka.
Tippe's retrospective account, written in 2000, may be influenced by
the recollection of that history. At this time, the military used popular
anger and dissatisfaction to argue that all Acehnese were separatists.
But this sentiment does not indicate that the 1976 movement had such
widespread, even if latent, support. The interaction of mass anger and
intellectual criticism was a recurrent theme in discourses that distinguished so-called rational and irrational demands for justice.

Tippe attempted to counter the historical arguments that were often
made in the media and by many Acehnese in order to underline the
main distinction between East Timor and Aceh. In Aceh, he argued,
dissatisfaction with the central government was the primary problem.
He cited the senior intellectuals' opinion as more realistic, that "Aceh
wants to free itself from the frame of NKRI [Unitary State of the Republic of Indonesia] because of mistreatment with all its consequences"
(2000, 39). Like Wahab, he located blame and lack of credibility with
the central government, which he distinguished from the military. Unlike Wahab, however, he was extremely critical of the central government. He wrote that, in the context of government mistreatment, "the
spirit of separatism seems to be more of a seed that is sown by the government itself aware or unaware." What it would mean for issues of resolution and accountability that the government had sown seeds with
possible awareness was not discussed; Tippe does not consider whether
the government might have been aware that it was sowing the seeds of
discontent or the ways in which it might have done so.

Tippe based his argument on the comment of university chancellor
Dayan Dawood that in "reality the referendum is a last resort if it really
appears that the center will do nothing." According to Tippe, Dawood
located the crisis of confidence in the central government, "which
[did] not seem to be serious about understanding the people's aspirations, especially regarding the excesses of DOM" (2000, 35).[42] Rather
than read this as a counterargument to the idea that the people were
all separatists and as an opening for resolution, Tippe recast the desire

for Referendum as irrational vengeance. Entirely absent from Tippe's discussion was the role of the military in committing the excesses that the government mishandled. The excesses were so visible that he had to address them in some way, so Tippe analyzed Referendum as an expression of resentment and an act of revenge:

In another language, the attitude of Acehnese who want a referendum is an act of pouting because they are resentful (*sakit hati*) that the central government is not serious about Aceh. This pouting attitude often is also a result of the sting to their self-respect because of unjust treatment, which was humiliating, or disregard, which pushes the opposite reaction to avenge their resentment. If it is already like this, the dominant factor will be actions that are not suspected, and in fact which are completely irrational. (2000, 36)

This passage begins by positing the conflict as a logical outcome of the mistreatment of the Acehnese by the civilian government, but then introduces the aspect of irrationality. To recast intellectuals' criticisms as mere pouting characterized the Acehnese as irrational, and their criticisms, not as balanced or just, but as pure emotion, rebellion for the sake of rebellion.[43] Victims' accounts attested that the treatment they received was unjust and humiliating, but their anger and resentment was directed toward the security forces and the military, which they held responsible. The central government was held accountable for the economic injustice. Tippe cleverly condensed the issues of economic and political justice to suit the interests of the military by pointing to others who should be held accountable.

The military's actions in Aceh, both in the past and the post-DOM period following Wiranto's unfulfilled promise that the national security forces would be removed from the region, were always cast in terms of the "sacred duty of the TNI to defend the Unitary Republic of Indonesia" ("Aparat Keamanan di Aceh Diminta Proaktif," *Media Indonesia*, 22 June 1999).[44] Military efforts to suggest that they were carrying out the government's instructions are ironic in view of the discursive and legal struggle over the chain of command. In most discussions, including Wiranto's apology, the excesses were attributed not to a systematic military policy but to the excess or "emotion" of individual agents or deserters of the military. Tippe's references to the government implied a certain chain of command at the same time that it avoided acknowledging military responsibility. If the military were to hold the civilian government accountable, surely it would have to expose the long chain of command between those whose hands were dirtied in the actual acts of violence up through the hierarchy to those high-ranking officers who interact with the government. In Tippe's detached and often accurate assessment of the political mood in Aceh, the military's historical role of implementing the violence disappears.

Exposure did not include the acknowledgement or redress of injustice that investigators had imagined it would. The occurrence of abuses during DOM has not often been denied, but reiteration of this fact has provided no resolution. The acknowledgment of mistreatment offered by Tippe's narrative was not a step towards acknowledgement, justice, and accountability; instead, the idea of injustice was deployed to portray Acehnese as pouting children. In other discussions, too, security forces categorized the Acehnese as irrational. Letjen Agum Gumelar affirmed that the demands for "justice, strengthening human rights and the desire for economic parity are rational" but pronounced the goal of Aceh Merdeka irrational ("Dibentuk, Tim Independen Tuntaskan Kasus Aceh: Teliti Pelanggaran HAM di Era Reformasi," *Republika*, 3 July 1999).

Converting the desire for redress into an irrational demand created a new narrative of separatism that, coupled with conditions of increasing violence attributed to the *provokator*, generated new rationalizations for military repression. Wiranto acknowledged that the Aceh problem was not "just a simple problem of security," but also included economic, political, social, and cultural matters. Accordingly, he argued, the Aceh problem would require a comprehensive solution. But security came first, as "we are facing an armed resistance and struggle for independence which we cannot tolerate." Wiranto observed that conditions in Aceh had become more complicated, perhaps indicating the various armed forces at work, since the withdrawal of troops. He divided Acehnese demands into two categories, rational and irrational: "The realistic raise problems of autonomy, economy, and culture, including religion. That can be handled well by dialogue through the regional government [DPRD]." He noted that "There have also been commitments to guarantee demands for economic parity between the center and region." The demand for independence was unrealistic, Wiranto contended: "There cannot be any thoughts such as this in the Republic of Indonesia. . . . The demand for Aceh Merdeka cannot be tolerated and cannot be communicated because it is non-negotiable (*harga mati*)" ("Wiranto Tentang Aceh: Tuntutan Merdeka Tak Realistis,"*Kompas*, 13 August 1999). This characterization of the Referendum was consistent with SIRA's statements. The lack of justice, in both economic equity and accountability for state violence and human rights abuses, was consistently seen as fueling the drive for Referendum.

Since the state was unable to provide justice through law and lacked credibility in implementing any promises, the only possibilities were, in SIRA's rhetoric, Referendum, or, in GAM's rhetoric, independence.

The security forces contributed to making these threats real by converting bluffs into nonnegotiable realities. Wiranto's statements re-creating the victims of injustice as dangerous, subversive threats to the state were enabled by the conversion of unresolved human rights violations into self-determination by armed or legal means. The role of the actual violence in threatening the nation was obscured by these military analyses, which suggested it was unrealistic to struggle with the excess of historic grievance.

Another example illustrates the conflation of economic redistribution and retributive justice in which the dignity of Aceh was at stake. In an interview, retired Lieutenant General Mochamad Jasin considered the matter historically:

> I worry that they are going to carry on their guerilla tactics for years to come. If it is like that, the problem can never end. Just look, Tgk. Daud Beureueh was a guerilla for eight years. Why is Aceh with so many contributions always neglected with promises made in vain? And GAM now, if they become big, there is no possibility that the guerillas can be crushed. ("Wawancara Khusus Letjen (Purn) Mochamad Jasin, Kalau Dikerasi, Orang Aceh Tambah Keras," *Media Indonesia*, 29 August 1999)

Just as the Acehnese drew on history to back their demands, the military used the same history to project armed struggle into the future to justify continued vigilance.

When the interviewer asked, "If the perpetrators of DOM were tried, wouldn't the uprising settle down?" Jasin replied, "No. The reason is that their goal is still independence (*merdeka*). But as someone who has experienced the period of struggle [national liberation], I do not agree with Aceh becoming independent. Do we want to become like Yugoslavia which is destroyed?" He points to the solution in a fairer distribution of resource wealth, 70 percent to Aceh and 30 percent to Jakarta ("Kalau Dikerasi, Orang Aceh Tambah Keras," *Media Indonesia*, 29 August 1999). In the context of criminality and extortion that pervade Aceh, any increased revenue would likely increase the amount of arms circulating in the province. Efforts to demilitarize Aceh have been striking by their absence.[45]

Implementation of Islamic Law (*Syariah*)

During Habibie's efforts to resolve the Aceh problem, most reformers in Jakarta agreed that Islamic law should be instituted in Aceh.[46] In the media and in parliamentary discussions, advocates pointed out that this promise made by Soekarno to Daud Beureueh remained unfulfilled.[47] Enacting Islamic law, *syariah or syariat* in Indonesian and Acehnese, they argued, would restore Acehnese faith in the central government.[48] The other popular justification for enacting Islamic law was to force GAM into a corner, implying that the various GAMs would have to follow Islamic behavior and conduct a moral struggle; if they did not follow Islamic law, the Acehnese would no longer be behind them ("RUU Pelaksanaan Keistimewaan. 80 Persen Hasil Gas Alam untuk Aceh," *Kompas*, 8 September 1999).[49] This argument echoed the underlying strategy of separating GAM from the people. At the time, NGO activists in Aceh, including legal aid groups, were opposed to Islamic law, and a coalition of women's groups worried that *Syariah* would disproportionately be applied to restrict women's activities.[50] Amid the voices of agreement and praise for the enactment of Islamic law in Aceh, the military representatives cautioned that civil law would still be required. The police in Aceh praised the decision noting that it would reduce sinful behavior (*maksiat*), such as drinking and gambling ("Selangkah Lagi Syariat Islam Berlaku di Aceh," *Republika*, 23 September 1999).[51] The Acehnese I interviewed, however, were troubled not by *maksiat* but by state violence.

Most people I spoke with were not opposed to the implementation of Islamic law. They always opened their comments by saying, "As a Muslim, I am very happy there will be Islamic law," but then explained that this would not solve the problem. The women's groups that criticized the initiative were intimidated and harassed. As some critics feared, the lack of formal mechanism and clear, coherent policy on Islamic law meant that Islam could be politicized as it was in many other areas of Indonesia and used as an excuse to "play judge oneself" or to justify vigilantism and offer a new narrative for violence occurring "horizontally" between individuals ("Presiden Gus Dur, Syariat Islam & Aceh," *Sinar Pagi*, 18 December 2000).

Acehnese intellectuals were also opposed to the implementation of *Syariah* law, not because of the practical problems of implementing punishments but because the necessary reeducation and resocialization would be expensive and, at the time that *Syariah* was passed, the center had made no commitment to economic autonomy for Aceh ("RUU Keistimewaan Dinilai Aceh Tidak Aspiratif," *Media Indonesia*, 24 September 1999). Despite worries about corrupt civil servants having their hands cut off and other theoretical dilemmas associated with Islamic law that were often used as illustrative points in arguments concerning the practice, in reality the application of Islamic law initially was—as women's rights activists feared—disproportionately applied to the matter of women, especially police and civil servants, wearing head scarves. Many Acehnese pointed out to me that historically Acehnese women did not wear headscarves; this practice was a more recent phenomenon due to a national resurgence in Islamic identity.

The formal institutionalization of Islamic law in Aceh was performed by Gus Dur and witnessed by other Islamic nations' representatives on the date claimed as GAM's anniversary, 4 December 2000, commemorating Hasan Tiro's declaration of Aceh Merdeka twenty-four years earlier. Many people worried that the implementation of *Syariah* would reinforce the perception that the Acehnese were fanatic Muslims, simultaneously making them less likely to get support in their claims against Indonesia from Western democracies and reducing the likelihood that they would be supported by Islamic countries on the grounds that their Islamic beliefs were marginalized by Indonesia. Many people worried, in the context of the "War on Terror," it could stigmatize them as "fundamentalist" Muslim rebels and terrorists. The radical Muslim fighters who launched campaigns for Muslims in Maluku never defended Acehnese Muslims against state-sponsored violence.[52] Some Acehnese felt that it was presumptuous and insulting of the center to give them the right to practice Islamic law when it was already the basis of culture and daily interaction. Acehnese clerics and intellectuals were offended when a young Muslim scholar from Java, Eep, was sent to prepare people for the implementation of Islamic law. Other people felt that the center granted them the right to institute Islamic law only to reduce their historical superiority in matters of religion; although this step should have been a victory for their cultural identity, it actually represented a reduction of it.

The discussions and commentary surrounding the implementation of Islamic law demonstrated that at the same time that a historical grievance was addressed, the history of violence was erased. The compounding of unfulfilled promises made by the center to Aceh was fundamental to the conflict and narrations of it. However, analyses that projected the current conflict backward to Daud Beureueh and Soekarno often failed to attend to the violence that has occurred since then. Since the implementation of Islamic law, violence has also occurred in the name of cleansing Aceh from sin. As one Acehnese man pointed out to me, "we now have to live with Islamic law, it is already in effect," but discussion of it never occurred throughout civil society because of the polarization aroused by separatism. Implementation of Islamic law was seen by many as an effort to undermine the popularity of Referendum and divert attention from the state violence that has occurred since the initial demands to form a more Islamic region.

One analyst said that Islamic law was a shortcut to restoring the dignity of Aceh, but might also be thought of as a shortcut to restoring the dignity of the law and the credibility of the government. In discussing the failed Humanitarian Pause, Amran Zamzami suggested to me that the government needed to take GAM to Mecca and make promises there, where they would mean something, or else GAM would lose its popular support. This statement assumes that the necessary strategy in Aceh was to reduce public support for GAM and therefore separatism. My interactions suggested the contrary: that those charged with resolving the conflict have often both deliberately and inadvertently increased popular support for Referendum and for independence. Zamzami's statement demonstrated the profound level of distrust in society and the government's lack of credibility. If promises had no meaning and institutions had no credibility, negotiation was nearly impossible.

Law, Justice, and the Exposure of State Violence

Commentaries on transitional justice debate the role of justice in authorizing law and legal institutions. Some theorists suggest that it is necessary to "sacrifice some justice now for more justice later," noting that a divided community cannot enforce a legal decision. Others argue that offering amnesty because legal institutions are too weak to enforce justice undermines law itself (on this debate, see Feher 1999). The Bantaqiah case demonstrates the fatal consequences of impunity from the law. The lack of political will to hold perpetrators accountable was noted by many Acehnese I spoke with. Legal institutions seemed incapable of providing justice; instead, law protected perpetrators. Indeed, the military's legal team in the Bantaqiah case demonstrated a great proficiency in exploiting the technicalities of law and legal procedure to advance their interests, appearing to support law while undermining the pursuit of justice.

In an anthropological consideration of the problem of retributive justice in the former Eastern European states, John Borneman wrote: "The jural reform in East-Central Europe . . . though ostensibly about eliminating past injustices, is more centrally about defining the future parameters along which the legitimate state not only has moral obligations but can itself claim to represent morality" (1997, 25). Aceh presents a unique problem for Indonesia not only in coming to terms with the past and creating a credible law but also in creating a moral grounding for the nation. Zamzami's exploration of the Bantaqiah case was explicitly an investigation of the lack of morality in Indonesia (2001). Others, most notably essayist Goenawan Mohamad, have written about what it means to be Indonesian in light of the blatant state involvement in ongoing violence (2001). The Aceh case discloses that narratives about violence authored in the interests of human rights and reform have not lead to accountability or an end to violence. Theoretical analyses have pointed to the disavowed violence that founds law and the disjuncture between law and justice (Benjamin 1986; Derrida 1992). Clearly, the impunity in Aceh reflects law's subordination to violence; however, I am interested in the realm of violence not fully disavowed and the productive indeterminacies of the dark pattern that produce social paranoia.

In Aceh, the problem is that the narrative link between justice and law has been severed and the violence that would invisibly authorize law is no longer entirely under the control of the state. The reform era exposed much state violence. The Bantaqiah trial demonstrated not only that the military was using excessive violence but that the narratives and public secrets that had secured the necessity of violence no longer held. At the same time, these narratives became all the more real as genuine separatist demands permeated society. Violence was no longer controlled or predictable. Formerly, violence had ensured stability and a semblance of legal order; now, scandalously, the law was in service of violence and violence raged out of control. Although discussions of justice often centered on "strengthening the law," the Bantaqiah case demonstrated that the problem was not a misapplication of law or a matter of implementation. Law was exposed as disconnected from justice and in servitude to violence itself.

Prior to the tsunami both "sides" appeared to have embraced violence as the means of addressing the past. Violence became endless, except for temporary pauses. There were too many weapons and militarized people in Aceh for the conflict to be resolved by simply withdrawing the TNI. "The dark pattern," unresolved by the transparency of the court, ensured that violence continued. Popular militancy continued as well. Until the tsunami, it was difficult to imagine a security operation that could bring violence under control in Aceh. One person told me that the people of Aceh were so traumatized that, even if the military were professional, the mere sight of a uniform would scare people.

Subsequent chapters take up the difficulty of addressing the legacies of the dark pattern and *provokator* in terms of historical narratives and their corrosive effect on state institutions. Law itself still seems to hold some promise for some people. Separating the police and military was one strategy to strengthen the law, but the shifting danger ascribed to separatists and criminals in Aceh complicated discussions of legitimate force. The post-Soeharto separation of police and military has been exploited by some military to avoid accountability for human rights violations. In Aceh, the cases selected for investigation occurred after the military was no longer responsible for security. In addition, when the danger is always cast as a danger to the nation, the law is subordinate. The TNI reiterated that the development of Aceh would be smooth if the political situation was stable, police functioned effectively, and law was strengthened ("Kostrad dan Kopassus Siap Terjun ke Aceh," *Republika*, 17 April 2001). But strengthening the law has meant that expressions of criticism and dissatisfaction are criminalized and treated as security problems; for example, Nazar, the head of SIRA, was jailed for "subversion." The legacies of the New Order continue to render law subordinate to violence and incapable of providing justice.

Why has justice not been achieved? The center's lack of political will is an obvious, but insufficient explanation. Through a range of different initiatives to address popular demands for justice, justice was replaced by the politicized demand for Referendum. Justice is doubly impossible in Aceh because of the problem of indeterminacy and logic of paranoia.

In the case of Aceh, the fundamental instability of terms has rendered language dysfunctional, and it is hard to imagine what would legitimate the law secured by the Indonesian state. Compensation plans were abstract and without concrete effects. Demands shifted to seeking justice through international mechanisms that might connect law and justice. In response to the failures of law, advocates sought to garner international support and to cast the struggle in terms of international norms, particularly by invoking the issue of genocide against the Acehnese, and by using the lack of justice in the existing legal system to assert the right to self-determination through Referendum. Converting all of the human rights abuses and "excesses" committed in the name of "hunting down separatist rebels to secure national integrity" into a right to independence has both retroactively proven the existence of rebels and diverted attention from the crimes that were committed. It has forced a discussion in which neutrality is impossible and there is no justice beyond politics. This conundrum is the work of the New Order ghosts that still haunt Indonesia.

Chapter 5

Neutrality and Provocation

Amid failed justice efforts and continuing state violence, Acehnese activists and nongovernmental organizations intensified calls for international attention. During Indonesia's post-Soeharto "reform" period, many international programs supported initiatives related to democratization. Acehnese organizations sought a national and international response to the reports of crimes perpetrated during DOM. Following the announcement that the East Timorese would vote in an internationally supervised process to determine their relationship to Indonesia, many Acehnese sought international support for a referendum in Aceh. In November 1999, the Referendum march drew as many as a million participants (*Suara Pembaruan,* "Sejuta Orang Turun ke Banda Aceh," 8 November 1999). The Henri Dunant Centre for Humanitarian Dialogue (HDC), a Swiss nongovernmental organization founded in 1999, brokered an agreement in which representatives of the armed forces of the Republic of Indonesia (TNI) and the Free Aceh Movement (GAM) signed a Joint Understanding for Humanitarian Pause in Davos, Switzerland, on 12 May 2000.[1] By their signatures, the parties formally agreed to a pause in the conflict to allow the distribution of humanitarian aid. Significantly, they also agreed to "to assist in the elimination of all offensive actions by armed elements which do not belong to the Parties to this Joint Understanding." The press and local people call these armed elements the "third force," or *provokator.* HDC correctly identified these armed elements as an important force in extending violence. As a result of the HDC mediation, the *provokator* and related figures in the conflict were eliminated. However, I argue, the logic of the *provokator* and the process through which they were eliminated fatally and irrevocably transformed the conflict.

Close kin of the "dark force," these mysterious *provocateurs* (the Indonesian term is a direct transmission from the French term for secret agents who instigate violent conflict) complicated the Aceh conflict. The *provokator,* "third force," and "the force that does not want Aceh to be safe" discursively and practically made the Aceh conflict irresolvable. The *provokator* troubled local people, and the dark force was part of the problem diagnosed by the state. In one protest a young man in a wheelchair held a sign "Free Aceh from the shackles of Provocation."[2] A photograph of the man and sign circulated in the January 1999 issue of an Acehnese tabloid with a story titled "When Referendum Begins to Threaten" ("Ketika Referendum Mulai Mengancam," *Kontras*, 20 January 1999). The article began with a series of questions. Did the people of Aceh really feel such intense antipathy toward Indonesia? Were these opinions appearing because they now had the freedom to express anything without fear of being arrested by intelligence? Or were the Acehnese denying the historical fact that the region had long supported the Republic? A text box titled, "Careful! The *provokator* Begins to Act" ("Awas! *provokator* Mulai Beraksi"), quoted student organizers of a demonstration in favor of Referendum who said that "other forces" had "infiltrated their action" and provoked the masses to violent acts. The students were there simply to ask for a referendum to see if the people still wanted to be united with Indonesia. In Aceh, *provokator* emerged coincident with "Referendum" as two critical and linked issues in discursive struggles over violence and justice. Referendum appeared as a nonviolent solution in which past violence could be resolved through political rights; the movement for justice was turned into a movement for sovereignty. A wide range of violence was displaced onto *provokator*, enabling an unlikely coalition of previously opposed interests to coalesce as nonviolent under the banner of Referendum in a discursive economy powered by violence and its representation. The notion of a third force or *provokator* allowed violence to continue with impunity. In the structure of the HDC agreement, the *provokator* became distinct from, and target of, an officially recognized GAM and the TNI.

Provokator and provocations were prominent political terms in post-Soeharto Indonesia, but they rarely appeared as more than snapshots and slogans. Provocations and *provokator* are explanations; they do not need to be explained. They are a type of public secret at the same time that they are a public threat. *Provokator* functions as an explanatory placeholder for an indeterminate threat and as a means of evading accountability for violence. *Provokator* are assumed to exist throughout Indonesia, but in Aceh, *provokator* took on greater force through their inclusion in the internationally brokered Humanitarian Pause.

This chapter examines the way in which the continuing lack of justice in conditions of rampant criminality produced a genuine armed separatist movement in place of what had formerly been the imagined enemies of an anxious military. The Humanitarian Pause played a pivotal role in this transformation because those who designed and advocated for it failed to understand, or ignored, the complexities of mistaking public secrets for truth. The Humanitarian Pause agreement failed to "free Aceh from the shackles of provocation" by eliminating the armed elements that belonged neither to GAM, the separatist rebels, nor to TNI, the Indonesian armed forces,[3] precisely because the agreement distinguished and formalized those elements in the logic of the *provokator*, which perpetuated violence and deferred justice. The "dark pattern" was the overlap between GAM and TNI in both the DOM and post-DOM periods. Instances of this overlap were widely known. The mysterious *provokator* deflected attention from this shadowy zone of conspiracy. Attributing violence that many people suspected was perpetrated by TNI to a third force made pursuing accountability difficult. Giving GAM a discursive and actual existence in the context of an international agreement distinguished a legitimate and recognizable GAM from criminal and "dark" elements. Despite its nonpolitical rhetoric, the agreement formally recognized GAM in a political context without offering a political solution. The Humanitarian Pause consolidated various "rebel" factions into a single force representing the people of Aceh's protest against Indonesian state violence in the politically and economically important space of international humanitarian mediation. Bringing to life the shadowy *provokator* enabled the idea of GAM to attach itself to outrage against injustice. The nonviolent Referendum movement shifted from publicizing the lack of justice and Jakarta's lack of credibility to popularizing the idea that only in separation, whether achieved through a popular vote or armed struggle, would there be any possibility of building a just society. But the militant movement to secure independence foreclosed the possibility of achieving justice.

In this chapter, I consider the *provokator* as a public secret, analyzing the work it did in 1999 as it haunted political discourse both nationally and locally, particularizing incidents of violence at the same time that it linked them, obstructing accountability, and making public secrets inscrutable. Then I expand the discussion of Referendum's insertion into the space of incalculable justice. Taking a controversial stance, the Acehnese Women's Congress did not support Referendum, but tried to maintain a position of neutrality. It became increasingly difficult for individuals and groups to continue to espouse nonviolence as the conflict dynamic shifted to a definition fixed by the international mediation. The Humanitarian Pause, despite its nonpolitical nature and formal neutrality, rendered the position of neutrality increasingly dangerous for members of Acehnese civil society. In adopting a neutral stance but configuring conflict protagonists as a polarized pair, the Humanitarian Pause made neutrality and more than tactical nonviolence almost impossible for most Acehnese. Finally, I consider the process by which the new term "GAM/Society" (GAM/Masyarakat) fused GAM and the people, rendering them indistinguishable in a conflict with the Indonesian state. This fusion figuratively pushed the Acehnese outside of the imagined Indonesian community and rendered them no longer Indonesian at the same time that the escalating state violence attempted to secure their participation in the Indonesian nation. At this stage, efforts were made to link GAM to other instances of unsolved violence in the capital.

The Emergence of *Provokator*

An understanding of the *provokator* illuminates the intersection between the discourse of elite intervention and "engineering" and instances of violence as they were imagined and experienced by those remote from control and others who held "the remote control," as the Jakarta military elite was described by an Acehnese human rights investigator.[4] In the post-Soeharto reform period, violence featured prominently in public discourse. The violence in these stories took several forms: violence by the state against its citizens; by "armed civilians" against the state and sometimes against ordinary people; by members of different religious or ethnic groups against rival groups; and a continuation of New Order criminal violence.[5] *provokator* permeated the stories of each type of violence.

The exposure of both state violence and violence described as "horizontal"—to indicate that it was occurring spontaneously between citizens—contributed to widespread anxieties over the fate of the nation for some and everyday existence for others. Stories that documented military involvement in past human rights abuses increased calls for an end to the military's dual social and political role. At the same time, however, stories of seemingly uncontrollable horizontal violence created the impression that the military was still necessary. Often, spontaneous violence was said to be provoked or engineered by various parties (sometimes specified, but most often not) to satisfy their own political or personal ends. Suspicions were never followed with conclusive investigations by either the media or the authorities, so popular rumors of manipulations were never proved or disproved. Nor were there plausible explanations of why the masses participated in this engineered violence. In the absence of resolution, these incidents took on a life of their own in public discourse. Intense struggles occurred as the violence was attributed to and claimed by different parties in locally specific, nationally complicated conflicts.

During the "reform" period, most incidents were said to be incited by *provokator*. The term appeared on the scene simultaneously with more widespread public acknowledgement of military involvement in violence and human rights abuses. Despite the frequent appearance of *provokator*, it was difficult to ascertain who they were. But the term did significant work in the political discourse. *Provokator* is the legacy of the maldistribution of power in the New Order and the final period of Soekarno's rule that preceded it, called Guided Democracy. For almost four decades, the militarized state was the most powerful political force in Indonesia. Citizens' attempts at political expression were consistently criminalized, manipulated, or redirected in the interests of power. The term *provokator* has antecedents in *Terlibat* (Involved), *Provokasi* (Provocations), and other terms used by the New Order regime to locate mysterious enemies elsewhere and avoid responsibility for violence that only it was powerful enough to cause. Critics used these terms to confirm that powerful interests were at work, but abstractly, so as not to become involved in political conflict and to avoid the risk of repression. After the Soeharto regime ended, the suspicion, or expectation, continued that conflicts would be manipulated by the powerful. At the same time, however, those in power were unable or unwilling to control local violence once engineered or ignited.

During the New Order period, most political activity was said not to represent the political aspirations of Indonesian citizens but to be organized by "masterminds" or "puppet masters." If no logical scapegoats were available, mass political action was said to be the result of nameless sinister provocations. A joint fact-finding team charged with investigating the 1998 riots in Jakarta that marked Soeharto's fall used the term *provokator* to suggest that the military was behind the riots. Building on the myth that the Indonesian people are incapable of acting alone, this report pointed to the organized nature of the mayhem, which it argued could only have been arranged by the military. *Provokator* emerged as a way to talk about elite and military manipulations of violence. A member of the joint fact-finding team, Hermawan Sulistyo, defines *provokator* as like a "fart: it can be felt, it can be smelled, but it does not have a shape." In writing their final report, he and his colleagues encountered "a creature (*makhluk*) which cannot be explained" (2000, 65).[6]

Munir, a national human rights activist, defined four types of *provokator*. First, *provokator* is an "accusation to the leader of a demonstration"; second, it is an accusation to those who "empower social groups"; third, it is most often used to "address the political actors who play one group of people against another through the issue of religion," including both the parties who spread "disinformation" to trigger the conflict and those who actually lead it; finally, the fourth use is addressed to "Satan," or "something which is used to deny a reality" (2000, 59).

The end of DOM inaugurated the dangers of *provokator* in Aceh. Initially, prominent Acehnese figures talked about the riots that marked the withdrawal of Kopassus troops as being "engineered" in order to "justify military behavior [repression] toward those who were accused of being GPK" (Ismail Hasan Meutereum [Ketua DPP PPP], "Sujud Syukur atas Pencabutan 'DOM'," *Kompas*, 10 August 1998). Students and NGO activists in Aceh were resolute in their demands that the "intelligence forces stop using provocations and intimidation toward civilians" ("Mahasiswa Aceh Berkabung di HUT RI," *Media Indonesia*, 18 August 1999; see also "Demonstrasi Desak KPU Tunda Pemilu di Aceh Berlanjut. Partai Hentikan Pengerukan Suara di Aceh," *Merdeka*, 7 June 1999). In Jakarta, Munir pointed to the efforts of "certain forces" in provoking the people to burn sites formerly used for torture and detention in Aceh ("Munir tentang Aceh: Ada Upaya Provokasi Membakar Bukti Bangunan Posko Tentara," *Kompas*, 24 August 1998). Initially, language about provocations was used to indicate the role of the security forces in instigating violence in post-DOM Aceh. In media and public discourse, the term was slippery. On the one hand, accusations that "certain forces" were provoking the violence in Aceh so that their abuses would be forgotten referred to the military; on the other hand, the possibility that GAM might be involved was not excluded. One newspaper editorial stated bluntly: "whoever they are, drag them to court so that the people know who they are" ("Siapa Penggerak Kerusuhan Itu?" *Kompas*, 5 September 1998). This was one of the first demands that *provokator* be unmasked so that people would know who they were. In November and December 1998, violence in Aceh continued with very few references to "provocations." During this period, most of the reported killings were of *cu'ak* (informers) by groups of unrecognized people.[7]

The military intensified the use of provocations in the Ahmad Kandang case with such expressions as the people "were provoked by Ahmad Kandang's gang . . . to put the women and children in front" ("Baku Tembak di Lhokseumawe, 5 Orang Tewas," *Republika*, 4 January 1999). In Jakarta, the Lhok Nibong incident provided the impetus to start "Operation Authority" to find "the armed forces members who have been kidnapped by people who were provoked by GPK Hasan Tiro" ("Aparat Sudah Kuasai Situasi Aceh," *Media Indonesia*, 5 January 1999). Consistent with the military's strategy of locating the source of grievance in poor economic conditions, spokesmen reiterated that the Aceh Merdeka group would not succeed in provoking the people if the local economy improved ("Kol Inf H Johny Wahab S.Sos: 'Motifnya Mendirikan Aceh Merdeka'," *Media Indonesia*, 10 January 1999).

The association of Aceh Merdeka and *provokator* animated the binary opposition between TNI and its enemy. The idea of *provokator* converted the struggle from one in which the TNI pointed to GAM and GAM pointed to TNI into a more complicated discourse in which violence that each projected onto the other fragmented and ricocheted in multiple directions. Each conflict protagonist was able to exclude its connections with the other by displacing them onto the *provokator*. In contrast to early DOM rhetoric in which much violence was attributed to separatists mimicking the military to discredit them in the eyes of ordinary people, the *provokator* came to life as a separate force that doubled narratives of violence, pointing not to its other but toward a mysterious "third element."

Provokator concerned elite Acehnese political figures as well. Hasballah M. Saad described the problem of provocations as part of the "vacuum" left by the departure of the security forces in the absence of adequate preparations for local authorities to take over security ("Pangab Adakan Pertemuan Tertutup dengan Tokoh Aceh: ABRI Disarankan Jangan Pakai Kekerasan," *Republika*, 6 January 1999).[8] A member of the human rights commission (Komnas HAM), Albert Hasibuan, stated that whoever violated human rights in Aceh must be brought to court and tried, including Ahmad Kandang, once described as a separatist, who had "become a *provokator*" ("GPL dan Aparat Sama-sama Razia KTP 'Achmad Kandang Harus Ditangkap'," *Republika*, 8 January 1999). GAM was no longer in the position of liminal criminality it had occupied immediately after the end of DOM.

In February 1999, after the announcement of the Referendum for East Timor, security forces invoked *provokator* as an agent for playing people against each other, corresponding to the third usage Munir defined. A military spokesman stressed that *provokator* were not necessarily outsiders, but could be "local" people who were "happy when people [were] enemies" and sought "to ruin the unity of this nation" ("Pangdam Bukit Barisan: Aceh Masih Perlu Penanganan Serius," *Republika*, 25 February 1999).[9] This description of people who fomented factionalism was the most explicit statement provided by security forces regarding who *provokator* were and where they came from. In a rhetorical near-convergence, Daud Yusuf, a prominent spokesman for the armed wing of GAM, linked *provokator* with the idea of Referendum. He urged Acehnese to avoid the bloodshed that had occurred in East Timor and to be careful of *provokator* who were using the student movement to spread the idea of Referendum ("Kerusuhan Lhokseumawe, 50 Warga Diperiksa," *Kompas*, 22 April 1999).

PROVOKATOR AND THE GENERAL ELECTIONS

The national election in June 1999 consolidated the idea of *provokator* as an out-of-control force in the violence in Aceh. Student activist Aguswandi suggested that "morally, the election is handicapped in

Aceh"; the elections could not be fair and safe because people were still traumatized by the military's violence, the military still acted violently and arbitrarily, and *provokator* abounded ("Wawancara Khusus Aguswandi Pemilu di Aceh Harus Diboikot," *Media Indonesia*, 16 March 1999). Preparations for the election in Aceh were marred by violent incidents attributed to *provokator*. Stories of killings, intimidation, and destruction of polling places and ballot boxes were frequent. *Provokator* were said to intimidate all those who were involved in the preparations for elections by likening ballot boxes to their coffins. Most people I spoke with were unable to attribute the violence to either the military or GAM.[10] They were most inclined to suspect the military or "imitation GAM," which typically was a shielded reference to the military. Through the repeated use of the terms, conditions of instability, and incomprehensibility of overwhelming low-grade violence, *provokator* and their relatives, "the force that does not want Aceh to be safe" and unidentified people, solidified a category distinct from both the military and the separatists but utterly mysterious in its own ends and affiliations.

In discussions of the terror association with the elections, local police officers lamented the lack of manpower and equipment that prevented them from taking over the security situation.[11] The head of police for North Aceh attributed violence to "*remote control provokator* who worked in Lhokseumawe but lived in Jakarta." He emphasized that "clearly the puppet master (*dalang*) of the riot is in Jakarta." These *provokator* manipulated the security forces and people against each other in an attempt to create conditions in which the elections failed ("Korban Tewas 24, Lhokseumawe Mulai Tenang," *Suara Pembaruan*, 4 May 1999).[12] This idea is strikingly similar to the popular notion that GPK masqueraded as the military to discredit the national armed forces among the people they served. The idea of *provokator* who played different forces against each other was typically used to describe horizontal conflicts, such as the conflict between Muslims and Christians in Maluku. In Munir's account, the *provokator* functioned to give vertical conflicts the veneer of horizontality. Yet the term worked more powerfully than as a mere veneer; if this was a conspiracy, as activists often surmised, it took on a life of its own. In an atmosphere where paranoia is justified rather than psychotic, institutions fail. Under the sign of the *provokator*, violence spun out of control, and in a context with no accountability, violence readily became horizontal.

Curiously, in the military statement that the *provokator* played people and security forces against one another, the language and logic of horizontal conflict were applied to a vertical conflict between the state and the people. At this point, the rhetoric of separatism had not yet been extended to include the entire population of Aceh based on their

Acehnese identity. This statement twisted the rhetoric of subversives and separatists working to divide the military and the people, for as the legitimate controllers of the means of violence the military should not be susceptible to being played against the people it is supposed to protect. If security forces were disciplined, they should be immune to such temptations—unless the provocations followed through their chain of command.

ADDING A THIRD FORCE TO THE GAM-TNI CONFLICT

In both media accounts and conversation, *provokator* were ever-present in igniting the violence sweeping Aceh, but they were never caught despite the professed best efforts of security forces. *Provokator* were said to throw grenades, fire guns, and burn buildings. Both civilian and military were casualties of *provokator*. *Provokator* were impossible to unmask. If by chance they were unmasked, they became a single, undisciplined armed forces member (*oknum*) who did not represent any systematic plan of the military, or they were declared GAM separatist rebels.

Prior to the election, the police forces in Aceh explained the difficulty of arresting "unidentified people who disturb the peace": "There are some people who have been caught for doing provocative actions, but when they are asked who stands behind them, they answer there is no one" ("Kalau Perlu, Munir akan Diperiksa. *Provokator* Aceh Sulit Ditangkap," *Media Indonesia*, 29 May 1999). Although the idea of *provokator* and unidentified persons suggests uncoordinated individual activities, continuing New Order logic decreed that there must be a mastermind behind them. With the ready label of *provokator*, isolated criminal events were consolidated into a particularly virulent danger that might arise anywhere at any time.

The figure of the *provokator* extended the logic of earlier accusations by TNI that GPK/GAM had committed crimes in the guise of TNI to discredit it. In the DOM situation, when GAM rarely made public statements, there was no denial. GAM remained a nearly invisible, shadowy force and was often conflated with various security disruptors. In the post-DOM situation, particularly after Wiranto said that GAM members who had fled to Malaysia could return, identifiable GAM spokespeople might reject these claims. Furthermore, the suggestion might remind listeners of the discredited rhetoric of DOM. *Provokator* provided a convenient label for violent acts. This violence could not be immediately attributed to former detainees or returnees from Malaysia. In the period when violence was attributed to the *provokator*, GAM developed a reputation as a force for the people; it became possible to think that among the many acts committed under the guise of various GAM strains was a positive, pure GAM that acted with the interests of ordinary people in mind.

In the post-DOM period, both GAM and TNI attributed violence to *provokator*. For example, in discussing the threats directed toward political parties prior to the election, one political party head blamed *provokator*, not Aceh Merdeka. National military spokesmen announced that the local military had arrested a "*provokator* of GAM" who "was creating terror to discredit the military and police" ("Pemilu di Aceh Utara Sesuai Jadwal," *Media Indonesia*, 5 June 1999). Similarly, GAM spokesman Maulida announced that GAM would conduct a "sweeping" operation to find *provokator* to guard against the "staining of the good name of GAM" ("Laporan Republika dari 'Sarang' GAM 'Mana Mungkin Kami yang Membakar'," *Republika*, 12 June 1999).[13] Maulida suggested that the *provokator* were trained "like Kopassus," the Special Forces units responsible for much of the DOM violence. He attempted to turn the idea of the *provokator* directing the people on its head, noting: "the people already know that the ones who are doing the provocations are Kopassus, not just anyone. It is not that the people don't want to take the risk to destroy the provokators, but it is not possible for them to resist carelessly" ("Wawancara Khusus Teungku Maulida Tak Mungkin Bangsa Aceh Meneror Sesamanya," *Media Indonesia*, 13 June 1999). What the people might have suspected but hesitated to admit was that some GAM might also be Kopassus members, disavowed or otherwise.

Many people I spoke with at the time of the national elections were suspicious of the *provokator*. At that point, it seemed realistic to them that the military was deliberately creating violence, or that military people might be pretending to be GAM. Eventually, various types of political and criminal violence coalesced in the term *provokator*. In one incident at the time of the elections, local people captured four *provokator*; three acknowledged being members of TNI, and one was a civilian.[14] The local military command verified to the state news agency that the three suspects had been taken to the police for investigation ("Isu Kerusuhan di Aceh Utara tak Terbukti," *Media Indonesia*, 8 June 1999). Two days later, the regional military commander, Johny Wahab, denied that three TNI had been captured by the people, but stated instead that three members of TNI had been killed by unidentified people. In Jakarta, the military stated that the three "were no longer members of Kostrad or Kopassus" (Subagyo HS [KASAD], quoted in "Tentang Tiga Orang TNI Yang Diduga Sebagai *provokator*. Danrem: Mereka Sedang Cari 'Orang Pintar'," *Republika*, 11 June 1999). Wahab then accused GAM of hypocrisy for accusing TNI of acting as *provokator* when in fact GAM had done so itself ("Tentang Tiga Orang TNI Yang Diduga Sebagai *provokator* Danrem: Mereka Sedang Cari 'Orang Pintar'," *Republika*,

11 June 1999). A GAM spokesperson claimed to have captured ten individuals who often acted as *provokator* using GAM's name.[15] At the same time, security forces reportedly captured a GAM sympathizer posing as a Kopassus member. A Jakarta military source suggested that provocations done in Aceh were intended to "turn around the actual conditions." This case, he argued, was clear proof that there was a "systematic effort by the GPL Hasan Tiro to spread propaganda as if TNI were still actively spreading members of Kopassus in Aceh" (Mayjen TNI Syamsul Ma'arif, quoted in "Kapuspen TNI: Tidak Ada Lagi Kopassus di Aceh," *Kompas*, 12 June 1999). These accusations and denials echoed the previous logic of GPK trying to discredit the military by mimicking it. However, as these examples make clear, the discourse became much more complicated when GAM mimicked TNI rhetoric. It is clear during this period that many violations were committed by the TNI, and even other forces, and there was no process of investigation or accountability to end the dynamic of accusations, denials, and disavowals that brought *provokator* to life amid general conditions of insecurity.

At the time of the elections, Aceh was rife with rumors of a secret operation directed by prominent Kopassus members. Many people I spoke with warned me that motorcycle taxi drivers, trash collectors, and others were undercover Kopassus agents who were smuggled back in various guises. Later news suggested that prominent Special Forces members had been touring Aceh, but they denied that it was a secret operation.[16]

Provokator were also blamed for large-scale displacement. The camps for internally displaced people (IDPs) were widely publicized by the media. The police suggested that people did not need to flee but merely to contact the local police and military to get rid of the *provokator* who were scaring them ("Ban Meledak, Lima Orang Tertembak di Aceh," *Republika*, 14 June 1999). In visiting the IDP camps, it was difficult to ascertain what threat people were fleeing, but it was obvious that they were afraid. The camps I visited were typically watched over by young, aggressive men who described how the population had been terrorized by the TNI entering and destroying homes. Sometimes these youths identified themselves as GAM; other times they did not. These men were organizing the camps and the movement of people, and it was very difficult to speak to individuals without the "coordinators" overseeing the interaction. According to many analysts, the internal displacement of people was calculated to attract international attention.

Criminal activity, glossed as provocations in some reports, continued despite the large military presence in Aceh. Many high-level figures, including President Wahid, acknowledged military involvement in the violence ("Presiden: Penggerak Pengacau Aceh dari Jakarta," *Republika*,

3 May 2000). While the veracity of these suspicions is extremely important and exceedingly difficult to document, the effects of rampant criminality and the rumors themselves were easily documented. Tolerating criminal activity extended practices of terror that were committed systematically by the military during DOM. The multiplying effects of ongoing random criminal activity included a pervasive sense of lawlessness, as security forces were unable to resolve even one incident of theft or extortion. Gradually, citizens felt powerless to effect any change, depoliticizing society through criminal activity—the obverse of the previous New Order practice of criminalizing political activity. Suspicion destroyed weak civil society alliances or efforts toward reconciliation. As many Acehnese emphasized, "before it was clear who the enemy was; now no one knows who is a friend and who is an enemy."[17]

The Logic of Referendum

Before the post-Referendum violence in East Timor and the election campaign in Aceh, I thought that Referendum sounded like a fair and democratic idea for Aceh. I admit that I might have been suffering from the tendency to romanticize the underdog resistance that had afflicted many of my activist friends in Jakarta. I was surprised when two Acehnese NGO leaders were discussing the idea of a referendum with much suspicion at my house in Jakarta in early 1999. Where I, naively, saw a genuine expression of political aspiration, they saw the potential for "engineering." They feared that people might be fooled into thinking that this demand was their own will. One activist started his explanation with the obvious and undeniable evidence of official involvement: the huge, professionally painted letters that spelled out Referendum on the main road connecting Medan and Banda Aceh. I agreed that the letters were impressive. He was right that no one could have painted such evenly spaced, uniform, multicolored, thickly painted letters (with exactly the same texture and effect as the traffic markings on the road) if they were acting covertly. He said it was not merely that the security forces allowed Referendum to be painted on almost every visible surface in Aceh. There was also the question of materials. Where would loosely organized students get the money and ability to coordinate such a massive project? One student-painter had told him that a man they did not know had come up when they were making banners and given them the paint as a donation. People who were driving by and did not want to give money to the painters were insulted and intimidated. It was obvious that the security forces had not done everything in their power to prevent the painting. I countered that some people had been stopped from painting Referendum ("Tiga Mahasiswa Ditangkap: Akan Tuliskan 'Referendum' di Atap Terminal," *Kompas*, 23 February 1999), but he pointed out that this occurred only after the idea of Referendum "already existed." Once such permanent letters had been painted there were some efforts to paint over them, which emphasized their erasure by the security forces. And, as many people came to believe that Referendum was the voice of the people against the security forces, when Referendum banners were removed, the anger of the people was directed toward the military ("Spanduk Referendum Dicopot, Massa Marah," *Kompas*, 14 April 1999). He concluded his argument that "referendum [was] a provocation that [was] fishing (*pancing*) for people's anger."

The appearance of the word Referendum and its invocation by a range of opposing forces and actors positioned it as a key term structuring the discourse of "the Aceh problem." The physical presence of a million people gathered to demand Referendum on 8 November 1999 in Banda Aceh moved the demand from threat to real force. It was striking to many people, myself included, that the Referendum gathering could assemble so many people without incident. Indeed, amid constant violence between security forces and rebels, it was startling that "civil society" and the "ordinary people" could express their aspirations without a single incident of violence.

I was not in Banda Aceh for the historic event, but in Jakarta. I had scheduled an interview with an elite Acehnese man who was reputed to be very close to certain people in the military. He had told me himself in an earlier conversation that he was "teaching Wiranto to play bridge, because he [Wiranto] did not understand matters of strategy." Following the interview, I was invited to brunch with the whole family. I ended up in a car with the man, his wife, and his driver. His wife engaged me in conversation regarding life in Indonesia, how many times I had been to Aceh, and so forth. The man was on the phone. He sounded so anxious that we fell silent. His adamant voice was startlingly loud: "whatever happens, it must not be from either the TNI or the GAM. Nothing should happen, but if it does, it will be because of the *provokator*." The term *provokator* was invoked in advance as a cover for whatever violence might occur. The conversation ended shortly thereafter. It was as if the conversation had not happened after he hung up as he began to tell me, in Indonesian, about the restaurant where we would soon be dining and the occasion to be celebrated.

Writing Referendum on banners, roads, and buildings brought Referendum to life in a way not dissimilar from the logic of the term *provokator*. Once Referendum was popularized ("socialized"), it became a word that everyone could gather behind, a word that would transcend the many differences amongst its proponents. Referendum appeared, existed, interrupted discourse, and seemed to be the voice of the people, but the material and political conditions of its production were often obscured by its ubiquity and seemingly universal appeal. Referendum, at the moment that it was made real by the appearance of mass support, seemed to be the voice of everyone Acehnese.

I had an opportunity to see how the name of SIRA, the Central Committee for Referendum Aceh, could be used on banners without the group's authorization. In Banda Aceh I was in the car with an older activist. He worked with NGOs and was known to have many connections in Jakarta, though, unlike many others in a similar position, he had remained in Aceh. He recalled Gus Dur's widely publicized comment on his trip to Cambodia: "If there is a referendum in East Timor, why can't there be one in Aceh. That is called unfair" ("Presiden KH Abdurrahman Wahid: Aceh Takkan Lepas Dari RI," *Kompas*, 9 November 1999). Suddenly, he was calling out on his cell phone ordering a banner to be charged to his account with the words "If East Timor can have a referendum, why not Aceh—Gus Dur" and signed SIRA. There was nothing covert about the operation; he asked for it to be put up on the corner we were passing at that moment. When I passed by the next day, there it was. The man had numerous affiliations and had publicly supported Referendum. This banner was no different from the others that were crowded onto available spaces in Banda Aceh in preparation for the upcoming visit of ministers likely to be widely covered by national media. The man who had this banner made met with all the ministers. He had many forums in which to express his opinion. At no time did I hear him identify himself as a member of SIRA, which had separate meetings with the ministers.

One of the most prominent and frequently photographed images of Referendum was the wrought iron billboard in the front of the Great Mosque in Banda Aceh, which read: "The People of Aceh want a Referendum Stay with or Separate from the Republic of Indonesia." The permanence of this billboard made it easy to forget how it came to exist. Amien Rais and Abdurhaman Wahid, who later became Indonesia's third president, were present for the uncovering of this banner. The day after they gathered with other prominent Muslim leaders for a ceremony to uncover the billboard with a prayer, black paint was thrown at it. Religious leaders suggested that it was a "test" from those who did not want to understand the Aceh problem, while students and NGOs cast it as "a form of terror toward peaceful concepts which were developing in society" ("Papan 'Referendum', Dilumuri Cat Hitam," *Kompas*, 18 September 1999). This billboard appeared after the issue had taken hold and people felt that it represented their own voice.

The issue of whose voice Referendum represented and the security forces' toleration of, or cooperation with, the campaign created controversy among activists. The authenticity of Referendum as the voice of the people generated fierce debate between two people who had worked together on building civil society and investigating human rights abuses during DOM. I quote at length from their exchange. This e-mail message circulated among several groups, although none of the recipients still had a copy of it, and some of them had erased their hard drives because of military harassment. I have replaced the names with A and B to protect the identities of those involved, even though it was a semipublic exchange.

B began by quoting A's argument:

The referendum issue is a phenomenon that shows how the demand of many different groups in Acehnese society have not been heeded and fulfilled by the government of RI [Republic of Indonesia], so . . . there needs to be pressure to raise their bargaining position, to free themselves from the shackles of the repressive regime which oppressed them. The problem is, if legal justice cannot be given by the government of RI, what more can be hoped from RI?

Referendum appeared in A's analysis to be a tactic to increase leverage in negotiations with the central government that had failed to provide legal justice. Referendum was a last resort in the absence of other options.

B presented a critique of Referendum: "I am of the opinion that the referendum issue is an issue which is very strategic and chosen to shift the issue from 'the demands to resolve the human rights violations in Aceh during the duration of DOM' and the circulation of that issue." B noted that people who raised the issues were not aware of the "issue shifting" and could not control the issue they initiated. He used the example of the iron billboard in front of the Great Mosque:

The hero of referendum from SIRA [Muhammad Nazar] said in *Kompas*, when answering a question of one of the congress attendees, that to build the Billboard referendum in front of the Great Mosque in Banda Aceh, he received an eighteen million Rupiah donation from the Regional Military Commander [Syafuddin Tippe]. To you . . . I want to ask, what is this a symptom of? Is it enough to justify the action of Mr. Muhammad Nazar who said that for the interest of referendum he would accept donations from anyone who is sympathetic to the struggle?

For B, the donation was evidence that the leaders of the movement could not control the issue. A did not deny the receipt of donations, but argued the TNI could not be behind Referendum because they have forced "people to erase the referendum writings by licking them with their tongues." B responded that the goal was not to support the campaign, but merely to make Referendum into the key issue in order to distract attention from the human rights violations of the past.

At the very moment that Acehnese civil society appeared to be gaining strength, bitter disagreements appeared among activist groups. Throughout this exchange, the antagonists reiterated the importance of democracy and respecting differences of opinion, but both sides personalized the disagreement, and commentary became snide. What seemed to be at stake was who had the right to serve as the representative of the suffering people. Referendum fissured the opposition. In an atmosphere of suspicion permeated by the idea that things were never quite what they seemed and were "controlled from behind," it was hard to be certain what conflicting interests might be operating under the umbrella of Referendum. Following the Humanitarian Pause agreement, which was not favored by the security forces and might be considered one of the outcomes of the manifestation of the Referendum march, the security forces became less sympathetic to SIRA.

As the anniversary of the million-person march approached, SIRA members were quoted in local newspapers reporting that the people were calling every day to find out if there was to be another event, suggesting that another gathering was the will of the people (*Kontras*, 21 November 2000). The victims' congress had drawn many people to Banda Aceh and increased media attention without producing substantial progress toward resolution. Prior to the first anniversary, SIRA conducted its own poll, which found that 92 percent of the people favored *merdeka*, independence.

Around this time, several people from Aceh with whom I met in Jakarta told me that there was a lot of intimidation; people were afraid both of going to the gathering and of not going. SIRA decided not to call off the march, and despite much criticism defended its decision in the interests of the people. I spoke with someone at the U.S. embassy who had frequent contact with Nazar. This official said he was angry that Nazar had gone ahead with another mass rally to mark the anniversary; the decision was irresponsible, as it was clear that there would be considerable violence. There was. Reports varied, counting between fourteen and over one hundred fatalities (*Kontras*, 21 November 2000). SIRA members said that the violence was not their responsibility, but was evidence of the cruelty of the armed forces. A poll conducted by a local newsweekly in Aceh indicated that readers overwhelmingly faulted the military for the violence. Acehnese sources stated that there was intensive sweeping and intimidation of transportation operators leading up to the event. By that time, SIRA had alienated many of its more elite sympathizers, and the defense minister was emphatic that the center would not tolerate any sort of referendum.

Nazar did not appear at the second SIRA meeting. He was in hiding as the police had summoned him in conjunction with banners displayed by SIRA on 17 August that were considered subversive. Subsequently, other members of SIRA came to my house to try to convince me to act on Nazar's behalf and to reiterate that the international community had to do something. I reminded them I was a researcher and suggested other members of the international community that might be more able to assist them. I then challenged them by saying I had heard that people were forced into signing the questionnaires that they were reporting to me as solid evidence that the position they represented was the genuine will of the people and that therefore I, as someone from a democratic country, must support it. They defended the practice of requiring a signature and address to legitimate the authenticity of the ballot. I countered that others had told me that often the village head position was controlled by GAM and they were afraid of abstaining or not voting for independence.[18] They insisted their poll was democratic.

A month later in Jakarta, I met with another Acehnese student from an Islamic group in a crowded restaurant after the fast ended. He leaned forward and told me that he could not say it in Aceh, but that people were scared. He could not tell me this in Aceh because one never knew who anyone was. Looking around cautiously several times despite the din of the restaurant, he told me there were people who felt forced into going to the demonstration, who knew that they would be harassed by the security forces but were more afraid not to go. He said that the polling had been accompanied by intimidation as well.

Advocating Referendum had not been synonymous with advocating independence at the outset, but then the relationship between GAM and SIRA shifted. Initially, GAM commented that the Referendum was an effort to provoke the people. However, following the arrest of M. Nazar and the efforts of the security forces to link GAM and SIRA, GAM leaders were quoted as saying that SIRA was the child of GAM ("Pahlawan Baru Ciptaan Jakarta," *Majalah Tempo*, 3 December 2000). National media sources suggested that "naively" Jakarta had created a new hero by acting as if SIRA were the enemy of Indonesia. On 20 November 2000, Nazar went to the police to respond to his summons. Official sources justified Nazar's arrest as an effort to "strengthen law" in Aceh (Brigjen Pol Drs Chaerul R. Rasyidi, quoted in *Kontras*, 29 November 2000). In an interview, Nazar said that the "police do not want to arrest me, they want to stop the demand for Referendum" ("Pahlawan Baru Ciptaan Jakarta," *Majalah Tempo*, 3 December 2000). Referendum, like *provokator*, took on a life of its own; arresting one person could not diminish the power of the logic in extending conflict dynamics.

The Referendum movement was able to claim the power of the "floating mass" developed during the Soeharto period.[19] For the first year, there were almost no dissenting voices. In February 2000, a year after the youth conference that established SIRA, the Acehnese Women's Congress (*Duek Pakat Inong Aceh*, DPIA) brought together women from all over Aceh. After an intense nine-hour debate and a walkout by a minority of the participants, the congress decided not to support Referendum. One spokeswoman stated: "the women of Aceh want to position themselves as neutral" ("Perempuan Aceh Abaikan Soal Referendum," Satunet.com, 29 February 2000). The participants refused both autonomy and Referendum and concluded: "We want to live peacefully in Aceh." Despite the results of the congress, women were active participants in the drive for Referendum. One participant explained that the women had chosen to emphasize their desire for peace through the twenty-two point list of recommendations, which focused on stopping violence, instituting Islamic law, and trying perpetrators for past rights violations. She stated that while women answered they wanted *merdeka*, freedom, if they were asked individually, they would specify freedom from fear; in a larger group, however, they would answer "freedom, meaning separation from Indonesia" ("Referendum Aceh Lebih Banyak Mudharatnya Daripada Manfaatnya," Satunet.com, 10 March 2000). The Women's Congress voiced the desire to shift the conflict away from the politicized terms of the Referendum campaign. However, Referendum already controlled the terms of discussion.

Like the letters on the street, very few people recall where Referendum came from, or how it spread—suddenly it was everywhere, marking the landscape and political discourse. Initially, it seemed like an umbrella under which Acehnese could gather without being forced to articulate their views on independence. As the frequent killings in 2000–2001 of figures once considered neutral indicate, there was no space outside the conflict. The injustice became much more profound as the undeniable facts of violence that occurred during and after DOM were widely known and yet remain unresolved many years later.

The Humanitarian Pause and Nonpolitical Neutrality

The agreement establishing the Humanitarian Pause was signed between representatives of the armed forces of the Republic of Indonesia and GAM. The relationship between GAM military commanders and the exiled leadership was not clear to many people, and the Indonesian military was not involved in discussions leading up to the agreement.

Just before the agreement was announced, I spoke with a cabinet member and minister charged with the Aceh problem. He very confidently and excitedly explained to me his plans for resolving the conflict in Aceh. First he described the Bantaqiah hearing,[20] and then he moved to the Pause. I expressed my doubts as to how it would work, especially if no one had definite control over what was happening on the ground. In particular, I mentioned the pervasive rumors and perceptions among the Acehnese I spoke with that the military was behind the ongoing violence. His eyes lit up as he indicated that this was the very problem he could solve. Putting one hand in the air, he said: "This is GAM." Then he raised the other hand and, waving it, said: "This is the Police." Bringing both hands together in a deafening clap, he exclaimed: "This is the army—Finished."

The Pause did not "finish" off the army as he suggested it might, in part because of a lack of clarity about who GAM was at this point. In 1998 and 1999, I met and interviewed many of those originally accused of being members of Aceh Merdeka. None of them identified with the resurgent GAM between the end of DOM and the beginning of the Pause. None of them at this point were familiar with Abdullah Syafi'ie. One person said there was another group that worked "directly," implying the use of arms, which he referred to as "Arjuna's group." Other than Arjuna, he did not know anything about the armed activities of GAM. He had learned of Arjuna in the 1990s when he was jailed with a person who had been arrested for sheltering Arjuna, who had himself escaped.

One version of Arjuna's story was printed in a national newspaper in July 1999:

Arjuna, 37 years old, former commander of the GAM troops in the Pidie region, now says he is pensioned. From 1989–1992, Arjuna became a guerilla for GAM under the umbrella of Hasan Tiro. Because he was being chased by the military in Aceh, he fled and hid himself in Malaysia. For five years he exiled himself, and in 1997 he made a *comeback* [English in original]. . . . Then, in October 1998, this former GAM activist who had been trained in Libya from 1989–90 evacuated to Jakarta with his wife and child. Arjuna admitted that in 1992–8 the majority of the activities when they were under the group of Hasan Tiro made the people of Aceh suffer. When reform occurred the local government of Aceh pleaded with the GAM group in the mountains to descend and those in foreign countries to return to Aceh. Based on this, Arjuna returned and wanted to help resolve the problem in Aceh.

When asked by the newspaper reporter about the rumors that he had been "close to the military," Arjuna responded, "I returned to Indonesia based on the request of the government, if that which is named government already includes ABRI and local government. When I returned to Indonesia, because those who control the government are ABRI and civilians, I have to automatically report that I am no longer with the group of Hasan Tiro. Based on that, there is a connection with the government and ABRI" ("Arjuna. Harus Berlaku Syariat Islam di Aceh," *Media Indonesia*, 25 July 1999). Before the execution of the Pause agreement, there was much suspicion about the connections between the Indonesian military and the armed rebel factions. After the Pause, many of the individuals jailed early on became familiar with and identified with the armed faction.

Most sources saw the swiftly executed Humanitarian Pause agreement as one of Abdurrahman Wahid's initiatives. The president and his supporters may have seen this agreement with GAM as the last hope to forestall the domino-style disintegration of Indonesia, starting with East Timor and Aceh. When the agreement was announced, however, Wahid's critics condemned the signing as a "blunder" (Dewi Fortuna Anwar, quoted in "Akbar wants govt to explain RI-GAM truce signing abroad" *Jakarta Post*, 16 May 2000) that threatened Indonesian sovereignty by internationalizing a local conflict, which recalled criticism of President Habibie's decision to allow East Timor a referendum ballot and disclosed the anxiety of elite Jakarta reformers about attempting political resolution of regional conflicts.

Despite the fact that an evaluation of the initiative disclosed that the Henri Dunant Center staff who mediated the negotiations were aware of the many factions in GAM, they decided to accept the signatures of the overseas contingent. The relationship between these symbolic leaders and the armed resistance was not clear. Beyond the exiled leadership and those arrested and jailed in the early DOM period, there were very few resistance figures associated with GAM.[21] Splits and factions had developed among the opposition. By virtue of the Humanitarian Pause agreement, one group inherited the resistance title and other groups were eliminated, sometimes literally. The Humanitarian Pause marginalized the MP-GAM faction, which advocated nonviolent resolution of the Aceh conflict. Teungku Don Fadli, their exiled leader, was killed on the first day the agreement was implemented. No one was convicted for his murder, nor was his killing given much coverage in the newspapers.

Prior to the agreement negotiated with GAM, the Henri Dunant Center had embarked upon a broad-based civil society initiative. Representatives of several groups and organizations had held a series of meetings. Then, with the approval of GAM figureheads, the community dialogue called the Congress of Acehnese People, or KRA, was abruptly canceled. I met with several leaders who had been engaged by the HDC local representatives for this dialogue. One religious leader felt particularly betrayed by the sudden shift. He felt that the HDC had abandoned him and others involved in order to work exclusively with GAM as the representative of the Acehnese, even though it was not at all clear who GAM was.

I traveled to several different villages at the start of the Humanitarian Pause to get a sense of how people understood the arrangement. Some people I met were very irate. One community leader complained about the wording of the posters designed for community education, which emphasized that the Humanitarian Pause was not a political solution. When I went to inspect the poster with the humanitarian worker with whom I was traveling, we were immediately surrounded by a large group of people at the market. One woman advanced, visibly upset, and asked if we were from the Pause. We said we were not. She asked what it meant that it was not a political solution. She said the people were tired; they wanted a political solution, and if this was not a political solution the internationals should leave. Some civilians asked if the signing of the Humanitarian Pause meant that Aceh would never be safe again.

To eliminate the low-grade criminality consolidated by the term *provokator* would have required a political solution. In his analysis of *provokator*, Munir concluded that the only solution to the problem was political. He suggested that the forces that had the power to agitate local situations must be brought under control; however, he placed equal emphasis on creating a society that was empowered and "clever" enough to maintain a distance from such provocations and able to exert social control over elite political and military forces (Munir, quoted in Stanley 2000, 63). The Humanitarian Pause did the opposite, resulting in a highly polarized, militarized resistance toward state authority that lacked credibility. The fundamental problem with the agreement is that, in the name of neutrality, HDC played along with the rhetoric that everyone at the time knew was just a way to avoid holding the military accountable for violence, or to avoid admitting that it was impossible for the reformers to do that. When known perpetrators are not held accountable, the system of mediation and dialogue is impossible. In this situation, not only were the perpetrators known, but there was an effort to pretend that they were not part of the system. The HDC colluded with this act of misrepresentation and injustice. Even if these are only rogue elements, they still corrupt the system, since the military cannot discipline them, the state cannot monopolize violence, and the law cannot enforce verdicts that are true. If these were not rogue elements, "single bad guys," or *provokator* belonging to the "dark pattern," but rather figures who acted on the basis of covert collusion between armed groups and the security forces, then the agreement actually perpetuated the conditions for the continuation of violence.

Early human rights investigations document abuses committed by GAM as well as by the Indonesian armed forces.[22] Many Acehnese civilians I interviewed expressed fear of both GAM and the TNI. The relationship between GAM and ordinary citizens was difficult to ascertain. Prior to the Humanitarian Pause, most Acehnese differentiated between the many strains of opportunist or engineered GAM and pure GAM that had the best interests of the people in mind. The effect of the Humanitarian Pause agreement was not only to make shadowy *provokator* real but also to consolidate and legitimate a public GAM. After the Pause, ideas of "engineered" or "fake" GAM disappeared and its violence was attributed to the *provokator*,[23] rendering the "pure" GAM increasingly viable as a symbol of resistance. At the same time, an armed GAM became increasingly visible with named commanders for various regions.

In order to oppose the central government, a person had to identify as GAM; positions on the committees were available only to self-described GAM members. NGOs that had formerly spoken out against GAM violence were marginalized, blacklisted, and had little access to the funding that the Pause offered.[24] Activists who suggested that GAM did not represent the only voice of the Acehnese people were frequently harassed and intimidated by members of GAM and by police and military officials. At the village level, GAM had greater access to mobilize support and recruit, sometimes forcefully. Indeed, GAM orchestrated an effective performance for the international community. The strong support of certain NGOs, intellectuals, and other figures for GAM during the Pause does not indicate that they had been silent supporters of GAM; rather, it indicates the lack of options for political expression. At the same time, key intellectuals and civil society figures shifted to support GAM even if they did not take positions on committees. Although the Pause did not "legalize" GAM, it created a situation in which the conflict became polarized between GAM and the Indonesian state. Individuals who had been arrested and tried as AM/GAM in the pre-DOM period were placed on the committees, which assumed a false continuity between earlier incarnations of Aceh Merdeka and the GAM that emerged at that time.

In the initial phase of the Pause, there was a decrease in media reports of violence, but many Acehnese reported that everyday violence, intimidation, and terror intensified. Average daily death tolls did not decline significantly. At the end of the Pause, the situation was more militarized and there were increased reports of violence, especially low-grade incidents and killings of individuals. The stated objectives of the agreement, to eliminate the *provokator* and reduce violence to facilitate the distribution of humanitarian aid, were not met. Many civil society groups reported decreased international funding and increased local extortion. Violence formerly attributed to the *provokator* continued a similar pattern, but the term "unidentified person" named perpetrators in killings reminiscent of the "mysterious" state-sponsored murders of the 1980s.

The agreement itself catalyzed the discursive struggle to represent violence and human rights abuses in Aceh in a translation process from abuse to compensation, basing political rights on victimization. In this context, justice circulated as a political commodity always unattainable. The issue became what to do in the face of the overwhelming impossibility of attaining justice for past crimes. In a discourse that equated justice for past abuses with the right to self-determination, independence became the goal of struggle. This shift reinforced a belief held by some of the population—though not always by those who were direct victims of violence—that independence, through whatever means, compensated for the past denial of rights. Discussions of justice were hijacked by Referendum into nonnegotiable mandates for independence. Ultimately, this move became one of the logics by which violence was perpetuated as the only means of resolution. The conflict in Aceh shifted from a problem of separatism justifying a military repression to separatist sentiment widely enforced and popularized by increasingly public GAM separatists and decentralized violence, which the military was unable or unwilling to control.

Making All Acehnese GAM

Following the Humanitarian Pause, a new category was added to terms used to describe the conflict: GAM/Masyarakat (GAM/society). Joining GAM to society rendered the conflict as one between all Acehnese, by virtue of their Acehnese identity, and the Indonesian military state. While I have pointed to the porous boundaries of the GAM, particularly emphasizing its relationship to the TNI, I do not intend to imply that GAM was not part of a separatist movement operating in Aceh. The figure of Hasan Tiro has remained a central focus around which dissatisfaction coalesces. The Humanitarian Pause legitimated GAM as the only voice of dissent and marginalized civil society organizations advocating human rights. The impression was that all Acehnese were represented by, sympathizers with, or members of GAM; every Acehnese was enrolled at least discursively in an armed separatist conflict. The construction of the silent majority of Acehnese as supporters of independence and the visible recognition of armed separatists coincided with military rhetoric declaring the impossibility of distinguishing GAM and ordinary people. "Excess" was converted to a "proportional" defense of national unity. Casualties could then be counted as GAM/Masyarakat, eliminating the possibility of "innocent" victims. All violence was resignified as political. The drive to "separate the people from the separatists," which had been a staple of military rhetoric, was abandoned. The people and enemy were no longer distinguishable. The terms and implementation of the Humanitarian Pause enabled these conversions to take place.

The agreement formally empowered GAM to distribute funds and to represent the Acehnese people while addressing injustice. Many other organizations lent their credibility to authorize the conflict configuration outlined by HDC, even when they knew that conditions on the ground were much more complicated. Human rights organizations in Aceh, Jakarta, and Western countries endorsed the Pause. When I first visited Aceh in 1996, I met a very impressive and diverse group of people working for human rights. Creative and critical, they seemed focused on the issue of human rights instead of the political rivalries that dominated the Jakarta-based NGOs I had observed. Less than three years after Wiranto's apology, "politics," "interests," and "intrigues" had replaced the solidarity and purpose of this group.

I was struck by how deeply divided Acehnese activists had become when I read a memo from a longtime human rights advocate to Amnesty International and Human Rights Watch, which had been concerned with state violence in Aceh since 1989. The author contacted me in 2003 and told me that someone needed to explain what had happened in Aceh. He had always been cagey about giving any direct information, so I was surprised when, after generalities couched in cryptic references, he said that he would give me copies of his writings and notes. When we met the next day he handed me a package of photocopies, neatly bound in red, yellow, and green plastic binders. I was surprised to find a few bright green A4-sized Fuji photo albums as well. He muttered that I might also need photos. I did not open the albums at the time; his car was waiting, and he had arrived half an hour before our scheduled meeting in a hurry. I never asked him who took the photos or how he came to have them. They were graphic images of the abuses perpetrated in Aceh. The documents were meticulous human rights reports with cross-checked references on every case of violence that occurred after the end of DOM. I had seen him work; I knew that he read every newspaper, noted each death or violent incident, and called throughout his extensive networks to confirm the names, dates, and other details.

His memo, "Blueprint of the Aceh Case: Notes for HRW and AI" (Human Rights Watch and Amnesty International), is a thirteen-page

document tracing how the Humanitarian Pause and other international involvement had polarized civil society and human rights organizations. It is dated May 2001, a year into the Humanitarian Pause.
The analysis locates the central problem in Aceh as arms trafficking
rather than ideological or political differences.

The main problem in Aceh at this moment is that the lives, property and dignity of civilian inhabitants (*penduduk sipil*) are threatened by armed groups. Not
one person or institution or regulation (*aturan*) can protect and guarantee the
safety/survival of anyone. The government also is not capable of doing anything to safeguard (*menghindari*) citizens from acts of violence by armed
groups, even though thousands of personnel from TNI/Polri have been sent
there. The government seems not to have sufficient capability to protect citizens or even to run the civil government and to enforce civil order.

Many people agreed that the government lacked the capacity to control
the violence in Aceh at that time. He stated clearly that the situation is
"not caused by the Separatist Movement in Aceh becoming more powerful and widespread, but because of the problems in the government
itself."

A final section of the memo is devoted to the relationship between
GAM and NGOs in Aceh, Jakarta, Europe, and the United States. The
author points to divisions among former friends and critics of the government, listing the final "choices" that individuals have made regarding which side to support in the joint security committees that were the
basis for monitoring the Humanitarian Pause. He notes that the first
meeting between NGO members and GAM developed through a meeting arranged to rescue a Javanese researcher who was working on a
book about the violence of the security forces at a strategic torture post.

The author explains why he cannot support GAM: he is Acehnese, he
has spent his life in Aceh, he knows many of the GAM "higher-ups," and
he is certain that they are not struggling for the people of Aceh. He was
writing at a moment when the Humanitarian Pause had failed and the
president had signed an instruction granting the military much greater
powers to crush the rebel movement. The NGO activists whom this author identifies as GAM, primarily based on the roles they filled representing GAM on the committees, were being evacuated by international
NGOs, and their views were dominating representations and analyses of
the conflict. He details the implication of national and international organizations in the division of NGOs, especially in terms of their attitude
toward GAM violence:

A section of NGOs in Aceh and those supported by national and also international NGOs closed their eyes and justified the acts of GAM which were sadistic
and barbaric to the civilians in Aceh, and they . . . considered that raising the

cases of human rights violations that were done by GAM against civilians (*warga sipil*) in Aceh would weaken the struggle of GAM against TNI. And, they . . . said that violence (read: barbarity) which has been done by GAM against civilians in Aceh is the price that has to be paid for a struggle toward independence. For them, what has to be raised is the cruelty/barbarity which has been done by TNI/Polri, and at the same time that which is done by GAM has to be justified. And this attitude is believed and worked for by NGO activists and students who are a component of GAM in Aceh. At the same time, the other group of NGOs in Aceh still considers that both TNI/Polri and GAM have committed human rights violations in Aceh that are equally cruel and barbaric. The NGOs that take this attitude have been viewed as an enemy that has to be marginalized (*disingkirkan*) by the NGOs that are a component of GAM and at the same time are also viewed as an enemy by TNI/Polri.

Many other activists in Jakarta and Aceh had commented on the violations committed by GAM. What distinguishes this document is its insistence on locating accountability for the escalation of the conflict.

The author examines how certain activists from the GAM component were evacuated:

But, strangely, when the attitude of TNI/Polri has become strict and harsh in facing the GAM, especially after the Presidential Instruction 4/2001, in fact those who have been voicing and campaigning to the international world about the need to "evacuate activists" from Aceh are all NGO activists from the component of GAM; at the same time NGO activists not from the GAM component say that this is the moment for us to remain in the midst of the civilians (*rakyat sipil*) to help them to not become a senseless victim from the actions of TNI/Polri in implementing the Presidential Instruction 4/2001.

If the international NGOs or Western countries want to save/rescue Acehnese from violence of "armed groups," then what they must do is to evacuate all of the Acehnese who are not GAM from Aceh. If they do not do that, then indeed international NGOs [and] national organizations . . . must later be asked to take responsibility for the killings of thousands of civilians (*rakyat sipil*) in Aceh and they indirectly have protected people (activists) who for this long have worked to plant the seeds that have finally come to fruition in [Presidential Instruction No. 2/2001 that authorized military operations in Aceh].

The author's disappointment with the organizations he addresses is profound: they have been working in Aceh for ten years; unlike HDC, they have credibility, and they do not need to make their reputation on the Aceh case. But "it is possible that HRW and AI are pulled to support the romantic illusion (*romantisme semu*) because they do not know the human rights violations of GAM." He then details several cases.

Moving Violence to Jakarta

A day before the second scheduled hearing for former President Soeharto, in September 2000, a bomb exploded in Jakarta at the stock exchange building (BEJ) parking lot killing ten people, mostly drivers. Initially, police suggested that the bomb had been placed by "an evil group" to create terror. Several days later, it was announced that members of the group arrested were Acehnese. M. Nazar, the head of SIRA, linked the arrests with government efforts to end the negotiations then going on in Sweden with GAM, stating: "I am certain that the police are only trying to corner Acehnese who are outside of Aceh. They deliberately will make this a propaganda tool so that later they can be made [victims of] *sweeping*" ("Polisi Akui Tangkap Pelaku Pemboman," *Republika*, 25 September 2000). Subsequently, the police announced that the low-ranking military involved were also Acehnese ("Dua TNI Terlibat Pengeboman," *Media Indonesia*, 26 September 2000).[25] The head of the police said that "institutionally, it is certain TNI is not involved, but there are oknum, including those arrested . . . both people are from Aceh, Pidie."[26] Accusations of the military were often deflected by identifying crimes as the work of *oknum*. *Oknum* signified disavowed military members, acting without orders, or retroactively declared deserters. Linking *oknum* to Aceh potentially could have greatly extended the violence that could be attributed to the Acehnese and especially to GAM. Displacing criticism and suspicion of the military onto the Acehnese, the Special Forces spokesman explained: "We (Kopassus) have an open attitude. We intensified our investigation because there were members of ours who had deserted, and also there was a suspicion that Kopassus members were involved in the bombing." To solidify the link to Aceh, the spokesman noted that an unspecified number of Special Forces members from Aceh had asked for leave to return to Aceh a month prior to the bombing. When they returned to Jakarta, they were "lost." The territorial head of TNI underlined the military's willingness to be investigated. He promised: "TNI will not ever obstruct authorized institutions from inspecting its members if there is proof" (Letjen Agus Wijoyo, *Kepala Staf Teritorial TNI*, head of TNI Territorial Operations, quoted in "Dua TNI Terlibat Pengeboman," *Media Indonesia*, 26 September 2000). That the purpose of investigations might be to obtain such proof, or that if there was already credible proof investigations would not be required, was never discussed by the TNI when it expressed its desire to cooperate. The military stated that it would take all necessary measures to investigate the involvement of its members in this and other bombings that were suspected (based on the materials used) to be the work of military agents ("Pengebom Lainnya Diduga Lari ke Surabaya: Dua TNI Diserahkan ke Polisi," *Media Indonesia*, 27 September 2000).

The attorney general confirmed that it was clear there were "military elements" involved and noted that the problem was whether the police could effectively resolve the matter ("Pengebom Lainnya Diduga Lari ke Surabaya: Dua TNI Diserahkan ke Polisi," *Media Indonesia,* 27 September 2000). The TNI said it would "not protect and cover up" for members of the army who had been involved in "criminal and terror cases" because "it soiled the reputation of the military as an institution," not because they were opposed to impunity or wanted to support rule of law (see also "Widodo Mengaku, Kontras Anggap Janggal," *Sinar Pagi,* 27 September 2000). Megawati, in her capacity as vice president, said that she could not accept that the Special Forces were continually cornered because of the actions of a few members, such as the stock exchange bomb and the kidnapping of activists ("Wapres Minta Kopassus Jangan Dipojokkan," *Media Indonesia,* 28 September 2000).[27] At the highest levels of legal and civilian authority, military involvement is acknowledged, but attributed to individuals acting alone.

The logic by which military institutions would not be held accountable for the behavior of their members, who had increased access to the means of violence through their institutional association with the TNI, was facilitated by the inverse logic whereby, by virtue of the fact that there were Acehnese suspects, these crimes were the work of GAM. The conversion of suspects who are both military deserters and Acehnese to a part of the armed wing of Aceh Merdeka (AGAM) was accomplished through the confession of a businessman, who reportedly said that "the funds for the BEJ bombing were paid purely by AGAM" ("Ibrahim blak-blakan kepada polisi AGAM Terlibat Peledakan Bom," *Poskota,* 27 September 2000). An unnamed commander of AGAM quickly denied this accusation via cell phone: "That is not true! We never do anything as shameful and cruel that sacrifices the lives of people who have not sinned [innocent victims]."

Acehnese politicians criticized the assumption that Acehnese individuals were acting on behalf of "the" Acehnese. The head of the regional parliament (Ketua DPRD) stated that "If among the suspects who the police have arrested there were some from Aceh, it is only a coincidence. They have not acted in the name of the ethnic group of Aceh." He emphasized that "it does not need to be linked to the ethnicity of Aceh because the people of Aceh are also a part of the people of Indonesia" (Tgk M. Yus, quoted in "Polri Jangan Diskreditkan Suku Aceh," *Media Indonesia,* 27 September 2000). Strikingly, military efforts to contain Aceh as part of the Indonesian nation increased as political discourse increasingly rendered the Acehenese outside of the nation. In Jakarta, there was suspicion "of what was behind" linking suspects from Aceh with GAM and the conflict in Aceh (Ghazali Abbas Adnan, MPR member from Aceh, quoted in "Kasus Bom Sudutkan Orang Aceh," *Sinar Pagi,* 28 September 2000). NGO critics in Jakarta tried to dissociate GAM from the bombers by the fact that the capital was outside AGAM's sphere of operations ("Widodo Mengaku, Kontras Anggap Janggal," *Sinar Pagi,* 27 September 2000).

The official investigation found, based on the evidence of the bomb material, that TNI members must have been involved. According to official statements, however, "the involvement of TNI members is only because of an economic consideration. It is not because they were assigned by their unit" to infiltrate GAM (Wakakoserse Brigadir Jendral Arsyad Mbai, quoted in "Polisi: Jaringan Pelaku Bagian Dari GBPK GAM Peledakan Gedung BEJ Bermotif Politis," *Sinar Pagi,* 6 October 2000). Among the many coincidences of this case, in the course of a routine investigation the police discovered part of a network to send arms to Aceh ("Tersangka Pengebom BEJ. Terkait Jaringan Pemasok Senjata ke Aceh," *Kompas,* 28 September 2000). But this news did not inspire a more thorough investigation of the TNI's role in arming GAM. Financial transfers that pointed to the possibility that GAM figures in Singapore[28] were involved corroborated the existence of the arms network. Police concluded: "The indication that GAM is involved is in fact true. It is proven by the flow of money to and from the suspect and at the same time there is an effort to supply ammunition purchased with that money" ("Polri Umumkan 13 Tersangka Peledakan Bom," *Kompas,* 6 October 2000). M. Nazar, head of SIRA, stated that the security forces engineered the whole incident as "part of a grand scenario of the security apparatus to build public opinion which corners GAM" ("Lagi, Tersangka Pengebom BEJ Diciduk," *Republika,* 6 October 2000). The leader of the armed wing of GAM, Abdullah Syafi'ie, denied that GAM had done the bombing, stating "we are not terrorists" and protesting that GAM was always blamed ("Panglima GAM: GAM Tak Terlibat Kasus Peledakan di Jakarta," *Kompas,* 7 October 2000). The spokesperson of the joint committee on security for the Humanitarian Pause denied involvement in the bombing and underlined that the Acehnese who were detained "have no connection with GAM" ("Dua Mayat Ditemukan, Tiga Diculik di Aceh Utara. GAM Bantah Terlibat Kasus Peledakan Bom," *Media Indonesia,* 7 October 2000). A GAM spokesperson in Sweden stated: "this is the work of Indonesian intelligence. We have been faithful to the Humanitarian Pause Agreement. We do not take aggressive actions anywhere, including Aceh."[29] The bombing coincided with negotiations to extend the Pause for another three-month period. Initially, Komnas HAM emphasized that there would be no reason for GAM to carry out these bombings unless "the process in Geneva was stopped, then it would make sense that GAM was motivated to increase their attacks" (Asmara Nababan, quoted in "Penangkapan Pembom BEJ [2-Habis]. Begitu Banyak Kebetulan," *Republika,* 28 September 2000). Logics of what existing conflict forces might do substituted for the investigation and process of accountability for the violence which had been committed. Most striking in these discussions is the government's assertion that every one who is Acehnese is GAM and any TNI who commits a crime is an *oknum* for which the military are not responsible.

Critics of the Henri Dunant Centre hold them "morally accountable for the more than one thousand lives lost in Aceh since the pause," as one observer put it to me in August 2001.[30] The agreement not only failed to provide the promised solution but also irrevocably altered the terms and realities of the conflict. The brief window for dialogue passed and the conflict was transformed into a more intractable one. The substitution of romantic rebels for unpalatable realities allowed HDC to create an agreement and project that conformed to their desire to remain neutral and nonpolitical in a situation that was considered highly volatile.[31] This substitution enabled a whole chain of substitutions that obscured the consequences of HDC's desire for neutrality by retroactively rendering the conflict intractable from the start, in accordance with other state, military, national, and local narratives, and not a conflict that was intensified and escalated by an ill-conceived intervention. In Aceh during the Humanitarian Pause, neutrality became a dangerous, even fatal position for Acehnese who might have been able to mediate a solution or initiate dialogue with terms other than Referendum and independence.[32]

Other analysts defend HDC's decision to limit participation in negotiations to the Indonesian government and GAM on the grounds that the goal was to first reach a cease-fire and then subsequently initiate wider discussions. They also note that GAM "was not willing to participate as just one among many Acehnese groups" (Aspinal and Crouch 2003, 48). In this framework the existence of GAM determines the conflict analysis. The only alternative mentioned for the government would have been to divide factions of GAM on the ground from those in Sweden, which is dismissed as based on wishful thinking that Jakarta exaggerates splits in the movement to discredit it. One Acehnese man I spoke with was extremely suspicious of the strange convergences between the TNI and GAM, but followed a similar logic when he suggested that GAM would have spoiled an agreement that they were not involved in and that the main goal was to bring the arms under control, which required GAM's cooperation.

These analyses fail to understand that the terms of the HDC agreement actually contributed to bringing into existence an increasingly popular and militant GAM which retroactively appears inevitable. The existence of GAM as a conflict protagonist does significant work in structuring the conflict dynamic. Alternative narratives and policies would have resulted in different outcomes.

In these analyses, even though the goal is to bring arms under control, GAM's weapons empower it to set the terms of the negotiations and limit the power of other groups. Taking seriously the number of weapons circulating in this conflict that originate from the TNI suggests other alternatives. A policy of bringing weapons under control, accounting for how they escaped the military, and holding the military accountable for contributing arms to its enemy would have significantly altered the conditions of uncontrollable violence that foreclosed dialogue. One of the most striking scenes during my visit to Aceh on the first anniversary of the tsunami was attending the final decommissioning ceremony for GAM. Weapons were destroyed in public, ensuring that at least these weapons would not be endlessly passed between shadowy forces. As impressive as the destruction of the weapons was, it does not extinguish the other conflict logics that make the conflict endlessly renewable. Destroying weapons to prevent their use is extremely important. As difficult as rounding the weapons up was, assigning liability for the decisions that made an armed GAM logically and materially inevitable is much more difficult.

Provokator both enables and mirrors the rhetoric of neutrality. Structurally, in mediating between two opposed groups, it was convenient to have a third mysterious force to which to attribute violence. The logic of *provokator* points to a lack of accountability and a lack of knowledge. HDC was a new organization that employed individuals with conflict resolution experience, but no knowledge about Aceh. Claiming that it was impossible to conduct any negotiations in which GAM was not the sole representative of the Acehnese is predicated on the existence of a coordinated armed force; it would not make sense to expect that any agreements reached would be effectively implemented if the force in question were not presumed to be organized in a chain of command. This assumption ignores the widespread violence that was attributed to the *provokator*, the blatant abuses perpetrated by the TNI, and the undeniable overlap between TNI and its enemy. Yet, existing forms of liability and evidence make it extremely difficult to demonstrate that the conflict could have developed otherwise and that the retroactively inevitable rebels might not have taken the role they did in a mediation that assumed a different conflict pattern. Just as existing separatist rebels make it difficult to hold the TNI accountable, a GAM widely claimed to be representative by a range of groups including former human rights defenders and intellectuals makes it difficult to hold only HDC "morally accountable" for all the deaths occurring after its intervention.

Referendum initially promised a nonviolent solution to the conflict, but it fell prey to the logic of the *provokator*. After considerable violence between variously named factions, the myth of Referendum persisted. The statement Nazar made from his jail cell in June 2001 epitomized this idea: "hand things over to the people, respect their rights, because it is the most democratic and there won't be any lives sacrificed" ("Granat Meledak di Banda Aceh, Lima Orang Dilarikan ke RS," *Kompas*, 24 June 2001). This preference for nonviolent and democratic means bespeaks a logic similar to that of the HDC's insistence on neutrality and nonpolitical solutions. Many people in Aceh revealed to me a great fear of not identifying with the independence movement.[33] In light of how many lives have been lost since the end of DOM, particularly during the Humanitarian Pause, and in view of the devastating scorched earth campaign initiated by TNI and proxy militias in East Timor after its decision to separate from Indonesia, it is difficult to imagine that a referendum would have been peaceful.

The terms of the Humanitarian Pause produced a particular conflict formation that was nearly irresolvable. Problems with subsequent mediations derive from this configuration; the failed negotiations enabled the brutal military operations that preceded the tsunami. The Pause ended with Abdurrahman Wahid's Presidential Instruction authorizing military operations in April 2001. His failed attempts at resolution through dialogue may have been one of the factors that paved the way for his replacement by Megawati Soekarnoputri as president in July 2001.

Megawati had strong ties to the military; she was an adamant nationalist unwilling to compromise on regional demands. Nevertheless, the HDC worked to renew dialogue and ultimately was able to negotiate the Cessation of Hostilities Agreement (COHA) in December 2002 (see Aspinal and Crouch 2003). This agreement provided a very brief interlude of peace to ordinary people, and the hostilities resumed, although initially violence was less frequent. The agreement provided for international monitoring, peace zones, and a process of dialogue among all elements of Acehnese society. The agreement broke down at a final round of negotiations in Tokyo in May 2003 because the two sides were irreconcilably divided on the future status of Aceh, as independent or part of Indonesia. GAM representatives were arrested and jailed, and within hours President Megawati had signed a Presidential Decree imposing martial law throughout Aceh. Though the military claimed that the objective of this campaign was to "win hearts and minds," the government and military failed to provide evidence that the operation differed from previous security operations. The sense of grievance and in-justice increased as the state seemed determined to impose a military solution to the "Aceh problem." Many analysts noted that military oper-ations would fail to diminish the desire for independence (Sukma 2004, ICG 2003), yet no alternatives were proposed. These military op-erations remained in effect when Aceh was struck by the Indian Ocean tsunami in December 2004.

Chapter 6
The Tsunami and the Cease-Fire

On 26 December 2004, a tsunami devastated Aceh. It spared Aceh's valuable natural gas fields, tropical forests, and other natural resources, but destroyed the capital city, Banda Aceh. Approximately 160,000 people, 3 percent of the total population but a quarter of the population in the capital, were killed. Most people lost everything. One man I spoke with stuffed his wallet in his pocket as he ran; later, even though he had money, doctors at the hospital would not treat him, assuming he would not survive. No one was unaffected. The televised scenes of bulldozers burying the dead were arresting, reminding me of the rumors that bulldozers had been used to bury victims during DOM. The waves burst open prisons, releasing some prisoners, drowning others. Military units sustained losses. Ships were tossed inland and buildings were washed out to sea. There were miraculous stories of survival such as mosques standing untouched amid rubble and devastation, and countless stories of coincidences and split-second decisions that spared some but doomed others.

At that time, Aceh was under a state of emergency imposed by President Megawati in 2003 after the failure of the final round of negotiations to extend the Cessation of Hostilities. Under martial law, access to Aceh was tightly controlled, especially for foreign journalists and international aid groups. After the tsunami, government missions, aid organizations, and journalists crowded in to address the catastrophe. That Aceh had been the scene of conflict for three decades was repeated in coverage of the tsunami, but the intersection of the conflict and its legacies with the natural disaster and reconstruction was not well analyzed.[1]

Many commentators outside Indonesia expressed the hope that the separatist rebels and the Jakarta government would cooperate in relief efforts and that humanitarian considerations would prompt the negotiation of a lasting peace. Many Acehnese expressed these hopes as well. Some public discourse interpreted the tsunami as Allah's punishment for widespread corruption, which encompassed violence, graft, and collusion as well as for sin and immorality. The Free Aceh Movement

Figure 4. Billboard in Lhokseumawe urging people to repent for their sins, February 2006.

(GAM) immediately declared a unilateral cease-fire. Yet violent incidents continued in the aftermath of the tsunami. GAM spokesmen emphasized the losses their fighters had suffered and reiterated that they posed no threat; they were adamant that they had faithfully adhered to their cease-fire. The Indonesian security forces (TNI) and the police persisted in exaggerating the danger posed by rebels. Intense national and international attention made it more difficult for the security forces to continue ascribing their own violence to the rebels. A shooting at a military post near the UN compound two weeks after the tsunami raised concerns among international aid workers. Two soldiers were shot; one was killed. No foreigners were injured. The TNI initially blamed GAM, but subsequently the Indonesian foreign minister acknowledged that the act was committed by a "stressed soldier" (AP, 10 January 2005) This small admission indicated a major reversal of the prevailing pattern, in which the state invariably accepted the military's claims that various enemies had perpetrated violence actually authored by the military.

Violence had been a productive and profitable resource in Aceh for many years, but after the tsunami it was a threat to international donors and their programs. The tsunami is the critical turning point in many chronologies of the negotiations that resulted in the 15 August 2005 Memorandum of Understanding (MOU), which resolved contested issues and laid the basis for a peace settlement. In early 2004, Vice President Kalla had called together a secret committee of advisors to design a peace process for Aceh that would include substantial economic concessions to the rebels (ICG 2005).[2] After the tsunami ravaged Aceh's coastline in December, the process was dramatically accelerated. International funds and attention focused on Aceh increased the political stakes for both sides. GAM gave up the demand for independence and agreed to surrender its weapons. Jakarta conceded greater autonomy to Aceh, giving it the ability to tax its citizens, jurisdiction over natural resources, the right to have local political parties, and the power to institute particular roles such as "head of state" (*wali Negara*, the title Hasan Tiro had assumed in exile). Amnesty for the rebels, the release of political prisoners, and the reintegration of former combatants were negotiated. The government of Indonesia agreed to allow access for an international monitoring mission. Most analyses suggested that the losses sustained and the scale of the catastrophe prompted both sides to negotiate in better faith and with greater flexibility.

The MOU created agreement on principles and required the drafting and ratification of a law on governing Aceh to implement them. Negotiating that law took almost one year; it was finally passed by the Indonesian parliament in August 2006. When local elections were held in December 2006, former GAM members won many political offices, including the highest-ranking position in the local government, Aceh's governor. Not only was this the first time that GAM could openly campaign and seek political power, it was also the first election in Indonesia in which independent candidates and local parties were allowed. The election campaign confirmed splits within GAM between the exiled leadership and local commanders that had been rumored for some time; many internationally known GAM representatives disappeared or were marginalized, while figures from the new generation of armed forces moved into prominent positions. Following GAM's electoral victory in Aceh, legislators in Jakarta drafted a law stipulating that local parties cannot contest national elections ("Govt drafts local parties regulation for Aceh," *Jakarta Post* Web site, 6 February 2007). This measure shields the unitary Indonesian state from the threat of regionally based parties; Aceh's interests will still have to be articulated by national parties in Jakarta.

I was invited to join a delegation of scholars and activists to observe

Figure 5. Billboard in Lhokseumawe picturing the MOU, December 2005.

the progress of post–tsunami reconstruction in December 2005. Our group met with representatives from the government Agency for Rehabilitation and Reconstruction (BRR); savvy, English-speaking GAM leaders returning from exile for the first time in decades; members of the international Aceh Monitoring Mission (AMM),[3] international funding agencies, Acehnese academics and politicians, and nongovernmental organizations. We witnessed key public events, including the final ceremony for the decommissioning of GAM fighters, which was marked by the public destruction of weapons. We visited the barracks that housed tsunami survivors and listened to residents' complaints about the struggles of daily life and delays in rebuilding housing. I attended a commemoration of the tsunami in one barrack where everyone prayed together and shared a meal of sacrificed cows.

After these official meetings, I spent time talking with old friends, attending focus group discussions and public forums concerning the Draft Law on Governing Aceh (RUUPA, Rencana Undang Undang Pemerintahan Aceh), and meeting with a diverse group of new civil society organizations dedicated to monitoring the judicial system, preventing corruption and revitalizing Acehnese culture. The scene in Aceh was strikingly different from all the other times I had been there. A year after the tsunami, many signs of the destruction remained, but reconstruction and monitoring efforts were staffed by numerous expatriates who flocked to new coffee houses and restaurants. Acehnese students whom I had met in 1999 had returned from exile to take up positions with international organizations; they frequented the same places. Conversations were audible, interrupted, and overheard, not whispered and cryptic. International Women's Day was marked by a demonstration in front of the Great Mosque; protestors held signs reminding passersby of the injustices women had suffered from the conflict and under Islamic law. At moments, it seemed that anything could be said, reminding me of the euphoria that had accompanied Soeharto's fall in 1998 (Figure 6).

I was eager to hear what people were saying about the fact that the MOU foreclosed judicial investigation and prosecution of past human rights abuses. I expected to find human rights advocates heatedly debating the issue of accountability for violence. After all, their political activism was founded on exposing human rights violations, especially in the immediate aftermath of DOM. Instead, I found they were focused on the urgent problems of sustainability, livelihoods, and other reconstruction issues. Their most vigorous critique concerned the politics of who implemented programs, why the expatriate staff earned such disproportionately high salaries, who among their Acehnese friends had taken jobs with international NGOs and who had remained outside and critical of the process. Almost all of them criticized the cash-for-work programs implemented by international NGOs, saying that they had destroyed community solidarity and made it difficult to implement community organizing programs. The neighborhood cooperation that they had identified as part of Acehnese cultural tradition (*adat*) had been eroded by the practice of paying wages for cleaning up, building schools, and other public projects. Now, they said, they could not even convene focus group discussions or trainings without paying "sitting money" to those who attended. They realized that people needed money after the disaster, but explained that people participated not to facilitate the cleanup work they would have had to do anyway but because they wanted the money. These activists' frustration seemed to arise from the fact that they thought the disaster would spur social solidarity through mutual assistance but, instead, they felt it had only accelerated the spread of capitalism and individualism. They pointed to the beggars in the streets, reminding me that Aceh never had beggars before.

Figure 6. International Women's Day demonstration in front of the Great Mosque, Banda Aceh, December 2005.

The issue of accountability came up almost exclusively in response to my direct questions. Several former human rights activists told me that justice had not been forgotten, but now was not the time to seek it. They repeated the dominant rationale that people just wanted peace. Some people told me that it was too dangerous to investigate the past. Many people were preoccupied with bringing their struggle for rule of law and democracy into the realm of public policy. Moving forward was the priority, and the new law that would detail how various points of the MOU were to be realized was a critical step. Continuing the struggle that began under the banner of Referendum, they said that the Acehnese must secure as much power as possible through legislation and elections.

The MOU and the Elections

The Memorandum of Understanding between GAM and the government of Indonesia resolves the conflict between these two distinct sides. It addresses many dimensions of governance in Aceh, including political participation and the economy, human rights and the rule of law, amnesty, the reintegration of rebel fighters into society, security arrangements, the establishment of the Aceh Monitoring Mission, and a process of settling disputes. The MOU left much of the framework for implementing the substantive points unspecified and to be established in a law on governing Aceh. Most Acehnese I spoke to emphasized that the English version, "Law on Governing of Aceh," was what the MOU stipulated, while the Indonesian version, which could be translated 'Laws on the implementation of government in Aceh,' was an effort to reduce the authority of Aceh and diminish its rights to meaningful self-governance, as opposed to previous initiatives promising autonomy within Indonesia. Special autonomy legislation passed by the Indonesian Legislative Assembly (DPR) in July 2001, called the law on Nanggroe Aceh Darussalam (NAD, the Acehnese term for Aceh as a political entity), had already established a symbolic head of state (*Wali Negara*), the authority to implement Islamic law, and the direct election of the governor. In addition, the 2001 law promised that 80 percent of petroleum and natural gas revenues would be returned to Aceh. The law on governing Aceh was to provide much greater authority to the region. But the final version ratified by the DPR was significantly weakened from the versions submitted and reduced the authority granted by the 2001 law.

The months that I was in Aceh and Jakarta (December 2005–March 2006) coincided with an intense period of drafting and lobbying for this law. I found cautious optimism and near consensus about the Acehnese draft. There was a strong sense that all components of Acehnese society had come together in countless meetings and agreed on a version of the law to submit to Jakarta. Individuals expressed various dissatisfactions with parts of the law, but all said they could not risk being divided in negotiations; they had to lobby for what came to be called the "All-Aceh" draft. Given the extensive polarization and distrust that was expressed in other contexts, and that I knew continued to mark social and political relations, I was surprised by the seeming consensus on the draft law. The "All-Aceh" version was submitted by the Acehnese parliament, making use of formal state channels. At one point, a GAM version was submitted that differed from the "All-Aceh" version.[4] In failing to ratify the draft prepared in a consultative process by the Acehnese, the central government demonstrated yet again a disregard for Acehnese citizens exercising their political rights through official channels, in addition to confirming suspicions that the center was not negotiating in good faith.[5]

Discussions on the law and the future of Aceh were most heated around issues of local parties, independent candidates, and when local elections would take place. Strategizing and speculation about who would represent GAM and how GAM would perform in the upcoming elections were central to discussions about their role and how "civil society" would relate to GAM in the future. Jakarta-based NGO allies attended some of these meetings. In addition to seeking guidance on what their Acehnese colleagues wanted them to lobby for in Jakarta, these individuals recognized the importance of the Aceh election as a precedent for national electoral reform. Women's organizations lobbied for provisions to increase women's political participation. In meetings and discussions, political issues, such as the formation of local parties, filled the available time, and the issues of human rights and past violence were deferred. Everyone told me that the important thing was to get the law passed to ensure the Acehnese had as much political power as possible. When I asked about the past, people said it was important, but now was not the time to confront it. I was told people did not want to upset the fragile peace, they wanted to resume their normal lives, or it would be better to deal with this problem after the Acehnese had more political power.

I thought that residual fear and continuing intimidation from both armed parties might be contributing to the lack of interest in discussing the past. In early 2006, it was not clear who would win the elections, how GAM would perform as a political party, and who would exercise power. It was wise not to say much about the past. GAM had reason to fear disclosure of the abuses perpetrated by fighters who were being reintegrated and stood to attain valuable resources, political offices, and positions in the Indonesian military or police, as provided in the MOU. GAM also had reason to fear what the still-powerful military might to do disrupt an agreement they were not enthusiastic about. For example, disgruntled members of TNI might engineer violence to create conditions that would necessitate their return. Opening a discussion of the past might derail the fragile peace process. The official processes, narratives, institutions, and mediations all constrained the space for discussing the past. The MOU establishes a human rights tribunal for violations occurring after the MOU was signed and projects an Acehnese Commission for Truth and Reconciliation subordinate to a national level commission. The 2004 law mandating the national Commission for Truth and Reconciliation was declared unconstitutional in December 2006. Consequently, there is no longer a basis for establishing the Aceh commission.[6]

These processes and institutions have made it impossible to distinguish rumors and suspicions from actions for which individuals might be held accountable. Rumors that have not been disproved could return and disrupt the fragile peace. If there is no discussion or acknowledgment of the overlap between rebels and security forces and no process for holding individuals accountable for the crimes they committed that resulted in losses of life, property, and dignity, then it is difficult to imagine how politics and law, which everyone hopes will displace the violent conflict, will function effectively.

Many former human rights activists were involved with economic development programs, trying to ensure that aid reached those who needed it most. They spoke in terms of *eko-sok*, economic and social rights, distinguishing them from the individual political rights that they had worked for previously. As they looked toward the future, they focused on the substantive changes that might be made through a more democratic governance system. They spoke of a GAM that existed, had to be reckoned with politically, and might even be their best representative. Yet, although we did not discuss the matter, I could not imagine that they had forgotten their earlier doubts about GAM. Seven years before, some of them had struggled to convince me that GAM was the product of the security forces and was intended to distract attention from their own violations during DOM. On the other hand, GAM might become the best vehicle for implementing the changes they hoped for. I took their silence on the issue to be the most meaningful comment I would hear and turned to the present, observing what was happening and what futures were being imagined. I still wondered how it would be possible to build a future with so many residual fears and the complex legacies of the dark pattern and *provokator*.

It makes perfect sense that the parties negotiating the MOU, GAM and the Indonesian government, agreed not to examine past violations. The MOU stipulates that GAM fighters will be granted amnesty by the government of Indonesia; and subsequent statements by high-ranking military suggested that the TNI should also be granted amnesty. GAM rhetoric consistently made justice for past violence a political rather than a legal issue. As early as 1999, Syafi'ie told me that independence would be justice and that there would be no need to have a legal process to adjudicate DOM violations. If political settlements were to replace legal prosecutions, then the past apparently could be resolved through political demands and GAM's transformation into a political party. Indeed, the electoral victories of "ex-GAM" candidates in Aceh's December 2006 elections is a political development that opens new, nonviolent channels for redressing past inequalities and grievances.

Now former GAM leaders will have to demonstrate that when they hold power they can improve conditions for the Acehnese.

Troubles with terminology have persisted. One striking aspect of the election campaign was the contradictory status ascribed to GAM itself. On the one hand, GAM as an organization of violent separatist rebels had officially ceased to exist as a condition of the cease-fire. On the other hand, if GAM did not exist, then the Indonesian military state had no partner with whom to make peace. The new acronyms did not fully replace former designations of the combat structure, but the newly disallowed terms seemed to point to more stable referents than they had in the past. Concurrently, civil society activists who had not aligned themselves with GAM, especially those committed to non-violence, found themselves sidelined from the political process. Some supported "ex-GAM" leaders, while others did not. Out of a shifting array of multiple political and military formations, the MOU created two clearly delimited antagonists, imposing order but also distorting the situation on the ground. The political campaign could not contain these distortions as multiple individuals sought to take on the power of being (ex-)GAM.

Despite concerns about what might go wrong based on ample past experience, the elections went smoothly. The period leading up to the vote was marred only by minor incidents of violence related to tensions and splits within GAM. Former GAM combatants won many offices throughout Aceh. Most attention focused on the governor's race. Both major tickets included a candidate for governor who was visibly affiliated with GAM and a candidate for lieutenant governor who was visibly not. Hasan Tiro's group ultimately supported Hasbi Abdullah and Humam Hamid. Hasbi is the younger brother of a prominent AM member in exile. He had been in Aceh and was repeatedly jailed as a GAM member during DOM, and he had served on one of the earlier Humanitarian Pause committees. Humam, a well-known intellectual and political figure who remained in Aceh throughout DOM, had the backing of the primary national Islamic party (the PPP). They were opposed by Irwandi Yusuf and Muhammad Nazar, who ultimately broke with the international leadership. Irwandi, an academic who joined GAM in 1990[7] and was in jail during the tsunami but survived by knocking a hole in the roof, had experience in the armed struggle and represented second-generation GAM (ex-combatants identified by the acronym KPA) with the monitoring mission. Nazar, the young leader of SIRA (Central Information Committee on Aceh Referendum) who rose to prominence by organizing the Referendum march, had previously maintained a strict distinction from GAM. Initially, both tickets received endorsements from Hasan Tiro's prime minister in exile, Malik Mahmud, demonstrating the complexity of GAM's transition to a political organization and betraying fractures between groups acting in its name prior to the elections. The organization of ex-combatants initially remained neutral, but ultimately supported the winning ticket of Irwandi and Nazar.[8] I was impressed with the speech I heard Irwandi deliver at the decommissioning ceremony in December 2005. He drew on the metaphor of building a traditional chair, noting that the coarse work of felling the tree and cutting the structure had been done with armed struggle but now it was time to take up other tools, words, to finish the fine work and to make the beautiful Acehnese carving. He has expressed a willingness to take on a number of tough issues in Aceh, including corruption. He has declared his own wealth and has very little. Irwandi presents himself as secular and intends to review controversial aspects of the implementation of Islamic law.[9] He is concerned with finding livelihoods for former combatants and ending extortion, tasks that are closely linked (Figure 7).

Perhaps the tsunami washed away so much of the past that Irwandi and Nazar will be able to build a new future unencumbered by its dark legacies. Their victory may herald the change that many Acehnese have sought since 1998. Indeed, in the tense months following the tsunami before the MOU was signed, some Acehnese said if peace could not be achieved after something as extraordinary as the tsunami, it meant there would never be peace in Aceh. Since the MOU there has been visible optimism. If people in Aceh can be optimistic after so many disappointments, then perhaps those analyzing the situation from afar ought to write a happy ending to this tale. Yet, I am suspicious of agreements signed in far-away capitals that are grounded on conflict narratives that do not take into account all the conflict's victims and have no legal provision to hold anyone liable for so many violent deaths. The most optimistic view is perhaps the most cynical: if the manipulations of those in power created conditions of possibility for violence that was enacted locally, then a top-down solution is an effective approach to resolving the conflict. The likelihood that TNI and GAM members were behind-the-scenes collaborators in the shadowy past may facilitate their working relationship as they go forward in public. If violence itself became the key resource during much of the conflict, then ending violence requires conditions in which keeping the peace is a prerequisite for access to funds; peace must pay dividends.[10] Still, I remain deeply troubled by the histories that are widely known but cannot be openly acknowledged. Like many Acehnese and Indonesian human rights activists, I am haunted by well-documented stories of murder, vengeance, and collusion that are hard to forget, persistent public secrets that are not quite

Figure 7. Destruction of GAM weapons, December 2005.

denied. I fear that the tsunami has not swept away memory and the suspicion generated by the past.

I was especially struck by one Acehnese analysis of the conflict, which
discloses the complexities of the past and makes clear why it must be
reckoned with. I turn to this viewpoint before considering how the legacies of violence infect the political process with paranoia that is not entirely irrational.

"What is the philosophy of a person who raises kites?"

At the end of January 2006, I met with a young man who had become
involved in conflict resolution after the Humanitarian Pause. He had
grown up in one of the areas most affected by the conflict, and his
family had lost members to both GAM and TNI. We had not met before, and he did not know most of the NGO people I did; an international aid worker had suggested I contact him. We set up a meeting
to discuss conditions in Aceh and his current work. In the second
hour, our conversation moved into his analysis of the conflict. He
had made vague references to things that were not exactly as they

seemed or should be; such remarks were familiar to me from conversations with other people on previous visits. I asked direct questions to see if he would confirm what he was alluding to, including what he thought about the many signs or stories of cooperation between GAM and TNI.

He answered after letting me know that these comments could not be attributed to him: "I often say that the Aceh conflict is like a person who flies kites. What is the philosophy of a person who raises kites? Actually TNI." I must have looked puzzled, because he paused and repeated "kite" in English. He continued:

It's like this. In '98 the current was *civil society on the top* [English in original], because *civil society* was capable of toppling (*menggulingkan*) Soeharto. And the predictions were that TNI was going to fall to null in terms of their position. Those people, the children of powerful people, automatically had a strategy. Their strategy was fishing, fishing so that that [TNI's position] would return. Because Wiranto in his speech in Lhokseumawe had said that at that moment the security conditions in Aceh had been handed over to the *ulamas* (religious leaders). So, what happened there a day after that, rocks were thrown at local buildings; a few stores were burned down . . . [names different buildings and describes the destruction]. What is very funny was that it was done by school children with a few different kinds of uniforms. But, unfortunately, the shirts of their uniforms were fine, but the hair on their legs was thick. They were already old like that, and at that moment, it happened, Gerakan Aceh Merdeka (Free Aceh Movement) was heard. And in my opinion, GAM, that was the military.

He explained the dynamic and conditions at that moment. He used an Indonesian expression, *gayung bersambut,* "something is expected and then it is there," and then stated in English, "This condition creates the space for GAM."

However, this was not a preexisting or hidden GAM in Aceh. He explained: "Thus at that moment, it was known that in Aceh there was no longer any GAM at all. All the GAM were in Malaysia and Batam. The ones who were really GAM, yeah? Those ones, they were in Batam. Ahmad Kandang was in Batam at that moment. And the majority of them were in Malaysia, like Ishak Daud and Muzakir Manaf; they also had gone to Malaysia at that moment." I was surprised to hear Ahmad Kandang cited as true GAM. Many others had pointed to him as one of the clearest examples of how the TNI had produced its enemy in 1998.

The idea that there is a real GAM elsewhere, or individuals who are "really" GAM, complicates his analysis of the TNI "giving" the kite, which is actually their existence, to GAM:

Now, with conditions like this, this kite was already in the air, the kite was already raised by TNI, then given to GAM, "here it is you guys raise it up." Finally it was up. But, at the moment that it was raised, the wind was too good; the wind was a wind that was strong. And, the philosophy of the kite raiser is that when it catches a strong wind, constant and stable, it will not come down again, not at any time.

Recalling his opening comments on the position of civil society at the end of DOM, the strong wind likely included the prominent role played by civil society organizations in Soeharto's downfall, national sentiments favoring reform, the overwhelming outrage inspired by accounts of DOM violence, and international support for the East Timor referendum.

Then, in the very next sentence, he seems to cast doubt on the idea that objective conditions, with strong grievances and more open political spaces, had kept the kite up in the air. Perhaps aware of my puzzlement, he continued:

And even if it was actually like that, it will not want to come down ever, and this is what happened. So, don't be surprised if in Lhokseumawe there are machines from Bandung, from Pindad [state munitions factory], and even the purchase of quite a lot of weapons from Bandung. GAM doesn't at all [*pause*]. . . . Ah, this is their philosophy actually, the ones who raise the kites just want to initiate them, but the wind is just too good. And automatically, yeah, if he wants the kite to come down again the string must be broken. So, now that is GAM.

He suggested that the security forces wanted to start GAM, but that it got out of their control. One reason the story of the TNI creating GAM seems so implausible is that GAM has become so popular. If it was a fabrication, then why did society support it, why did it become real? Quite often, observers and analysts assume that the visible overlaps between GAM and TNI are aberrations, isolated incidents that are insignificant in light of the apparently overwhelming support of the 'people' for GAM.

He repeated that in the connection of GAM and society, what was expected happened: Acehnese "society, in my analysis, is like a person who is floating in the river when it is flooded." He paused, so I asked him to explain.

Automatically he is going to look for something to grab on to, and as we know, on the edge of the river there is mostly grass. The people of Aceh know that GAM is just grass, something that they cannot actually hold onto, but who knows if this grass might be bamboo, because bamboo is a kind of grass. Who knows if the grass this time is bamboo grass and not tall coarse grass (*rumput ilalang*)? That is why it fits. . . . From one side it is terrible; from another side it is an opportunity. So that is why it is like this.

The expression that something "cannot be held" is frequently used to suggest that someone's word cannot be trusted, or that they behave inconsistently. The idea that everyone knew GAM could not be held onto complicates the appearance of popular support for the rebels.

I said there were not many people who said things like this so clearly, even though many people hinted at similar issues and others emphasized the abuses perpetrated by GAM. He told me not to be mistaken because not all the people, even in GAM, knew this. I asked him to explain:

What I mean . . . the majority . . . maybe, yeah, maybe people who raised the kites are already dead like Abdullah Syafi'ie, Rahman Paloh, GAM commander in Lhokseumawe, Ahmad Kandang, and then Ishak Daud, these people are the only ones who know, the rest of them do not know. I am not sure that Irwandi knows because Irwandi came in late.

I asked if the first generation of Aceh Merdeka, such as Hasbi Abdullah, knew. He replied:

So, it is like this, so what I meant, those who were used, and even like this, yeah, even GAM members who were given the kite to raise, sometimes they were not aware "oh, I am being ordered to raise this, oh." They felt that "I am flying kites," without being aware.

I asked him to explain more about what they were not aware of.

So, it is like this, they feel that "these are the kites that I have raised." They are not aware that the kite was actually given to them. So if you want to get an acknowledgement from him, he won't acknowledge it. If I talk to GAM like this, maybe I would be killed. "What do you know about our struggle from 1976, that is not it . . . hoh, *bullshit*" [English in original]. Indeed, it is true, from the year '76 they became like this, like this, like this. But, we are talking about the *moment*. And, don't be surprised that GAM has a *strict point* [English in original], they do not want to compromise on issues like this. Later it will be said that this disrupts all kinds of things. So, they are not going to be open about issues like this. So, I say that I see this as my analysis of just an ordinary Acehnese person.

The fact that the TNI had provided weapons and ammunition was not something that most GAM members would have denied. When I met with a GAM fighter and representatives to the HDC committees in 2000, they were very forthcoming about the levels of support provided by TNI.[11] The idea that the TNI had created their organization as he suggests would be much more disruptive.

Even though this man noted problems of the current GAM through the kite metaphor, he was not immune to hope that there might be a pure GAM.

At one point I was asked: "Do you or don't you like GAM?" Actually, it is true I would like to be free from Indonesia without GAM.
D: What do you mean?
Not GAM as an organization, but as the rogue elements/agents. For example, if as the concept survives it can help the people of Aceh, I will support it.

His comments implied that while he did not trust the current GAM as an organization, given its ties to the TNI and rogue elements, he considered the original concept of Aceh Merdeka worth supporting. As critical as he is of the current organization, he asserts a historical continuity between it and the 1976 movement.

He described some recent work he had done along these lines. When he finished, I asked him about the role of HDC in empowering GAM as a representative and how this changed the conflict.[12] He said it was part of GAM's lobbying efforts:

The problem is that at the time of the Humanitarian Pause I think almost 75 percent of Acehnese society supported GAM. So if, for example, civil society was not included at that moment, its context was not too large, because that moment really was the height of GAM's strength. How could it reach that peak? Because from 1998 to 2001 the government did nothing. There was no counter of any kind, be it information or development. If the government could have countered the issue in Aceh or countered it with development it would be a very different issue. And besides that, a justification of information [propaganda] happened in Aceh at that time. So you can imagine the socialization that was done by GAM from *meunasah* to *meunasah* (small buildings for prayer) from mosque to mosque and from place to place, without any kind of counter from any side. Automatically what was said was already [what was] true. And indeed there was nothing, including me at that time. I mean, in early 1999, around that time. Because I did not have any kind of access to true information, did not know who they were; what I knew was only the people around me, all that shaped my opinion. So, HDC was not wrong if they did not want to look any further [to see] what the actual problem was. They thought that [they] had spoken with lots of people who had the same voice that doing something then was right. So, this is what I mean, what happened then. They did not want to know more *beyond* [English in original] [what they heard]. . . . Don't be mistaken, at that time there was no one who was bold enough to challenge GAM, there was no one. Not even to contradict them; if we were neutral it was already dangerous. "So you are not of Acehnese blood." Yeah, it was like that, indeed it was a bit difficult to position oneself then. So the objective meaning from a reality was not there, because the people did not speak from their heart then. It was the same when they spoke to TNI.

The difficulty of criticizing GAM and still being "Acehnese" cannot be emphasized enough, especially in 1999. He comments that he opposes GAM, but not the concept, and he prefers their goal, independence, without their individual agents. He endeavors to demonstrate greater fidelity to the goal than those who have claimed it—that is, to be more Acehnese in his spirit of independence and to distinguish that spirit from GAM's claim to it.

It is striking that the demand for justice and the articulation of an Acehnese identity centered on justice was replaced by the drive for independence. Then the demand for independence was exchanged for political office in a deal predicated on the absence of juridical examination of the injustices, crimes, and grievances that fueled these very campaigns. The military made direct contributions to the formation and popularity of GAM. Through inaction, the civilian government provided further impetus for ordinary Acehnese to choose GAM in a conflict resolution process structured without other alternatives by HDC and the civilian government. His comments reminded me that the process of "socialization," creating public awareness and dissemination of information, continued. A short time later, when I attended an information session on the MOU in Lhokseumawe, the Indonesian representative failed to appear, and the GAM representative told the crowd that without GAM there would have been neither peace nor development.

We had scheduled a brief meeting because his job required much travel and he was off the next morning, but he still wanted to explain how the problem continued into the present. People said only what they thought the powerful international forces wanted to hear. Like the kite-raising process he had spoken of earlier, this pattern extended the conflict dynamics: "In my view, the *peace process is still honeymoon* [English in original]. Psychologically, GAM still feels that they have weapons and that the people are still afraid of them. Psychologically, TNI still feels that they have many friends." Various "nonorganic" backup units that were not under the control of the local military command had been removed but, perhaps institutionally and certainly individually, soldiers still had an exaggerated sense of their power. The people were still "afraid of GAM as if they still have weapons, and still afraid of TNI as if they are still repressive." He thought that this situation would change:

My prediction is that when *freedom of expression* [English in original] arises Aceh will be a bit different, in that when the people are bold enough to challenge GAM, when they are bold enough to speak in the coffee shop the way that I am talking, for example, it will already be different. The people are not yet bold to speak like I am.

He was waiting for the moment when the people were brave enough to refuse the demand of a local GAM figure for a cigarette, for example. He reminded me that the Acehnese were "tough" and, as a result, a dangerous situation that tested the peace process could develop. Refusing extortion demands and openly discussing the overlap between TNI and GAM pose different challenges to the peace process.

In his comments, GAM slides back and forth between a fabrication of the TNI—a kite that has its own momentum and seems to exist independently of the process that put it in the air, an opportunity to achieve better conditions for Acehnese—and the individual local agents who ask for cigarettes. In the past, information was hard to come by; intimidation was pervasive. In his story, the people know that GAM is slippery and cannot be held. But, in the absence of better alternatives, they grasp for it and hope that it turns out to be better than they suspect or fear.

In his analysis, there seems to be a GAM that is not a fabrication of the security forces. In early 2006, as in 1999, every suspicion of an imitation or false GAM called into being the hoped-for or imagined existence of a real GAM that had the people's best interest in mind: a pure GAM. No judicial or investigative process has examined the relationship between GAM and TNI. In the Independent Commission report, at the very same time that the dark pattern is invoked to describe the contribution of the security forces to GAM, the dissatisfaction and critique are consolidated with armed struggle of suspicious or separatist origins. Similarly, at the same time that it documents military manipulations and overlap with their enemy, the report invokes a second-generation GAM that has appeared in response to popular grievances and lack of response from the Indonesian government. The existence of a real GAM makes it impossible to account for the overlap between TNI and GAM, and the overlap makes it possible for a real GAM to come into existence.

Both individual and societal processes would be needed to address the dark pattern that is made inscrutable by the figure of the *provokator*. It is difficult to conceive of the conditions that would make it possible for ordinary people to talk in coffee shops about the TNI passing the kite to GAM. If this overlap were discussed, it would be difficult to imagine that GAM could provide an opportunity for a better future. GAM has become the only opportunity for seeking justice and change. Both TNI and GAM have an interest in not recalling the process of raising the kite. It is not clear whether the string has been cut, or who is holding it. The kite metaphor resonates with a long history of masterminds moving masses that is characteristic of Indonesian politics and security forces' rhetoric and policy of threat perception and response. The timing and conditions that made the kite fly, along with the conditions that made many Acehnese grasp it, remove the analysis from the realm of a conspiracy theory that attributes too much power to an extremely weak, often incompetent, and uncoordinated state and military apparatus. At the same time, this metaphor obscures the precise decisions made and actions taken over and over again to make the kite seem to be flying under its own power, or out of control of the initiator. It covers up the decisions made over and over to hope that there was a pure GAM despite known overlaps. And it does not address the liabilities of the civilian state for failing to hold the military accountable, failing to address the problem of "single bad guys" that it acknowledged was significant and to some extent recognized, and failing to make decisions and enact policies that would have provided concrete opportunities for Acehnese to pursue justice and a better future in the framework of Indonesia. The failure to "counter" in any concrete or symbolic form, the failure to support individuals who might not have chosen this kite as their best option, has produced a conflict configuration that retroactively appears inevitable. Closer inspection reveals a series of decisions and actions that produced the current conflict. Pragmatic concerns about an extremely powerful military that made it impossible to hold known perpetrators accountable judicially have corrupted the law.

Some international observers may hope that, once Irwandi has consolidated power and established functioning state institutions, at least a limited investigation of violent "excesses" could be carried out. It is unlikely that regional truth and reconciliation commissions will be established following the defeat of national commission legislation by the constitutional court. Even if a commission were to be established to examine Aceh's past, it would be feasible to focus only on *oknum*, "rogue elements," of TNI and on *provokator* or extortionists posing as GAM. Double agents, "deserters" who moved between sides, and collaborators whose identities are known to relatives and co-villagers of the dead and disappeared would remain immune, along with TNI and GAM commanding officers. The "dark pattern" would continue to lurk in the shadows, just as the kite would continue flying with a visible GAM holding the string. The fact that ex-GAM governs Aceh as a result of an internationally brokered cease-fire might suggest that TNI's liability for mass death could be adjudicated, yet the political bargain between GAM and the Indonesian state makes the region's autonomy dependent on recognition from the center. And the Indonesian state itself remains insecure relative to its own military, always poised to assert its leading role in the face of recurrent unrest. So, mistrustful silence continues.

Despite the rhetoric of winning hearts and minds and trying to keep the military from getting out of control, civilians did very little. This does not mean that the military should be excused; quite the contrary. But, by giving in to the discursive construction of all Acehnese citizens as GAM supporters, civil society is also being let off the hook for its failure to protect democratic rights or otherwise counter the conflict. The state failed to be more than a corrupt front for a military bully. This process was preventable, but became irreversible. Neither economic reforms and democratic processes nor justice through law, were it attainable, would have worked the same way prior to the tsunami as they would have in 1998. GAM's electoral victory may allow it to exercise power nonviolently, though it secured that power through the use of violence. In the meantime, human rights advocates who sought nonviolent solutions and struggled to maintain neutrality in the earlier phases of the conflict either allied themselves with GAM or have been marginalized.

Retroactively existing separatist rebels, renewed threats of vengeance, and indeterminate patterns of violence all limited the state's liability for acknowledged violence. The appearance of instability or of a threat to the republic in the present justifies the military's continued prominence and aggression. The Indonesian armed forces have a long history of manufacturing threats to bolster their importance and justify their political role. In fact, during 1998–1999 many people believed that cases of mysterious violence that erupted across the archipelago were provoked or engineered by the military.[13] The Acehnese case, however, differs in important ways from both historic and contemporary cases of manipulated conflicts. Official analyses developed a conflict logic that proved irresistible to both sides. Indeed, the solidification of the "sides," especially the rebel force GAM, resulted from the logic outlined in official reports and policies. The logic itself became evidence; a compelling narrative about ideologically motivated violence between existing forces framed incidents that were otherwise ambiguous. International mediations based on official interpretations of the conflict solidified a visible and existing GAM as representative of the people of Aceh.

Both GAM and the military had an interest in understanding the conflict as one that had been waged by GAM over a long period of time. Individuals claiming to represent GAM enjoyed an increased social status from their struggle. The economic benefits were also significant. Representatives of GAM exercised considerable leverage in distributing funds under the Humanitarian Pause. Individuals claiming to represent GAM systematically extorted "taxes" from the population. Reconstruction programs and future governance reward those identified as (ex-)GAM, while programs to compensate victims of either TNI or GAM violence have not been prioritized. For the military, narrating the struggle as protracted and the rebels as recalcitrant shifted discussions of accountability. A visible and armed GAM that claimed a long history of struggle justified past military policies that were excessive in their implementation. The military's role in producing its enemy disappears.

In a two-sided conflict, acts of violence could be attributed to either side, enabling relativist analysis of violence. Although these developments may appear inevitable, as if efforts toward resolution were overtaken by increasingly violent social protest expressed through the GAM movement, I have argued that it is precisely narratives about second-generation separatists and subsequent policy decisions that have produced the situation those narratives predicted. The hypothetical existence of a conflict protagonist, GAM, that waged a continuous struggle came to be inevitable retroactively and obscured the concrete processes through which GAM came into being, especially the dark pattern in which the security forces contributed substantial resources to their enemy to distract attention from their own crimes. Retroactive inevitability, by which a solid GAM appears and claims a continuous history of struggle, has made the process of creating GAM inscrutable, and as a result assigning liability and holding the security forces accountable for the dark pattern has been impossible. GAM's continued existence has provided a renewable source of ammunition to extend this conflict and avoid judicial inspection of the past. Relativism and the interests of both GAM and TNI foreclose investigation of past violations, especially during DOM. Without reviewing the past, the logic of an insecure state may persist. Civilian leaders in Aceh and Jakarta have failed to confront the weakness of the state, especially its inability to control the powerful military. The law remains subordinate to the power of violence. Corrupt institutions cannot enforce a situation where individual acts have consequences. The possibility of horizontal violence may threaten the fragile peace. New anxieties and new latent dangers may arise.

Counter-Narrative

How lasting can a peace be that is based on historical narratives constructed through the active collaboration, perhaps even collusion, of some parties to the conflict but do not take into account the voices and viewpoints of those who suffered from the violence it visited upon them? This is not simply an argument that the voices of the victims must be heard and acknowledged in some kind of official context (e.g., Minow 1998). The victims of human rights abuses have testified, and their stories have not been denied. Neither am I suggesting that these agreements will be disrupted by conflicts between individuals when "freedom of expression" develops. Rather, I am concerned with the legacies of the dark force. What kinds of new inequalities will be institutionalized by these agreements and the initiatives and programs designed to support them? How much faith can less powerful people place in institutions of justice if the military leaders who perpetrated systematic campaigns of terror against civilians enjoy immunity from prosecution? Those whose grievances turn on economic inequality and lack of democratic political participation may find opportunities for expression and redress as GAM shifts from a separatist force to one focused on prosperity and democracy in Aceh, but this remains to be seen. How will continuing problems of governance be addressed if they are perpetrated by Acehnese rather than the central government? To what extent will the terms of GAM's political triumph allow for a working-through in which agents acknowledge their complicities? Was the tsunami powerful enough to cast contradictions, complexities, and complicities irretrievably into oblivion? Do the possibilities of peace and the bright future of prosperity and self-governance foreclose, or render unnecessary, accountability for the past?

It is almost impossible to demonstrate that conflict situations could have developed differently, and as a result it is nearly impossible to assign liability for the escalation of particular conflicts. To demonstrate how different narratives about the past developed through the analytic tools explored in Chapter 1 would result in different consequences, I sketch how a different narrative might perform different political work.

A historical narrative that highlights the discontinuities between the "generations" of political rebels—the 1950s DI/TII movement for an Islamic nation within a federal state, the 1976–1979 Aceh Merdeka liberation movement for self-determination and control over economic resources, and the 1998–1999 civil uprising against military domination and authoritarian rule—would suggest different relationships between recent and past violence. Reading the current situation in light of this alternative narrative would require acknowledging that Aceh Merdeka articulated a nonviolent critique of unjust patterns of economic development but was violently suppressed in a military campaign that repressed many more Acehnese than had supported AM. Recognizing that this group was distinct from what later became known as GAM would trace a clear line between political-economic radicalism and armed separatism. This alternative genealogy of Acehnese rebellion entirely excludes what the military called GPK and characterized as a criminal gang, but it holds open the possibility that GAM itself, in its post-1998 incarnation in Aceh, was produced through armed conflict among the state security forces, renegade elements of those forces, remnants of rebel forces, and corrupt and ruthless opportunists. Taking this possibility seriously would mean that the Indonesian military and GAM were as much collaborators as opponents in the protracted conflict that victimized the people of Aceh throughout the 1990s.

Seeing GAM as it emerged from DOM in the late 1990s as more aligned with the military itself than with AM's intellectual, nonviolent critique of resource exploitation articulated in the name of regional identity would demand military accountability and economic reform rather than campaigns to eradicate separatism. GAM could no longer be presented as a threat to the integrity of the Indonesian state, a group committed to pursuing its nonnegotiable demand for independence through violent means. If GAM were seen as a shadowy extension of the Indonesian military, its nightmare alter ego, with whom it was often exchanging personnel, weapons, and disguises, and with whom it collaborated in carrying out mass abduction, murder, rape, and torture, then the role of the separatist threat and the violence it justified in perpetuating the military's control of Aceh and its supremacy in the Indonesian state would be clarified.

This counternarrative may be more totalizing than is warranted, but dismissing it out of hand forecloses important analytic and political possibilities. Have such possibilities already been foreclosed by the election, the win, the big shift of hope, and the happy ending? At the very least, TNI contributed to GAM's existence by naming the violent separatist group as its antagonist in order to justify indiscriminate violence in Aceh, and the state's cooperation with HDC inscribed this conflict discourse in the international intervention. If the dynamic interactions between GAM and TNI were taken seriously, reformers and political elites in Jakarta would have to consider the problem of an uncontrollable military rather than, or at least in addition to, violent separatists. This understanding of the conflict dynamics could focus attention on the state's use of force to address political critiques, its failure to address widespread human rights violations, the lack of human rights protections, and the failure of legal institutions.

Constructing alternative accounts of political violence requires us to document and analyze conflict dynamics and processes. Studying the processes and dynamics through which conflicts emerge, develop, and mutate as they continue or resume is different from trying to historicize identities and discover truer histories (Scott 1999). Studying the conflict dynamic discloses how historical narratives shift over time, serve

particular strategies, and command different resources. Indeed, historical narratives are themselves crucial to the consolidation of the conflict
protagonists and their mobilization of various forces into oppositional
arrays. In conflict situations, narratives and evidence about what happened in the past and what it means for the present are valuable and
contested. Thus, making particular versions of history dominant and
unassailable makes it especially difficult to return to the process of consolidating conflict protagonists, or to question certain forms and terms
that structure the conflict. Disarming the infinite supply of ammunition
provided by their existence requires innovative analyses and policies. If
the movement that grew to be a threat to the state started off as a nonviolent critique of inequality, what guarantee is there that the new local
political parties and their efforts to improve the conditions for their
constituents will not develop into a similar threat? What will stop the
logic of insecurity?

Law and Corruption

While I am troubled by the disappearance of certain historical narratives, I do not think that narration and disclosure of the past in and
of itself is healing, although this rationale justifies the prominent
role given to truth commissions and tribunals in some political transitions. In the Indonesian case, instead of a problem of trauma, I perceive a problem of corruption—not in the familiar form of graft, the
commonplace misuse of public office for private financial gain, but
in a pervasive societal form, a radical disconnection between agency
and liability that undermines the possibility of communal solidarity
as well as institutional legitimacy (Drexler 2006c). The point of a
process of adjudication in Aceh would not be to hear the facts, which
are widely known, but to free the society of the corrosive power of
mistrust, to ensure that actions have consequences, and to distinguish truth from falsity. The retroactive inevitability and imagined
continuity of GAM's current existence makes it impossible to hold
the military accountable for the dark pattern and its own crimes, as
the Bantaqiah case demonstrates. The acceptance of this narrative
signifies the refusal of society to recognize collective culpability, so—
with demoralizing circularity—everything remains corrupt. At this
point, it seems, most people who aspire to political power are complicit in suppressing their awareness of the dark pattern without
counteracting its existence. These corruptions will not disappear
after former GAM combatants are inaugurated into political offices
in an autonomous Aceh. Returning to the story of the kite, it is possible that newly elected governor Irwandi does not know the kite was

handed off to the now-deceased figures who were part of the dark pattern. If this is the case, his ability to govern may be undermined by a failure to understand the complex political relationships and debts that he will have to contend with. If he is privy to the kite's handoff, then he will be indebted to the kite launchers—the military—and may have his own insecurities about his legitimacy. If he is operating in a system where he knows things are not exactly as they appear, it may be significantly harder to bypass the politics and move to a new form of clean governance. Or, he may believe, as GAM representatives told me in 2000, and as many members of the Timorese resistance also told me, that the "truth" and "rightness" of GAM's struggle motivated good-hearted soldiers labeled rogue elements by their TNI commanders to lend material support to GAM. The dark pattern may, in fact, be a source of legitimacy.

In January 2006, I talked with one old friend who seemed uninterested in the draft law. He said there were too many "interests," too many people and groups motivated by self-interest, for him to be optimistic about the outcome. He told me the past was important, but he had very little to say about the Truth and Reconciliation Commission. He said that the people knew who the perpetrators were, though they would not acknowledge it publicly by making accusations. He was worried primarily about a "horizontal" conflict between victims of the TNI and victims of GAM. Failure to understand the overlap between GAM and TNI reinforces the sense that there are two groups of victims, not victims of two apparent forces that are much less distinct than they appear or present themselves as being. Just before a visible, active GAM emerged from the shadows, a consensus had developed among Acehnese to demand justice. The vertical nature of the violence was unambiguous, in contrast to outbreaks of violence elsewhere in Indonesia. That moment of possibility passed quickly as conflict protagonists were consolidated and alternatives to armed and electoral separatism were ruled out of order. Failure to understand how the conflict dynamic worked will make it much more difficult to achieve meaningful reconciliation and a functioning rule of law. Legacies of both the dark pattern and the branch system through which intelligence operations were perpetrated during DOM threaten the credibility of state institutions and social relations.

Shadowy, unknown agents committing acts of violence and terror that intimidate and depoliticize citizens, as well as painful betrayals, suspicions, and desires for vengeance, are often consolidated under the rubric of the legacies of authoritarianism that truth commissions and tribunals are designed to resolve. These transitional institutions quite often fail. In East Timor, after similar Indonesian military operations, even well-funded, internationally supported and staffed institutions have failed (Drexler 2006c; Cohen 2002; AI/JSMP 2004; ICG 2002). If a truth commission or tribunal is ever established in Aceh, it will not be as extensive or internationally supported. At this point, it is likely that the promise of a truth and reconciliation commission stipulated by the MOU will be endlessly deferred. This deferral allows Acehnese to blame Jakarta for foreclosing this discussion. The range of complicities and corruptions associated with the *provokator* and the dark pattern—not just TNI contributing to GAM, but all the people who overlook this overlap to champion GAM as the voice of the people and justify acts of violence perpetrated in its name—will not be examined. Like the *provokator*, they will remain individual and particular, not recognized as systematic or social.

Guided by psychoanalytic theory and practice—in which individuals resolve traumas by narrating past experiences and integrating them into their present so they can move forward free from the fractures in memory, spoiled identities, and paralysis that trauma imposes—national and transnational institutions have been designed to facilitate a collective resolution of traumatic political violence during transitional periods. Aceh has not had such a process. Some of the conditions that make it unsafe to discuss the past will be perpetuated until there is a process where the past can be addressed. Until these suppressed but commonly known historical truths are addressed, historical narratives about continuous rebellion and second-generation separatists can trigger conflict dynamics. The ammunition of GAM's existence may perpetuate the threats of conflict at the same time that it corrupts the institutions that might be capable of resolving the conflict. In this case, the relationship between narration and institutions will be critical in determining whether an exploration of the past provokes violence or contributes to conditions in which trauma can be worked through.

Dominick La Capra distinguishes working through trauma from acting out and the compulsion to repeat by the victims' ability to "gain critical distance . . . and to distinguish between past, present, and future" (2001, 143–44). According to La Capra, by "working through" the past and distinguishing the present, a person who has been victimized and traumatized by violence "acquires the possibility of being an ethical and political agent," recovering the ability to act in his or her own life with the expectation that justice and accountability, rather than terrifying randomness, cycles of vengeance, and naked force, prevail. The inscrutability of the dark pattern extends its legacies and hinders efforts to work through the past. The Independent Commission 1999 report may be quite right that the dark pattern will only end through resolution in an extraordinary trial; other judicial settings are corrupt and would be incapable of delivering a legitimate verdict that does not continue to deny and obscure widely known public secrets about the military's involvement in myriad forms of violence. Perhaps the tsunami was such an extraordinary event that these patterns have been broken. GAM's unilateral cease-fire and TNI's admission that what was attributed to GAM was actually a "stressed soldier" reversed certain discursive elements of the dark pattern.

Ethnocultural explanations for the repetition of trauma and persistence of violent rebellion dominate understandings and policies on Aceh. In addition to the psychosocial model, another predominant Western European and American explanatory framework for such conflicts posits "undying hatreds" between different ethnic, religious, and/or cultural groups that are involved in civil wars. Thus, "reconciliation" is not simply between perpetrators and victims who must, or wish to, continue living together, but between different groups who have seen their interests, or even identities, as opposed. Political factions that use violence are often defined in ethnocultural terms by Western analysts, rather than being regarded as groups generated by leaders who appeal to such differences to legitimate their aspirations to power and mobilize supporters. The tendency is to regard non-Westerners as atavistic, backward people controlled by ancient antagonisms and doomed to act them out forever unless restrained by outside intervention in the form of peace treaties or political settlements and armed peacekeeping forces or monitors. In Indonesia, indeed, the notion of a vengeful Acehnese character exists to justify repression by the center.

In the case of Aceh, narratives of traumatic repetition and ethnocultural fanaticism are as unfounded as the dominant conflict narrative of historically continuous rebellion. The extension of violence has been caused by the everyday practices, institutions, and politics that shape memories and perpetuate conditions in which past patterns are reproduced. An analytic of corruption helps us to understand the failure of transitional policies, investigations, and mediations to legitimate law and end cycles of violence. Legal institutions are corrupted when they fail to establish appropriate relationships between narrative meanings and social consequences. When legal processes grant immunity to identified perpetrators, fail to recognize known victims, and confuse these two categories of action, corruption becomes systemically contaminating. In social-historical contexts in which violence is widely presumed to have been carried out through conspiracies as well as conflicts between groups of suspicious loyalties and to have involved personal vengeance as well as political principles, corruption makes legal institutions a means of extending the pattern instead of an alternative to violence.

The legitimacy of legal institutions in post-conflict situations rests on their ability to shift relationships of dominance, subordination, and marginality, not merely to endorse the status quo. The Indonesian state is extremely weak and unable either to shift relationships of dominance or to name and judicially examine the dark pattern. The undeniable overlap between TNI and GAM is made inscrutable through the figure of the *provokator*. The Bantaqiah tribunal was supposed to end the dark pattern and demonstrate that the state had a monopoly on violence, but the verdict confirmed that violence remained out of the law's control. The report that developed evidence for this and other cases of human rights abuses suggests that the dark pattern, the process by which TNI contributed to the second-generation GAM, was developed to offer the security forces immunity and deniability: "it can crush the morale of the TNI foot soldiers if TNI seems to be the *single bad guys* in Aceh." The problem is that real lives were lost fighting imaginary enemies. The commission noted that the dark pattern could only be resolved in court. In the trial, the dark pattern was judicially illegible (Felman 2002a), and the suggestion that Bantaqiah was a member of GAM or GPK was not examined in that context. Indeed, the trial did not challenge the rhetoric of an existing movement that threatened the state. Rather, it depended on the logic of a GPK enemy figure. The masterminds of the massacre were not tried, even though the conspiracy was admitted; the charge of premeditated murder was dropped for lack of evidence. The failure to provide justice contributed to the conditions that made a second-generation GAM come into existence as a popular force. The denial of justice reinforced anxieties at the center about the impossibility of winning Acehnese hearts and minds. The trial corrupted the law by silencing particular narratives and legitimizing other narratives that reproduced the conditions for the repetition of violence.

As the Bantaqiah case demonstrates, the process by which the enemy is fabricated and overlaps with the TNI is inadmissible and corrupts the law. The failure of the law reinforces the logic that there is no other choice than to grasp the second-generation GAM and suggest that the object of the widely known manipulations of the security forces is an "imitation" GAM. The failure of the law works to endorse the grievance narrative espoused by the second-generation GAM and to remove the pursuit of justice for past violence from the law to politics.

Trials, policies, mediations, and official investigations enforce particular narratives so that they have social and political consequences and exclude other narratives so that pervasive patterns of violence are hidden from prosecutorial and social visibility. Such powerfully perverse logics are at work even when these institutions, such as investigations and tribunals, cannot enforce their narratives by rendering judgments. The primary perpetrators are not on trial, and important narratives—especially regarding the central role of the Indonesian military in creating the separatist enemy—cannot be articulated in the courtroom. Moreover, the legally constructed narratives say one thing, yet another is known, and the gap between common knowledge and enforceable truth undermines the legitimacy of legal institutions. In both situations, the linkage between narrative meanings and social consequences is disrupted, and legal institutions become complicit in corruption. The extension of violence is secured by institutional forms that enable specific acts of violence to be perpetrated in the first place and to remain immune to legal justice afterwards, laying the groundwork for intractable conflicts.

Prosecutions failed to address the existence and ramifications of systematic, state-sponsored violence enacted through "criminals," *provokator*, and the dark pattern of overlap with "GAM," dissolving the organized campaign of terror into a series of discrete incidents embedded in local antagonisms and involving spontaneous, excessively violent acts. In addition to the complex, often contradictory relationship of its agents with GAM, the Indonesian military has a history of using the branch system to militarize civilians and create social polarization. Typically, in its DOM operations to find enemies within society, any association, or even an accusation of association with the targeted group was license for abuse. The system exploited social and personal animosities, and in turn was exploited by some people against others whom they considered their enemies. A person could report a personal enemy as a rebel and assist the security forces in his or her abduction. A person who could not withstand torture and interrogation could implicate someone else as the state's enemy to take his or her place. Being an informant or assisting Special Forces operations was rewarded with significant privileges, especially the hope of safety for one's family. The military sowed seeds of dissension and suspicion whose ramifications continue in Acehnese communities today.

Current institutions may be undermined by memories that fall outside of official narrations. At the same time, individual and social memories may be violated by current institutional practices and policies. A TNI that cooperates with its enemy to sustain an independence struggle obviously contradicts the Indonesian narrative of armed separatist warfare. This history is rife with ambiguities that connect second-generation GAM with Indonesian security forces. The TNI that may arm and collaborate with criminal and separatist elements needs the independence forces not to be defeated in order to continue a conflict that sustains its own existence.

A collective working-through—developing conditions in which actions have predictable and appropriate consequences—depends on the judiciary to institutionalize truth by demonstrating beyond a reasonable doubt that the truth is true, that falsity is false, and that there is a recognizable process for distinguishing between them. When the process of "justice" reduplicates the corruption and deceptions that characterized the original crimes, mistrust in institutions of governance and social polarization are perpetuated. Each repetition of a politically expedient narrative that does not align with past experiences diminishes the social legitimacy of new institutions. Each pragmatic use of the symbols and conflict narrative involving GAM versus the TNI reinforces the decision not to investigate human rights violations and undermines the power and legitimacy of law.

The situation in Aceh illuminates the intricate relationship between institutional corruption and the corruption of social memory and historical narrative. Corruption propagates through the interdependent elements within a social system. The distortion of any component or function undermines the whole and either brings it to a crashing halt or, more insidiously, perverts the entire process. Definitions of textual corruption point to the process by which meanings are distorted in the process of narration or silencing. In this account, exclusions—not only that which cannot be spoken or heard, but also that which those who know are unwilling to repeat because there is no telling who is who and no protection from dangerous consequences—are as important as trauma-induced gaps in testimony.

Definitions of corruption drawn from computer programming provide a surprisingly apt metaphor for understanding the complex process by which institutional corruption and corruptions of memory intersect and compound one another. In some situations, data that appears to be lost still resides in system memory, but it is impossible to locate because critical links have been severed. In a process invisible to most ordinary users, the computer maintains a "hidden" inventory of where various files are stored. When this master list of named pathways is damaged or distorted, other data files may become inaccessible even if they remain "true." Corruption is as much a matter of connections made or lost as it is of errors, distortions, and deceptions that ramify through a system. An analogous process occurs when forensic evidence and remembered facts exist, but become unreadable in the courtroom because politically expedient narratives have retold, revised, and renamed these events. Links among current, recent, and historical events are severed as well. Yet the remembered truths remain, constantly threatening to disrupt the new, apparently seamless narrative that is based on exclusions from accessible memory. Rumors circulate in the gap between knowledge and narrative.

When institutions of governance and social institutions are themselves corrupt, they can no longer guarantee distinctions between truth and falsity, or validate certain actions and choices while they invalidate others. Mistrust permeates everyday life and shapes institutional logics. In societies marked by the pervasive mistrust produced by long periods of corrupt governance and mass violence, revelations are not therapeutic. Societies are not self-healing; truth and reconciliation are complex societal processes requiring the restoration of connections between actions and consequences and the rebuilding of everyday trust. In situations like that in Indonesia, tribunals cannot even demonstrate definitively that true things are true. Any testimony or evidence that circulates through these institutions becomes corrupt because of the pervasive, destabilizing power of suspicion. Transitional justice institutions are undermined by the justified and sensible paranoia of masses of ordinary people. Falsity, too, cannot be demonstrated; by definition, conspiracies cannot be disproved. The court faces the essential double bind that its judgments fail to align with social truth and it lacks sufficient authority to make judgments that reverse social perceptions and dispel rumors. Separated from truth and justice by politics and expediency, the law suffers an irresolvable corruption.

Can politics replace law as the adjudicator of justice in Aceh? A doubtful proposition, as both the history of other postconflict situations and this region's own past indicate. Visible leaders of "second-generation" GAM may not have participated directly in the handoff of the kite, but they know enough to have questions about the integrity of their organization; otherwise they would not have survived the political realignments that followed the tsunami. Most of the group's current leaders have an excess of knowledge; they know things are not as they seem and their power is not quite legitimate. In the absence of justice, they—like everyone active in Acehnese and Indonesian politics—are subject to a deeply rooted paranoia. Paranoia in this social rather than psychological sense arises when neither law nor history can function to settle vital questions. Not only justice, but also knowledge is corrupted. In the therapeutic sense, to free the self from the paranoia that attends irreconcilable conflicts that cannot be entirely excluded from consciousness, one side has to give up its truth claims. In this social sense, however, both sides make the same truth claim: they agree on the convergent narrative of a two-sided conflict. The international recognition conferred on this claim does not make it true to the people on the ground. It remains dependent on the power of its enforcers and always subject to their violent excesses.

Those who have an excess of knowledge about things that are not admitted publicly include those in power, who know that they have debts to other sides and remain vulnerable to exposure; those who may have doubts about the newly invented ex-GAM and its leaders; and the survivors of a regime of violence and indeterminacy. If paranoia is a structure of knowing rather than a substance or content of knowledge, then no evidence or information can cure this excess. No matter how many acts of massive violence are revealed, no matter how much transparency is offered, how strong a light of international observation and analysis is directed to the object of scrutiny—including this work—doubt remains, for the "dark pattern" does not disappear from the shadows that are hidden in common sight. If all this murkiness stemmed merely from the endless finger-pointing to displace guilt onto others, then the tsunami ended that. GAM was disciplined and gave up the power of the threat, while the TNI was forced to admit a single, symbolic act of excess. If all agreed to close off the past, perhaps this exercise in denial could work. But if what interrupted this endless spiral of paranoia was a natural disaster, to which Indonesia seems particularly vulnerable, then the return of relative security is likely to raise the risks of a reprise. Natural disaster is not a sustainable governance solution that can be counted upon to intervene every time dark patterns threaten to escape control, corrupt authority, and rend the social fabric asunder. Violence is likely to end only when accountability for the past joins nonviolence as the sole effective and legitimate means of political action. Without justice, violence remains an option to the closely joined protagonists in this protracted conflict, and paranoia remains a reasonable outlook on a world in which nothing is at it seems.

Paranoia, with its excess knowledge, cannot be resolved by legal institutions. The logic of paranoia continues to incorporate all "facts" into its logic of suspicions that cannot be grounded or disproved. Paranoia does not end even with death. Who was Abdullah Syafi'ie, and when did he die? Syafi'ie is no longer, but suspicion survives. Suspicion that permeates society produces powerful, concrete effects, shaping the conflict dynamic and institutionalizing the slippery protagonists whose boundaries are blurred despite policies and realities that posit them as distinct. This corrosive, destabilizing paranoia extends the spiral of latent dangers and actual violence.

In Aceh, the prolonged repetition of everyday practices of mass violence, coercion, torture, betrayal, and collusion have created conditions in which certain recollections are dangerous. The consequence of discussing what is commonly known may be to forfeit whatever possibilities for a better future have been achieved through protracted struggle. In this process of corruption, narrative logics make certain "truths" temporarily inaccessible, or make certain forensic facts obvious but undermine their ramifications and excuse their liabilities. Adjudication is limited beforehand by impunity. Not only is knowledge of the dark pattern inadmissible in current contexts, it is irresolvable through the law in its current institutional form. These practices and the conditions they enforce caused a spiral of violence and suspicion to reproduce itself endlessly until the tsunami put a stop to ordinary life in Aceh and required people to rebuild their society from the ground up.

While legal institutions were incapable of resolving the dark pattern's productive indeterminacy, the tsunami may have destroyed the conditions of possibility for this spiral, which is governed by the logic of paranoia. The tsunami's destruction may have broken survivors' connections with the past that could be used to reenliven fighters, fantasies, and insecurities. The conflict dynamic before the tsunami allowed no possibility for the TNI to admit that GAM was not a self-perpetuating threat, and no possibility for GAM to assert that they were not separatists and that their mere existence did not threaten the state. My suspicion is that no amount of "evidence" would prove or disprove the dark pattern of the past. Yet, its logic still has the potential to undermine the new institutions of governance in Aceh.

The institutions of governance now have whatever credibility they enjoy from seeming clearly and cleanly demarcated from the past, and (ex-)GAM elected officials gain legitimacy from appearing to have opposed the state until they could assume local power. Many activists give the new incarnation of GAM the benefit of the doubt, hoping it is the "pure" GAM they imagined. But inquiring into the past, examining the process by which GAM became the viable alternative to the state, scrutinizing the dark pattern in which enforcers of security and agents of subversion change places and costumes, and investigating other productive indeterminacies remain impossible. Only effective governance, in which the state is capable of uttering felicitous performatives, could begin to undo the widespread suspicion and corrosive mistrust, not only of those in power but also among the people themselves, that is the legacy of the dark pattern in Aceh.

Irwandi's savvy plan to address corruption may resolve paranoia by not addressing it at all. If he can eradicate the persistent problem of graft and the misuse of public resources for personal gain, he may effect a performative in which ex-GAM becomes what GAM itself never could quite be: a popular force with the people's best interests in mind. In focusing on corruption, which has been the governing metaphor for the inadmissible logics of the dark pattern, Irwandi may through an adroit sleight of hand appear to solve these more fundamental and pervasive problems as well. In response to a situation where the state has been unable to govern effectively, utter felicitous performatives, to transform relationships of power, if Irwandi and Nazar can govern well and maintain at least the illusion of transparency, perhaps the paranoia of the past will slip quietly out to sea. Guaranteeing a modicum of security and exercising a monopoly of force would, in this context, be considerable achievements.

The potential threats to this scenario are both internal and external. To understand the internal threats, it is helpful to consider the relationship between the performative and paranoia. Rereading Walter Benjamin's famous "Critique of Violence" (1986), which identifies law's dependence on extralegal violence through the figure of the police, and Derrida's commentary on it (1992), which subsumes Benjamin's concern in a problem of the performative, Eric Santner (1996) suggests that Daniel Paul Schreber's concept of paranoia is best understood as a crisis of investiture—that is, the sense those who are placed in positions of power have of the sources from which their position derives. This sort of paranoia arises when the person in a position of authority has the "finer sensibility" to perceive the missing link at the origin of institutional authority. The New Order state seeks to resolve concerns about its own legitimacy by appropriating death through criminality (Siegel 1998), setting in motion a spiral of political violence that could never definitively establish its legitimacy but, rather, constantly undermined its authority and militarized the entire society. Will those ex-GAM officials who know about the dubious origins of their organization, or those who share complicated histories with the Indonesian military suffer from a similar crisis of legitimacy?

The external threats may come from Jakarta. Recent draft legislation limiting the jurisdiction of local parties to local politics, containing GAM in Aceh without representation in the national parliament, suggests that factions in Jakarta still believe that this resolution to the Aceh conflict threatens the unitary state. Violence may not be profitable in Aceh in the immediate future, but impunity for crimes in Aceh is not likely to end the logics of an insecure state, which were never limited to Aceh; rather, the escape from liability here simply transfers these anxieties to different contexts. Adherence to the internationally monitored agreement may produce an impression of legitimacy for the Indonesian state, but will it make the insecure state legitimate in its own eyes?

NOTES

Introduction

1. One writer and journalist frequently posed these questions to me; F. X. Rudy Gunawan takes them up at length in a book about victims of forced disappearance (1998). Nugroho's account of the disappeared (1999) is unique in its focus on society's cowardice in following the state's rhetoric blaming the victims, branding them communists, criminals, and other subversives. Heryanto (2006) offers an insightful and detailed analysis of state terror in Yogyakarta, arguing that even after the end of the New Order, state terrorism continues to work. Gordon (1996) and Taussig (1992) inspired my attention to the issue of disappearances.

2. The calls that focused on exposing Soeharto's role in the coup attempt to disguise what was actually a power struggle within the military. The military warned that personal memoirs, even of those involved in the events, did not constitute evidence; "Wiranto: Memoar Jangan Diklaim Sebagai Pelurusan Sejarah," *Republika*, 12 April 1999. Examples of notable testimonies include A. Latief (1999) and Sudisman (2000); also see the Air Force account in Katopo (1999).

3. The mass killings were not discussed as part of the initial calls to straighten history. In contrast to scholarship that discusses China's recollection of "bitter stories" that both recall and repress memories of widespread violence (Anagnost 1997; Mueggler 2001), in Indonesia stories of the 1965 killings were virtually absent from public discourse during the New Order. For translated stories, see Aveling (1975), Foulcher (1990), and a more recent collection of poems, essays and stories on forty years of humanitarian violence, H. Latief, Miryanti, and Mahendra (2005). Indonesia's foremost author, Pramoedya Ananta Toer, was detained in 1965 and confined on Buru Island, a penal colony, until 1979. While on Buru, he wrote a quartet of novels thematizing national consciousness in the early twentieth century, which were banned by the New Order. Sulami, a prominent human rights advocate whose activism began in the Indonesian women and youth movement during the revolutionary period and joined the precursor to the Indonesian Women's Movement (Gerwani) in 1950, was imprisoned from 1967 to 1984, and after her release worked for human rights. She joined with Pramoedya to form an organization with other ex-political prisoners aimed at

exposing the truth about the 1965 killings. Their efforts to rebury the remains of those killed in 1965–1966 met with violent opposition. Pramoedya and Sulami's activities are not discussed under the rubric of "straightening history," but as relating to the problem of injustice; see Sulami (1999). Oral histories about the killings are collected in Roosa, Ratih, and Farid (2004). See also "Keluarga Korban Pembunuhan 1965–1966 Tuntut Soeharto," *Sinar Pagi*, 16 April 1999; "Komnas HAM Diminta Teliti Korban Pembunuhan Pasca G30S/PKI," *Kompas*, 30 April 1999. Sulistyo (2000b) offers one of the first Indonesian scholarly examinations of the killings. For international scholarship on the mass killings during the New Order, see Cribb (1992) and his 2002 review essay. Robinson (1995) details mass violence in Bali. Geertz's cultural reading of the killings (1973) has been critiqued by Pecora (1989) and George (2004). The relationship between culture and violence in Indonesia in other contexts has been explored by a number of scholars; see for example, Collins (2002), George (1996), Hoskins (1996), Steedley (1999). On the legacy of violence in Indonesia, see Dittmer (2002). For analyses of culture and violence beyond Indonesia, see Daniel (1996) and Rosaldo (1980).

4. Siegel (1998) provides a notable exception, tracing how the 1965 killings are related to the mysterious killings of 1983. Stoler (2002b) notes that focusing on the killings obscures the vibrant civil society that existed during the 1950s and the alternative futures that might have followed. Bourchier and Legge (1994), Lev (2005), and Nasution (1994) have documented key aspects of the 1950s political institutions and culture that disappeared under Soeharto. Farid (2001) sketches legacies of these killings.

5. For important exceptions, see Nugroho (1999), Roosa, Ratih, and Farid (2004), and Rochijat (1985). Heryanto's analysis of "fatally belonging" (2006) sheds light on this complex dynamic.

6. During Soeharto's rule, very few accounts challenged the official history of the supposed communist coup attempt: Notosusanto, Nugroho, and Saleh (1968). Official versions of the "incident" disseminated in film (see Sen 1994), textbooks, and museums (McGregor 2003) emphasized the brutality of the communists, especially the allegation that members of Gerwani, a mass-based women's movement considered part of the then-legal Indonesian Communist Party, danced naked to arouse the generals who were then killed, castrated (a claim that was refuted in Anderson (1987), based on examination of the official autopsy report) and otherwise mutilated, and left in a hole. Post-Soeharto scholarship demonstrated that the women depicted in official photographs as Gerwani were prostitutes who were arrested, tortured, and forced to pose for the photos (Stanley 1999). The earliest critical analysis of the coup is found in Anderson and McVey (1971). For the most recent English-language account, see Roosa (2006). During the "reform" period, a number of accounts were published in Indonesian; notable were the Air Force's account in Katopo (1999) and testimonies from those wrongly accused, for example, A. Latief (1999) and Sudisman (2005). For critical analyses of the Soeharto regime and its use of history, see Warman (2004a, b), Sasongko (2005). Budiawan (2004) explores the process of remembering the past. For a range of English-language accounts of history and memory after Soeharto, see Zurbuchen (2005).

7. Gupta (1995) is a pioneering example of such a project. Smith (2006) offers a nuanced example of corruption as a national discourse in Nigeria, noting how discourses of widespread complicity point to both intractability and possibilities for change. See also Hasty (2005). These studies emphasize the im-

portance of studying practices of corruption to track lived experiences of the state. My notion of corruption differs from these works in exploring public discourse of corruption as a way to consider the social legitimacy of institutions and the legacies of state violence. For an institutional analysis of corruption in Indonesia, see Pompe's (2005) outstanding history of Indonesia's supreme court.

8. Stoler (2002a) focuses on the "content of the form" to analyze how colonial archives were technologies of colonial rule. Official histories were an important part of the state's "ideological armory" (Bourchier 1994, 50; see also McGregor (2005); Sen (1994). For challenges to New Order history after the fall of Soeharto, see Warman (2004a, b), Farid (2001), and Zurbuchen (2005).

9. Bertrand (2004) uses a historical institutionalist model to argue that "ethnic violence tends to occur during periods of renegotiation of national models and state institutions." Sidel (2006) maps changes in the modalities of religious violence as religious authority and representation have shifted. In contrast, I look at how historical narratives have themselves become resources for extending violence and how lack of legitimacy of state institutions has decreased the effects of institutional shifts.

10. Peng Cheah (2003) links the state's enemies within to its relationship with the nation through a reading of Pramoedya Ananta Toer's novel *House of Glass*. On the notion of internal enemies and the haunting of past violence outside Indonesia, see, for example, Daniel (1996), Nelson (1999), Taylor (1997), Warren (1993). Feldman (2005) describes how states are constituted through current threats. Zulaika and Douglass (1996) analyze productive narratives of terrorism as threat. Gordon (1996) develops a method for finding the points at which specters haunt the present. Taussig (1992, 1997) offers useful concepts for considering the state and violence. Other studies point to the impunity with which the Indonesian state has perpetrated violence toward its citizens; see, for example, Purdey (2006), Tanter, Ball, and van Klinken (2006), Nevins (2004).

11. West and Sanders (2003) and Marcus (1999) provide examples of ethnographies of suspicion and conspiracy logics.

12. Departing from Austin (1975 [1955]), a number of scholars have developed the performative, see for example, Butler (1997), Derrida (1992), and Felman (2002b).

13. Writing about the post-Soeharto witch killings in East Java, James Siegel describes the witch as the result of a peculiar performative where effects come into being not through the intention of a first-person speaker, but through multiple third persons (2006).

14. Conversations with Sebastiaan Pompe helped me to clarify this point.

15. Marzuki Darusman, presentation at International Crisis Group Seminar on Truth and Reconciliation in Indonesia, Hotel Borobodur, Jakarta, 11 September 2000.

16. H. S. Dillon, presentation at International Crisis Group Seminar on Truth and Reconciliation in Indonesia.

17. Goenawan Mohamad, presentation at International Crisis Group Seminar on Truth and Reconciliation in Indonesia.

18. The term civil society is used to refer to a broad range of nonstate actors that sought to develop a new political culture with room for expressions of difference and critique; I do not wish to imply a coordinated agenda. I am aware of the difficulty of defining and realizing "civil society"; however, it remained a powerful ideal for many activists I encountered.

19. Conversations with Yazir Henri underlined the ethical dilemmas of reproducing "public record" testimonies. He addresses some of these issues in Henri (2003).

20. Sukanta (1999a) offers an eloquent Indonesian-language account of the struggle to maintain personal dignity; see also the English-language analysis in Budiawan (2005).

Chapter 1. Analyzing Conflict

1. On the religious violence and terrorism industry and its experts, see John Sidel's (2006) thoughtful and thorough analysis, which discloses the role of secular and other organizations in extending religious violence.

2. I obtained identification and permission as part of group of U.S.-based scholars in Indonesia at that time. Of this group, I was the only person to travel to Aceh. I traveled with Australian monitors outside Banda Aceh. With Vanessa Johanson and Edward Aspinal, I coauthored a "Report on the 1999 Elections in Aceh" for the Australian Council for Overseas Aid. Johanson and I attended the meeting with Syafi'ie; Aspinal remained in Banda Aceh that day because of concerns about his personal safety.

3. Official rationales for this were based not on intimidation but on concerns expressed by religious experts that the dye would interfere with people's ability to clean themselves for prayer.

4. Aceh Merdeka translates literally as a declarative statement, "Free Aceh." Hasan Tiro reportedly "declared" Aceh Merdeka on 4 December 1976, in his capacity as the leader of the Acheh Sumatra National Liberation Front (ASNLF). Since 1999, 4 December has been celebrated as the founding of the Free Aceh Movement. The distinctions between ASNLF and the current GAM, especially the transformation of a national liberation front that included other ethnic areas in Sumatra into a separatist armed group, have been obscured over time by the processes discussed here.

5. The sovereignty that AM and GAM sought to restore was from the mythic past that preceded Dutch colonialism; Indonesian and Javanese colonialism are described as the latest in a continuous history of colonial domination.

6. Syafi'ie used *bangsa*, an Indonesian/Melayu word which can be translated as nation, people, or race. It is frequently used in statements designating the Indonesian nation, *bangsa* Indonesia. He selected this common term for nation, which the Acehnese had previously used in claiming their belonging to the Indonesian nation, to distinguish the Acehnese nation from the Indonesian nation.

7. Merry (2006) has described the translation of global human rights norms into local contexts, with a particular attention to the individuals who mediate between international and national contexts. Hasan Tiro and Abdullah Syafi'ie do a similar kind of mediation and call our attention to the contradictions that "middle" figures must negotiate over time.

8. Of black boxes Latour writes: "no matter how controversial their history, how complex their inner workings, how large the commercial or academic networks that hold them in place, only their input and output count" (1987, 3). My principles in this chapter are developed from Latour's formulations; readers familiar with Latour's work will recognize parallels and points of connection.

9. For example, in intelligence reports (*Laporan Penugasan Tim Pase 4* 1995),

official government investigations (Independent Commission 1999), histories of the conflict (Sulaiman 2000; Tippe 2000), and national media reports (e.g., in *Kompas*).

10. I was inspired by Bruno Latour's *Science in action* (1987) in developing this series of principles for analyzing violent conflict. Issues of narration, history, violence, and representation have been prominent in anthropology for over a decade; as a result, a vast body of literature on these themes bears on the principles developed here. These principles are sufficiently abstract to be used to analyze both violent conflicts and the industry of policy analysis and expertise that accompanies them (Mitchell 2002). Considering the resonance of principles that Latour developed to analyze technoscience in a dramatically different context underlines the force of knowledge and expertise in conflict situations. Scholars who inspired my thinking on these principles include Judith Butler on the relationship between discourse and materiality (1993); Marguerite Feitlowitz on violence and language (1998); Michel Foucault on genealogy (1977); Walter Benjamin on the appropriations of history of violence (1989); Joan Scott on the conditions of possibility for representation of experience (1990). In thinking through the challenges of ethnographic analysis of the inseparability of conflict discourse and materiality, I found Jeanne Favret-Saada's ethnography of witchcraft very helpful; she demonstrates that "the act in witchcraft is the word" (1977, 9).

11. The literature on the relationship between history and the nation is extensive; see Anderson (1983), Chaterjee (1993), Duara (1995), D. Scott (1999), Kelly and Kaplan (2001). On the uses of history in struggles for sovereignty, see McGranahan (2005), Slyomovics (1998). On the narration of conflict, see Brass (1997).

12. It is beyond the scope of this chapter to address the distinctions between AM 1976 and GAM 1979. Very few sources exist to document these distinctions. During the period in which I conducted fieldwork and interviews (1998–2006), obtaining retrospective data on this issue was impossible, given the high stakes of the contemporary claims made on behalf of GAM. I highlight the distinctions between AM and GAM and the various forces that operated under the label of GAM over the thirty-year period. Some of the AM 1976 participants may have seen their actions as an extension of the 1950s DI/TII struggle; others I spoke with recalled AM as an intellectual critique of natural resource extraction; and still others may have had connections to Hasan Tiro. Critically important distinctions have been collapsed into the terms and narratives that structure current political discourse.

13. The state plays an important role in naming its others. James Siegel describes how the Indonesian state has been challenged by threats it struggled to name (1998). Ariel Heryanto details how various threats develop in interrogation (2006). Begona Arextaga (2000) looks at the fictional character of state narratives about terrorism, pointing to how these narratives "embody" the state. See also Zulaika and Douglass (1996).

14. Morris (1983) refers to the declaration of Negara Aceh Merdeka and the movement as the Aceh National Liberation Front. Other sources, such as Jihad (2000), and the group's own Web site use ASNLF.

15. For example, the Human Rights Watch/Asia Watch 1990 report referred to a Tiro/ASNLF-authored document, *A Black Paper Documenting Javanese/ Indonesian Crime of Genocide against the People of Acheh/Sumatra 1990* (no longer available on the ASNLF Web site). Although cautious in the use of ASNLF

materials, HRW's use of this document contributes to the linkage of human rights in Aceh to Hasan Tiro and AM.

16. Joan Scott makes this point eloquently in arguing that testimonies obscure the wider conditions of possibility for subject formation (1991).

17. Kammen and Widjajanto explain that during the New Order there was no need for an official policy called "DOM"; the state did not recognize any legal limitations on its use of force, so no special zones or states of emergency had to be declared in unstable provinces. The military campaigns in Aceh bore specific names; the Red Net Operations were run successively by Kolakops Jaring Merah (Red Net Operations Implementation Command) and Kopassus (the Special Forces) with Tribuana units (2000, 10). I have used DOM following popular usage throughout my analysis.

18. "Kronis Pelanggaran HAM di Aceh," *Kompas*, 5 August 1998; "Farida Ariani dan Korban Perkosaan," *Kompas*, 21 August 1998; "Dialog Mensos dengan Korban DOM: Perhatikan Kami, Tegakkan Hukum," *Kompas*, 7 November 1998; "Korban Jaring Merah di Bukit Tengkorak," *Majalah Gatra*, 8 August 1998.

19. "Kepiluan Itu Langsung Menyergap: Korban DOM kembali bersaksi," *Kompas*, 31 October 1998; "Hasballah M. Saad: Kekejaman Luar Biasa pada Peradaban Manusia," *Media Indonesia*, 31 January 1999.

20. "Kerangka-kerangka itu Bukti Nestapa di Aceh," *Majalah D&R*, 29 August 1998; "Diduga Kuat Ada Pembantaian," *Kompas*, 23 August 1998; "Korban Jaring Merah di Bukit Tengkorak," *Majalah Gatra*, 8 August 1998; "Aceh: Siapa Harus Minta Maaf Padamu," *Majalah Gatra*, 8 August 1998.

21. *Pak* is a Javanese/Indonesian title of respect. SCTV, a privately owned television station, had interviewed Syafi'ie.

22. He asked the military to appear in uniform in response to complaints that there were long-haired, pierced mobile police brigade officers. Later, military spokesmen denied that there were still Brimob [Mobile Police Brigade members] with long hair, but said that before there had been; see "Komandan Kodim Pidie Bantah Aparat Lakukan Penyisiran," *Kompas*, 20 March 2000.

23. *Pantau* magazine documents the use of this term to misrepresent the conflict in Aceh. According to *Pantau*, what are called armed conflict or exchanges of fire often are in fact attacks on unarmed civilians. "Militerisasi Kosakata," *Pantau: Kajian Media dan Jurnalisme*, edition 6, October–November 1999.

24. Confidential personal communication, 13 June 2001.

25. Gerakan Separatis Bersenjata (Armed Separatist Group) retained the acronym GSB that formerly meant Gerakan Sipil Bersenjata (Armed Civilian Movement).

Chapter 2. Struggling with History

1. I first discussed these themes in "Histories of Struggle, Struggling with History: Aceh in Reform(ing) Indonesia," presented at the Association for Asian Studies annual meeting in 2000, as part of a panel in honor of Daniel S. Lev's retirement. Subsequently, I circulated an extended version of the paper at the Workshop on History and Memory in Contemporary Indonesia, University of California Los Angeles, 6 April 2001, organized by Tony Reid and Mary Zurbuchen. An earlier version was also included in my 2001 Ph.D. dissertation. In 2005, Tony Reid wrote about these themes, drawing on many of the same examples.

2. Koetaradja, a powerful sultanate, had continued to resist the imposition of Dutch rule.

3. This speech is cited by Hasjmy in 1995; however, references to other regions purchasing airplanes have been eliminated.

4. Most discussions of the plane focus on the Dakota plane called RI-001 Seulawah (Acehnese for Golden Mountain). Although sources claimed as many as three planes were purchased with the funds collected at that time, most suggest that it was two. The others do not appear to have been named, and it is more difficult to trace their histories. An early air force history lists the planes and notes that the second plane donated by Aceh was later given to Burma (*Sewindu Angkatan Udara Republik Indonesia 9 April 1946–9 April 1954*, 1955). There appear to have been only seven planes of this type at that time, making the Acehnese donation quite significant. None of the other planes is listed as donated by a particular region or given a name. The fate of Seulawah is not clear, a 2003 article notes that it was taken to Calcutta for servicing in the early 1950s, on the way back from helping Burma, and finally was exhibited in Jakarta as the Republic's first plane. According to the article, it had been taken to a technical facility in Bandung, where it was likely "cannibalized for other planes." One replica of the plane can still be flown, for joyrides or parachuting ("Gunung Emas yang Raib," *Majalah Tempo*, 24 August 2003, 53).

5. Aceh was spelled Atjeh in the spelling system developed by the Dutch and used at that time.

6. Most sources suggest that Soekarno called Aceh the "daerah modal" in recognition of the province's important role in 1948, both in maintaining the Republic and in donating the airplanes. The phrase is used without elaboration or citation in both official histories (Department of Education and Culture 1978; Soemargono et al. 1992) and Acehnese sources (Hasjmy 1995; Jakobi 1998, 1992). It was also frequently invoked in print media after 1998 (for example: "Tanah Rencong dan Jasanya bagi Indonesia," *Kompas*, 15 August 1999; "Achmad Tahir: Aceh Ditetapkan Daerah Modal Perjuangan RI," *Suara Pembaruan*, 2 November 1998; "Aceh Cinta Republik, Kecewa pada Pemimpin," *Kompas*, 25 November 1999; "Rakyat Merasa Dibohongi," *Suara Pembaruan*, 23 September 1999; "Mengapa Aceh Bergolak Sepanjang Masa?" *Kompas*, 15 April 2001). Neither newspaper reports nor collected documentation of Soekarno's visit to Aceh published in 1948 directly call Aceh a *daerah modal (Perkundjungan Presiden Soekarno ke Atjeh*, 1948; "Mengikuti Perdjalanan Presiden," *Waspada*, 18 June 1948; "Presiden ditengah2 rakjat Atjeh," *Merdeka*, 19 June 1948; "Pres. Soekarno ditengah-tengah Rakjat tanah Rentjong," *Merdeka*, 22 June 1948; "Presiden berdjumpa dgn rakjat Djambi," *Waspada*, 24 June 1948). An unpublished pamphlet, T. Alibasyah Talsya's "History and Documents of the Rebellion in Atjeh," uses the phrase in the context of lamenting Soekarno's failure to fulfill promises that the state would be based on religion. Talsya writes that the government does not understand what the people of Aceh want, and that "Atjeh, which before was *daerah modal* to uphold and maintain the Republic of Indonesia has been forgotten day by day by the Indonesian government" (n.d., 27 [inscribed by the author to the national library in July 1958]). Talysa, who worked as a journalist and later was a member of the Indonesian Army in Sumatra, later wrote a three-volume series on the struggle for independence in Aceh based on daily notes from that time (according to the introduction). The second volume, *Modal Perjuangan Kemerdekaan 1947–1948 (Capital for the Independence Struggle)*, contains the speech cited. Hasjmy wrote the foreword to Talsya's 1990 book, and

appears to have highlighted and popularized the title of "daerah modal," citing Sekarno's 1948 Biruen speech in his 1995 book. Interestingly, Hasjmy is listed as the editor of the 1948 publication, *Perkundjungan Presiden Soekarno ke Atjeh (President Soekarno's Visit to Atjeh)* that includes speeches and photos from June 1948. The Biruen speech is not included in this collection; Soekarno's visit to Biruen is mentioned with the note that "the President's speech here was of the same kind as the speech at Koetaradja." In 1992, the Foundation of the Seulawah RI-001 (named after the airplane) published a book by A. K. Jakobi, *Aceh Daerah Modal: Long March ke Medan Area,* that cites a 1991 interview with Ibnu Sa'dan, former secretary to the military governor of Aceh, then eighty-five years old, that quoted a version of Soekarno's *daerah modal* statement from a meeting with military commanders in Biruen, 17 June 1948. I was unable to locate an original transcript of the Biruen speech in the national library or national archives; Hasjmy's library in Banda Aceh also did not have the Biruen speech, though it did have copies of the Koetaradja speech, which was also reprinted in *Bung Karno dan Rakjat Atjeh,* published in conjunction with the founding of Sjiah Kuala State University in Banda Aceh in 1961.

7. The official history of Taman Mini echoes Soekarno's comments: "The extension of Aceh appears to be a[n] airplane with the identification R.I. 001 Seulawah . . . because this plane seems to be capital (*modal*) for struggle, this is a donation from the society (*masyarakat*) to the original independence of the Republic of Indonesia" (Suradi, Kutoyo, Masjkuri, Wahyuningsih, and Sukrani 1989, 58).

8. Soekarno does not recall his earlier proclamation of Atjeh as a *daerah modal* in Biruen; he attributes the initial statement to Saleh's prompting. He clearly proclaims the importance of Atjeh as a *daerah modal* in this speech.

9. Pemberton discusses how the donations from Java became "authentic" even though they were all newly created. Siegel notes that the airplane was at odds with the "authentic" as well, since it is not a symbol of the timeless past but refers to a specific history and has a power of reference that provokes stories. He seeks to find the airplane's equivalent in language.

10. Soeharto stated: "The publication of *The Dutch Colonial War in Acheh* represents a significant contribution to our knowledge of the history of our own struggle. The history leads us to a deep consciousness that ever since earlier times there has been difficult and long struggles against oppression and at the same time struggles for our independence and self-esteem throughout our country" (English in the original).

11. Soeharto elaborated: "Our great history of our past earlier times and the strenuous and persistent struggle of our nation in the past have strongly motivated us to carry on our development duties which are also very great, today as well as in times to come."

12. Resink (1968) contradicts the popular Acehnese claim that this was the only treaty signed with an independent sultanate.

13. On 11 October 1873, the *Times* of London editorialized: "the concession to a foreign state of a right to annex territory in exchange for dominions ceded to us is hardly consonant with modern English notions of our proper relations to inferior races."

14. The historian Anas Machmud (1988) interprets the surrender of the Sultan differently: "The sovereignty of Aceh was never handed over to any foreign nation, and therefore the sovereignty of Aceh has been joined to become one with the sovereignty of the Indonesian nation which is deeply rooted in the instincts of the Indonesian people to live as a free nation" (19).

15. Both cite Van't Veer (1969). In contrast to the authors of *DCWA*, Reid contends that the continuing struggle against the Dutch was not a form of protonationalism; rather, the potential of Islam as a unifying force was realized in the early twentieth century.

16. See Hoskins (1987) for another example of how the central state appropriated the heroism of other region's resistance to Dutch colonialism.

17. Ibrahim Hasan is unpopular in Aceh, primarily because he is credited with inviting an increased Indonesian military presence to fight off separatist and criminal threats in 1989.

18. In 1990, rising violence in Aceh led to a military intelligence strategy intended to teach the "Acehnese to defend the country," including the formation of paramilitary groups, armed with knives, to catch the GPK, the security disruptors gang.

19. It is impossible to estimate what proportion of Indonesians have seen this film, but most people I spoke with had seen it many times. It was shown at the 2000 Jakarta International Film Festival as one of two "classic" Indonesian feature films.

20. Dhien is portrayed as a brilliant military strategist, an unflinchingly brave killer, and a just defender of the right cause, but, like all heroines under the New Order, she is primarily a good wife and mother. Filmmaker Eros Djarot stated: "I wanted to show heroine Tjoet Nya' Dhien as a hero on the field of war, but also a woman with a husband and children, a woman (*wanita*) who is still dominated by the feelings of a woman (*perempuan*) . . . it turns out, history was only as a background." "Eros Djarot Tawarkan Dialog," *Kompas*, 13 November 1988.

21. None of the people I asked about this film were struck by the strangeness of using the Indonesian flag in a film set in the period before independence.

22. This acknowledgment contrasts with the claims made by Hasan Tiro.

23. Most accounts I heard and read blamed Soekarno for reneging on this promise. The more complicated reality was that the entire government had done so. As prime minister, Natsir traveled to Aceh to meet with Daud Beureueh who threatened to resign with all the local officials if Aceh were not declared an autonomous province. Natsir explained that the government was bound by an agreement reached between the Republic and the Federated States under which Aceh formed a part of North Sumatra. Natsir promised to work for a more just solution, and Beureueh dropped his opposition. Natsir's cabinet fell before he was able to fulfill his promise. Two years later Beureueh joined the Darul Islam movement. I am grateful to Audrey Kahin for clarifying this for me.

24. Law PP UU no. 8/Des/WKPM/1949, 17 December 1949. See also Syah and Hakiem (2000); *Panji Masyarakat* 34, 8 December 1999, 30.

25. Cited in Tiba (1999, 55–57), and in the commentary of the United Development Party Fraction in discussion of the Draft Law Initiative on Implementation of the Distinction of Aceh as a Special Region, delivered by FPPP-DPR RI spokesperson Dr. H. Muchtar Aziz on 19 August 1999, reprinted in Syah and Hakiem (2000, 98).

26. From the 1940s to the 1960s, the DI/TII (Darul Islam/Tentara Islam Indonesia, or Darul Islam/Indonesian Islamic Army) struggled in various regions of Indonesia, not just Aceh, for the creation of an Islamic state.

27. For example, Muchtar Aziz stated in a parliamentary session discussing the implementation of the law on Aceh's status as a special region in 1999:

"Imagine, Aceh Darussalam, which was before a sovereign nation, after joining the Republic of Indonesia suddenly is valued the same as a residency in the Province of North Sumatra. This disappointment gave birth to the DI/TII movement." Quoted in Syah and Hakiem (2000, 97).

28. Morris continued: "The situation was much the same as it had been twenty five years before when a Darul Islam leader [S. M. Amin] commented: 'Advocates of autonomy for Aceh were unable to ignite the people's imagination; the people were unwilling to sacrifice themselves for an autonomy of uncertain character and extent.' Save for some younger Acehnese—who originally accepted the assumptions of the technocratic representation of Aceh's marginality but then rejected its limited and compromising goals—the Aceh Merdeka ideology of ethnic separatism was not a call which could rally the Acehnese populace. The Aceh Merdeka movement continued beyond the time of my field research in Aceh; small groups under the Aceh Merdeka banner continued to attract sympathy, but its leadership and ideology limited widespread participation."

29. Sunda is the region of West Java from which Karto Suwiryo, the founder of DI/TII, hails. The Sundanese have a distinct language and culture.

30. Hasan Tiro's ancestor, Saman (1826–1891), was honored by Sultan Muhammad Daud Syah (1878–1903) with the right to collect taxes for the war effort from local people (*hak sabil*). See Alfian (1987) and Sulaiman (2000).

31. The term Tiro used for the state is "Negara Republik Indonesia." In later campaigns, TNI and hardliners focused on NKRI, "Negara Kesatuan Republik Indonesia," with a K standing for unity. The unitary state had not yet been established in 1948, but Tiro started off by linking Aceh's history to the Indonesian state, not the nation (*bangsa*).

32. "One" is emphasized by the spaces punctuating the word.

33. Zentgraff was a prominent Dutch historian.

34. For the wider context of Dutch scholarship on regional histories and the challenge to nationalist history writing, see van der Kroef (1958). For an innovative analysis of the role of history in the limits of the nation in Irian Jaya, which has also been viewed as a separatist threat by the Indonesian state, see Rutherford (2003). Post-New Order recollections of rebellion in South Sulawesi are discussed in Bhakti (2005). On prerevolutionary historical writing among Sumatra's Batak, see Rodgers (2005). Steedley (2000) considers memory artists' recollections of revolutionary displacement on Sumatra.

35. The article was based on correspondence from January 1904. Because it simplifies original historical sources, I cite it not as a definitive record of Dutch colonial policy, but rather as an indication of how Dutch policies were recalled in the present.

36. Confidential interview, Jakarta, 26 September 2000.

Chapter 3. Threat and Violence

1. Moerdani's biography (Pour 1993, 19) discusses his experience in RPKAD (Resimen Para Komando Angkatan Darat, Army Para-Commando Regiment) defending national unity against internationally supported regional rebellions during the 1950s. Anxiety about international support of disintegration developed during this period; see Kahin and Kahin (1995).

2. The killings were reportedly the worst from January to June 1966. In 1999 I spoke with a man who recalled organizing youth for the killings. His explana-

tion of why they were necessary reiterated the official national version: there had "been a coup of the legitimate government, an effort to overturn the Pancasila"; however, in Aceh it was different, because they were fighting for Islam. I was confused, wondering how any Acehnese could have been members of the communist party. He explained that the animosity between *uleebalang* (hereditary chiefs) and *ulamas* (religious leaders) had motivated *uleebalang* to side with the communists. The "people were deceived," signing up to receive tools and joining the farmers' organization (BTI) affiliated with the PKI. An earlier social revolution against the *uleebalang* had cleared the way for the implementation of the new Republican institutions (Reid 1979). Playing off the *uleebalang* and *ulamas* was a key component of the Dutch policy devised by Snouck Hurgronje (1906). He advocated securing the allegiance of the *uleebalang*, whom he correctly identified as independent of the sultanate, and isolating the more popular *ulama* in matters of religion, using force if necessary. As Jim Siegel points out, Snouck saw this disjunction as a form of conflict between Islam and indigenous custom (2000). Siegel traces the special position of the *ulama* as a liminal figure able to form close ties with villagers.

3. Confidential interview, Banda Aceh, September 1999. In the same discussion, this man indicated that these groups were likely a creation of military intelligence, which tried to link them to the previous DI/TII uprising. Asia Watch noted in its 1990 report that Lieutenant General Ali Moertopo, the Deputy Head of BAKIN (the Indonesian state intelligence agency), brought together leaders of the West Java DI/TII movement prior to the 1977 election to reactivate the movement. "He reportedly told them that their activities in support of an Islamic state were needed to stop the spread of communism after the fall of Viet Nam, but his real reason, it is now believed, was to discredit the Muslim parties before the election by associating them with extremism. Close to 1,000 people suspected of having attended meetings with former Darul Islam members were arrested between 1977 and 1979 and accused of being members of a non-existent organization called Komando Jihad or the Holy War Command. Since Aceh had its own Darul Islam Movement some of the arrests there in the late 1970s were also by-products of Murtopo's electoral machinations." Asia Watch/Human Rights Watch (1990, 3).

4. Aceh's rich natural resource base, especially natural gas (LNG) and oil, was exploited by the highly centralized New Order state to acquire vital revenues. The economy of Aceh remained extremely underdeveloped throughout the New Order period. Tim Kell notes that Soeharto "implicitly acknowledged that . . . exploitation was occurring" (quoting "Jangan Berkesan Buruk terhadap Pemerintah," *Kompas*, 29 May 1992). Kell cites reports which indicate that in 1983 Aceh "contributed 11 percent to Indonesian exports" while receiving the same grant from the central government as other regions which contributed less than .01 percent to national exports (1995, 53). It is difficult to obtain precise figures for the value of resources obtained from Aceh. Syarifudin Tippe, a military officer with experience in Aceh, cited research by Dr. Djalaluddin Hasan (Head of Commission B of the Regional Parliament, DPRD I Aceh) reproducing figures from the APBN (national budget) indicating that Aceh contributed 10 percent of oil and 43 percent of natural gas income totaling Rp. 10,515.91 billion for 1999 (with an exchange rate at that time of approximately 8000 Rp. to 1 $U.S.). The return to Aceh from the central government averaged less than 5 percent of the value of resources exploited. Tippe (2000).

5. Honna traces the social gap issue nationally in internal military documents (1999, 143).

6. Confidential interviews. A note on Tiro's misuse of DI/TII funds appeared in the Indonesian media, possibly as a move to discredit him: "Antara Ganja dan 'Aceh Merdeka'," *Editor*, 15 April 1989, 13. Sulaiman notes that Tiro and Beureueh met in the early 1970s (2000, 18).

7. This history was recounted to me by Abdullah Syafi'ie during an interview in Aceh on 8 June 1999, and it appears in many later books and media accounts. Although various accounts recall the details of Tiro's homecoming and the promotion of the idea of an independent Aceh, none of the people with whom I spoke described any ceremony on 4 December. They repeated the date as if it were memorized, rather than pertaining to an event they recalled from their own experience.

8. Malik emphasized: "it is futile to struggle with an oath of 'one nation, one state and one language.'" He continued: "'we struggled for the independence of 13,000 islands of Indonesia. What is that liberation if it is based on 13,000 independences?" He blamed the lack of unity on underdevelopment in Irian Jaya and other places. "Terlalu Pagi Menilai 'Deklarasi Aceh Merdeka'," *Kompas* 7 June 1977.

9. *Pancasila* refers to the five principles of state ideology: belief in one supreme god, requiring all citizens to belong to one of the five major world religions; just and civilized humanitarianism; Indonesian unity; popular sovereignty governed by wise policies achieved through deliberation and consensus; and social justice for all Indonesian people. These principles were enshrined in the national constitution, in place of a Jakarta Charter that would have made all Muslims responsible to Islamic law.

10. Sudomo included PRRI/Permesta (Revolutionary Government of the Republic of Indonesia/Universal Struggle Charter), a regional though not separatist uprising based primarily in northern Sulawesi and central Sumatra in the late 1950s, DI/TII, and G30S/PKI (September 30th Movement/Communist Party Indonesia), the so-called abortive communist coup of 30 September 1965. "Kas Kopkamtib: Munculnya 'Aceh Merdeka' Peringatan Bagi Bangsa Indonesia," *Kompas*, 11 June 1977.

11. Many people told me this in interviews; Kell (1995) makes a similar point.

12. Accounts vary on when Hasan Tiro fled Aceh; it is likely that he had already left.

13. Anxieties about powerful external forces supporting internal enemies correspond to the historical experience of outside support for regional rebellion, see Kahin and Kahin 1995.

14. I have tried to maintain the distinction between GAM and AM. But making this distinction is difficult when citing others' analyses, since few people now consider GAM and AM separate. Many of those arrested in the initial repression of AM distinguished that group from the GAM that later emerged, but in casual speech even they used the two terms interchangeably.

15. The weapons available during this period were most likely left over from DI/TII.

16. He used the English term "embryo."

17. It is highly unlikely that an Acehnese separatist would have taken the code name of Arjuna, a primary figure in the *wayang* shadow plays performed in Java.

18. The term Gerombolan Pengacau (Gang of Disruptors) was extended to

Gerombolan Pengacau Kemanan (Gang of Security Disruptors), and then, keeping the same acronym, GPK, the Gang was changed to a movement, resulting in Gerakan Pengacau Keamanan. GPK was used in Irian Jaya and East Timor during this period. In 1980-1982, gang and movement were often used in the same article.

19. The accusation was made by Asisten Intel Kowilhan I Kolonel Goenarso.

20. For an excellent analysis of the military's rhetoric in the post-DOM period, which quantitatively analyzes the frequency with which such terms as "exchange of fire" were used by military spokespeople and reproduced by the media, see "Kemelut Aceh," *Pantau: Kajian Media dan Jurnalisme*, edition 6, October–November 1999.

21. The article does not explain how there could still be six members if there were six prior to Zubair's killing.

22. The final four were Hasan Tiro, who named himself Head of State of Free Aceh (Hasan Tiro *yang menamakan dirinya* Wali Negara Aceh Merdeka); Doctor Husaini Abdullah, Minister of the Interior (Mendagri Aceh Merdeka); Doctor Zaini, Minister of Public Health (Menkes);and Daud Paneuh, Commander in Chief of Armed Aceh Merdeka (Panglima Bersenjata Aceh Merdeka). The article lists the others arrested in this campaign, noting that all had been caught with weapons and documents.

23. See Siegel, "Possessed," an essay added to the new edition of *The Rope of God* (2000). Acehnese marijuana is said to have the highest THC content of any in the world and was traditionally used as a condiment.

24. In private, many people reported that incidents of extortion and intimidation "in the name of GAM" were a significant source of the movement's income. Official GAM sources say that all of the movement's income was generated from freely given donations. It may be that the existence of an underground economy in marijuana allowed many donations from the military to remain unacknowledged.

25. Operation Wibawa, the same name given to the post-DOM operation.

26. The dictionary defines *dibina* as "to build, construct, establish, or cultivate." I translate it as "cultivated" because a senior member of the military describing this period noted that the rebels had been *dipelihara* (taken care of, protected, raised), created (stated in English in the interview), and cultivated (stated in English).

27. In contrast to the previous round of arrests, in which the names and positions of each person were given, during this period the names were omitted, resembling regular criminals in typical reports in Indonesia. For a discussion of criminality in Jakarta, see Siegel (1998). The identities of the guilty were indistinct, and no evidence linked them to GAM.

28. On 11 July 1990, Hasan met with President Soeharto and requested that extra troops be brought in to secure Aceh for development. "Syarwan Hamid Siap Diperiksa Untuk Kasus Aceh," *Republika*, 18 November 1999; "Masalah Aceh. Tiga Mantan Jenderal Keberatan Penuhi Panggilan DPR," *Republika*, 26 November 1999; "DPR Tak Mampu Korek Para Jenderal," *Kompas*, 30 November 1999. For his 1999 testimony, see *Risalah Rapat Dengar Pendapat Umum Pansus Tentang Permasalahan Di Daerah Istimewa Aceh* 1999.

29. According to Loren Ryter, GPK initially referred to the youth wing of the Muslim party (PPP), which refused to give up the name. The security forces then used the term to describe subversives, and it stuck (personal communication, 2000). Geoffrey Robinson (1998) has analyzed how the *rawan* (troubled)

areas in which GPK is a perceived threat might in fact be *rawan* because of the security forces. Campaigns against GPK were simultaneously conducted in East Timor and Irian Jaya.

30. Many people I spoke with during the late New Order and reform periods expressed suspicions about what they perceived to be a deliberate strategy of raising vague threats and possibilities through their denial. For example, the death of B. Lopa was immediately reported as "not by poison," causing people to suspect foul play.

31. Some GAM sources acknowledged that there had been training in Libya. I am interested here in the effects of this shift on the narration of the conflict rather than whether fighters trained in Libya, although that now seems to be the consensus among analysts, observers, and participants.

32. The man called "Robert," whose real name was Dharma Bakti, was born in Banda Aceh. His father was Acehnese, and his mother was originally from Tapanuli Selatan. The emphasis on non-Acehnese figures was a strong contrast to the final round of labeling GAM/*masyarakat*, in which GAM and the people became indistinguishable.

33. In the 1987 elections the government party, Golkar, finally succeeded in capturing enough votes to displace the previous majority Muslim party, PPP. On electoral politics during this period, see Kell 1995.

34. This village-level campaign is described in "Dari Pembunuhan Hingga Referendum," *Kompas*, 14 January 2000.

35. The location where these bodies were found was not the same as the place where the National Human Rights Commission excavated.

36. Soeharto claims in his autobiography that brutal shock therapy is necessary to show that there is still someone who can control criminality; *Soeharto*, 364.

37. For discussion of the economic and political problems associated with this project, see Kell (1995).

38. Currently, conflicts have developed in Irian Jaya for what may be very similar reasons. Robinson's analysis of the relationship between military operations and abuses and "trouble spots" (1998) applies to the conflicts there as well.

39. Later the report describes the appearance of this witness, who had been tortured.

40. Despite its internal contradictions, the pattern of remarking that people are becoming less enamored of the opposition's ideology and casting all of society as probable or potential members of the clandestine resistance is common in Indonesia. In Timor, many observers noted, some government officials thought that the people would not select independence, and yet operationally they treated all the people as potential enemies or informers.

41. Another report describes the work of cultivated agents in determining that DI/TII weapons were found during this operation. "Since DI/TII was eradicated by the national army of Indonesia, there is still the possibility that the weapons are being stored by ex-DI/TII who are still living or other groups." Laporan Khusus, 25 June 1995, No. R/14/LAPSUS/1995, 2.

42. The military contracted soldiers to provide security for corporations. For example, Exxon Mobil employed a significant number of soldiers to secure its operations during the 1990s.

43. At this point Bantaqiah was a recognized figure, but not necessarily part of GAM. By including this testimony, GAM publishers in exile attempted to link themselves with movements occurring in Aceh.

44. The second ceremony was held in a crowded military compound, and a week before it people were urged to attend. "Lhokseumawe Rusuh," *Kompas*, 1 August 1998.

45. Many people doubted that the troops had been completely withdrawn, and militarization occurred under new rationales. So this promise was not fully realized. But the ceremony occurred, which had important ramifications in discussions of security forces' violence.

46. Confidential interview, Medan, November 1999.

47. On 6 December 2000, four humanitarian workers from Rehabilitation Action for Torture Victims in Aceh (RATA), a group sponsored by the Danish government, were traveling in North Aceh to pick up victims for treatment. Their vehicle was stopped by TNI members out of uniform. They were tortured and shot in the head. One escaped and reported the incident. He fled Indonesia in fear of his safety. For other instances of humanitarian workers being abused by the security forces, see Human Rights Watch Press Statement, 8 December 2000. http://hrw.org/english/docs/2000/12/08/indone644_txt.htm (accessed 1 November 2006).

48. Some accounts saw this accident as an indication that he was unfamiliar with firearms.

49. The vehicle used for the robbers' escape had a police license plate, according to some sources, and was later found in the forest near Kandang, 8 kilometers from Lhokseumawe. "BCA Lhokseumawe Dirampok," *Kompas*, 5 February 1997.

50. Kol Dasiri Musnari Komandan Korem 011/LW was replaced by Johny Wahab shortly after this incident.

51. Ninjas were men who appeared in black with their faces masked who were believed to be military agents. Ninjas were involved in other cases in Indonesia, especially the killings of suspected witches in East Java from December 1998 to February 1999. James Siegel describes the representation of ninja associated with the Indonesian army, "they are merely a power that operates in any world and that appear there without explanation" (2006, 165).

52. The team included Albert Hasibuan, Soegiri, and Koesparmono Irsan, and was scheduled to be in Aceh 6–8 January, 1999.

53. Supposedly, his only identifiable feature was a crippled foot, the result of a motorcycle accident; "Mencari Ahmad di Desa Kandang," *Majalah D&R*, 18–23 January 1999.

54. In the same interview, the youth offered other examples, including an incident of simultaneous sweeping done by ABRI and GAM; although they were no more than 200 meters apart, they did not confront each other, but only terrorized civilians. He was a very young "DOM victim" who fit the typical profile of those whom GAM tried to recruit.

55. These figures are in the Confidential Presidential Decree Team report; other accounts vary on the number of victims. See "Korban Tewas 24, Lhokseumawe Mulai Tenang," *Suara Pembaruan*, 4 May 1999. Military sources described the victims as GPK. However, one was a seven-year-old child. "Mereka Tiarap, Tapi tetap ditembak," *Media Indonesia*, 10 May 1999.

56. Following the end of DOM, Syahputra frequently gave media interviews as a spokesperson for GAM in the Pase region.

57. In an article discussing the return of the military member taken hostage, he said he had brought his short-wave radio and gun because he was afraid he would be kidnapped. "Tentara dan Warga Bentrok di Aceh," *Kompas*, 4 May 1999.

58. The head of Habibie's Special Team on Aceh, Usman Hasan, diagnosed four possible sources of the trouble: remaining non-organic troops who had not left, troops who had returned to Aceh, civilians, and imitation GAM. See "Sulit Dimengerti, Penembakan Orang-orang tak Bersenjata," *Media Indonesia,* 5 May 1999.

Chapter 4. Translating Violence into Politics

1. There were infrequent reports of military tribunals, but this was the only case that was tried by a tribunal that was not exclusively military.
2. "DPR Bentuk Tim Pencari Fakta Aceh dan Irja,"*Kompas,* 22 July 1998; "TPF DPR ke Aceh Disambut Mahasiswa,"*Kompas,* 27 July 1998; "TPF DPR Prihatinkan Tindak Kekerasan di Aceh,"*Kompas,* 29 July 1998.
3. In 2000, playwright Ratna Sarumpaet thematized the issue of rape in her production on Aceh, *Alia, Luka Serambi Mekah.*
4. The generals called to the parliamentary session in November 1999 used this argument. I heard many stories of Abdullah Syafi'ie successfully evading Indonesian soldiers by shifting his fanny pack to his chest, covering his head with a scarf, and putting a women's sarong over his pants.
5. Photos of women in *jilbab* (Islamic head covering) wielding AK-47s were extremely popular in the media. In some photos these women's fear and discomfort are visible; they appear unfamiliar with holding a weapon.
6. Marzuki became attorney general under the Wahid administration, but he did not investigate cases related to Aceh.
7. "Sujud Syukur atas Pencabutan 'DOM',"*Kompas,* 10 August 1998; "Menhankam/Pangab Jendral Wiranto: Pasukan Bukan Organik Aceh Dikembalikan ke Pangkalannya," *Suara Pembaruan,* 8 August 1998; "Dicabut, Status 'DOM' Aceh * Panglima ABRI Jendral Wiranto Mohon Maaf,"*Kompas,* 8 August 1998.
8. *Risalah Rapat Pendapat Umum Pansus Tentang Permasalahan Di Daerah Istimewa Aceh* (1999); see also "Mengenai 'Peristiwa Aceh',," *Suara Pembaruan,* 28 August 1998; "Korban Jaring Merah Di Bukit Tenkorak," *Majalah Gatra,* 8 August 1998.
9. "21 Kerangka Jenazah di Aceh Masih Diperiksa," *Suara Pembaruan,* 25 August 1998; "Menhankam/Pangab Sesalkan Pernyataan Komnas HAM,"*Kompas,* 27 August 1998; "Data Komnas HAM Soal Aceh Belum Final,"*Kompas,* 28 August 1998.
10. I recall speaking to an Acehnese man at an event in Jakarta designed to raise money and awareness of the situation in Aceh. A skit acted out the violence between "TNI" and "GAM." Many people in the crowd laughed at the dramatization of the ambiguity of the conflict as one person repeatedly switched sides. The Acehnese man I spoke with was aghast that people could be laughing when the scenes featured Acehnese people dying. Events such as this were limited to the period before the Humanitarian Pause, before there was a visible and violent GAM.
11. Interview with Munir of *Kontras,* Jakarta, 7 July 1999.
12. Confidential interview, Jakarta, November 2000.
13. Confidential interview, Los Angeles, April 2001.
14. In addition to the killing at Bantaqiah's Islamic school, the four other priority cases included the rape of Sumiati on 16 August 1996 in Pidie (the military perpetrator had acknowledged his act, but was not held responsible); kidnappings and killings at Rumoh Gedong torture post in 1997–1998; mur-

ders at Idi Cut (seven civilians were killed on 2 February 1999 by the army in what appeared to be revenge for kidnapping of eight army members by unidentified forces); and shootings at the KKA intersection on 3 May 1999 (39 civilians were fatally shot and 125 wounded by the army).

15. This report is the most comprehensive statement of the transitional government's understanding of the Aceh problem and it guided policy on Aceh during a period of national reform and international attention. Aceh was a critical test for the government in achieving legal supremacy to the military. The report catalogs the state's anxieties about the undeniable evidence of the past crimes of still-powerful armed forces. The report is one of the clearest and most sustained examples of how the state organized evidence that threatened its legitimacy. In 1999 the "Aceh Problem" was a political problem, and discussions in Jakarta focused on how to do justice regarding the admitted violations committed in Aceh. In 2003, it again became a military problem, as civilian politicians authorized a state of emergency to combat armed separatists.

16. I quote from this confidential report at length, citing page numbers in the text. Copies of the Report and Executive Summary are in the author's possession.

17. "Markas Tgk Bantaqiyah Digempur, 31 Tewas," *Media Indonesia,* 27 July 1999; "Kekerasan Tewaskan Puluhan Warga Sipil di Aceh,"*Kompas,* 27 July 1999; "Komisi Independen untuk Aceh Terbentuk. Tragedi Beutong Ateuh Tewaskan 52 Orang," *Republika,* 31 July 1999.

18. One eyewitness report suggested the military were from several different battalions and units. "Bantaqiah Sengaja Dihabisi? Tragedi Beutong Target Siapa?" *Kontras,* 4 August 1999.

19. Bantaqiah's *dayah* was located in Beutong Ateuh, which consisted of four villages: Blang Meurandeh, Blang Pu'uk, Kuta Teungoh, and Babah Suak. According to Zamzami (2001), the total population of these four villages was approximately 1,826 people in 1999.

20. The *Majalah Tempo* article compared this movement to other social protests against new values conducted with and without violence, such as Samin in Java.

21. The project was valued at over 400 million Rupiah in November 1990. Bantaqiah sent a letter to the local military official (*Danrem*) stating that he refused to move to the lower area in December 1990. The official reason that the project could not be built in Bantaqiah's area was that there was no road; however, as documented by Serambi newspaper at that time and noted by Amran Zamzami, since 1982 as much as 956 million Rupiah had been allocated for building a mere 35.5 km of road. See Zamzami 2001, 30.

22. It is extremely difficult to document the marijuana trade. I heard an unconfirmed rumor that Bantaqiah had been involved in large-scale marijuana deals. At this time, it was said that Bantaqiah was in Tommy Soeharto's group, making the post-Stock Exchange bombing efforts to link GAM and Tommy especially ironic.

23. Danrem 011/Lilawangsa, the commander of the Korem. Aceh is divided into two Korems, Lilawangsa and Teuku Umar.

24. He was said to be on leave because of psychological illness, but the leave paperwork presented was signed after he had become a fugitive. *Kontras* noted the inconsistencies in the dates.

25. Colonel Syarfril Armen, Danrem 011/Lilawangsa Kodam I Bukit Barisan.

26. The independent team reports this telegram as STR 232, while the court refers to STR 232a; no mention or explanation was made of this discrepancy.

27. Although this information is not in the testimony, the statement may have been made in the original questioning. His refusal indicates that other soldiers could have known that the order was illegal, but the decision does not pursue the implications. The "reasonable person" test is often used to determine guilt in trials of soldiers for crimes against humanity who argue that they were only following orders.

28. This information was included in the manuscript of Zamzami's "Peradilan Koneksitas, Sebuah Jalan Tengah" (91), but does not appear in the published book.

29. Unfortunately, the copy of the report I was given was missing the page after this one. I do not know whether this omission was deliberate. There was no way to recover the missing page.

30. For a military denial of "wild" Special Forces that occurred before the Bantaqiah case, see the report in the military's newspaper: "Menhankam/ Pangab: Tak Ada Pasukan Kopassus Liar di Aceh," *Harian Umum* ABRI, 24 February 1999.

31. On 27 January 1999, Habibie announced there would be a referendum in East Timor with the options of *pelepasan* (independence) if the offer of autonomy was rejected. See "Timtim Dilepas Bila Status Khusus Otonomi Luas Ditolak," *Suara Pembaruan*, 28 January 1999. On 30 August 1999, the referendum occurred and on 3 September 1999, the results were announced in New York: the majority of East Timorese voters, 344,480, or 78.5 percent, rejected special autonomy, while only 94,388, or 21.5 percent, accepted it.

32. James T. Siegel has discussed at length the problem of the student movement asking the state for permission to hold a referendum rather than starting a revolution. His analysis raises many interesting points (see "Possessed," a new essay added to *The Rope of God* in 2000). However, SIRA did hold its own poll, which alienated many of its international supporters. It is essential to consider the international context in which this conflict was situated and the participants' keen consciousness of this context. Referendum was an effort to be as neutral as possible in order to attract as wide a range of support as possible, both internationally and from the elder generation, who were still powerful though they could have been considered less credible because of their associations with the past regime. The referendum umbrella was not revolutionary, but endeavored to provide a narrative and strategy in which all Acehnese could be accommodated.

33. Including Bustari Mansur (Wakil Gubernur) and Teungku Muhamad Yus (Ketua DPRD I Aceh), both mentioned in "Referendum di Aceh Itu Harga Mati,"*Kompas*, 9 November 1999.

34. Nur Asikin was one of the few women prominent in the Referendum movement. She and one other speaker that day later became GAM representatives under the Humanitarian Pause agreement. Cut Nur Asikin was part of the minority group who staged a walkout from the Aceh Women's Congress after it decided despite extreme intimidation not to make a statement for referendum but instead to make a statement in favor of peace and moving beyond politics to move beyond violence.

35. To which many Acehnese replied: "if a couple wants a divorce, does the whole village have to vote on it?" Acehnese do not consider themselves "children" in the family model that the New Order tried to develop. Since the revo-

lution, the center has considered Aceh as one of many subordinates, while Aceh has seen itself as a partner in shaping the nation.

36. President Megawati signed Law No. 18/2001 regarding regional autonomy, titled Nanggroe Aceh Darussalam, on 9 August 2001. See "Presiden Tanda Tangani UU Nanggroe Aceh,"*Kompas*, 16 August 2001. Describing the proposed legislation, a member of parliament said that for eight years Aceh would receive 70 percent of gas revenues from resources in Aceh; in the ninth year, it would receive only 50 percent. However, he noted that later it could be renegotiated. See "DPR Sahkan RUU NAD," *Koran Tempo*, 20 July 2001.

37. Yusril became prominent in the reform era as both minister of laws and legal institutions and minister of justice; he retained a place in Megawati's cabinet as Minister of Law and Human Rights. For a discussion of his position in the Wahid administration (Menteri Hukum dan Perundang-Undangan), see "Menteri Harus Mampu Hidup Sederhana," *Suara Pembaruan*, 29 October 1999. His position in Megawati's administration (Menteri Kehakiman dan HAM) is discussed in "Kabinet Gotong Royong Diumumkan. Megawati: Kedudukan Presiden Tak Tergantung DPR,"*Kompas*, 10 August 2001.

38. One person I interviewed recalled using kerosene lanterns to light porches during DOM because there was no electricity to meet the military's demand for illumination. For data on the problem of economic exploitation, see Tippe (2000, 44–49) and Kell, 1995.

39. Interviews in Banda Aceh, October 1999.

40. Many ordinary Acehnese reiterated that if there were independence everyone would be rich. GAM propaganda includes figures, but wealth is difficult to calculate in a context where rebels as well as the military practice extortion.

41. Kol. Inf Johny Wahab was Danrem 011 Lilawangsa, located in Lhokseumawe.

42. In September 2001, after Dawood advocated dialogue between the government and GAM, he was killed by two unidentified gunmen on a motorcycle. See *AFP*, 6 September 2001.

43. For an example of military descriptions of Indonesians in general as prone to running amok, see "Zacky: TNI Telah Berusaha Atasi Kerusuhan,"*Kompas*, 12 May 2000.

44. See also "KSAD: Pasukan TNI di Aceh Tidak Akan Ditarik," *Media Indonesia*, 18 June 1999; "Kekuatan Pasukan di Aceh Akan Ditambah," *Republika*, 22 June 1999; "Dibentuk, Tim Independen Tuntaskan Kasus Aceh," *Republika*, 3 July 1999. For a similar civilian viewpoint, see the comments of Akbar Tanjung, speaker of the DPR, quoted in "Rakyat Berhadapan Dengan TNI," *Sinar Pagi*, 5 August 1999. For an analysis of the use of "amok" see Good and Delvecchio Good (2001).

45. In 2001, after the Stock Exchange bombing in Jakarta, there were discussions of the need to stop weapons being bought from Thailand, but little discussion of the sale of arms from the TNI to Aceh. See "Pengiriman Senjata ke Aceh Digagalkan," *Media Indonesia*, 12 May 2001; "Presiden Wahid Sampaikan Terimakasih Kepada Thailand. Arus Senjata ke Aceh Minta Diawasi," *Media Indonesia*, 15 May 2001; "Polisi Cari Pelaku Penyeludupan Ribuan Amunisi and Senjata ke Aceh," *Poskota*, 30 July 2000.

46. On the importance of Islamic law in the context of "political disappointment," see Confidential Report, 476–79.

47. Lev 1972 is the classic work on Islamic courts. For an overview of the

relationship between Islam and the state in historical perspective, see Effendy 2003. Essays in Salim and Azra 2003 consider the complexities of *Syariah* in Indonesia. For a review of the application of *Syariah* law in Aceh after the MOU, see International Crisis Group July 2006. Bowen 2003 is an exemplary study of the relationship of Islam and public reasoning in the Gayo region of Aceh.

48. "RUU Keistimewaan Aceh Diharapkan Bisa Jadi Solusi Konflik," *Republika*, 20 August 1999; "RUU tentang Aceh Segera Jadi UU," *Media Indonesia*, 21 August 1999; "Makmun Daud Beureueh: Aceh Harus Tetap Bersatu Dengan RI," *Republika*, 23 August 1999.

49. For GAM reaction, see "AGAM Tolak NAD dan Merdeka dari Pemerintah RI," *Waspada*, 16 October 2000.

50. For an example of the use of Islamic law to justify harassment of prostitutes, see "Hukum Rajam Bagi Pezinah dan Pencuri di Aceh," *Republika*, 6 December 1999. On women's obligation to wear head coverings, see "Mesjid Raya, Kawasan Wajib Jilbab Pertama di Aceh," *Republika*, 27 September 1999.

51. In the 1980s, the issue of immoral and undisciplined behavior had been a problem in the new industrial zone; see Kell (1995).

52. These groups first appeared in Aceh after the tsunami as volunteers to assist in the proper burial of victims.

Chapter 5. Neutrality and Provocation

1. Following the first agreement in 2000, the HDC remained involved in facilitating a second cessation of hostilities agreement in 2002. For an overview of HDC's role in Aceh, see Huber (2004).

2. The Indonesian text uses *bebaskan*, which means to release or free, rather than *merdeka*, which is typically translated as free in the name of the rebel group. *Merdeka* is also translated as independent; its use invokes revolutionary struggles for independence from the Dutch.

3. In the context of the agreement, TNI refers to both the armed forces and the police forces, which had recently been separated from the military. Relationships between various elements of the armed forces and the police were extremely tense in Aceh during this period.

4. Confidential interview, Jakarta, 7 November 1999.

5. For an analysis of the reporting on criminality and its construction as a category, see Siegel (1998).

6. Sulistyo described the knowing smile of the police officers in the Joint Fact Finding Team (TGPF) charged with investigating the May 1998 riots; even if they knew who it was (as it seems they did), they knew no one would be bold enough to arrest that person. He proposed that journalists and others follow the wealthy because money was what makes the *provokator*; if reporters followed them for days, the public could discover what they were doing.

7. The unidentified groups were referred to as *orang tak dikenal* or *kelompok orang tak dikenal.*

8. Hasballah, who was once detained on charges of being GAM, served as human rights minister during the reform period.

9. Pangdam I Bukit Barisan Mayjen Rachman Gaffar's rhetoric nearly reproduces Soeharto's commentary in Aceh regarding the communist party twenty years before.

10. As an official election monitor in Aceh, I had the opportunity to interview

local government officials, security forces, police, NGOs, students, and voters. Results of this observation are reported in Aspinal, Drexler, and Johanson 1999.

11. Interviews, June 1999. ABRI changed its name to TNI, and the police were separated from the national armed forces. "Polri Pisah Dari ABRI," *Suara Pembaruan*, 1 April 1999; "Dari ABRI ke TNI," *Media Indonesia*, 6 April 1999.

12. English in original. Letkol Pol Drs Iskandar Hasan explained the Desa Paloh Lada incident, in which 24 civilians were killed.

13. Maulida was often suspected of being a double agent for the TNI.

14. "Dua Anggota TNI Ditemukan Tewas di Dalam Karung," *Media Indonesia*, 10 June 1999; "Berbagai Insiden Warnai Pelaksanaan Pemilu Di Aceh," *Suara Pembaruan*, 8 June 1999

15. "Berbagai Insiden Warnai Pelaksanaan Pemilu Di Aceh," *Suara Pembaruan*, 8 June 1999; "Dua Anggota TNI Ditemukan Tewas di Dalam Karung," *Media Indonesia*, 10 June 1999

16. The Kopassus group was code-named Tim Elang. "Suasana mencekam, warga pilih diam di rumah. Kontak Senjata di Aceh, 6 Tewas," *Poskota*, 6 August 1999; "Gerak-geriknya Mencurigakan. Tiga Anggota TNI Diamankan Masyarakat," *Republika*, 8 June 1999

17. Confidential interview, Medan, 10 June 2000.

18. At this time, many reports in the local and national media focused on the absence of local officials, calling it a "paralysis" of the Indonesian government in Aceh.

19. The "floating mass" was a concept developed during the New Order, when social and political organizations were not able to organize at the local level as it would lead to disunity and interfere with the New Order development project. The mass of the people, in contrast to Soekarno's direct addresses to them, would express themselves politically only once every five years in general elections.

20. He claimed to have Sujono "in safe keeping," but Sujono disappeared.

21. When the *Far Eastern Economic Review* featured a photo of Hasan Tiro in 1999, many Acehnese I spoke with said that it was the first time they had seen an image of him.

22. In an article titled "Deadly Suspicion," Schwarz (1991) cited Ramli Ridwan's statement that ABRI provoked more fear among local people than did the separatist rebels. See AI 1993.

23. In public statements, GAM blamed violent incidents on *provokator*. Prior to the agreement, when GAM was still an underground movement, it was difficult to discern who the actual perpetrators were. Both TNI and GAM could have disavowed members. In this atmosphere, several strains of GAM were distinguished, including a GAM *provokator* to which most criminality was attributed.

24. Conversations with international organizations disclosed that their funding decisions were not immune to the polarizing distrust among civil society groups. Lists circulated by e-mail of organizations that would not be eligible for funding that came through the pause mechanism. Precise figures for the amount of aid distributed in conjunction with the Pause have been difficult to document, though, it appears much less than was promised. The amount of money that would have been liable to appropriation by GAM members for purchase of weapons cannot be ascertained.

25. One was from Kostrad (Territorial) and the other from Kopassus.

26. Pidie, perhaps not entirely coincidentally, is also Hasan Tiro's place of origin.

27. The activists mentioned were supporters of Megawati who were abducted in the military's July 1996 raid on her headquarters.

28. In particular, GAM Minister Malik, who was also important in securing GAM's participation in the Pause.

29. Bakhtiar Abdullah did admit that he had not met Malik from Singapore, indicating the fractures among people who spoke in the name of GAM and were identified with it. Bakhtiar took the opportunity to deny responsibility for other violent incidents in Aceh that remained unsolved and had been blamed on GAM. Specifically, he noted the death of Ismail Syahputra, which had provoked much speculation regarding the possibility that he had been a double agent for GAM and TNI. He also noted the death of the Deacon of IAIN, Ar-Ranniry. See "Dua Mayat Ditemukan, Tiga Diculik di Aceh Utara. GAM Bantah Terlibat Kasus Peledakan Bom," *Media Indonesia,* 7 October 2000.

30. Acehnese who spoke with HDC representatives at various points, as well as people who have read the confidential internal evaluation of the project, all indicated that HDC was aware of the relevant information that it chose to ignore.

31. People involved in the humanitarian aid industry whom I knew in Jakarta made cynical comments about the competition among international groups to find the messiest, most volatile, most worthwhile, and highest-risk conflict to resolve.

32. Consider, for example, the mysterious deaths of T. Johan, Dyan Dawood, and S. Idris.

33. This conclusion is based on interviews conducted prior to the military operations authorized by Presidential Instruction, Inpres No 4/2001. These operations reportedly resulted in 1000 deaths during the first six-month period. Interviews conducted in 2006 suggested that fear of challenging or not identifying with GAM remains, though some people expressed hope that this would change after the elections. For discussion of the military operations, see "Indonesia Tuding GAM Tolak Perundingan," *Media Indonesia,* 22 April 2001; "Inpres Aceh Diperpanjang Empat Bulan," *Media Indonesia,* 10 October 2001; "Seribu Tewas Selama Inpres No 4 di Aceh," *Media Indonesia,* 12 October 2001.

Chapter 6. The Tsunami and the Cease-Fire

1. For a discussion of controversies surrounding one program to relocate displaced peoples to barracks, see Hedman (2005).

2. This group of advisors included Hamid Awaluddin, Minister of Justice and Human Rights; Sofyan Djalil, Minister of Communication and Information; and Major General Syafuddin Tippe, former commander of Korem 012, the regional military command in Banda Aceh. The team had been in contact with rebels in exile.

3. The HDC was not involved in these negotiations or the monitoring mission. The agreement was brokered by the Crisis Management Initiative (CMI) based in Helsinki, which describes itself as "an independent, nongovernmental organisation responding to challenges in sustainable security."

4. The version from the Acehnese parliament (DRPD) stated that Islamic law would be the foundation for good governance, while the GAM version did not include this introductory paragraph. The DPRD version stated that candidates for political office must be Indonesian citizens and not have been sen-

tenced to jail for any criminal act except for *makar*, the GAM version that they must be Acehnese or live in Aceh and never have been sentenced to jail for corruption. The DPRD required local parties to have at least 50 percent Indonesian citizens and 30 percent women on their boards of directors and stipulated that the goal of local parties was to work for the rights and welfare of Aceh in the frame of NKRI; the GAM version did not include any of these requirements. The GAM version gave Aceh's government the right to work directly with international organizations for development and other financial matters, health, humanitarian, and social issues, and democracy and to have representatives in other countries. The DPRD acknowledged that the TNI will remain in Aceh to protect against external threats. The GAM version specified that the DPRA (their version replaces the D for regional parliament with an Acehnese parliament) must be consulted in advance regarding troop movements and numbers in Aceh and must agree to them in writing. The GAM version advocated significant funds to educate a wider age range (youth 6–18 years old have the right to basic education, in contrast to those aged 7–15 in the other version), emphasized international cooperation, and stipulated a second-language curriculum for English and Arabic as well as allowing courses to be taught in Acehnese. Under the section on culture, the DPRD version also advocated teaching in the regional language. The GAM version obliged the governments of Indonesia and Aceh to collect data on victims of the conflict as historical documents, to maintain mass graves for both the tsunami and the conflict as historical monuments, and to build a museum for the armed conflict and a monument for the humanitarian tragedy. In terms of human rights, the DPRD version was much more detailed, anticipating violations through their prohibition, while the GAM version incorporated universal human rights standards. The DPRD version obliged the government to protect the rights of minorities and to form a Human Rights Court and Truth and Reconciliation Commission within one year of the passing of this legislation. Subsequently, the DPRD version stated that the Truth and Reconciliation Commission would be derived from the national commission. The DPRD also stated that a UN Special Rapporteur would be called upon to investigate crimes against humanity in Aceh. The GAM version stated that the governments of Indonesia and Aceh are obliged to rehabilitate the victims of conflict: the government of Indonesia is obliged to give Aceh funds to rehabilitate public and individual property destroyed as a result of the conflict, land or work must be given to victims, and a joint commission shall be formed to resolve issues related to reintegration and rehabilitation between GAM and Indonesia. The GAM version specified that Aceh has its own flag, anthem, and symbols. The DPRD version required a special police force and court system for implementing Islamic law, while the GAM version did not. In the DPRD version the *wali Negara* has primarily symbolic functions, while the GAM version detailed extensive rights, responsibilities, and immunities of the head of state, including the right to resolve disputes between various other bodies and institutions in Aceh. The DPRD version outlined detailed requirements for identity cards for Acehnese, while the GAM version did not. In addition, the DPRD version has a section on customary law (*adat*) that was not in the GAM version.

5. For an analysis of how the "All-Aceh" version differs from the versions drafted by the DPR, see ICG March 2006.

6. The sections of the law on the human rights tribunal and the commission for truth and reconciliation were rife with technical problems. The MOU sim-

ply states "A Human Rights Court will be established for Aceh." According to the law, the human rights tribunal will examine any violations occurring after the MOU was signed. This tribunal depends on national legislation that establishes such tribunals, but does not establish one in Aceh. An additional legislative process built on a political consensus would be required to amend the existing law or to establish parallel structures in Aceh. The MOU declares that "A Commission for Truth and Reconciliation will be established for Aceh by the Indonesian Commission of Truth and Reconciliation with the task of formulating and determining reconciliation measures." The legislation for the national commission was ratified, the commissioners were tested and ranked, but they were never appointed by the President of Indonesia. In 2006, human rights activists requested the Constitutional Court to review articles declaring that compensation would only be granted to victims after perpetrators had been given amnesty, and that once cases had been resolved through the commission they could not be brought to court. In other cases, the Constitutional Court had modified only articles; the human rights advocates who initiated the review were shocked by the court's decision to declare the entire law unconstitutional. The court did recommend the creation of new legislation in line with the constitution and international law.

7. The details of his early involvement with GAM are not clear. He went to the U.S. to study veterinary science in 1993. Some people told me that they thought he joined the movement after DOM. He was arrested in 2003 and remained in jail until the tsunami.

8. For a detailed account of splits in GAM prior to the election, see ICG November 2006.

9. On the implementation of Islamic law, see ICG July 2006.

10. Making peace profitable was one of HDC's strategies, but it did not work. The funds for tsunami reconstruction and the tax on reconstruction have created a much higher peace dividend and much greater opportunities for corruption.

11. In Jakarta, I met with several publicly acknowledged GAM figures during the Humanitarian Pause. One man whom I had not met before was introduced as a GAM fighter. I rarely taped interviews, but on this occasion I was supposed to get an "official statement" from GAM about the Pause. He was an animated and forthcoming speaker. I asked what he could tell me about how GAM was armed and financed. Most people answered such questions vaguely, which gave me the impression that they themselves did not know or preferred not to know that information. This man had no reservations; he rapidly fired off a list of weapons and prices. The supplier was the TNI through the Pindad factory in Bandung. I was stunned, even suspicious of his blatant disclosure of TNI support for GAM. I moved to turn off the tape, reminding him that it was running. He was unconcerned about being recorded. He thought I was shocked that the TNI was helping GAM. The other representatives joined in, detailing the support of the military. Anecdotes recalled particular incidents of certain military members' help, as well as reiterating the more general availability of weapons. Finally, I asked why the TNI would do this. In their view, these donations proved the justness of their cause. They explained: "Some of the soldiers have seen how badly the people of Aceh were treated. They leave us their weapons." Others had economic motivations and sold their weapons when they left; "soldiers make very little money, they need extra money." Others simply "were involved" with GAM, perhaps as double agents.

12. I had encountered many people during that period who were suspicious of GAM. I also met community leaders who had been interviewed by the HDC and had presented an alternative view, which HDC chose to disregard.

13. Gerry van Klinken (2001) argues that more attention needs to be paid to the role of society in violence that is said to be engineered.

Glossary

Indonesian and Acehnese Terms

adat—custom
bahasa—language
bangsa—nation, people, race
bebaskan—to release
connexitas—joint civilian-military
cu'ak—informer
daerah istimewa—special territory
dalang—puppeteer, mastermind
desirtir—deserter
dibina—cultivated
eko-sok—economic and social rights
eksesekses—excesses
ganga—marijuana
Hak Asasi Manusia (HAM)—human rights
hantu penasaran—curious ghosts
ilmu hantu—ghost science
merdeka—freedom
provokator—provocateur

Groups and Supposed Groups

ABRI—Indonesian armed forces and police until April 1999 when the name was
  changed to TNI and the police were separated
AGAM—armed wing of GAM
AM—Aceh Merdeka, Free Aceh
AMM—international Aceh Monitoring Mission
ASNLF—Aceh Sumatra National Liberation Front
BRR—Agency for Rehabilitation and Reconstruction in Aceh and Nias
DI/TII—Darul Islam/Tentara Islam Indonesia, Darul Islam/Indonesian Islamic
  Army
DOM—Daerah Operasi Militer, military operations zone
DPIA—Duek Pakat Inong Aceh, Acehnese Women's Congress
DPR—Dewan Perwakilan Rakyat, House of Representatives (Lower House of
  National Parliament)

DPRD—Acehnese regional parliament
GAM—Gerakan Aceh Merdeka, Free Aceh Movement
GBPK—Gerakan Bersenjata Pengacau Keamanan, Armed Movement to Disrupt Security
GHT—Gerakan Hasan Tiro, Hassan Tiro Movement
GPK—Gerombolan Pengacau Keamanan, Security Disruptor's Gang
GPK—Gerakan Pengacau Keamanan, Security Disruptor's Movement
GPL—Gerombolan Pengacau Liar, Gang of Wild Disruptors
GPLHT—Gerakan Pengacau Liar Hasan Tiro, Hasan Tiro's Wild Disruptors Movement
GSB—Gerakan Separatis Bersenjata, Armed Separatist Movement
GSB—Gerakan Sipil Bersenjata, Armed Civilian Movement
Golkar Party—Golongan Karya, The Group of Functionaries, political party for civil servants
HDC—Henry Dunant Centre for Humanitarian Dialogue
Humanitarian Pause—HDC brokered agreement between GAM and RI from May 2000 to April 2001
KGB—Komunisme Gaya Baru, New Style Communism
KKN—Korupsi, Kolusi, Nepotism, Corruption, Collusion, Nepotism
Komnas HAM—National Human Rights Commission
Kopassus—Indonesian Special Forces
Kopkamtib—Operational Command for the Restoration of Security and Order
LBH—Lembaga Bantuan Hukum, Legal Aid Foundation
Merdeka—Independence
MOU—Memorandum of Understanding
MPR—Majelis Permusyawaratan Rakyat, the People's Consultative Assembly (Upper House of National Parliament)
NAD—Nanggroe Aceh Darussalam, official name of the province of Aceh since 2001
NKRI—Negara Kesatuan Republik Indonesia, Unitary State of the Republic of Indonesia
OTK—Orang Tak Kenal, Unidentified Person
Pansus Aceh—Special Session of the National Parliament to discuss Aceh
Pertamina—staterun oil company
Pengacau Hasan Tiro—Hasan Tiro disruptors
PKI—Indonesian Communist Party
Polri—Polisi Republik Indonesia, Police of the Republic of Indonesia
PPP—Partai Persatuaan Pembangunan, Islamic Party under the New Order
RI—Republik Indonesia, Republic of Indonesia
RPKAD—Resimen Para Komando Angkatan Darat, Army paracommando regiment, precursor to Kopassus
SIRA—Central Information Committee for Referendum Aceh
TNI—Tentara Nasional Indonesia, Indonesian armed forces
TPO—Tenaga Pembantu Operasi, civilian operations assistants for Indonesian special forces

References

Indonesian and Acehnese Periodicals

Adil Tabloid (Jakarta)
Angkatan Bersenjata (TNI newspaper, Jakarta)
Antara (Jakarta)
Editor (Jakarta)
Harian Umum ABRI (ABRI newspaper, Jakarta)
Jakarta Post (electronic version)
Kompas (Jakarta)
Kontras (Banda Aceh)
Koran Tempo (Jakarta)
koridor.com (Jakarta)
Majalah D&R (Jakarta)
Majalah Forum Keadilan (Jakarta)
Majalah Gatra (Jakarta)
Majalah Interview (Jakarta)
Majalah Tajuk (Jakarta)
Majalah Tempo (Jakarta)
Media Indonesia (Jakarta)
Merdeka (Jakarta)
Panji Masyarakat (Jakarta)
Pantau: Kajian Media dan Jurnalisme (Jakarta)
Poskota (Jakarta)
Rakyat Merdeka (Jakarta)
Republika (Jakarta)
Satunet.com (Jakarta)
Serambi Indonesia (Banda Aceh)
Sinar Pagi (Jakarta)
Suara Acheh Merdeka (London)
Suara Karya (Jakarta)
Suara Pembaruan (Jakarta)
Waspada (Medan)
Warta (Medan)

266   References

Books and Articles

Note: Many Indonesians are known by only one name.

Alfian, T. Ibrahim. 1987. *Perang di Jalan Allah.* Jakarta: Pustaka Sinar Harapan.

Alfian, Ibrahim, Muhamad Hasan Basry, Ismail Sofyan, and Lian Sahar, eds. 1997. *The Dutch colonial war in Acheh (DCWA).* Banda Aceh: Documentation and Information Center of Aceh.

Amnesty International. 1993. *Indonesia: "shock therapy"—Restoring order in Aceh, 1989–1993.* London: Amnesty International.

Amnesty International and Judicial System Monitoring Programme. 2004. *Justice for Timor Leste: The way forward.* ASA 21/006/2004.

Anagnost, Ann. 1997. *National past-times: Narrative representation and power in modern China.* Durham, N.C.: Duke University Press.

Anderson, Benedict. 1983. *Imagined communities: Reflections on the origin and spread of Nationalism.* London: Verso.

———. 1987. How Did the Generals Die? *Indonesia* 43 (April): 109–35.

Anderson, Benedict, and Ruth Thomas McVey (with Frederick P. Bunnell). 1971. *A preliminary analysis of the October 1, 1965, coup in Indonesia.* Ithaca, N.Y.: Cornell Modern Indonesia Project.

Arendt, Hannah. 1964. *Eichmann in Jerusalem: Report on the Banality of Evil.* New York: Penguin.

Arextaga, Begona. 1997. *Shattering silence: Women, nationalism, and political subjectivity in Northern Ireland.* Princeton, N.J.: Princeton University Press.

———. 2000. A fictional reality: Paramilitary death squads and the construction of state terror in Spain. In *Death squad: The anthropology of state terror,* ed. Sluka, 46–49.

Asia Watch/Human Rights Watch. 1990. *Indonesia: Human rights abuses in Aceh.* New York, 27 December.

Aspinal, Edward, and Harold Crouch. 2003. *The Aceh peace process: Why it failed.* Policy Studies 1. Washington, D.C.: East West Center.

Aspinal, Edward, Elizabeth Drexler, and Vanessa Johanson. 1999. *Report on the 1999 elections in Aceh.* Melbourne: Australian Council for Overseas Aid, July.

Aveling, Harry, ed. and trans. 1975. *Gestapu: Indonesian short stories on the abortive communist coup of 30 September 1965.* Working Paper 6. Honolulu: University of Hawaii Southeast Asian Studies.

Bal, Mieke, Jonathan Crewe, and Leo Spitzer. 1999. *Acts of memory: Cultural recall in the present.* Hanover, N.H.: University Press of New England.

Benjamin, Walter. 1986. Critique of violence. In *Reflections: Walter Benjamin essays, aphorisms, autobiographical writings,* ed. Peter Demetz, 277–300. New York: Schocken Books.

———. 1989 (1940). Theses on the philosophy of history. In *Critical theory and society: A reader,* ed. Stephen Bronner and Douglas MacKay Kellner, 255–63. New York: Routledge.

Bertrand, Jacques. 2004. *Nationalism and Ethnic Conflict in Indonesia.* Cambridge: Cambridge University Press.

Bhakti, Andi F. 2005. Collective memories of the Qahhar Movement. In *Beginning to remember: The past in the Indonesian present,* ed. Zurbuchen, 123–49.

Blueprint of the Aceh case: Notes for Human Rights Watch and Amnesty International. 2001. Confidential document in author's possession.

Borneman, John. 1997. *Settling accounts: Violence, justice, and accountability in postsocialist Europe.* Princeton, N.J.: Princeton University Press.

Bourchier, David. 1994. The 1950s in New Order ideology and politics. In *Democracy in Indonesia: 1950s and 1990s*, ed. Bourchier and Legge, 50–62.

Bourchier, David, and John Legge, eds. 1994. *Democracy in Indonesia: 1950s and 1990s*. Clayton, Australia: Monash University Centre of Southeast Asian Studies.

Bowen, John R. 2003. *Islam, law and equality in Indonesia: An anthropology of public reasoning*. Cambridge: Cambridge University Press.

Brass, Paul R. 1997. *Theft of an idol: Text and context in the representation of collective violence*. Princeton, N.J.: Princeton University Press.

Brison, Susan J. 2001. *Aftermath: Violence and the remaking of a self*. Princeton, N.J.: Princeton University Press.

Budiawan. 2004. *Mematahkan Pewarisan Ingatan: Wacana Anti-Komunis dan Politik Rekonsiliasi Pasca-Soeharto*. Jakarta: ELSAM Lembaga Studi dan Advokasi Masyarakat.

———. 2005. Tortured body, betrayed heart: State violence in an Indonesian novel by an ex-political prisoner of the "1965 Affair." In *Violent conflicts in Indonesia*, ed. Coppel, 242–57.

Bung Karno dan Rakjat Atjeh. 1961. Banda Aceh: Panitia Persiapan Pendirian Universitas Negri Sjiah Kuala.

Butler, Judith. 1993. *Bodies that matter: On the discursive limits of "sex"*. New York: Routledge.

Buruma, Ian. 1994. *The wages of guilt: Memories of war in Germany and Japan*. New York: Farrar, Strauss and Giroux.

Caruth, Cathy, ed. 1995. *Trauma: Explorations in memory*. Baltimore: Johns Hopkins University Press.

Chaterjee, Partha. 1993. *The nation and its fragments: Colonial and postcolonial histories*. Princeton, N.J.: Princeton University Press.

Cheah, Peng. 2003. The haunting of the people: The spectral public sphere in Pramoedya Ananta Toer's Buru Quartet. In *Spectral nationality: Passages of freedom from Kant to postcolonial literatures of liberation*, chap. 6, 239–306. New York: Columbia University Press.

Cohen, David. 2002. Seeking justice on the cheap: Is the East Timor tribunal really a model for the future? *AsiaPacific Issues: Analysis from the East West Center* 61 (August).

Collins, Elizabeth Fuller. 2002. Indonesia: A culture of violence. In *The legacies of violence in Indonesia*, ed. Lowell Dittmer. Special issue *Asian Survey* 42, no. 4 (July–August): 582–604.

Coppel, Charles A., ed. 2005. *Violent conflicts in Indonesia: Analysis, representation, resolution*. London: Routledge Curzon.

Cribb, Robert. 1990. *The Indonesian killings 1965–1966: Studies from Java and Bali*. Clayton, Victoria: Monash University Center of Southeast Asian Studies.

———. 2002. Unresolved issues in the Indonesian killings of 1965–1966. In *The legacies of violence in Indonesia*, ed. Dittmer, 550–63.

Daniel, E. Valentine. 1996. *Charred lullabies: Chapters in an anthropography of violence*. Princeton, N.J.: Princeton University Press.

Das, Veena. 2004. "The signature of the state: Paradoxes of illegibility" In *Anthropology in the margins of the state*, ed. Das and Poole, 225–52.

Das, Veena, and Deborah Poole, eds. *Anthropology in the margins of the state*. Santa Fe, N.M.: School of American Research Press.

Departmen Pendidikan dan Kebudayaan, Pusat Penelitian Sejarah dan Budaya. 1977/1978. *Sejarah Daerah Propinsi Daerah Istimewa Aceh*. Jakarta: Proyek Penelitian dan Pencatatan Kebudyaan Daerah.

Derrida, Jacques. 1992. Force of law: The 'mystical foundation of authority.' In *Deconstruction and the possibility of justice*, ed. Drucilla Cornell, Michel Rosenfeld, and David Gray Carlson, 3–67. New York: Routledge, Chapman and Hall.

Dittmer, Lowell, ed. 2002. *The legacies of violence in Indonesia*. Special issue, *Asian Survey* 42, no. 4 (July–August).

Douglas, Lawrence. 2001. *Memory of judgment: Making law and history in the trials of the Holocaust*. New Haven, Conn.: Yale University Press.

Drexler, Elizabeth. 2001. Paranoid transparencies and fatal neutralities: Aceh's historical grievance and Indonesia's failed reform. Ph.D. dissertation, University of Washington.

———. 2006a. History and liability in Aceh, Indonesia: Single bad guys and convergent narratives. *American Ethnologist* 33, no. 3: 313–26.

———. 2006b. Provoking separatism, authenticating violence: Aceh's humanitarian pause. In *Violent conflicts in Indonesia*, ed. Coppel, 163–73.

———. 2006c. Transitional institutions and the corruption of truth, memory and justice. Paper presented to the seminar on Institutions of Truth and Memory: Resolving the Legacies of Mass Violence, May 18–25, 2006, Rockefeller Brothers Study Center Workshop, Bellagio, Italy.

Duara, Prasenjit. 1995. *Rescuing history from the nation: Questioning narratives of modern China*. Chicago: University of Chicago Press.

du Toit, André. 2000. The moral foundations of the South African TRC: Truth as acknowledgment and justice as recognition. In *Truth v. Justice*, ed. Rotberg and Thompson, 122–40.

Eda, Fikar W., and S. Satya Dharma. 1999. *Sebuah Kesaksian: Aceh Menggugat*. Jakarta: Pustaka Sinar Harapan.

Effendy, Bahtiar. 2003. *Islam and the state in Indonesia*. Singapore: Institute of Southeast Asian Studies; Athens: Ohio University Press.

Farid, Hilmar. 2001. Out of a black hole: After the New Order, the lid on Indonesia's past is beginning to lift. *Inside Indonesia* (October–December).

Favret-Saada, Jeanne. 1977. *Deadly words: Witchcraft in the Bocage*. Cambridge: Cambridge University Press.

Feher, Michel. 1999. "Terms of reconciliation," in *Human rights in political transitions: Gettysburg to Bosnia*, ed. Carla Hesse and Robert Post. New York: Zone Books.

Feitlowitz, Marguerite. 1998. *A lexicon of terror: Argentina and the legacies of torture*. New York: Oxford University Press.

Feldman, Gregory. 2005. Essential crises: A performative approach to migrants, minorities, and the European nation-state. *Anthropological Quarterly* 78, no. 1: 213–46.

Felman, Shoshana. 2002a. *The juridical unconscious: Trials and traumas in the twentieth century*. Cambridge, Mass.: Harvard University Press.

———. 2002b. *The Scandal of the speaking body: Don Juan with J. L. Austin or seduction in two languages*. Stanford, Calif.: Stanford University Press.

Felman, Shoshana, and Dori Laub. 1992. *Testimony: Crises of witnessing in literature, psychoanalysis, and history*. New York: Routledge.

Foucault, Michel. 1977. Nietzsche, genealogy, history. In *Language, countermemory, practice*, ed. Donald F. Bouchard, 139–64. Ithaca, N.Y.: Cornell University Press.

Foulcher, Keith. 1990. Making history: Recent Indonesian literature and the events of 1965. In *The Indonesian killings 1965–1966*, ed. Cribb, 101–20.

Freidlander, Saul. 1992. *Probing the limits of representation: Nazism and the "Final Solution"*. Cambridge, Mass.: Harvard University Press.

Geertz, Clifford. 1973. *Interpretation of cultures*. New York: Basic Books.

George, Kenneth M. 1996. *Showing signs of violence: The cultural politics of a twentieth-century headhunting ritual*. Berkeley: University of California Press.

———. 2004. Violence, culture, and the Indonesian public sphere: Reworking the Geertzian legacy. In *Violence: Culture, performance, and expression*, ed. Neil L. Whitehead, 25–54. Santa Fe, N.M.: SAR Press.

Good, Byron J. and Mary-Jo DelVecchio Good. 2001. "'Why do the masses so easily run amuk ...?': Madness and violence in Indonesia politics." *Latitudes Magazine* [Bali] 5.

Goodale, Mark. 2006. Introduction to anthropology and human rights in a new key. *American Anthropologist* 108, no. 1: 1–8.

Gordon, Avery F. 1996. *Ghostly matters: Haunting and the sociological imagination*. Minneapolis: University of Minnesota Press.

Greenhouse, Carol J., Elizabeth Mertz, and Kay B. Warren, eds. 2002. *Ethnography in unstable places: Everyday lives in contexts of dramatic political change*. Durham, N.C.: Duke University Press.

Gunawan, F. X. Rudy. 1998. *Orang Hilang: Sebuah Catatan Lepas di Sekitar Korban Penculikan*. Jakarta: Penerbit Pabelan Jayakarta.

Gupta, Akhil. 1995. Blurred boundaries: The discourse of corruption, the culture of politics, and the imagined state. *American Ethnologist* 22, no. 2: 375–402.

Hacking, Ian. 1995. *Rewriting the soul: Multiple personality and the sciences of memory*. Princeton, N.J.: Princeton University Press.

Hamber, Brandon E. and Richard A. Wilson. 2002. Symbolic closure through memory, reparation, and revenge in post-conflict societies. Journal of Human Rights 1, no. 1 (March): 35-53.

Hasan, Yusmar Basri, and Amrin Imran, eds. 1997. *Ilmu Pengetahuan Sosial 2: untuk sekolah Dasar Kelas 4*. Jakarta: Departmen Pendidikan dan Kebudayaan, Balai Pustaka.

Hasjmy, A. et al., eds. 1995. *Lima Puluh Tahun Aceh Membangun*. Banda Aceh: MUI Propinsi Daerah Istimewa Aceh.

Hasty, Jennifer. 2005. The pleasures of corruption: Desire and discipline in Ghanaian political culture. *American Ethnologist* 20, no. 2: 271–301.

Hayner, Priscilla B. 2001. *Unspeakable truths: Confronting state terror and atrocity. How truth commissions around the world are challenging the past and shaping the future*. New York: Routledge.

Hedman, Eva-Lotta E. 2005. Back to the barracks: *Relokasi Pengungsi* in post-tsunami Aceh. *Indonesia Journal* 80: 1–19.

Henri, Yazir. 2006. Reconciling reconciliation: A personal and public journey of testifying before the South African Truth and Reconciliation Commission. In *Political transition: Politics and cultures*, ed. Paul Gready, 262–75. London: Pluto Press.

Heryanto, Ariel. 2006. *State terrorism and political identity in Indonesia: Fatally belonging*. London: Routledge.

Hoffman, Daniel. 2002. "Violent events as narrative blocs: The disarmament at Bo, Sierra Leone." *Anthropological Quarterly* 78, no. 2: 329–53.

Honna, Jun. 1999. The military and democratisation in Indonesia: The developing civil-military discourse during the late Soeharto era. Ph.D. dissertation, Australian National University, Canberra.

———. 2003. *Military politics and democratization in Indonesia.* London: Routledge Curzon.

Hoskins, Janet. 1987. The headhunter as hero: Local traditions and their reinterpretation in national history. *American Ethnologist* 14, no 4 (November): 605–22.

———, ed. 1996. *Headhunting and the social imagination in Southeast Asia.* Stanford Calif.: Stanford University Press.

Huber, Konrad. 2004. *The HDC in Aceh: Promises and pitfalls of NGO mediation and implementation.* Policy Studies 9. Washington, D.C.: East West Center.

Human Rights Watch. 1992. Indonesia: Commission of Inquiry needed for Aceh. *Asia Watch* 4, no. 5 (19 February).

Hurgronje, Snouck. 1906. *The Achehnese.* Trans. A. W. S. Sullivan. 2 vols. Leiden: E.J. Brill.

Independent Commission. 1999. *Laporan: Komisi Independen Pengusutan Tindak Kekerasan Di Aceh (Bab 1–9: Prosedur, Temuan, Analisis, Kesimpulan dan Rekomendasi).* Report: Independent commission for the investigation of acts of violence in Aceh (chapters 1–9: procedure, findings, analysis, conclusions and recommendations). Presidential Decree No. 88/1999, Jakarta. Confidential document, copy in author's possession.

Indonesian Legal Aid Foundation. 1991. *Resume Hasil Observasi Proses Peradilan Kasus Aceh.* Jakarta: Yayasan Lembaga Bantuan Hukum Indonesia, July.

International Crisis Group. 2002. Indonesia: The implications of the Timor trials. *Asia Briefing* 16. Jakarta and Brussels, 8 May.

———. 2003. Aceh: How not to win hearts and minds. *Asia Briefing* 27. Jakarta and Brussels, 23 July.

———. 2005. Aceh: A new chance for peace. *Asia Briefing.* 40. Jakarta and Brussels, 15 August.

———. 2006a. Aceh: Now for the hard part. *Asia Briefing* 48. Jakarta and Brussels, 29 March.

———. 2006b. Islamic law and criminal justice in Aceh. *Asia Report* 117. Jakarta and Brussels, 31 July.

———. 2006c. Aceh's local elections: The role of the Free Aceh Movement (GAM). *Asia Briefing* 57/ Jakarta and Brussels, 29 November.

Ishak, Otto Syamsuddin. 1999. Secara Kultural Orang Aceh Pemberani. In *Sebuah Kesaksian: Aceh Menggugat,* ed. Fikar W. Eda and S. Satya Dharma. Jakarta: Pustaka Sinar Harapan.

———. 2003. *Sang Martir: Teungku Bantaqiah.* Jakarta: Yappika Seri 6: Resolusi Konflik.

Jakobi, A. K. (Tgk.) 1992. *Aceh Daerah Modal: Long March ke Medan Area.* Jakarta: Yayasan "Seulawah RI-001"/PT Pelita Persatuan.

James, Wilmot, and Linda van de Vijver. 2000. *After the TRC: Reflections on truth and reconciliation in South Africa.* Athens: Ohio University Press; Cape Town: David Phillip.

Jeganathan, Pradeep. 2000. On the anticipation of violence: Modernity and identity in Southern Sri Lanka. In *Anthropology, development and modernities: Exploring discourses, counter-tendencies and violence,* ed. Alberto Arce and Norman Long, 112–26. London: Routledge.

Jelin, Elizabeth. 2003. *State repression and the labors of memory.* Trans. Judy Rein and Marcial GodoyAnativia. Minneapolis: University of Minnesota Press.

Jihad, Abu. 2000. *Hasan Tiro dan Pergolakan Aceh.* Jakarta: PT Aksara Centra.

Kahin, Audrey R., and George McT. Kahin. 1995. *Subversion as foreign policy: The secret Eisenhower and Dulles debacle in Indonesia.* Seattle: University of Washington Press.

Kammen, Douglas, and Bambang Widjajanto. 2000. The structure of military abuse. *Inside Indonesia* (April–June).

Katopo, Aristides, ed. 1999. *Menyingkap Kabut HALIM 1965.* Jakarta: Sinar Harapan.

Kell, Tim. 1995. *The roots of Acehnese rebellion, 1989–1992.* Ithaca, N.Y.: Cornell Modern Indonesia Project.

Kelly, John D., and Martha Kaplan. 2001. *Represented Communities: Fiji and world decolonization.* Chicago: University of Chicago Press.

Kelsall, Tim. 2005. Truth, lies, ritual: Preliminary reflections on the Truth and Reconciliation Commission in Sierra Leone. *Human Rights Quarterly* 27: 361–91.

Kenang-kenanangan Peresmian Pembukaan Taman Mini Indonesia Indah. 1975. Jakarta: Badan Pelaksana Pembangunan dan Persiapan Pengusahaan Projek Miniatur Indonesia "Indonesian Indah."

Kleinman, Arthur, Veena Das, and Margaret M. Lock. 1997. *Social suffering.* Berkeley: University of California Press.

Kritz, Neil J., ed. 1995. *Transitional justice: How emerging democracies reckon with former regimes.* Washington, D.C.: U.S. Institute of Peace Press.

LaCapra, Dominick. 2001. *Writing history, writing trauma.* Baltimore: Johns Hopkins University Press.

Laporan Penugasan Tim Pase 4 di daerah operasi Aceh Periode Nov 1994 s/d Nov 1995. Jakarta. Confidential document, copy in author's possession.

Latief, A. 1999. *Pledoi Kol Soeharto Terlibat G 30.* Jakarta: ISAI.

Latief, H., Miryanti, and Mahendra. 2005. *Tragedi Kemanusiaan 1965–2005.* Bandung: Penerbit Malka.

Latour, Bruno. 1987. *Science in action: How to follow scientists and engineers through society.* Cambridge, Mass.: Harvard University Press.

Lev, Daniel S. 1972. *Islamic courts in Indonesia.* Berkeley: University of California Press.

———. 2005. Memory, knowledge and reform. In *Beginning to remember: The past in Indonesia's present,* ed. Mary S. Zurbuchen, 195–208.

Lembaga Ilmu Pengatahuan Indonesia (LIPI) Research Team. 2001. *Bara Dalam Sekam: Identifikasi Akar Masalah dan Solusi atas Konflikkonflik Lokal di Aceh, Maluku, Papua, dan Riau.* Jakarta: Mizan.

Machmud, Anas. 1988. *Kedaulatan Aceh yang tidak pernah diserahkan kepada Belanda adalah bahagian dari kedaulatan Indonesia.* Jakarta: PT Bulan Bintang.

Malamud-Goti, Jamie. 1996. *Game without end: State terror and the politics of justice.* Norman: University of Oklahoma Press.

Marcus, George.1999. *Paranoia within reason: Conspiracy as explanation.* Chicago: University of Chicago Press.

Mariati, Syarifah. 1999. Catatan Seorang Janda [Notes of a widow]. In *Nyala Panyot Tak Terpadamkan.* Banda Aceh: Flower Aceh.

Markas Besar Angkatan Udara Republik Indonesia Biro Penerangan. 1954. *Sewindu Angkatan Udara Republik Indonesia 9 April 1946–9 April 1954.* Djakarta: Markas Besar Angkatan Udara Republik Indonesia Biro Penerangan.

McGranahan, Carole. 2005. Truth, fear and lies: Exile politics and arrested histories of the Tibetan resistance. *Cultural Anthropology* 20, no. 4: 570–600.

McGregor, Katharine E. 2003. Representing the Indonesian past: The National Monument History Museum from Guided Democracy to the New Order. *Indonesia* 75 (April): 91–122.

————. 2005. Nugroho Notosusanto: The legacy of a historian in the service of an authoritarian regime. In *Beginning to remember: The past in Indonesia's present*, ed. Zurbuchen, 209–32.

Merry, Sally Engle. 2006. "Transnational human rights and local activism: Mapping the middle." *American Anthropologist* 108, no. 1: 38–51.

Minow, Martha. 1998. *Between vengeance and forgiveness: Facing history after genocide and mass violence.* Boston: Beacon Press.

Mitchell, Timothy. 2002. *Rule of experts: Egypt, techno-politics, modernity.* Berkeley: University of California Press.

Mohamad, Goenawan. 2001. On being Indonesian. *Latitudes Magazine* (Bali), 6 (July).

Morris, Eric E. 1983. Islam and politics in Aceh: A study of center-periphery relations in Indonesia. Ph.D. dissertation, Cornell University.

Mueggler, Erik. 2001. *The age of wild ghosts: Memory, violence, and place in Southwest China.* Berkeley: University of California Press.

Munir. 2000. Mencari Provokator. In *Indonesia di Tengah Transisi*, ed. Stanley.

Nasution, Adnan Buyung. 1994. Human rights and the *Konstituante* debates of 1956–59. In *Democracy in Indonesia: 1950s and 1990s*, ed. Bourchier and Legge, 43–49.

Nelson, Diane M. 1999. *A finger in the wound: Body politics in quincentennial Guatemala.* Berkeley: University of California Press.

Nevins, Joseph. 2004. *A not-so-distant horror: Mass violence in East Timor.* Ithaca, N.Y.: Cornell University Press.

Nordstrom, Carolyn, and Antonius C. G. M. Robben. 1995. *Fieldwork under fire: Contemporary studies of violence and survival.* Berkeley: University of California Press.

Notes and Events of 1998. Confidential document, in author's possession.

Notosusanto, Nugroho, and Ismail Saleh. 1968. *The coup attempt of the "September 30 Movement" in Indonesia.* Jakarta: Pembinging Masa.

Nugroho, Bimo, ed. 1999. *Dicari: Orang Hilang.* Jakarta: ISAI.

Osiel, Mark. 1997. *Mass atrocity, collective memory, and the law.* New Brunswick, N.J.: Transaction.

Pecora, Vincent P. 1989. The limits of local knowledge. In *The new historicism*, ed. H. Arman Veeser, 243–76. New York: Routledge.

Pemberton, John. 1994. *On the subject of "Java".* Ithaca, N.Y.: Cornell University Press.

Pendjelasan Tentang Projek Miniatur Indonesia "Indonesia Indah". 1971. Jakarta: Badan Pelaksana Pembangunan dan Persiapan Pengusahaan Projek Miniatur Indonesia "Indonesian Indah."

Polim, Mohammad Ali Panglima. 1996. *Sumbangsih Aceh Bagi Republik.* Jakarta: Pustaka Sinar Harapan.

Pompe, Sebastiaan. 2005. *Indonesian Supreme Court: A study of institutional collapse.* Ithaca, N.Y.: Southeast Asia Program Publications at Cornell University.

Popkin, Margaret, and Naomi Roht-Arriaza. 1995. Truth as justice: Investigatory commissions in Latin America. *Law and Social Inquiry* 20, no. 1: 79–116.

Pour, Julius. 1993. *Benny Moerdani: Profile of a soldier statesman.* Trans. Tim Scott. Jakarta: Yayasan Kejuangan Panglima Besar Sudirman.

Purdey, Jemma. 2006. *Anti-Chinese violence in Indonesia, 1996–1999.* Honolulu: University of Hawaii Press.

Putusan, Pengadilan Negeri Banda Aceh (Decision of National Court, Banda Aceh). 2000. No. 11/PID/B/Koneks/2000/PNBNA, 17 May 2000. Perkara Pidana, Terdakwa: Anton Yuliantoro, dkk.

Rahmany, P. Dyah. 2001. *Rumoh Geudong: Tanda Luka Orang Aceh*. Banda Aceh: Cordova Institute for Civil Society Empowerment.

Reid, Anthony. 1969. *The contest for North Sumatra: Atjeh, the Netherlands, and Britain, 1858–1898*. Oxford: Oxford University Press; Kuala Lumpur: University of Malaya Press.

———. 1979. *The blood of the people*. Kuala Lumpur and Oxford: Oxford University Press.

———. 2005. *An Indonesian frontier: Acehnese and other histories of Sumatra*. Singapore: Singapore University Press.

Resink, Gertrudes Johan. 1968. *Indonesia's history between the myths: Essays in legal history and historical theory*. The Hague: W. van Hoeve.

Risalah Rapat Dengar Pendapat Umum Pansus Tentang Permasalahan Di Daerah Istimewa Aceh. 1999. Official Parliamentary transcript, 29 November.

Robinson, Geoffrey. 1995. *The dark side of paradise: Political violence in Bali*. Ithaca, N.Y.: Cornell University Press.

———. 1998. *Rawan* is as *rawan* does: The origins of disorder in New Order Aceh. *Indonesia* 66 (October): 127–56.

Rochijat, Pipit. 1985. Am I or am I not PKI? Trans. Ben Anderson. *Indonesia* 40 (October): 37–56.

Rogers, Susan. 2005. *Print, poetics and politics A Sumatran epic in the colonial Indies and New Order Indonesia*. Leiden: KITLV Press.

Roosa, John. 2006. *Pretext for mass murder: The September 30th Movement and Suharto's coup d'état in Indonesia*. Madison: University of Wisconsin Press.

Roosa, John, Ayu Ratih, and Hilmar Farid, eds. 2004. *Tahun yang tak pernah berakhir: Memahami pengalaman korban 65: Esai-esai sejarah lisan*. Jakarta: Lembaga Studi dan Advokasi Masyarakat (ELSAM) bekerja sama dengan Tim Relawan Untuk Kemanusiaan [dan] Institut Sejarah Sosial Indonesia.

Rosaldo, Renato. 1980. *Ilongot headhunting, 1883–1974: A study in society and history*. Stanford, Calif.: Stanford University Press, 1980.

Ross, Fiona C. 2001. Speech and silence: Women's testimony in the first five weeks of public hearings of the South African Truth and Reconciliation Commission. In *Remaking a world: Violence, social suffering, and recovery*, ed. Veena Das, Arthur Kleinman, Margaret Lock, Mamphele Ramphele, and Pamela Reynolds, 250–80. Berkeley: University of California Press.

———. 2003. *Bearing witness: Women and the Truth and Reconciliation Commission in South Africa*. London: Pluto Press.

Rotberg, Robert I. 2000. Truth commissions and the provision of truth, justice and reconciliation. Introduction to *Truth v. Justice: The morality of truth commissions*, ed. Robert I. Rotberg and Dennis Thompson, 3–21. Princeton, N.J.: Princeton University Press.

Rutherford, Danilyn. 2003. *Raiding the land of the foreigners: The limits of the nation on an Indonesian frontier*. Princeton, N.J.: Princeton University Press.

Ryter, Loren. 1998. Pemuda Pancasila: The last loyalist free men of Soeharto's Order? *Indonesia* 66: 45–73.

Salim, Arskal, and Azyumardi Azra, eds. 2003. *Shari'a and politics in modern Indonesia*. Series on Islam. Singapore: Institute of Southeast Asian Studies.

Santner, Erik L. 1996. *My own private Germany: Daniel Paul Schreber's secret history of modernity*. Princeton, N.J.: Princeton University Press.

Sarumpaet, Ratna. 2000. Alia: Luka Serambi Mekah [Performance]. Jakarta: Taman Ismail Marzuki, 12–17 May.

Sasongko, H. D. Haryo. 2005. *Korupsi Sejarah dan Kisah Derita Akar Rumput.* Jakarta: Pustaka Utan Kayu.

Scarry, Elaine. 1985. *The body in pain: The making and unmaking of the world.* Oxford: Oxford University Press.

Schwarz, Adam. 1991. Deadly suspicion. *Far Eastern Economic Review,* 25 July.

Scott, David. 1999. *Refashioning futures: Criticism after postcoloniality.* Princeton, N.J.: Princeton University Press.

Scott, Joan W. 1991. The evidence of experience. *Critical Inquiry* 17 (Summer): 773–97.

Sen, Krishna. 1994. *Indonesian cinema: Framing the New Order.* London: Zed Books.

Shaw, Rosalind. 2007. Memory frictions: Localizing the Truth and Reconciliation Commission in Sierra Leone. *International Journal for Transitional Justice* 1, no. 2.

Sidel, John T. 2006. *Riots, pogroms, jihad: Religious violence in Indonesia.* Ithaca, N.Y.: Cornell University Press.

Siegel, James T. 2000 (1969). *The rope of God.* Ann Arbor: University of Michigan Press.

———. 1997. *Fetish, recognition, revolution.* Princeton, N.J.: Princeton University Press.

———. 1998. *A new criminal type in Jakarta: Counter-revolution today.* Durham, N.C.: Duke University Press.

———. 2006. *Naming the witch.* Stanford, Calif.: Stanford University Press.

Sjamsuddin, Nazaruddin. 1985. *The republican revolt: A study of the Acehnese rebellion.* Singapore: Institute of Southeast Asian Studies.

Sluka, Jeffrey, ed. 2000. *Death squad: The anthropology of state terror.* Philadelphia: University of Pennsylvania Press.

Slyomovics, Susan. 1998. *The object of memory: Arab and Jew narrate the Palestinian village.* Philadelphia: University of Pennsylvania Press.

Smith, Daniel Jordan. 2006. *A culture of corruption: Everyday deception and popular discontent in Nigeria.* Princeton, N.J.: Princeton University Press.

Soeharto. 1988. *Soeharto: Pikiran, Ucapan dan Tindakan Saya.* Jakarta: PT Lantoro Gunung Persada.

Soekarno. 1948. *Perkundjungan Presiden Soekarno ke Atjeh.* Koetaradja: Semangat Merdeka Bahagian Pustaka.

———. 1959. Speech of President Soekarno, Meulaboh, Atjeh, 4 September 1959.

Soemargono, K. et al. 1992. *Buku Profil Propinsi Republik Indonesia.* Jakarta: Yayasan Bhakti Wawasan Nusantara with Majalah Telestra.

Stanley. 1999. Penggambaran Gerwani Sebagai Kumpulan Pembunuh dan Setan (Fitnah dan Fakta Penghancuran Organisasi Perempuan Terkemuka). Paper presented at seminar, "Tragedi Nasional 1965," Masyarakat Sejarawan Indonesia, Serpong, 8 September.

———, ed. 2000. *Indonesia di Tengah Transisi.* Jakarta: Propatria.

Steedley, Mary M. 1993. *Hanging without a rope: Narrative experience in colonial and postcolonial Karoland.* Princeton, N.J.: Princeton University Press.

———. 1999. The state of culture theory in the anthropology of Southeast Asia. *Annual Review of Anthropology* 28: 431–54.

———. 2000. Modernity and the memory artist: The work of imagination in Highland Sumatra, 1947–1995. *Comparative Studies in Society and History* 42, no. 4 (October): 811–46.

Stoler, Ann L. 2002a. Colonial archives and the arts of governance: On the content in the form. In *Refiguring the archive,* ed. Carolyn Hamilton, Verne Harris,

Jane Taylor, Michele Pickover, G. Reid, and R. Saleh, 83–102. Cape Town: David Philip.

———. 2002b. On the uses and abuses of the past in Indonesia: Beyond the mass killings of 1965. *Asian Survey* 42, no. 4 (July–August): 642–50.

Stoler, Ann L., and Karen Strassler. 2000. Castings for the colonial: Memory work in "New Order" Java. *Comparative Studies in Society and History* 42, no. 1 (January): 4–48.

Sudisman. 2000. *Kritik Oto Kritik: Seorang Politbiro CC PKI.* Jakarta: Teplok Press.

Sukanta, Putu Oka. 1999a. *Merajut Harkat.* Yogyakarta: Pustaka Pelajar.

———. 1999b. *Nyala Panyot Tak Terpadamkan.* Banda Aceh: Flower Aceh.

Sukma, Rizal. 2004. *Security operations in Aceh: Goals, consequences, and lessons.* Policy Studies 3. Washington, D.C.: East West Center.

Sulaiman, M. Isa. 2000. *Aceh Merdeka: Ideologi, Kepemimpinan dan Gerakan* (Free Aceh: Ideology, leadership, and movement). Jakarta: Pustaka AlKautsar.

Sulami. 1999. *PerempuanKebenaran dan Penjara.* Jakarta: Cipta Lestari.

Sulistyo, Hermawan. 2000a. Mengadili Provokator. In *Indonesia di Tengah Transisi,* ed. Stanley, 65–68.

———. 2000b. *Palu Arit di Ladang Tebu: Sejarah Pembantaian Massal yang Terlupakan (1965–1966).* Jakarta: KPG.

Sundar, Nandini. 2004. Toward an anthropology of culpability. *American Ethnologist* 31, no. 2: 145–63.

Suradi, H. P., Sutrisno Kutoyo, Masjkuri, Wahyuningsih, and T. A. Sukrani, eds. 1989. *Sejarah Taman Mini Indonesia Indah.* Jakarta: Departemen Pendidikan dan Kebudayaan,

Syah, Kaoy, and Lukman Hakiem. 2000. *Keistimewaan Aceh Dalam Lintasan Sejarah: Proses Pembentukan UU No. 44/1999.* Jakarta: Pengurus Besar AlJami'iyatul Washliyah.

Talsya, T. Alibasjah. 1955. *Sedjarah dan Dokumen-Dokumen Pemberontakan di Atjeh.* Djakarta: Penerbit Kesuma (inscribed and received by the National Library Collection on 10 July 1958).

———. 1990. *Modal Perjuangan Kemerdekaan (Perjuangan Kemerdekaan di Aceh): 1947–1948.* Banda Aceh: Lembaga Sejarah Aceh.

Tanter, Richard, Desmond Ball, and Gerry van Klinken, eds. 2006. *Masters of terror: Indonesia's military and violence in East Timor.* Oxford: Rowman and Littlefield.

Taussig, Michael. 1984. Culture of terror—space of death: Roger Casement's Putumayo report and the explanation of torture. *Comparative Studies in Society and History* 26: 467–97.

———. 1992. *The nervous system.* New York: Routledge.

———. 1997. *The magic of the state.* New York: Routledge.

———. 1999. *Defacement: Public secrets and the labor of the historical negative.* Stanford, Calif.: Stanford University Press.

Taylor, Diana. 1997. *Disappearing acts: Spectacles of gender and nationalism in Argentina's "Dirty War".* Durham, N.C.: Duke University Press.

Tiba, Sofyan Ibrahim. 1999. *Referendum Aceh dalam Pantauan Hukum.* Banda Aceh: Gua Hira'.

Tippe, Syarifudin. 2000. *Aceh di Persimpangan Jalan (Aceh at the Crossroads).* Jakarta: Cidesindo.

Tiro, Hasan M. Di. 1948. *Perang Atjeh 1873M.–1927M (The Atjeh War 1873–1927).* Yogyakarta: pamphlet.

———. 1958. *Democracy for Indonesia.* Reprint Jakarta: Teplok Press, 1999.

————. 1965. *The Political Future of the Malay Archipelago.* New York, 3 January.

————. 1968. *Atjeh Bak Mata Donya.* New York.

Toer, Pramoedya Ananta. 2003 (1993). *House of glass.* Trans. Max Lane. Victoria: Penguin Australia.

van der Kroef, Justus M. 1958. On the writing of Indonesian history. *Pacific Affairs* 31, no 4 (December): 352–71.

Van Dijk, C. 1981. *Rebellion under the banner of Islam: The Darul Islam in Indonesia.* The Hague: Martinus Nijhoff.

van Klinken, Gerry. 2001. The Maluku wars: Bringing society back. *Indonesia* 71: 1–26.

Van't Veer, Paul. 1969. *De Atjehoorlog.* Amsterdam: Arbeiderspers.

Warman. 2004a. *Pelurusan Sejarah Indonesia.* Jakarta: Tride.

————. 2004b. *Soeharto Sisi Gelap Sejarah Indonesia.* Jakarta: Ombak.

Warren, Kay B. 1993. *The violence within: Cultural and political opposition in divided nations.* Boulder, Colo.: Westview Press.

————. 2000. Death squads and wider complicities: Dilemmas for the anthropology of violence." In *Death squad: The anthropology of state terror,* ed. Sluka, 226–47.

West, Harry G., and Todd Sanders, eds. 2003. *Transparency and conspiracy: Ethnographies of suspicion in the New World Order.* Durham, N.C.: Duke University Press.

Wilson, Richard A. 1997. *Human rights: Culture and context.* London: Pluto Press.

————. 2001. *The politics of truth and reconciliation in South Africa: Legitimizing the post-apartheid state.* Cambridge: Cambridge University Press.

Zamzami, Amran. 2001. *Tragedi Anak Bangsa: Pembantaian Teungku Bantaqiah dan Santri-santrinya.* Jakarta: Bina Rena Pariwara.

————. n.d. *Peradilan Koneksitas; sebuah jalan tengah.* Unpublished manuscript.

Zulaika, Joseba, and William Douglass. 1996. *Terror and taboo: The follies, fables and faces of terrorism.* New York: Routledge.

Zurbuchen, Mary S., ed. 2005. *Beginning to remember: The past in the Indonesian present.* Singapore: Singapore University Press; Seattle: University of Washington Press.

Index

Acknowledgments

Many people and institutions have contributed to this project. I owe a special debt to the late Daniel S. Lev, whose support, critical engagement, and exemplary work on Indonesian politics have inspired this project from the beginning. I learned much about historiography from Tani Barlow, who also provided insightful comments on an earlier draft and valuable support at critical moments. Ann Anagnost pointed me toward the performative and other provocative ideas; I am grateful for her thoughtful comments on an earlier version, as well as her encouragement and support throughout the process. I am especially indebted to Audrey Kahin, who generously shared materials from her own research and read the entire manuscript offering valuable comments. Sebastiaan Pompe has been a critical interlocutor and friend over the past decade; after discussing the project for years, he read the entire manuscript and offered further comments. Susan Rogers generously offered detailed critical comments that improved this manuscript tremendously.

I learned much about Indonesia from Ben Anderson, John Pemberton, Jim Siegel, and Anna Tsing. I am grateful to Ben Anderson for naming the moral bullies, he may not remember doing so, but it made an important difference. Scott Mobley read early drafts and made thoughtful suggestions. Sarah Elter Van Hoy provided crucial insights on paranoia. Hairong Yan pushed me toward creative interpretations of corruption early on. Peter Moran shared his wisdom on the fieldwork process and much else.

I am deeply indebted to the many people across Indonesia who spoke with me in confidence about topics large and small in the course of this project. Since few would agree with everything I say in this book and even listing their names here might be doing them a disservice, I trust that they know who they are and will accept my heartfelt thanks while remaining anonymous. I am most indebted to a small group of nongovernmental organizations that were active in Aceh in 1996. Their solidarity and courage inspired me to begin my research in Aceh. Their fragmentation a few years later prompted me to reflect on political transformations in a particular way. I look forward to a time when I can thank them all in public.

Many people contributed to my understanding and enjoyment of Indonesia. Emmy Hafild and Dhana Dharsono, as well as Ibu Jenny, Pak Rusdy, and Shanty Harmayn, and Bert Hoffman opened their homes to me many times for extended periods of time. Niesdri Foster and Vevi Aningsih patiently helped me learn Indonesian. Taufik Abdullah, Nelly Paliama, and Parsudi Suparlan facilitated different aspects of my research. The late Amran Zamzami discussed the Bantaqiah trial at length with me. A number of individuals and organizations contributed to my understanding of the legacies of the past throughout Indonesia, especially, Hilmar Farid, Agung Putri, Usman Hamid, Ifdhal Kassim, Bimo Nugroho, Jhonson Panjaitan, Robert Robertus, Stanley, and many others at ELSAM, ISAI, Kontras, PBHI, PSHK, and YLBHI. I thank the late Munir for conversations and insights as I began this project; his unsolved murder is a reminder of the challenges and risks taken by those who continue to work against impunity. I am grateful to a number of people for generously sharing their time and thoughts, especially: Milisa Day, Sisa DeJesus, F. X. Rudy Gunawan, Maria Hartiningsih, Marc Herman, Guy Janssen, Doug Kammen, Chalid Mohammad, Goenwan Mohammad, (alm.) Ridwan Monti, Sigit Murdawa, Nezar Patria, Prabandari, Teresa Birks, Loren Ryter, Marsillam Simantunjak, Jeremy Wagstaff, Jati Waluyo, and Juliana Wilson. My research assistant, Kamaludin Suganda contributed exceptional intelligence and dedication to this project. Dwi Agus Y proofread the manuscript.

The Department of Anthropology at Michigan State University provided leave time and engaging colleagues. The Fulbright New Century Scholar program created a context for stimulating discussions with a number of scholars, especially, Rebecca Bryant, John Darby, Courtney Jung, Barbara Oomen, Jillian Schwedler, and Dan Rabinowitz. Coorganizing a Bellagio workshop with Rebecca Bryant provided the opportunity to think through the institutionalization of histories and memories. I thank audiences at Cornell University, Melbourne University, Ohio University, University of California-Los Angeles, University of Maryland, and University of Michigan for their comments and questions. Ken George and Geoffrey Robinson were especially helpful at the early stages of this project. I am also grateful to Kamari Clarke, John Davis, Steve Esquith, Marguerite Feitlowitz, Leonard Feldman, Mariane Ferme, Yazir Henri, Alex Hinton, Robert Hitchcock, Najib Hourani, Carla Jones, Mindy Morgan, Brandt Peterson, Kristen Peterson, Lisa Robinson, and

Susan Slyomovics for conversations and comments on different aspects of the project, and to others too numerous to mention who have contributed to this effort since I began.

A Blakemore Foundation Fellowship enabled me to study Indonesian language and gain invaluable experience in Indonesia. My dissertation research was sponsored by the Indonesian Institute of Research (LIPI) and funded by a Fulbright-Hays Award. Subsequent research in Indonesia and East Timor was funded by a Fulbright New Century Scholar Fellowship and a Michigan State University Intramural Research Grant Program New Faculty award, and again sponsored by LIPI. The Department of Anthropology at Michigan State University provided research funds as well. The Center for the Advanced Study of International Development and Women in Development at Michigan State University provided support for the completion of this manuscript. A Cornell University Southeast Asia Program Fellow in Residence Award provided a stimulating atmosphere and extensive library resources. Ben Abel at the Echols Collection at Cornell University helped to track down references.

An earlier version of chapter one was first published in *Anthropological Quarterly* 80, no. 4 (2007). Earlier versions of portions of Chapters 4 and 5 appeared in *American Ethnologist* 33, no. 3 (2006) and *Representing Violent Conflict in Indonesia*, ed. Charles A. Coppel (London: Routledge, 2005) respectively. All are used here with permission. I am grateful to G. M. Sudarta and M. Edward Sampee for permission to reprint their cartoons, which originally appeared in *Kompas* 27 November 1999 and *Kontras* 4 December 1999 respectively.

Peter Agree has been an outstanding editor, patiently guiding me through the publication process, and an ideal correspondent asking thought provoking questions as well as answering my mundane questions. Grey Osterud recognized what this project was about immediately and her editorial expertise and friendship were indispensable in refining and clarifying it. Both have read numerous drafts of this manuscript offering thoughtful comments every time. I also thank Alison Anderson, Chris Hu, and the rest of the Penn Press team for their work on this book.

I am grateful to my brother, Ray Drexler, as well as Min Lo Jantz, Sara Ranney, Eric Terman, and Mari Philipsborne for their friendship and interest in this project. I am especially indebted to my parents, Jane and Ray Drexler, for their generous support and encouragement. There are no words adequate to thank them for all they have given me. This book and much else would be unimaginable without H. Nazaruddin Ibrahim. For his unwavering love and exceptional wisdom, I dedicate this book to him.

I alone am responsible for any errors and opinions expressed in this work.

East Lansing
February 2007